DATE DUE

			PRINTED IN U.S.A.

SOMETHING ABOUT THE AUTHOR

In Memory of Dennis Mason

ISSN 0276-816X

something ABOUT THE AUTHOR

**Facts and Pictures about Authors
and Illustrators of Books for Young People**

EDITED BY
ANNE COMMIRE

VOLUME 43

GALE RESEARCH COMPANY
BOOK TOWER
DETROIT, MICHIGAN
48226

Editor: Anne Commire

Associate Editors: Agnes Garrett, Helga P. McCue

Assistant Editors: Dianne H. Anderson, Eunice L. Petrini, Linda Shedd

Sketchwriter: Rachel Koenig

Researchers: Kathleen Betsko, Catherine Ruello

Editorial Assistants: Lisa Bryon, Elisa Ann Ferraro

Permissions Assistant: Susan Pfanner

In cooperation with the Young People's Literature staff

Associate Editor: Joyce Nakamura

Assistant Editor: Cynthia J. Walker

Research Coordinator: Carolyn Kline

External Production Supervisor: Mary Beth Trimper

External Production Assistant: Darlene K. Maxey

Internal Production Associate: Louise Gagné

Internal Senior Production Assistant: Sandy Rock

Layout Artist: Elizabeth Lewis Patryjak

Art Director: Arthur Chartow

Special acknowledgment is due to the members of the *Contemporary Authors* staff
who assisted in the preparation of this volume.

Publisher: Frederick G. Ruffner

Editorial Director: Dedria Bryfonski

Director, Literature Division: Christine Nasso

Senior Editor, Something about the Author: Adele Sarkissian

Library of Congress Catalog Card Number 72-27107

ISBN 0-8103-2253-6

ISSN 0276-816X

Computerized photocomposition by
Typographics, Incorporated
Kansas City, Missouri

Printed in the United States

Contents

A

B

C

D

V

W

Introduction

As the only ongoing reference series that deals with the lives and works of authors and illustrators of children's books, *Something about the Author (SATA)* is a unique source of information. The *SATA* series includes not only well-known authors and illustrators whose books are most widely read, but also those less prominent people whose works are just coming to be recognized. *SATA* is often the only readily available information source for less well-known writers or artists. You'll find *SATA* informative and entertaining whether you are:

> —a student in junior high school (or perhaps one to two grades higher or lower) who needs information for a book report or some other assignment for an English class;

> —a children's librarian who is searching for the answer to yet another question from a young reader or collecting background material to use for a story hour;

> —an English teacher who is drawing up an assignment for your students or gathering information for a book talk;

> —a student in a college of education or library science who is studying children's literature and reference sources in the field;

> —a parent who is looking for a new way to interest your child in reading something more than the school curriculum prescribes;

> —an adult who enjoys children's literature for its own sake, knowing that a good children's book has no age limits.

Scope

In *SATA* you will find detailed information about authors and illustrators who span the full time range of children's literature, from early figures like John Newbery and L. Frank Baum to contemporary figures like Judy Blume and Richard Peck. Authors in the series represent primarily English-speaking countries, particularly the United States, Canada, and the United Kingdom. Also included, however, are authors from around the world whose works are available in English translation, for example: from France, Jean and Laurent De Brunhoff; from Italy, Emanuele Luzzati; from the Netherlands, Jaap ter Haar; from Germany, James Krüss; from Norway, Babbis Friis-Baastad; from Japan, Toshiko Kanzawa; from the Soviet Union, Kornei Chukovsky; from Switzerland, Alois Carigiet, to name only a few. Also appearing in *SATA* are Newbery medalists from Hendrik Van Loon (1922) to Robin McKinley (1985). The writings represented in *SATA* include those created intentionally for children and young adults as well as those written for a general audience and known to interest younger readers. These writings cover the spectrum from picture books, humor, folk and fairy tales, animal stories, mystery and adventure, science fiction and fantasy, historical fiction, poetry and nonsense verse, to drama, biography, and nonfiction.

Information Features

In *SATA* you will find full-length entries that are being presented in the series for the first time. This volume, for example, marks the first full-length appearance of Enrico Arno, Dick Bruna, Grahame Corbett, Gail E. Haley, Jim Henson, David Levine, and Robert Tallon, among others. Since Volume 25, each *SATA* volume also includes newly revised and updated biographies for a selection of early *SATA* listees who remain of interest to today's readers and who have been active enough to require extensive revision of their earlier entries. The entry for a given biographee may be revised as often as there is substantial new information to provide. In Volume 43 you'll find revised entries for Beverly Cleary, Charles I. Coombs, Walter Farley, Patricia Miles Martin, and Alice Mary Norton.

Brief Entries, first introduced in Volume 27, are another regular feature of *SATA*. Brief Entries present essentially the same types of information found in a full entry but do so in a capsule form and without illustration. These entries are intended to give you useful and timely information while the more time-consuming process of compiling a full-length biography is in progress. In this volume you'll find Brief Entries for Jeni Bassett, Lorinda Bryan Cauley, Cherry Barbara Lockett Grimm, Dorothy F. Haas, P. J. Petersen, Ilse Plume, and Piero Ventura, among others.

Obituaries have been included in *SATA* since Volume 20. An Obituary is intended not only as a death notice but also as a concise view of a person's life and work. Obituaries may appear for persons who have entries in earlier *SATA* volumes, as well as for people who have not yet appeared in the series. In this volume Obituaries mark the recent deaths of Louise Seaman Bechtel, Elizabeth Cleaver, Lester Cooper, Robert Nathan, and others.

Each *SATA* volume provides a cumulative index in two parts: first, the Illustrations Index, arranged by the name of the illustrator, gives the number of the volume and page where the illustrator's work appears in the current volume as well as all preceding volumes in the series; second, the Author Index gives the number of the volume in which a person's biographical sketch, Brief Entry, or Obituary appears in the current volume as well as all preceding volumes in the series. These indexes also include references to authors and illustrators who appear in *Yesterday's Authors of Books for Children.* Beginning with Volume 36, the *SATA* Author Index provides cross-references to authors who are included in *Children's Literature Review.*

You will also find cross-references to authors who are included in the *Something about the Author Autobiography Series,* starting with Volume 42. This companion series to *SATA* is described in detail below.

Illustrations

While the textual information in *SATA* is its primary reason for existing, photographs and illustrations not only enliven the text but are an integral part of the information that *SATA* provides. Illustrations and text are wedded in such a special way in children's literature that artists and their works naturally occupy a prominent place among *SATA*'s listees. The illustrators that you'll find in the series include such past masters of children's book illustration as Randolph Caldecott, Kate Greenaway, Walter Crane, Arthur Rackham, and Ernest L. Shepard, as well as such noted contemporary artists as Maurice Sendak, Edward Gorey, Tomie de Paola, and Margot Zemach. There are Caldecott medalists from Dorothy Lathrop (the first recipient in 1938) to Trina Schart Hyman (the latest winner in 1985); cartoonists like Charles Schulz, ("Peanuts"), Walt Kelly ("Pogo"), Hank Ketcham ("Dennis the Menace"), and Georges Rémi ("Tintin"); photographers like Jill Krementz, Tana Hoban, Bruce McMillan, and Bruce Curtis; and filmmakers like Walt Disney, Alfred Hitchcock, and Steven Spielberg.

In more than a dozen years of recording the metamorphosis of children's literature from the printed page to other media, *SATA* has become something of a repository of photographs that are unique in themselves and exist nowhere else as a group, particularly many of the classics of motion picture and stage history and photographs that have been specially loaned to us from private collections.

What a *SATA* Entry Provides

Whether you're already familiar with the *SATA* series or just getting acquainted, you will want to be aware of the kind of information that an entry provides. In every *SATA* entry the editors attempt to give as complete a picture of the person's life and work as possible. In some cases that full range of information may simply be unavailable, or a biographee may choose not to reveal complete personal details. The information that the editors attempt to provide in every entry is arranged in the following categories:

1. The "head" of the entry gives

        —the most complete form of the name,
        —any part of the name not commonly used, included in parentheses,
        —birth and death dates, if known; a (?) indicates a discrepancy in published sources,

—pseudonyms or name variants under which the person has had books published or is publicly known, in parentheses in the second line.

2. "Personal" section gives

—date and place of birth and death,
—parents' names and occupations,
—name of spouse, date of marriage, and names of children,
—educational institutions attended, degrees received, and dates,
—religious and political affiliations,
—agent's name and address,
—home and/or office address.

3. "Career" section gives

—name of employer, position, and dates for each career post,
—military service,
—memberships,
—awards and honors.

4. "Writings" section gives

—title, first publisher and date of publication, and illustration information for each book written; revised editions and other significant editions for books with particularly long publishing histories; genre, when known.

5. "Adaptations" section gives

—title, major performers, producer, and date of all known reworkings of an author's material in another medium, like movies, filmstrips, television, recordings, plays, etc.

6. "Sidelights" section gives

—commentary on the life or work of the biographee either directly from the person (and often written specifically for the *SATA* entry), or gathered from biographies, diaries, letters, interviews, or other published sources.

7. "For More Information See" section gives

—books, feature articles, films, plays, and reviews in which the biographee's life or work has been treated.

How a *SATA* Entry Is Compiled

A *SATA* entry progresses through a series of steps. If the biographee is living, the *SATA* editors try to secure information directly from him or her through a questionnaire. From the information that the biographee supplies, the editors prepare an entry, filling in any essential missing details with research. The author or illustrator is then sent a copy of the entry to check for accuracy and completeness.

If the biographee is deceased or cannot be reached by questionnaire, the *SATA* editors examine a wide variety of published sources to gather information for an entry. Biographical sources are searched with the aid of Gale's *Biography and Genealogy Master Index*. Bibliographic sources like the *National Union Catalog*, the *Cumulative Book Index*, *American Book Publishing Record*, and the *British Museum Catalogue* are consulted, as are book reviews, feature articles, published interviews, and material sometimes obtained from the biographee's family, publishers, agent, or other associates.

For each entry presented in *SATA*, the editors also attempt to locate a photograph of the biographee as well as representative illustrations from his or her books. After surveying the available books which the biographee has written and/or illustrated, and then making a selection of appropriate photographs and illustrations, the editors request permission of the current copyright holders to reprint the material. In the case of older books for which the copyright may have passed through several hands, even locating the current copyright holder is often a long and involved process.

We invite you to examine the entire *SATA* series, starting with this volume. Described below are some of the people in Volume 43 that you may find particularly interesting.

Highlights of This Volume

DICK BRUNA......who became an author and illustrator of children's books when his own offspring grew old enough to read. At the time, this Dutch artist was greatly annoyed by the complexity of picture books. "They sometimes seemed to be written for parents," he recalls, "more than for children of a particular age." Bruna's extremely uncluttered works feature sparse texts and equally direct illustrations in bright, eye-popping primary colors. "If you make it that simple," he explains, "you leave the children a lot of room for their own imagination." Bruna is proud of the fact that his picture books have been used to aid handicapped youngsters. Surprisingly, he generally doesn't "feel all that comfortable with children. . . . I'm not sure what kind of attitude to adopt." He certainly has hit upon the right attitude in his children's books like *Miffy, The Apple, Tilly and Tess,* and *Snuffy.*

BEVERLY CLEARY......was born on a farm in Oregon where she spent six happy years of her childhood before her parents decided to move into the city. Cleary recalls the indignity she suffered as a "Blackbird" in the lowest level reading group in the first grade. Fortunately, Cleary became an avid reader when she reached the third grade. "Writing for young readers was my childhood ambition. . . ," she reveals. "I wanted to read funny stories about the sort of children I knew and I decided that someday when I grew up I would write them." True to her word, Cleary has been amusing young readers for over thirty years with the madcap antics of characters like Henry Huggins and Ramona Quimby. As a writer, Cleary sees herself collaborating with "the child within myself—a rather odd, serious little girl . . . seeking laughter in the pages of books." That ever-present girl has injected her fun-loving spirit into stories like *Henry and Ribsy, Beezus and Ramona, The Mouse and the Motorcycle, Jean and Johnny,* and the 1984 Newbery Award winner, *Dear Mr. Henshaw.*

WALTER FARLEY......author of *The Black Stallion,* one of the best-known horses in children's fiction. Generations of readers have followed the one-of-a-kind relationship between The Black, a furiously wild Arabian stallion, and Alec Ramsay, the young boy who tames him. A horse lover since childhood, Farley remembers his own boyhood encounter with the great racehorse, Man o' War. "What accounted for this stirring of the heart? . . . Was it the regal lift of his head, the giant sweep of his body, or the dignity with which he held himself. . .? Whatever accounted for it, I stood in his presence with quiet reverence. . . ." Farley knows that "there is no way to explain the *magic* that some people have with horses. It is almost a mystical gift." This sense of wonder and excitement can be found in his many adventures, including *The Black Stallion Returns, The Island Stallion,* and *The Black Stallion and Flame.*

GAIL E. HALEY......the only children's book illustrator to receive both the Caldecott Medal and the Kate Greenaway Medal, for *A Story, a Story: An African Tale* and *The Post Office Cat,* respectively. She grew up "a barefoot child" in an old rural North Carolina village called Shuffletown. Her fascination with the written word began with visits to the offices of the Charlotte *Observer* where her father was art director. For Haley, "telling stories and illustrating them is my invitation to children to join me in a world of fantasy. . . . My aim is not to manipulate children, but to encourage them to be active, imaginative, whimsical, and curious." Children can be all these things and more when they read Haley's books like *My Kingdom for a Dragon, Noah's Ark, The Green Man,* and *Birdsong.*

JIM HENSON......creator of the "Muppets." Although Kermit the Frog and Rowlf the Dog appeared on television shows during the late 1950s and 1960s, it was the debut of "Sesame Street" in 1969 that launched the meteoric success of Henson and his Muppets. That show produced "personalities" like Big Bird, Bert and Ernie, Oscar the Grouch, and Cookie Monster. Henson's own "Muppet Show" appeared in 1976, starring the inimitable Miss Piggy. Since then, the Muppets have been featured in over a dozen television specials and full-length films. Henson views his creations as "a medium of expression. They are, in a sense, my palette. They definitely aren't alive, but they do have a life of their own, much like characters in a book." They have, indeed, filled the pages of innumerable book adaptations, including *The Sesame Street*

Book of Letters; Cookie Monster, Where Are You?; The Muppet Show Book; A Day in the Life of Oscar the Grouch; Don't Cry, Big Bird; Miss Piggy's Treasury of Art Masterpieces; and *The Muppet Guide to Magnificent Manners.*

JIRI TRNKA......a Czechoslovakian puppeteer, stage designer, animator, and author/illustrator of children's books. Trnka's innovative and creative use of puppets in film paved the way for later artists in his field. He began his most noteworthy work as a puppet film producer in the mid-1940s and garnered many international awards for his films like "The Czech Year," "The Emperor's Nightingale," and "A Midsummer Night's Dream." Trnka's passion for the puppet film was rooted in his national heritage. "The Czech artists have always looked for the world's reality not in size but rather in depth. . . . Perhaps it is for this reason that we love puppets, because in this smallest of worlds we attempt to express everything about life, about beauty and about love." In 1968 Trnka received the Hans Christian Andersen Medal as a tribute to his illustrative work in more than fifty books for children.

These are only a few of the authors and illustrators that you'll find in this volume. We hope you find all the entries in *SATA* both interesting and useful.

Something about the Author Autobiography Series

You can complement the information in *SATA* with the *Something about the Author Autobiography Series (SAAS),* which provides autobiographical essays written by important current authors and illustrators of books for children and young adults. In every volume of *SAAS* you will find about twenty specially commissioned autobiographies, each accompanied by a selection of personal photographs supplied by the authors. The wide range of contemporary writers and artists who describe their lives and interests in the *Autobiography Series* includes Joan Aiken, Betsy Byars, Leonard Everett Fisher, Milton Meltzer, Maia Wojciechowska, and Jane Yolen. Though the information presented in the autobiographies is as varied and unique as the authors, you can learn about the people and events that influenced these writers' early lives, how they began their careers, what problems they faced in becoming established in their professions, what prompted them to write or illustrate particular books, what they now find most challenging or rewarding in their lives, and what advice they may have for young people interested in following in their footsteps, among many other subjects.

Autobiographies included in the *SATA Autobiography Series* can be located through both the *SATA* cumulative index and the *SAAS* cumulative index, which lists not only the authors' names but also the subjects mentioned in their essays, such as titles of works and geographical and personal names.

The *SATA Autobiography Series* gives you the opportunity to view "close up" some of the fascinating people who are included in the *SATA* parent series. The combined *SATA* series makes available to you an unequaled range of comprehensive and in-depth information about the authors and illustrators of young people's literature.

Please write and tell us if we can make *SATA* even more helpful to you.

Forthcoming Authors

**A Partial List of Authors and Illustrators Who Will Appear
in Forthcoming Volumes of *Something about the Author***

Abels, Harriette S.
Allen, Agnes B.   1898-1959
Allert, Kathy
Anders, Rebecca
Anderson, Leone C.   1923-
Andrist, Ralph K.   1914-
Appleby, Ellen
Atkinson, Allen
Austin, R. G.
Axeman, Lois
Ayme, Marcel   1902-1967
Bains, Rae
Baker, Olaf
Balderson, Margaret   1935-
Bartlett, Margaret F.   1896-
Bauer, Caroline Feller   1935-
Bauer, John Albert   1882-1918
Beckman, Delores
Beim, Jerrold   1910-1957
Beim, Lorraine   1909-1951
Bernheim, Evelyne   1935-
Bernheim, Marc   1924-
Birnbaum, Abe   1899-
Boegehold, Betty   1913-1985
Boning, Richard A.
Bonners, Susan
Bourke, Linda
Bowen, Gary
Bracken, Carolyn
Brewton, Sara W.
Bridgman, Elizabeth P.   1921-
Bromley, Dudley   1948-
Bronin, Andrew   1947-
Bronson, Wilfrid   1894-
Brooks, Ron(ald George)   1948-
Brown, Roy Frederick   1921-
Brownmiller, Susan   1935-
Buchanan, William   1930-
Buchenholz, Bruce
Budney, Blossom   1921-
Burchard, Marshall
Burke, David   1927-
Burstein, Chaya M.
Butler, Dorothy   1925-
Butler, Hal   1913-
Calvert, Patricia
Camps, Luis   1928-
Carley, Wayne
Carlson, Nancy L.
Carrie, Christopher
Carroll, Ruth R.   1899-
Chambliss, Maxie
Chang, Florence C.

Charles, Carole
Charles, Donald   1929-
Chartier, Normand
Chase, Catherine
Clarke, Bob
Cline, Linda   1941-
Cohen, Joel H.
Cole, Brock
Cooper, Elizabeth Keyser   1910-
Cooper, Paulette   1944-
Cosgrove, Margaret   1926-
Coutant, Helen
Croll, Carolyn
Dabcovich, Lydia
Daniel, Alan   1939-
D'Aulnoy, Marie Catherine
   1650(?)-1705
David, Jay   1929-
Davies, Peter   1937-
Davis, Maggie S.   1942-
Dawson, Diane
Dean, Leigh
Degens, T.
Deguine, Jean-Claude   1943-
Dentinger, Don
Deweese, Gene   1934-
Ditmars, Raymond   1876-1942
Drescher, Henrik
Dumas, Philippe   1940-
Dunn, Phoebe
East, Ben
Edelson, Edward   1932-
Edens, Cooper
Eisenberg, Lisa
Elder, Lauren
Elwood, Roger   1943-
Endres, Helen
Enik, Ted
Epstein, Len
Eriksson, Eva
Erwin, Betty K.
Etter, Les   1904-
Everett-Green, Evelyn   1856-1932
Ewers, Joe
Falkner, John Meade   1858-1932
Felix, Monique
Fender, Kay
Filson, Brent
Fischer, Hans Erich   1909-1958
Flanagan, Geraldine Lux
Flint, Russ
Folch-Ribas, Jacques   1928-
Foley, Louise M.   1933-

Fox, Thomas C.
Freschet, Berniece   1927-
Frevert, Patricia D(endtler)   1943-
Funai, Mamoru R.   1932-
Gans, Roma   1894-
Garcia Sanchez, J(ose) L(uis)
Garrison, Christian   1942-
Gathje, Curtis
Gelman, Rita G.   1937-
Gemme, Leila Boyle   1942-
Gerber, Dan   1940-
Goldstein, Nathan   1927-
Gorbaty, Norman
Gould, Chester   1900-1985
Graeber, Charlotte Towner
Gray, J.M.L.
Gusman, Annie
Halverson, Lydia
Harris, Marilyn   1931-
Hayman, LeRoy   1916-
Heine, Helme   1941-
Henty, George Alfred   1832-1902
Herzig, Alison Cragin
Hicks, Clifford B.   1920-
Higashi, Sandra
Hockerman, Dennis
Hollander, Zander   1923-
Hood, Thomas   1779-1845
Howell, Troy
Hull, Jessie Redding
Hunt, Clara Whitehill   1871-1958
Hunt, Robert
Inderieden, Nancy
Irvine, Georgeanne
Iwamura, Kazuo   1939-
Jackson, Anita
Jackson, Kathryn   1907-
Jackson, Robert   1941-
Jameson, Cynthia
Janssen, Pierre
Jenkins, Jean
Johnson, Harper
Johnson, Maud
Johnson, Sylvia A.
Kahn, Joan   1914-
Kalan, Robert
Kantrowitz, Mildred
Kasuya, Masahiro   1937-
Keith, Eros   1942-
Kiedrowski, Priscilla
Kirn, Ann (Minette)   1910-
Koenig, Marion
Kohl, Herbert   1937-

Kohl, Judith
Kredenser, Gail 1936-
Kurland, Michael 1938-
Lawson, Annetta
Leach, Christopher 1925-
Lebrun, Claude
Leckie, Robert 1920-
Leder, Dora
Le-Tan, Pierre 1950-
Lewis, Naomi
Lindgren, Barbro
Lines, Kathleen
Livermore, Elaine
Lye, Keith
Mahany, Patricia
Mali, Jane Lawrence
Marcus, Elizabeth
Marks, Rita 1938-
Marron, Carol A.
Marryat, Frederick 1792-1848
Marsh, Carole
Marxhausen, Joanne G. 1935-
May, Dorothy
Mayakovsky, Vladimir 1894-1930
McKim, Audrey Margaret 1909-
McLoughlin, John C. 1949-
McReynolds, Ginny
Melcher, Frederic G. 1879-1963
Meyer, Kathleen Allan
Miller, J(ohn) P. 1919-
Milone, Karen
Molesworth, Mary L. 1839(?)-1921
Molly, Anne S. 1907-
Morris, Neil
Morris, Ting
Moskowitz, Stewart
Muntean, Michaela
Murdocca, Sal
Nickl, Peter
Nicoll, Helen
Obligado, Lillian Isabel 1931-
O'Brien, John 1953-
Odor, Ruth S. 1926-
Oppenheim, Shulamith (Levey) 1930-
Orr, Frank 1936-
Orton, Helen Fuller 1872-1955
Overbeck, Cynthia
Owens, Gail 1939-
Packard, Edward 1931-

Parker, Robert Andrew 1927-
Paterson, A(ndrew) B(arton) 1864-1941
Patterson, Sarah 1959-
Pavey, Peter
Pelgrom, Els
Peretz, Isaac Loeb 1851-1915
Perkins, Lucy Fitch 1865-1937
Phillips, Betty Lou
Plowden, David 1932-
Poignant, Axel
Pollard, Nan
Pollock, Bruce 1945-
Pollock, Penny 1935-
Polushkin, Maria
Porter, Eleanor Hodgman 1868-1920
Poulsson, Emilie 1853-1939
Powers, Richard M. 1921-
Prager, Arthur
Prather, Ray
Pursell, Margaret S.
Pursell, Thomas F.
Pyle, Katharine 1863-1938
Rabinowitz, Solomon 1859-1916
Randall, E.T.
Rappoport, Ken 1935-
Reese, Bob
Reich, Hanns
Reid, Alistair 1926-
Reidel, Marlene
Reiff, Tana
Reiss, Elayne
Reynolds, Marjorie 1903-
Rhodes, J.H.
Richards, Dorothy Fay 1915-
Rippon, Angela
Robert, Adrian
Rohmer, Harriet
Rosier, Lydia
Ross, Pat
Roy, Cal
Rudstrom, Lennart
Sadler, Marilyn
Sallis, Susan
Satchwell, John
Schindler, Regine
Schneider, Leo 1916-
Sealy, Adrienne V.
Seidler, Rosalie
Shelton, Ingrid

Silbert, Linda P.
Slepian, Jan(ice B.)
Smith, Alison
Smith, Catriona (Mary) 1948-
Smith, Ray(mond Kenneth) 1949-
Smollin, Michael J.
Sorenson, Jane
Steiner, Charlotte
Stevens, Leonard A. 1920-
Stine, R. Conrad 1937-
Stubbs, Joanna 1940-
Sullivan, Mary Beth
Suteev, Vladimir Grigor'evich
Sutherland, Robert D. 1937-
Sweet, Ozzie
Tarrant, Graham
Thaler, Mike
Timmermans, Gommaar 1930-
Todd, Ruthven 1914-
Tourneur, Dina K. 1934-
Treadgold, Mary 1910-
Velthuijs, Max 1923-
Villiard, Paul 1910-1974
Vincent, Gabrielle
Wagner, Jenny
Walker, Charles W.
Walsh, Anne Batterberry
Walter, Mildred P.
Watts, Franklin 1904-1978
Wayne, Bennett
Weston, Martha
Whelen, Gloria 1923-
White, Wallace 1930-
Wild, Jocelyn
Wild, Robin
Winter, Paula 1929-
Winterfeld, Henry 1901-
Wolde, Gunilla 1939-
Wong, Herbert H.
Woolfolk, Dorothy
Wormser, Richard 1908-
Wright, Betty R.
Wright, Bob
Yagawa, Sumiko
Youldon, Gillian
Zaslow, David
Zistel, Era
Zwerger, Lisbeth

In the interest of making *Something about the Author* as responsive as possible to the needs of its readers, the editor welcomes your suggestions for additional authors and illustrators to be included in the series.

Acknowledgments

Grateful acknowledgment is made to the following publishers, authors, and artists for their kind permission to reproduce copyrighted material.

ATHENEUM PUBLISHERS, INC. Illustration by Gail E. Haley from *A Story, a Story: An African Tale,* retold by Gail E. Haley. Copyright © 1970 by Gail E. Haley./ Jacket illustration by Jack Gaughan from *Wraiths of Time* by André Norton. Copyright © 1976 by André Norton./ Illustration by William Van Horn from *Harry Hoyle's Giant Jumping Bean* by William Van Horn. Copyright © 1978 by William Van Horn. All reprinted by permission of Atheneum Publishers, Inc.

THE BOBBS-MERRILL CO., INC. Illustration by Robert Tallon from *Zoophabets* by Robert Tallon. Copyright © 1971 by Robert Tallon./ Illustration by Robert Tallon from *Rhoda's Restaurant* by Robert Tallon. Text copyright © 1973 by Robert Tallon. Illustrations copyright © 1973 by Robert Tallon./ Illustration by Robert Tallon from *The Thing in Dolores' Piano* by Robert Tallon. Copyright © 1970 by Robert Tallon. All reprinted by permission of The Bobbs-Merrill Co., Inc.

THE BODLEY HEAD LTD. Illustration by Susan Einzig from "The Little Horses," in *The Children's Song Book* by Elizabeth Poston. Musical settings copyright © 1961 by Elizabeth Poston. Illustrations copyright © 1961 by The Bodley Head Ltd./ Illustration by Ossie Murray from *Sally-Ann in the Snow* by Petronella Breinburg. Text copyright © 1977 by Petronella Breinburg. Illustrations copyright © 1977 by Ossie Murray. Both reprinted by permission of The Bodley Head Ltd.

THE CAXTON PRINTERS LTD. Illustration by Agnes Kay Randall from *Lucretia Ann on the Oregon Trail* by Ruth Gipson Plowhead. Copyright 1931 by Ruth Gipson Plowhead. Reprinted by permission of The Caxton Printers Ltd.

CHARIOT BOOKS. Illustration by Scott Gustafson from *The President's Stuck in the Mud and Other Wild West Escapades* by Stephen A. Bly. Text copyright © 1982 by Stephen A. Bly. Illustrations copyright © 1982 by Scott Gustafson. Reprinted by permission of Chariot Books.

COWARD, McCANN & GEOGHEGAN, INC. Illustration by Enrico Arno from *Brendan the Navigator: A History Mystery about the Discovery of America* by Jean Fritz. Text copyright © 1979 by Jean Fritz. Illustrations copyright © 1979 by Enrico Arno./ Jacket design by Rachel Isadora, photograph by Martha Swope, and Sidelight excerpts from *Worlds Apart: The Autobiography of a Dancer from Brooklyn* by Robert Maiorano. All reprinted by permission of Coward, McCann & Geoghegan, Inc.

THOMAS Y. CROWELL, CO. PUBLISHERS. Illustration by Judith Gwyn Brown from *Lavender-Green Magic* by André Norton. Copyright © 1974 by André Norton./ Illustration by Robin Jacques from *Dragon Magic* by André Norton. Copyright © 1972 by André Norton. Illustrations copyright © 1972 by Robin Jacques. Both reprinted by permission of Thomas Y. Crowell, Co. Publishers.

DELACORTE PRESS. Illustration by Lynd Ward from *Dream of the Blue Heron* by Victor Barnouw. Copyright © 1966 by Victor Barnouw./ Frontispiece illustration by Trina Schart Hyman from *For Reading Out Loud! A Guide to Sharing Books with Children* by Margaret Mary Kimmel and Elizabeth Segel. Foreword by Betsy Byars. Text copyright © 1983 by Margaret Mary Kimmel and Elizabeth Segel. Foreword copyright © 1983 by Betsy Byars. Illustrations copyright © 1983 by Trina Schart Hyman./ Illustrations by Ted Shearer from *Billy Jo Jive and the Walkie-Talkie Caper* by John Shearer. Text copyright © 1981 by Shearer Visuals, Inc. Illustrations copyright © 1981 by Ted Shearer./ Illustration by Ted Shearer from *Billy Jo Jive and the Case of the Midnight Voices* by John Shearer. Text copyright © 1982 by Shearer Visuals, Inc. Illustrations copyright © 1982 by Ted Shearer. All reprinted by permission of Delacorte Press.

DELL PUBLISHING CO., INC. Illustration by Beth and Joe Krush from *Emily's Runaway Imagination* by Beverly Cleary. Copyright © 1961 by Beverly Cleary./ Illustration by Louis Darling from *Henry and the Paper Route* by Beverly Cleary. Copyright © 1957 by Beverly Cleary./ Illustration by Beatrice Darwin from *Socks* by Beverly Cleary. Copyright © 1973 by Beverly Cleary./ Illustration by Paul O. Zelinsky from *Dear Mr. Henshaw* by Beverly Cleary. Copyright © 1983 by Beverly Cleary./ Illustration by Alan Tiegreen from *Ramona Quimby,*

Age 8 by Beverly Cleary. Copyright © 1981 by Beverly Cleary. All reprinted by permission of Dell Publishing Co., Inc.

J. M. DENT & SONS LTD. Illustration by Charles Mozley from *The Red Badge of Courage* by Stephen Crane. Illustrations copyright © 1971 by J. M. Dent & Sons Ltd. Reprinted by permission of J. M. Dent & Sons Ltd.

DILLON PRESS, INC. Photograph by Ann Newman from *China: From Emperors to Communes* by Chris and Janie Filstrup. Copyright © 1983 by Dillon Press, Inc. Photograph copyright © 1981 by Ann Newman. Reprinted by permission of Dillon Press, Inc.

DODD, MEAD & CO. Photograph by Paul Conklin from *Cimarron Kid* by Paul Conklin. Copyright © 1973 by Paul S. Conklin. Reprinted by permission of Dodd, Mead & Co.

DOUBLEDAY & CO., INC. Illustration by Enrico Arno from *Paul Bunyan and His Great Blue Ox*, retold by Wallace Wadsworth. Copyright © 1964 by Doubleday & Co., Inc. Text copyright 1926 by George H. Doran Co./ Sidelight excerpts from *How to Stay Out of Trouble with Your Horse: Some Basic Safety Rules to Help You Enjoy Riding* by Walter Farley. Copyright © 1981 by Doubleday & Co., Inc./ Illustration by Victoria Hodgetts from *Dream of the Dinosaurs* by Blake Christopher Hodgetts. Copyright © 1978 by Blake Christopher Hodgetts and Victoria Hodgetts./ Illustration by Patricia Mighell from *Hold Me Up a Little Longer, Lord* by Marjorie Holmes. Copyright © 1971, 1972, 1973, 1974, 1975, 1976, 1977 by Marjorie Holmes Mighell./ Illustration by Betty Fraser from *I've Got to Talk to Somebody, God: A Woman's Conversation with God* by Marjorie Holmes. Copyright © 1968, 1969 by Marjorie Holmes Mighell. All reprinted by permission of Doubleday & Co., Inc.

E. P. DUTTON, INC. Illustration by Grahame Corbett from *Who Is Hiding?* by Grahame Corbett. Copyright © 1982 by Grahame Corbett./ Illustration by Charles Mozley from *The Red Badge of Courage* by Stephen Crane. Illustrations copyright © 1971 by J. M. Dent & Sons Ltd./ Jacket illustration by David K. Stone from *The White Jade Fox* by André Norton. Copyright © 1975 by André Norton./ Jacket illustration by Jack Crane from *The Opal-Eyed Fan* by André Norton. Copyright © 1977 by André Norton./ Jacket photograph by Peter K. Fine from *It's Crazy to Stay Chinese in Minnesota* by Eleanor Wong Telemaque. All reprinted by permission of E. P. Dutton, Inc.

EXETER BOOKS. Illustration by Jiri Trnka from "The Bremen Town-Musicians" by The Brothers Grimm, in *Favorite Tales from Grimm and Andersen.* Copyright © 1959, 1961 by Artia./ Illustration by Jiri Trnka from "The Snow Queen" by Hans Christian Andersen, in *Favorite Tales from Grimm and Andersen.* Copyright © 1959, 1961 by Artia./ Illustration by Jiri Trnka from "The Swineherd" by Hans Christian Andersen, in *Favorite Tales from Grimm and Andersen.* Copyright © 1959, 1961 by Artia./ Illustration by Jiri Trnka from "The Ugly Duckling" by Hans Christian Andersen, in *Favorite Tales from Grimm and Andersen.* Copyright © 1959, 1961 by Artia. All reprinted by permission of Exeter Books.

EMIL FINK VERLAG. Illustrations by Berta Hummel from *The Hummel-Book,* poems and preface by Margarete Seemann. Translation by Lola C. Eytel. Illustrations copyright 1934 by Emil Fink Verlag. All reprinted by permission of Emil Fink Verlag.

THE FOLIO SOCIETY (London). Wood engraving by Joan Hassall from *Sense and Sensibility* by Jane Austen. Reprinted by permission of The Folio Society (London).

FOUR WINDS PRESS. Jacket illustration by Ronald Himler from *As the Waltz Was Ending* by Emma Macalik Butterworth. Copyright © 1982 by Emma Macalik Butterworth. Reprinted by permission of Four Winds Press.

FUNK & WAGNALLS, INC. Illustration by Ingrid Fetz from *The Wisher's Handbook* by Francine Jacobs. Text copyright © 1968 by Francine Jacobs. Illustrations copyright © 1968 by Ingrid Fetz. Reprinted by permission of Funk & Wagnalls, Inc.

GAMBIT INC., PUBLISHERS. Illustration by David Levine from *Pens and Needles: Literary Caricatures,* selected and introduced by John Updike. Illustrations copyright © 1969 by David Levine. Introduction copyright © 1969 by John Updike./ Illustration by David Levine from *The Fables of Aesop,* selected by David Levine. Copyright © 1965 by David Levine. Both reprinted by permission of Gambit Inc., Publishers.

GARLAND PUBLISHING, INC. Illustration from *Elsie Dinsmore* by Martha Finley. Reprinted by permission of Garland Publishing, Inc.

GRAIL. Sidelight excerpts from *Sketch Me, Berta Hummel! Biography of Sister Maria Innocentia* by Sister M. Gonsalva Wiegand. Reprinted by permission of Grail.

GREENWILLOW BOOKS. Illustration by Kevin Henkes from *Clean Enough* by Kevin

Henkes. Copyright © 1982 by Kevin Henkes./ Illustration by Rachel Isadora from *Backstage* by Robert Maiorano and Rachel Isadora. Text copyright © 1978 by Robert Maiorano and Rachel Isadora. Illustrations copyright © 1978 by Rachel Isadora Hite. Both reprinted by permission of Greenwillow Books.

GROSSET & DUNLAP. Illustration by Ben Carlton Mead from *Coronado's Children: Tales of Lost Mines and Buried Treasures of the Southwest* by J. Frank Dobie. Copyright 1930 by The Southwest Press. Reprinted by permission of Grosset & Dunlap.

HARCOURT BRACE JOVANOVICH, INC. Illustration by Enrico Arno from *The Wicked Enchantment* by Margot Benary-Isbert. Copyright 1955 by Harcourt Brace and Co./ Illustration by Enrico Arno from *Down from the Lonely Mountain: California Indian Tales*, retold by Jane Louise Curry. Copyright © 1965 by Jane Louise Curry./ Illustration by Douglas Hall from *Storm from the West* by Barbara Willard. Copyright © 1963 by Barbara Willard. All reprinted by permission of Harcourt Brace Jovanovich, Inc.

HARPER & ROW, PUBLISHERS INC. Illustration by Eros Keith from *In a Blue Velvet Dress* by Catherine Sefton. Text copyright © 1972, 1973 by Catherine Sefton. Illustrations copyright © 1973 by Eros Keith./ Illustration by Robert Quackenbush from *Six Silver Spoons* by Janette Sebring Lowrey. Text copyright © 1971 by Janette Sebring Lowrey. Illustrations copyright © 1971 by Robert Quackenbush./ Illustration by Irv Docktor from *The Casket and the Sword* by Norman Dale. Copyright © 1956 by Harper & Brothers. All reprinted by permission of Harper & Row, Publishers Inc.

THE HERITAGE PRESS. Illustration by Charles Mozley from *The Invisible Man* by H. G. Wells. Special contents copyright © 1967 by The George Macy Co. Inc. Reprinted by permission of The Heritage Press.

HOLT, RINEHART & WINSTON. Photograph by John E. Barrett from *Miss Piggy's Treasury of Art Masterpieces from the Kermitage Collection,* edited by Henry Beard. Copyright © 1982, 1983, 1984 by Henson Associates, Inc./ Illustration by Robert Tallon from *Fish Story* by Robert Tallon. Copyright © 1977 by Robert Tallon./ Illustration by Robert Tallon from *Rotten Kidphabets* by Robert Tallon. Copyright © 1975 by Robert Tallon./ Illustration by Robert Tallon from *Conversations: Cries, Croaks, and Calls* by Robert Tallon. Copyright © 1963 by Robert Tallon./ Illustration by Laszlo Matulay from *By His Own Might: The Battles of Beowulf* by Dorothy Hosford. Copyright 1947 by Henry Holt & Co., Inc. All reprinted by permission of Holt, Rinehart & Winston.

THE HORN BOOK, INC. Sidelight excerpts from *Illustrators of Children's Books: 1946-1956,* compiled by Bertha M. Miller and others. Copyright © 1958 by The Horn Book, Inc./ Sidelight excerpts from an article "The Album and the Artist," by Noel Streatfeild, April, 1964 in *Horn Book.* Copyright © 1964 by The Horn Book, Inc./ Sidelight excerpts from an article "Caldecott Medal Acceptance," by Gail E. Haley, August, 1977 in *Horn Book.* All reprinted by permission of The Horn Book, Inc.

HOUGHTON MIFFLIN CO. Jacket illustration by Diane de Groat from *O Zebron Falls!* by Charles Ferry. Copyright © 1977 by Charles Ferry./ Jacket illustration by Abigail Rorer from *Jeremy Visick* by David Wiseman. Jacket illustration copyright © 1981 by Abigail Rorer. Both reprinted by permission of Houghton Mifflin Co.

ALFRED A. KNOPF, INC. Illustration by Robert Tallon from *Latouse, My Moose* by Robert Tallon. Copyright © 1983 by Robert Tallon./ Photographs from *Of Muppets and Men: The Making of the Muppet Show* by Christopher Finch. Copyright © 1981 by Henson Associates, Inc. All reprinted by permission of Alfred A. Knopf, Inc.

THE LION PRESS. Illustration by Robert Tallon from *A.B.C....in English and Spanish* by Robert Tallon. Reprinted by permission of The Lion Press.

J. B. LIPPINCOTT CO. Illustration by Paul Bransom from *The Wahoo Bobcat* by Joseph Wharton Lippincott. Copyright 1950 by Joseph Wharton Lippincott. Reprinted by permission of J. B. Lippincott Co.

LITTLE, BROWN & CO. Illustration by Linda Allison from *The Reasons for Seasons: The Great Cosmic Megagalactic Trip without Moving from Your Chair* by Linda Allison. Copyright © 1975 by The Yolla Bolly Press./ Sidelight excerpts from *Some Part of Myself* by J. Frank Dobie./ Illustration by Tom Lea from *Apache Gold and Yaqui Silver* by J. Frank Dobie. Copyright 1928, 1931, 1938, 1939 by J. Frank Dobie./ Illustration by Charles Banks Wilson from *The Mustangs* by J. Frank Dobie. Copyright 1934, 1951, 1952 by The Curtis Publishing Co. Copyright 1936, 1949, 1950, 1951, 1952 by J. Frank Dobie./ Illustration by Tom Lea from *The Longhorns* by J. Frank Dobie. Copyright 1941 by J. Frank Dobie./ Illustration by Roland Rodegast from *Backyard Vacation: Outdoor Fun in Your Own Neighborhood* by Carolyn

PORTFOLIO PRESS. Photograph by Seymour Linden and Sidelight excerpts from *Hummel: The Complete Collector's Guide and Illustrated Reference* by Eric Ehrmann. Reprinted by permission of Portfolio Press.

PUFFIN BOOKS. Illustration by Michael Jackson from *Shadow in the Clouds* by Douglas Botting. Illustrations copyright © 1975 by Michael Jackson. Reprinted by permission of Puffin Books.

THE PUTNAM PUBLISHING GROUP. Jacket illustration by Robert Andrew Parker from *The Great Toozy Takeover* by Rosalie Kelly. Copyright © 1975 by Rosalie Kelly./ Illustration by Tom Hamil from *Kumi and the Pearl* by Patricia Miles Martin. Copyright © 1968 by Patricia Miles Martin and Tom Hamil./ Illustration by Leonard Vosburgh from *Yankee Privateer* by André Norton. Copyright 1955 by The World Publishing Co./ Illustration by Alberto Beltran from *The Incas: People of the Sun* by Victor W. Von Hagen. Copyright © 1961 by Victor W. Von Hagen. All reprinted by permission of The Putnam Publishing Group.

RANDOM HOUSE, INC. Sidelight excerpts from *Man o' War* by Walter Farley. Copyright © 1962 by Walter Farley./ Jacket illustration by Ruth Sanderson from *The Black Stallion* by Walter Farley. Copyright 1941, © 1969 by Walter Farley. Jacket illustration copyright © 1982 by Ruth Sanderson./ Illustration by Harold Eldridge from *The Black Stallion Returns* by Walter Farley. Copyright 1945 by Walter Farley./ Illustration by Angie Draper from *The Black Stallion and the Girl* by Walter Farley. Copyright © 1971 by Walter Farley./ Illustration by Milton Menasco from *Son of the Black Stallion* by Walter Farley. Copyright 1947 by Walter Farley./ Illustration by Joe Mathieu from *Christmas Eve on Sesame Street*, created by Jon Stone. Copyright © 1981 by Children's Television Workshop. All reprinted by permission of Random House, Inc.

SCHOCKEN BOOKS, INC. Illustration by Charles Mozley from *At the Back of the North Wind* by George MacDonald. Illustrations copyright © 1963 by The Nonesuch Press Ltd. Reprinted by permission of Schocken Books, Inc.

SCHOLASTIC, INC. Sidelight excerpts from *More Books by More People* by Lee Bennett Hopkins. Copyright © 1979 by Scholastic, Inc. Reprinted by permission of Scholastic, Inc.

CHARLES SCRIBNER'S SONS. Illustration by Gail E. Haley from *Go Away, Stay Away!* by Gail E. Haley. Copyright © 1977 by Gail E. Haley./ Illustration by Gail E. Haley from *The Green Man* by Gail E. Haley. Copyright © 1979 by Gail E. Haley. Both reprinted by permission of Charles Scribner's Sons.

TUNDRA BOOKS, INC. Illustration by Pat Bonn from *Ella: An Elephant—Un Elephant* by Jan Andrews. Copyright © 1976 by Tundra Books, Inc./ Illustration by John Lim from *Merchants of the Mysterious East* by John Lim. Copyright © 1981 by John Lim. Both reprinted by permission of Tundra Books, Inc.

THE VIKING PRESS. Jacket illustration by Carl Kidwell from *Granada, Surrender!* by Carl Kidwell. Copyright © 1968 by Carl Kidwell./ Jacket illustration by Bruce Waldman from *Iron Cage* by André Norton. Copyright © 1974 by André Norton./ Jacket illustration by Charles Mikolaycak from *Forerunner Foray* by André Norton. Copyright © 1973 by André Norton./ Illustration by Gail E. Haley from *The Abominable Swamp Man* by Gail E. Haley. Copyright © 1975 by Gail E. Haley. All reprinted by permission of The Viking Press.

WALKER & CO. Illustration by Bernard Colonna from *Star Ka'at* by André Norton and Dorothy Madlee. Text copyright © 1976 by André Norton and Dorothy Madlee. Illustrations copyright © 1976 by Bernard Colonna. Reprinted by permission of Walker & Co.

FRANKLIN WATTS, INC. Illustration from *Tomorrow's Home* by Neil Ardley. Copyright © 1981 by Franklin Watts, Inc./ Illustration by Charles Mozley from "Little Red Riding Hood," in *Famous Fairy Tales* by Charles Perrault. Copyright © 1959 by Franklin Watts, Inc./ Illustration by Charles Mozley from *A Vicarage Family* by Noel Streatfeild. Copyright © 1963 by Noel Streatfeild. All reprinted by permission of Franklin Watts, Inc.

ALBERT WHITMAN & CO. Illustration by Maj Lindman from *Snipp, Snapp, Snurr and the Gingerbread* by Maj Lindman. Copyright 1936, © 1964 by Albert Whitman & Co. Reprinted by permission of Albert Whitman & Co.

Sidelight excerpts from an article "Enrico Arno, Graphic Artist," by Fritz Eichenberg, May, 1956, in *American Artist*. Copyright © 1956 by *American Artist*. Reprinted by permission of *American Artist*./ Poster by Alan Tiegreen of Beverly Cleary's "Ramona." Copyright © 1984 by Beverly Cleary. Reprinted by permission of The American Library Association./ Sidelight excerpts from an article "A National Heroine and an International Favorite," by Shirley Fitzgibbons, winter, 1977 in *Top of the News*. Reprinted by permission of The American Library Association./ Sidelight excerpts from an article "Reducing the Gods to Scale," by Herbert Mitgang, March, 1976 in *Art News,* Volume 75, number 3. Reprinted by permission of *Art News.*/ Sidelight excerpts from *More Books by More People* by Lee Bennett Hopkins. Copyright © 1974 by Citation Press. Reprinted by permission of Curtis Brown Ltd./ Sidelight excerpts from an article "Writing for Young Adults," by Marjorie Holmes, August, 1983 in *Catholic Library World*. Reprinted by permission of *Catholic Library World.*/ Sidelight excerpts from an article "Low Man in the Reading Circle: Or, A Blackbird Takes Wing," by Beverly Cleary, June, 1969 in *Horn Book*. Reprinted by permission of Beverly Cleary.

Sidelight excerpts from "Laura Ingalls Wilder Award Acceptance," by Beverly Cleary, August, 1975, in *Horn Book*. Reprinted by permission of Beverly Cleary./ Sidelight excerpts from "Newbery Medal Acceptance," by Beverly Cleary, August, 1984 in *Horn Book*. Reprinted by permission of Beverly Cleary./ Sidelight excerpts from a letter from Walter Farley to Louise Bonino, March 19, 1942. Taken from a personal collection in the Rare Book and Manuscript Department of the Columbia University Libraries. Reprinted by permission of Columbia University Libraries./ Sidelight excerpts from an article "The Puppet Film as an Art," by J. Box, winter, 1955, in *Film Culture,* Volume 1, number 5-6. Reprinted by permission of *Film Culture.*/ Sidelight excerpts from *Man o' War* by Walter Farley. Copyright © 1962 by Walter Farley. Reprinted by permission of International Creative Management./ Illustration by Ted Shearer from the comic strip "Quincy," created and written by Ted Shearer, June 17, 1970. Copyright by King Features Syndicate, Inc. Reprinted by permission of King Features Syndicate, Inc./ Photograph from *Be Your Own Weather Forecaster* by Shaaron Cosner. Copyright © 1981 by Shaaron Cosner. Reprinted by permission of Julian Messner./ Cover illustration by Robert Tallon from *New Yorker*. Reprinted by permission of *New Yorker*.

Sidelight excerpts from an article "How the Muppets Got That Way," by Gerald Nachman, January 24, 1965 in *New York Post*. Reprinted by permission of *New York Post.*/ Sidelight excerpts from an article "Jim Henson Fights Trash with Trash," by George Maksian, March 18, 1973 in *New York Sunday News*. Copyright © 1973 by New York News, Inc. Reprinted by permission of New York News, Inc./ Sidelight excerpts from an article "The Muppets in Movieland," by John Culhane, June 10, 1979 in *New York Times* magazine. Copyright © 1979 by The New York Times Co. Reprinted by permission of The New York Times Co./ Sidelight excerpts from an article "Muppets on the Move," by Hank Nuwer, December, 1980 in *Saturday Evening Post*. Reprinted by permission of Hank Nuwer./ Sidelight excerpts from an article "Muppets on His Hands," by Don Freeman, November, 1979 in *Saturday Evening Post*. Copyright © 1979 by The Saturday Evening Post Co. Reprinted by permission of The Saturday Evening Post Co./ Sidelight excerpts from an article "The Muppet Family and How it Grew," by Robert Higgins, May 16, 1970 in *TV Guide*. Copyright © 1970 by Triangle Publications, Inc. Reprinted by permission of Triangle Publications, Inc.

Sidelight excerpts from an article "Behind Every Great Muppet . . . Stands Jim Henson, Who Has Crafted a Multimillion Dollar Empire Out of Bulbous Noses, Floppy Ears and Shaggy Humor," by Don Kowet, August 6, 1977 in *TV Guide*. Copyright © 1977 by Triangle Publications, Inc. Reprinted by permission of Triangle Publications, Inc./ Sidelight excerpts from an article "Ta-Dahhh! It's Jim Henson, Creator of Kermit the Frog and King of the Muppets," by Tom Shales, January 25, 1977 in *Washington Post*. Copyright © 1977 by *Washington Post*. Reprinted by permission of *Washington Post.*/ Illustration by Joe Mathieu from *Christmas Eve on Sesame Street,* created by Jon Stone. Copyright © 1981 by Children's Television Workshop. Reprinted by permission of Children's Television Workshop./ Sidelight excerpts from an article "Beverly Cleary: A Favorite Author of Children," by Margaret Novinger in *Authors and Illustrators of Children's Books,* edited by Miriam Hoffman and Eva Samuels. Reprinted by permission of Xerox Corp.

Appreciation also to the Performing Arts Research Center of the New York Public Library at Lincoln Center for permission to reprint the movie stills "The Great Muppet Caper," "The Muppet Movie," and "Sesame Street Presents: Follow That Bird"; and the television stills "Big Bird and Some of His 'Sesame Street' Friends" and "Dr. Teeth and The Electric Mayhem."

PHOTOGRAPH CREDITS

Neil Ardley: John Coles; Beverly Cleary: Sandra Hansen; Shaaron Cosner: John Nesti; Walter Farley: Virginia F. Stern; E. Christian Filstrup: David Bleiwith; Annegert Fuchshuber: Wolfgang Diekamp; Gail E. Haley: George Flowers; Kevin Henkes: Jon Henkes; James Maury

SOMETHING ABOUT THE AUTHOR

ADA, Alma Flor   1938-

PERSONAL: Born January 3, 1938, in Camaguey, Cuba; daughter of Modesto A. (a professor) and Alma (a teacher; maiden name, Lafuente) Ada; married Armando Zubizarreta, 1961 (divorced, 1971); married Jorgen Voss, 1984; children: (first marriage) Rosalma, Alfonso, Miguel, Gabriel. *Education:* Universidad Central de Madrid, diploma, 1959; Pontificia Universidad Catolica del Peru, M.A., 1963, Ph.D., 1965; Harvard University, post-doctoral study, 1965-67. *Home:* 639 Newlands Ave., San Mateo, Calif. 94403. *Office:* University of San Francisco, San Francisco, Calif. 94117.

CAREER: Colegio Alexander von Humboldt, Lima, Peru, instructor and head of Spanish department, 1963-65, 1967-69; Fulbright scholar and Mary Bunting Institute at Radcliffe scholar, 1965-67; Emory University, Atlanta, Ga., associate professor of romance languages, 1970-72; Mercy College of Detroit, Detroit, Mich., professor of language and co-director of Institute for Bilingual Bicultural Services, 1973-75; University of San Francisco, San Francisco, Calif., professor of education and director of doctoral studies, 1976—. Member of selection committee, Fulbright Overseas Fellowship Program, 1968-69, 1977-78; chairperson, National Seminar on Bilingual Education, 1974, National Policy Conference on Bilingualism in Higher Education, 1978, International Congress of Children's Literature in Spanish, 1978, 1979, 1981; publishing house consultant, 1975-82; visiting professor at University of Guam, summer, 1978, University of Texas, El Paso, summer, 1979; member of board, Books for Youth.

MEMBER: International Association for Children's Literature in Spanish and Portuguese (founding member and president), International Reading Association, Friends of International Books for Young People (IBBY), National Association for Bilingual Education (founding member of Michigan and Illinois branches), American Association of Teachers of Spanish and Portuguese, Modern Language Association of America, Mexican American Teachers Association. *Awards, honors:* Grants from Institute for International Education, 1965-67, Emory University, 1971, Michigan Endowment for the Arts, 1974; Mary Bunting Institute scholar at Radcliffe College and Harvard University, 1966-68; University of San Francisco Distinguished Research Award from the School of Education, 1984; University of San Francisco, Outstanding Teacher Award, 1985.

WRITINGS—For children; all published by Arica (Lima, Peru): *El enanito de la bared y otras historias* (title means "The Wall's Dwarf and Other Tales"), 1974; *Las pintas de las mariquitas* (title means "The Ladybug's Dots and Other Stories"), 1974; *Saltarín y sus dos amigas y otras historias* (title means "Springy and His Two Friends and Other Stories"), 1974; *La Gallinita Costurera y otras historias* (title means "The Little Hen Who Enjoyed Sewing and Other Stories"), 1974.

Reading series: *Hagamos caminos* (illustrated by Ulises Wensell; includes *Partimos* "We Start"; *Andamos* "We Walk"; *Corremos* "We Run"; *Volamos* "We Fly"; *Navegamos* "We Sail"; *Exploramos* "We Explore"), Addison-Wesley, 1985.

For children; translator from the English to the Spanish: Lucille Clifton, *El niño que no creía en la primavera* (translation of *The Boy Who Didn't Believe in Spring;* illustrated by Brinton Turkle), Dutton, 1975; Evelyn Ness, *?Tienes tiempo, Lidia?* (translation of *Do You Have Time Lydia?;* illustrated by E. Ness), Dutton, 1975; Norma Simon, *Cuando me enjojo* (translation of *When I Get Mad;* illustrated by Dora Leder), A. Whitman, 1976; Judith Vigna, *Gregorio y sus puntos*

ALMA FLOR ADA

(translation of *Gregory's Stitches;* illustrated by J. Vigna), A. Whitman, 1977; Barbara Williams, *El dolor de muelas de Alberto* (translation of *Albert's Toothache;* illustrated by Kay Chorao), Dutton, 1977; Barbara Brenner, *Caras* (translation of *Faces;* illustrated with photographs by George Ancona), Dutton, 1977; Mary Garcia, *The Adventures of Connie and Diego/Las aventuras de Connie y Diego* (text in English and Spanish; illustrated by Malaquis Montoya), Children's Book, 1978; Lila Perl, *Pinatas and Paper Flowers/Pinatas y flores de papel: Holidays of the Americas in English and Spanish* (text in English and Spanish; illustrated by Victori de Larrea), Clarion Books, 1982; Harriet Rohmer, *The Legend of Food Mountain/La leyenda de la montana del alimento* (text in English and Spanish; illustrated by Graciella Carrillo), Children's Book, 1982; Judy Blume, *La ballena* (translation of *Blubber*), Bradbury, 1983; Donald Charles, *El año de gato Galano* (translation of *Calico Cat's Year;* illustrated by D. Charles), Children's Book, 1985.

Compiler; all poetry and fairy tale books, except as noted; all published by Arica (Lima, Peru): *Poesia Menuda* (anthology; title means "Tiny Poetry"), 1970; *Poesia Pequena* (anthology; title means "Little Poetry"), 1973; *Poesia Nina* (anthology; title means "Child Poetry"), 1973; *Poesia Infantil* (anthology; title means "Poetry for Children"), 1974; *Fábulas de siempre* (title means "Everlasting Fables"), 1974; *Cuentos en verso* (title means "Stories in Verse"), 1974; *Vamos a Leer* (title means "Let's Read"), 1974; *Adivina adivinador* (title means "A Collection of Traditional Riddles"), 1974; *El nacimiento del Imperio Incaico* (history; title means "The Origins of the Inca Empire"), 1974; *El descubrimiento de America* (history; title means "The Discovery of the New World"), 1974; *El sueno de San Martín* (history; title means "San Martin's Dream"), 1974; *Las Aceitunas y la Cuchara* (drama; title means "The Olives" and "The Wooden Spoon"), 1974; *La Condesita peregrina y La Desposada del rey* (drama; title means "The Wandering Countess" and "The King's Bride"), 1974.

Also author of numerous textbooks, educational materials, and magazine articles in Spanish. Editor-in-chief, *Journal of the National Association of Bilingual Education,* 1975-77.

WORK IN PROGRESS: A book of poems to be published in Madrid, Spain entitled *Animalario;* three mystery novels for young adults that take place at different times during the Middle Ages in Spain.

SIDELIGHTS: "My vocation as a writer started as a young child. I couldn't accept the fact that we had to read such boring textbooks while my wonderful storybooks awaited at home. I made a firm commitment while in the fourth grade to devote my life to producing schoolbooks that would be fun—and since then I am having a lot of fun doing just that!

"My children have been a constant source of inspiration. My childhood vocation was actualized when my daughter at age three complained that I was writing ugly books (I was in the midst of a very scholarly work). One of my greatest joys is that my daughter collaborates with me and is beginning to translate some of my books into English."

ALLISON, Linda 1948-

PERSONAL: Born July 7, 1948, in San Bernardino, Calif.; daughter of Lewis and Marie (Maltos) Allison. *Education:* Received A.B. from University of California, Berkeley. *Home:* 2220 Sacramento St., Berkeley, Calif. 94720. *Agent:* Jim Robertson, Yollaboly Press, Covelo, Calif. 95421.

CAREER: Author and illustrator. *Awards, honors:* New York Academy of Sciences Children's Science Book Award honorable mention, 1980, for *The Wild Inside: Sierra Club's Guide to the Great Indoors; Blood and Guts: A Working Guide to Your Own Insides* was listed on the *New York Times* bestseller list for children's books.

*WRITINGS—*Juvenile: *The Reasons for Seasons: The Great Cosmic Megagalactic Trip without Moving From Your Chair* (self-illustrated), Little, Brown, 1975; (with David Katz) *Blood and Guts: A Working Guide to Your Own Insides* (self-illustrated), Little, Brown, 1976; *The Sierra Club Summer Book* (self-illustrated), Sierra Books, 1977; (with Stella Allison) *Rags: Making a Little Something Out of Almost Nothing* (illustrated with photographs by Tom Liden), C. N. Potter, 1979; *The Wild Inside: Sierra Club's Guide to the Great Indoors* (self-illustrated), Sierra Books, 1979; *Trash Artists Workshop,* Fearon Teacher Aids, 1981; (with D. Katz) *Gee Wiz! How to Mix Art and Science; or, The Art of Thinking Scientifically* (self-illustrated), Little, Brown, 1983.

WORK IN PROGRESS: Writing computer software for children's learning games.

A book is the only immortality.

—Rufus Choate

(From *The Reasons for Seasons: The Great Cosmic Megagalactic Trip without Moving from Your Chair* by Linda Allison. Illustrated by the author.)

ANDERSON, Grace Fox 1932-
(Grace Fox)

PERSONAL: Born May 14, 1932, in Melrose Park, Ill.; daughter of Edmund (a maintenance painter) and Phyllis (a homemaker; maiden name, Bloxham) Fox; married Vernon E. Anderson (a painting contractor), June 10, 1978; stepchildren: Mrs. Carol Gordon, Mrs. Lois Levin, Mrs. Linda Curry. *Education:* Wheaton College, B.A., 1954. *Politics:* Republican. *Religion:* Evangelical Christian (Protestant). *Residence:* Winfield, Ill. *Office:* Scripture Press Publications, 1825 College Ave., Wheaton, Ill. 60187.

CAREER: Baptista Film Co., Wheaton, Ill., photographer, 1952-56; Barber-Green Co., Aurora, Ill., commercial artist, 1956-64; Scripture Press Publications, Wheaton, Ill., editor of *Counselor,* 1964—, editor of children's books, 1975-79.

WRITINGS—Editor; juvenile; published by Victor Books: (Under name Grace Fox) *The Hairy Brown Angel, and Other Animal Tails* (illustrated by Darwin Durham), 1977; *The Peanut Butter Hamster, and Other Animal Tails* (illustrated by Richard Johnson), 1979; *Skunk for Rent, and Other Animal*

GRACE FOX ANDERSON

Tails (illustrated by D. Durham), 1982; *The Incompetent Cat, and Other Animal Tails* (illustrated by Janice Skivington Wood), 1985; *The Duck Who Got Goosebumps* (illustrated by J. S. Wood), 1986. Contributor of over 200 articles and stories to periodicals, including *Adventure, Counselor, Free Way, High, Moody Monthly, Standard, Living Today, Power for Living,* and *Teen Power.*

WORK IN PROGRESS: Collecting animal stories for two books.

SIDELIGHTS: "I write as a means of sharing my joy in Jesus Christ, my Saviour. Having experienced His forgiveness, as well as His power and grace and love in the common matters of life, I attempt to share through my writing and story collections the hope and help He offers each of us. The Bible, His Word, is my meat and drink—the foundation of my life, the source of my happiness and strength and creativity. I'd have little to say if it wasn't for what God has taught me through His Word and work in my life and the lives of those I've interviewed and written about. God has given me a great inner joy in life itself—in His creatures—in animals, growing things, and people (especially children). I taught Sunday school for over twenty-five years, loving the children and finding great satisfaction in teaching them the Bible.

"Sometimes I've felt I'd like two or three more 'gos' at life— say as a doctor (because I'm fascinated with medicine and nutrition and have worked as a volunteer in our local hospital's emergency room), or as an architect (I have notebooks of house plans I drew as a child of about ten and still enjoy planning out houses), or as a teacher (because of my joy in passing on knowledge to children). But God actually gave me the best of all worlds when He made me an editor. I deal with many subjects and can learn about them and share them with others."

HOBBIES AND OTHER INTERESTS: "Music is a part of me and has been most of my life. I've sung in church and school choirs for many years and play the piano and recorder. I love the classics but also appreciate other forms of music. I also enjoy working with my hands—cooking, sewing, crocheting, painting and drawing, miniatures, gardening. I'm active in sports such as swimming, biking, and hiking, and enjoy watching a good baseball game.''

ARDLEY, Neil (Richard) 1937-

PERSONAL: Born May 26, 1937, in Wallington, Surrey, England; son of Sydney Vivian (a clerk) and Alma Mary (Rutty) Ardley; married Bridget Mary Gantley (a researcher), September 3, 1960; children: Jane Catherine. *Education:* University of Bristol, B.Sc., 1959. *Home:* Lathkill House, Youlgrave, Derbyshire DE4 1WL, England. *Office:* 13a Priory Ave., Bedford Park, London W4 1TX, England.

CAREER: World Book Encyclopedia, London, England, editor, 1962-66; Hamlyn Publishing Group, London, editor, 1967-68; full-time writer, 1970—. *Member:* Royal Society of Arts (fellow, 1982).

WRITINGS—Juvenile: *Experiments with Heat,* Wolfe, 1970; *Life in the Open Sea,* Macdonald Educational, 1970; *Atlas of Space* (illustrated by John Smith), Macdonald Educational, 1970; (adapter) *How Birds Behave* (illustrated by David Andrews), Grosset, 1971; (editor) Elizabeth S. Austin and Oliver L. Austin, *The Look-It-Up Book of Birds* (illustrated by Richard E. Amundsen and George Thompson), revised edition, Collins, 1973 (Ardley was not associated with earlier edition); *Birds,* Sampson Low, 1974, edited by Jane Olliver and Valerie

Pitt, Warwick Press, 1976; *Atoms and Energy* (illustrated by Ron Jobson, Brian Pearce, and Michael Saunders), Sampson Low, 1975, edited by John Patton, Warwick Press, 1976, revised edition, Warwick Press, 1982; *Purnell's Find Out about Wonders of the World* (illustrated by Eric Jewell Associates and others), edited by Trisha Pike and others, Purnell Books, 1976; (editor) Vaclav Kvapil, *Exploring the Universe* (translated from the Czech; illustrated by Theodor Rotrekl), Hamlyn, 1976.

The Amazing World of Machines, edited by Deborah Manley, Angus & Robertson, 1977; *Let's Look at Birds* (illustrated by John Rignall, Richard Millington, and Graham Allen), edited by Jennifer Justice, Ward Lock, 1977, Derrydale (New York), 1979; *Man and Space,* edited by Philip Steele, Macdonald Educational, 1978, Silver Burdett, 1980; *The Scientific World* (illustrated by Terry Burton), Pan Piccolo, 1978; *Bird Life,* Sackett & Marshall, 1978; *People and Homes,* Macmillan (London), 1978; *Know Your Underwater Exploration,* Rand McNally, 1978 (published in England as *Underwater Exploration,* Purnell, 1978); *Musical Instruments* (illustrated by Annette Wade and Angus McBride), Macmillan (London), 1978, Silver Burdett, 1980; *Guide to Birds* (illustrated by Trevor Boyer), Pan Piccolo, 1979; *Purnell's Find Out about Birds,* Purnell, 1979; *Birds,* Macdonald Educational, 1979, Silver Burdett, 1980.

Stars (illustrated by Rhoda Burns and Robert Burns), Macdonald Educational, 1980, Silver Burdett, 1981; *Our World of Nature: A First Picture Encyclopedia* (illustrated by Chris

Each player controls a ship and tries to destroy the other ships. Guess which player is winning! ■ (From *Tomorrow's Home* by Neil Ardley.)

NEIL ARDLEY

Shields), Purnell Books, 1981; (with wife, Bridget Ardley) *1001 Questions and Answers,* Kingfisher Books, 1981, published in America as *The Arco Book of 1001 Questions and Answers,* Arco, 1984; (with others) *Nature* (illustrated by Stephen Adams and others), Pan Piccolo, 1981; *My Favourite Encyclopedia of Science,* Macdonald & Co., 1982; *First Look at Computers,* F. Watts, 1983; *Just Look at . . . Flight,* Macdonald Educational, 1984; *Space,* Macdonald Educational, 1984.

"World of Tomorrow" series; all juvenile; all published by F. Watts: *Transport on Earth,* 1981; *Out into Space,* 1981; *Tomorrow's Home,* 1981; *School, Work, and Play,* 1981; *Our Future Needs,* 1982; *Health and Medicine,* 1982; *Future War and Weapons,* 1982; *Fact or Fantasy,* 1982.

"Action Science" series; all juvenile; all published by F. Watts: *Working with Water,* 1983; *Using the Computer,* 1983; *Hot and Cold,* 1983; *Sun and Light,* 1983; *Making Metric Measurements,* 1984; *Exploring Magnetism,* 1984; *Making Things Move* (illustrated by Janos Marffy), 1984; *Discovering Electricity,* 1984; *Air and Flight,* 1984; *Sound and Music,* 1984; *Simple Chemistry,* 1984; *Force and Strength,* 1984.

Other: (Editor) Arrigo Polillo, *Jazz: A Guide to the History and Development of Jazz and Jazz Musicians,* translated from the Italian by Peter Muccini, Hamlyn (New York), 1969; *What Do You Know?,* Hamlyn, 1972; *The Earth and Beyond,* Macmillan (London), 1974; *Countries and Homes,* Macmillan (London), 1974; *Birds of Towns* (illustrated with photographs by Brian Hawkes), Almark, 1975; *Birds of the Country* (illustrated with photographs by B. Hawkes), Almark, 1975; *Birds of Coasts, Lakes, and Rivers* (illustrated with photographs by B. Hawkes), Almark, 1976; (with B. Hawkes) *Bird-watching,* Macdonald Education, 1978; *Birds of Britain and Europe* (il-

lustrated by Martin Camm), edited by Eric Inglefield, Ward Lock, 1978; (with Ian Ridpath) *The Universe,* Silver Burdett, 1978; *Illustrated Guide to Birds and Birdwatching,* Kingfisher Books, 1980; (with Robin Kerrod) *The World of Science,* Macdonald & Co., 1982; *Computers,* Warwick Press, 1983; *ZX Spectrum and Users Guide,* Dorling Kindersley, 1984.

Contributor to *The Joy of Knowledge Encyclopedia, Collins Music Encyclopedia, Great World of Science Encyclopedia, Ecology Encyclopedia, Our World Encyclopedia, Library of Modern Knowledge, World of Knowledge, Encyclopedia of Nature and Science, Caxton Yearbook,* and *The Complete Indoor Gardener.*

SIDELIGHTS: "My experience with World Book gave me an appreciation of the necessity to express ideas clearly and concisely. In my information books, I've tried to link this to a sense of wonder at the marvels of the world."

A musician as well, Ardley is both a composer and synthesizer player. He has been commissioned to produce pieces for music festivals.

ARMSTRONG, Louise

PERSONAL: Married Tom Hawley (an actor); children: two sons, Alexi and Noah (twins). *Education:* Studied music in Paris for one year. *Residence:* New York City.

CAREER: Author of books for children and adults; has worked variously as a painter, book reviewer, copywriter, and in advertising.

WRITINGS—All juvenile, except as indicated: *A Child's Guide to Freud* (illustrated by Whitney Darrow, Sr.), Simon & Schuster, 1963; *The Thump, Blam, Bump Mystery* (fiction; illustrated by Ray Cruz), Walker, 1975; *How to Turn Lemons into Money: A Child's Guide to Economics* (illustrated by Bill Basso; Junior Literary Guild selection), Harcourt, 1976; *How to Turn Up into Down into Up: A Child's Guide to Inflation, Depression, and Economic Recovery* (illustrated by B. Basso), Harcourt, 1978; *Kiss Daddy Goodnight: A Speak-out on Incest* (adult nonfiction), Hawthorn, 1978; *How to Turn War into Peace: A Child's Guide to Conflict Resolution* (nonfiction; illustrated by B. Basso), Harcourt, 1979; *Arthur Gets What He Spells* (fiction; illustrated by Syd Hoff), Harcourt, 1979; *Saving the Big-Deal Baby* (young adult fiction; illustrated by Jack Hearne), Dutton, 1980; *The Home Front: Notes from the Family War Zone* (adult nonfiction), McGraw, 1983.

SIDELIGHTS: "I . . . started writing children's books partly to amuse my twin sons, Alexi and Noah, but mostly because I can't help putting things on paper—any piece of paper. Most of my work starts out on the backs of envelopes.

"Money, of course, fascinates children. Mine get an allowance which they don't spend much. But they love getting it and counting it—and planning to spend it. Conversations about money led inexorably to long dinner-table explanations of how people earn money and why they have to spend it. And then goods and services, profit and loss, buying and selling—talking about it seemed awfully complex. I thought it could be made simpler. So I made a list of economic terms.

"I began the list on the back of an envelope containing the electric bill, continued it on a larger envelope, finished it off on the back of the telephone bill envelope. Then, with the words in hand, I went after the concepts. For some reason economics is neglected until kids get to college. But since I never went to college, I never did grasp it—until I made the list and worked out *How to Turn Lemons into Money.* I hope I can help kids understand why they can't get free ice-cream cones from the nice man on the corner. My kids have read the book. (They've begun selling their old books secondhand on the front stoop.) And now they sympathize with the ice-cream store man's problems.''

FOR MORE INFORMATION SEE: Authors of Books for Young People, 2nd edition supplement, Scarecrow, 1979.

ARNO, Enrico   1913-1981

PERSONAL: Born July 16, 1913, in Mannheim, Germany; came to United States in 1947; died April 30, 1981; married Inès Cortese, 1944 (divorced); married Paula von Heimberger; children: one stepdaughter. *Education:* Attended Vereinigte Staatsschulen für freie und angewandte Kunst, Berlin, Germany. *Residence:* Sea Cliff, Long Island, N.Y.

CAREER: Artist, illustrator, and teacher. Began career as illustrator for publishing houses in London, England and Rome, Italy; executed many commissions, including numerous murals and a postage stamp commemorating Fort Ticonderoga; designed book jackets, record covers, film illustrations, pos-

Enrico Arno, 1950.

ters, and advertising layouts; taught lettering at Pratt Institute and painting at Columbia University. *Awards, honors: The Shepherd's Nosegay: Stories from Finland and Czechoslovakia* and *The Tiger's Whisker, and Other Tales and Legends from Asia and the Pacific* were chosen one of American Institute of Graphic Arts Children's Books, 1958-60, *Men in Armor: The Story of Knights and Knighthood* and *Olode the Hunter and Other Tales* were chosen 1967-68.

ILLUSTRATOR—All for children: Jean Baptiste Molière, *The Misanthrope: Comedy in Five Acts, 1666,* translated from the French by Richard Wilbur, Harcourt, 1955; Margot Benary-Isbert, *The Wicked Enchantment* (ALA Notable Book), translated from the German by Richard Winston and Clara Winston, Harcourt, 1955; Marguerite A. Butterfield, *Adventures of Esteban,* Scribner, 1956; M. Benary-Isbert, *Blue Mystery,* translated from the German by R. Winston and C. Winston, Harcourt, 1957; Frances Winwar, *Elizabeth: The Romantic Story of Elizabeth Barrett Browning,* World Publishing, 1957; Harold Courlander and Albert K. Prempeh, *The Hat-Shaking Dance, and Other Tales from the Gold Coast,* Harcourt, 1957; Parker H. Fillmore, reteller, *The Shepherd's Nosegay: Stories from Finland and Czechoslovakia,* edited by Katherine Love, Harcourt, 1958; H. Courlander, *The Tiger's Whisker, and Other Tales and Legends from Asia and the Pacific,* Harcourt, 1959.

Adet Lin, *The Milky Way, and Other Chinese Folk Tales,* Harcourt, 1961; H. Courlander, compiler, *The King's Drum, and Other African Stories,* Harcourt, 1962; Sir Thomas Malory, *Le Morte d'Arthur,* Bramhall House, 1962; Eulalie S. Ross, editor, *The Lost Half-Hour: A Collection of Stories,* Harcourt, 1963; Elizabeth Borton de Treviño, *Nacar, the White Deer* (*Horn Book* honor list), Farrar, Straus, 1963; Anne Malcolmson, editor, *A Taste of Chaucer: Selections from the Canterbury Tales* (ALA Notable Book), Harcourt, 1964; Gina Bell-Zano (pseudonym of Jeanne Iannone), *The Wee Moose,* Parents Magazine Press, 1964; Wallace Wadsworth, reteller, *Paul Bunyan and His Great Blue Ox,* Doubleday, 1964 (Arno was not associated with earlier editions); Jane L. Curry, reteller, *Down from the Lonely Mountain: California Indian Tales,* Harcourt, 1965; Glanville Downey, editor and translator, *Stories from Herodotus: A Panorama of Events and Peoples of the Ancient World,* Dutton, 1965; Suzanne S. Morrow, *There Was a Time: The Story of Evolution,* Dutton, 1965; Mary Ray, *The Voice of Apollo,* Ariel Books, 1965 (Arno was not associated with earlier edition).

E. S. Ross, editor, *The Blue Rose: A Collection of Stories for Girls,* Harcourt, 1966; M. Ray, *The Eastern Beacon,* Ariel Books, 1966 (Arno was not associated with earlier edition); William W. Suggs, *Meet the Orchestra,* Macmillan, 1966; John Hampden, *The House of Cats, and Other Stories,* Farrar, Straus, 1967 (Arno was not associated with earlier edition); Myra C. Livingston, *Old Mrs. Twindlytart* (poems), Harcourt, 1967; Martha E. Almedingen, *The Story of Gudrun, Based on the Third Part of the Epic of Gudrun,* Norton, 1967; Olivia E. Coolidge, *The Golden Days of Greece,* Crowell, 1968; Richard Suskind, *Men in Armor: The Story of Knights and Knighthood,* Norton, 1968; Sesyle Joslin, *The Night They Stole the Alphabet,* Harcourt, 1968; H. Courlander and Ezekiel A. Eshugbayi, compilers, *Olode the Hunter, and Other Tales from Nigeria,* Harcourt, 1968 (published in England as *Ijapa the Tortoise, and Other Nigerian Tales,* Bodley Head, 1969); E. B. de Treviño, *Turi's Poppa,* Farrar, Straus, 1968; Stanley W. Angrist, *How Our World Came to Be,* Crowell, 1969; Joseph Gies and Frances Gies, *Leonard of Pisa and the New Mathematics of the Middle Ages,* Crowell, 1969; M. Jean Craig, *Pomando,* Norton, 1969; William Cole, compiler, *Rough Men,*

Gently the Dream Ship sailed over the roofs, and in spite of feeling bad Anemone was already fast asleep.
■ (From *The Wicked Enchantment* by Margot Benary-Isbert. Illustrated by Enrico Arno.)

Tough Men: Poems of Action and Adventure, Viking, 1969; R. Suskind, *Swords, Spears, and Sandals: The Story of the Roman Legions,* Norton, 1969.

R. Suskind, *The Barbarians: The Story of the European Tribes,* Norton, 1970; Mirra Ginsburg, editor and translator, *The Master of the Winds, and Other Tales from Siberia,* Crown, 1970; H. Courlander, compiler, *People of the Short Blue Corn: Tales and Legends of the Hopi Indians,* Harcourt, 1970; Sabra Holbrook, *Sir Tristan of All Time,* Farrar, Straus, 1970; Mannis Charosh, *Straight Lines, Parallel Lines, Perpendicular Lines,* Crowell, 1970; H. Courlander, compiler, *The Fourth World of the Hopis,* Crown, 1971; R. Suskind, *The Sword of the Prophet: The Story of the Moslem Empire,* Grosset, 1971; David I. Urquhart, *The Bicycle and How It Works,* Walck, 1972; D. I. Urquhart, *The Airplane and How It Works,* Walck,

1973; S. W. Angrist, *Closing the Loop: The Story of Feedback,* Crowell, 1973; S. W. Angrist, *Other Worlds, Other Beings,* Crowell, 1973; Robert Froman, *A Game of Functions,* Crowell, 1974; Jean Fritz, *Brendan the Navigator: A History Mystery about the Discovery of America,* Coward, 1979; Margaret K. Wetterer, *Patrick and the Fairy Thief,* Athenum, 1980; Freya Littledale, *The Magic Plum Tree: Based on a Tale from the Jataka,* Crown, 1981; (with Igor Tulipanov) J. B. Molière, *Four Comedies,* translated by Richard Wilbur, Harcourt, 1982.

Illustrator of filmstrips including "I, Juan de Pareja," based on the book by Elizabeth Borton de Treviño, Miller-Brody Productions, 1975, and "A Wind in the Door," by Madeleine L'Engle, Miller-Brody Productions, 1977. Contributor of illustrations to numerous periodicals, including *Holiday, Town & Country,* and *Life.*

SIDELIGHTS: Arno was born in Mannheim, Germany, and raised in Berlin, where he attended local schools. "... When I was twelve years old, I acted as a lion-handler during my summer vacation at the Berlin (Germany) Zoo. Every day I went there to draw animals, and every day the warden allowed me to carry the lion cubs from their cage to a fenced-in lawn. Lion cubs are heavy, their tongues are made of sandpaper (they

"Swedish Ole, the blacksmith, is the biggest man around here. When he puts shoes on a horse he takes the animal up on his lap like a baby." ■ (From *Paul Bunyan and His Great Blue Ox,* retold by Wallace Wadsworth. Illustrated by Enrico Arno.)

"Which way to Paradise?" Brendan called. . . . ■ (From *Brendan the Navigator: A History Mystery about the Discovery of America* by Jean Fritz. Illustrated by Enrico Arno.)

licked my hands, so I know!), and they have blue eyes. My drawings, though, were mainly of camels and dromedaries, which look like me (and of wart hogs, which look preposterous)." [Enrico Arno, "Meet Your Author," *Cricket,* April, 1978.[1]]

Arno studied to become a painter at the State Academy in Berlin, but later studied lettering and calligraphy. Arno's art studies were aborted, however, when the Nuremberg Laws of Nazi Germany declared Arno "a mongrel in the first degree" because he had a Jewish mother. Fortunately, he was able to work from Berlin through a British agent for several publishers in London, and later traveled to Italy.

In Italy Arno found employment with an Italian publisher, Mondadori, in Milan. When the Nazis began to take over Milan, Arno fled to Rome with homemade identification papers, but, again, the Nazis followed. In Rome he stayed in hiding until the Liberation, then found a job with the British Army Education. Later he worked for the Lux Film Company in Rome.

In 1947 he joined his mother in New York and worked there as a book-jacket and record-cover designer, as a children's book illustrator, and a map illustrator. His work as a technical illustrator required geographic accuracy and a special tech-

nique. ". . . It is understood that absolute faithfulness of reproduction (such as the tracing of the map in a suitable scale) is the basis, but it can never—in my experience—be used as it is. I start, therefore, from both ends, so to speak, and work towards a compromise; that is, I have first my tracing of an accurate map, then I start by placing the illustrative spots on a freehand drawing of the map, distorting the latter, of course, in the process. After that I put a squared grid over the topographic map and, according to the necessities of distortion that I gather from my freehand illustrative sketch, I distort the grid for my original scale map. In this way, I get the relative position of the chartered places right, but at the same time I have the required space for illustration where I need it and on the other hand, a 'foreshortened' view of those areas which would normally be blank space. Usually some adjustments have to be made freely to give the distanced transfer of the map a convincing look. Then I add my illustrative elements and normally I find that I have to distort the map some more here or there. My design then assumes, I believe, at least as much 'truth' as the ancient maps, which stressed the personal experience of the explorer more than the impersonal measurements. By this very procedure they strike us, even today, as being more informative than the cold, modern renderings of most accurate mechanically-registered data." [Fritz Eichenberg, "Enrico Arno, Graphic Artist," *American Artist,* May, 1956.[2]]

Arno's techniques varied according to the art project at hand. In his illustrations for children's books, for instance, he took great pains to use the most suitable material for a given purpose. "... The selections of a drawing pen was most important for my work while illustrating Margot Benary-Isbert's book, *The Wicked Enchantment*. I do not believe that drawing instruments or anything else, can be selected by brand names only. My approach is the most primitive—that of trying out. Of course, I cannot dip every drawing nib into India ink and draw with it in the supply store. I first select, therefore, those two or three that look most promising and press them gently on my fingernail to test their resiliency...."

"For a different purpose (the landscape drawing of a terraced mountain with house in Ischia), I found it necessary to make my own pen out of the plentifully growing reeds. This, as everyone knows, is the tool that Van Gogh used for his admirable drawings. The same pen can be used for its soft 'pictorial' quality, without the typical emotional Van Gogh handwriting that we invariably associate with his work in this medium.

"... About the relationship of the various elements that go into a piece of applied graphic art, I want to say that I feel that each job should have the unity of approach that only the same hand can guarantee it. This means that my belief in the *chef d'ouevre collectif* in the sense of the advertising agency procedure, where an ad is the result of the collective efforts of five or six specialists, is rather shaky. If I need a sculpture, as in the case of the *Arianna* cover for the Haydn Society, I do it myself. When I decided to use paper-sculpture for various jobs I took up photography, because no other person, not even one who was much more skilled in the craft than I, could possibly know my special intentions and requirements as I know them myself. The same is true of lettering which, to my way of thinking, has to be part of every design, not only as far as position and weight are concerned but also with regard to the single letter form. This means adaptation and, therefore, hand lettering in most cases."[2]

Besides his work in book illustration and graphics, Arno also produced filmstrips for Miller-Brody Productions, drawing full-color illustrations that were shown in synchronization with the text. He illustrated the filmstrip, "I, Juan de Pareja," based on the book by Elizabeth Borton de Treviño and "A Wind in the Door," by Madeleine L'Engle. Arno also painted murals, including the seventeen-foot mural for the Alco Company office in New York, and was chosen to design a postage stamp commemorating Fort Ticonderoga.

In addition to painting and illustrating, Arno taught lettering at Pratt University and painting at Columbia University. He made his home in Sea Cliff, Long Island, New York until his death on April 30, 1981.

HOBBIES AND OTHER INTERESTS: Puppetry.

FOR MORE INFORMATION SEE: American Artist, May, 1956; Martha E. Ward and Dorothy A. Marquardt, *Illustrators of Books for Young People*, Scarecrow, 1975; *Cricket*, April, 1978; Doris de Montreville and Elizabeth D. Crawford, editors, *Fourth Book of Junior Authors and Illustrators*, H. W. Wilson, 1978; Lee Kingman and others, compilers, *Illustrators of Children's Books: 1967-1976*, Horn Book, 1978. Obituaries: *Horn Book*, August, 1981.

It was a choice siesta spot, and Cottontail contentedly stretched out upon his back.... ▪ (From *Down from the Lonely Mountain: California Indian Tales*, retold by Jane Louise Curry. Illustrated by Enrico Arno.)

BARNOUW, Victor 1915-

PERSONAL: Born May 25, 1915, in The Hague, Netherlands; came to United States in 1919, naturalized citizen, 1924; son of Adriaan Jacob and Anne E. (Midgley) Barnouw; married Sachiko Miyagawa, January 7, 1964. *Education:* Attended Princeton University, 1933-35; Columbia University, A.B., 1940, Ph.D., 1948. *Home:* 2518 North Terrace Ave., Milwaukee, Wis. 53211. *Office:* Department of Anthropology, University of Wisconsin-Milwaukee, Milwaukee, Wis. 53201.

CAREER: Brooklyn College (now of the City University of New York), Brooklyn, N.Y., instructor in anthropology, 1945-48; University of Buffalo (now State University of New York at Buffalo), visiting assistant professor of anthropology, 1948-51; University of Pennsylvania, South Asia Regional Studies Department, researcher in South Asia, 1951-52, and in India, 1952-53; teacher at private school in Verde Valley, Ariz., 1953-54; University of Illinois at Urbana-Champaign, research associate, 1955-56, visiting assistant professor of anthropology, 1956-57; University of Wisconsin-Milwaukee, assistant professor, 1957-61, associate professor, 1961-65, professor of anthropology, 1965—, head of department, 1976-79, professor emeritus, 1982—. *Member:* American Anthropological

There was no telling who their visitor might be. ■ (From *Dream of the Blue Heron* by Victor Barnouw. Illustrated by Lynd Ward.)

Association (fellow). *Awards, honors:* Stirling Award from American Anthropological Association, 1968, for "Cross-Cultural Research With the House-Tree-Person Test."

WRITINGS: Acculturation and Personality Among the Wisconsin Chippewa, American Anthropological Association, 1950, reprinted, AMS Press, 1977; *Culture and Personality,* Dorsey, 1963, 4th edition, 1985; *Dream of the Blue Heron* (juvenile novel; illustrated by Lynd Ward), Delacorte, 1966; *An Intro-*

VICTOR BARNOUW

duction to Anthropology, Volume I: *Physical Anthropology and Archaeology,* Volume II: *Ethnology,* Dorsey, 1971, 3rd edition, 1978; *Programmed Learning Aid for Cultural Anthropology,* Learning Systems Co., 1972; *Plaid for Physical Anthropology and Archaeology,* Learning Systems Co., 1972; *Programmed Learning Aid for Physical Anthropology and Archaeology,* Learning Systems Co., 1973; (with Joseph B. Casagrande, Ernestine Friedl, and Robert E. Ritzenthaler) *Wisconsin Chippewa Myths and Tales and Their Relation to Chippewa Life,* University of Wisconsin Press, 1977; *Anthropology: A General Introduction,* Dorsey, 1979. Contributor of stories to popular magazines, including *Vogue* and *New Yorker.* Member of advisory aboard of *Journal of Psychological Anthropology.*

SIDELIGHTS: "Although my main profession has been teaching anthropology, I have also written fiction. My novel, *Dream of the Blue Heron,* was my major effort in this field. My fiction is 'anthropological,' usually being related to my field work. The novel, for instance, is about a Chippewa Indian boy."

BARTON, Harriett

BRIEF ENTRY: Born in Picher, Okla. Illustrator and designer of books for children. A graduate of the University of Kansas, Barton has provided illustrations for four books in Crowell's "Let's-Read-and-Find-Out Science Books" series. Critics have noted how her illustrations serve as visual aids to factual information provided in the texts. In a review of Phyllis S. Busch's *Cactus in the Desert* (1979), *Christian Science Monitor* observed: "[Barton's] bright illustrations spark this . . . carefully worded book. . . . Each drawing strengthens a point in the text." *Booklist* described her "large color and black-and-white cartoon-type illustrations" as "especially inventive" in Paul Showers's *You Can't Make a Move without Your Muscles* (1982). As the text introduces young children to the workings of the muscular system, *Horn Book* pointed out that "the drawings often help by juxtaposing a part of the body as seen on the surface with the same part seen with its muscles."

Barton also illustrated Showers's *No Measles, No Mumps for Me* (1980). "A simple, accurate account," stated *School Li-*

brary Journal, "of how immunization fights disease . . . [in which Barton's] drawings . . . give the book a pleasant, upbeat look." Also included in Crowell's series is a revised edition of F. M. Branley's *Rain and Hail* (1983). *School Library Journal* again noted that, in comparison to the now out-dated original illustrations, "Barton's new watercolors are good-humored pictures that add extra information." Her other illustrated works for children include *In the Witch's Kitchen: Poems for Halloween* (Crowell, 1980), compiled by John E. Brewton and others, and *Runaway Sugar: All about Diabetes* (Lippincott, 1981) by Alvin and Virginia B. Silverstein. *Residence:* New York, N.Y.

BASSETT, Jeni 1960(?)-

BRIEF ENTRY: Born about 1960. An illustrator of books for children, Bassett has studied painting at her mother's Art Workshop in Winter Park, Fla. In 1978 she received a gold medal in Scholastic's High School Art Exhibition. Among the nine books she has illustrated are four written by author Louise Mathews. Designed to aid children in mathematical concepts, these books feature an assortment of animal characters, verse, and amusing storylines. Multiplication is the focus in *Bunches and Bunches of Bunnies* (Dodd, 1978) as readers are treated to an increasing number of bunnies while performing the multiplying processes of one through twelve. *Booklist* observed that "the rabbits [pour] forth with disarming ease . . . , cavorting in growing spreads that vie for attention in and of themselves." Alligators replace bunnies in *Gator Pie* (Dodd, 1979), in which two young alligator friends become the lucky finders of a chocolate marshmallow pie; lucky, that is, until one hundred other alligators appear to claim their share. *Publishers Weekly* called the story "a wild fantasy, with effervescent paintings in full color and hints on handling fractions." Bassett and Mathews continue their successful format while exploring subtraction in *The Great Take-Away* (Dodd, 1980) and the difference between regular numbers and those that reflect place in *Cluck One* (Dodd, 1982).

Bassett's talented treatment of animals can also be seen in books like *In a Lick of a Flick of a Tongue* (Dodd, 1980) by Linda Hirschmann, *The Night Vegetable Eater* (Dodd, 1981) by Elke and Ted Musicant, and *The Biggest Pumpkin Ever* (Dodd, 1984) by Steven Kroll. Her latest illustrated works include Lisa Bassett's *A Clock for Beany* (Dodd, 1985) and Valrie Selkowe's *Spring Green* (Lothrop, 1985).

BEAMER, (G.) Charles, (Jr.) 1942-

PERSONAL: Born August 16, 1942, in Kansas City, Mo.; son of Dr. George C. (a professor of guidance and counseling) and Mary (a speech therapist; maiden name, Walker) Beamer; married first wife (divorced, 1975); married Alice Criswell (secretary), November 8, 1975; children: Stephanie, Lara, Christopher; stepchildren: Jodi Boggan Rush, Shannon Boggan. *Education:* North Texas State University, B.A., 1964; University of Texas at Austin, M.A., 1968. *Religion:* Christian. *Home:* 2306 Foxcroft, Denton, Tex. 76201.

CAREER: High school teacher of English at school in Georgetown, Tex., 1964-67; junior high school teacher of English at school in Austin, Tex., 1967-68; Steck Vaughn Co. (publisher), Austin, acquiring editor, 1968-69; teacher at Meridell Achievement Center in Jollyville, Tex., 1969-70; Graphic Ideas,

CHARLES BEAMER

Inc., Dallas, Tex., writer and editor, 1970-71; Miller Productions, Inc. (a multi-media production company), Austin, project writer, 1970-78; Education Service Center, Region XIII, Austin, educational writer, 1971-76; free-lance photographer, 1976—; Denton Senior High School, Denton, Tex., teacher of English, 1981-85. Talent Preservation Program Director, Georgetown High School, 1964-67; consultant to Behavioral Research Laboratories on programmed instructional materials, 1968; free-lance writer, 1970—; owner, Stillwaters Crafts Revival (crafts store), 1970-71; owner, Austin Writers Group (publisher), 1971—; consultant and writer for Dr. Pat Yeary on filming and documenting the World Dental Congress in Mexico City, 1972; career education consultant to Education Service Center, Region XIII, 1972-73; consultant to Gregg Division, McGraw-Hill on career education product development, 1973; consultant to Random House, Inc. on a series of readers, 1973; consultant to Houston Teachers' Supply Co. on conducting workshops on setting up learning centers, 1975; co-developer of the "Teacher Training Program" (for individualizing instruction and mainstreaming handicapped students), funded by Leadership Training Institute, United States Office of Education, and Dr. Maynard Reynolds, Director, 1975. *Member:* Author's Guild, Christian Writers' League of America. *Awards, honors:* Kathryn Morris Memorial Award, Poetry Society of Texas, 1969, for poem "Snap!"

"Aaiieesskreecht!" burst an earsplitting wail from the trees overhead. ■ (From *Magician's Bane* by Charles Beamer. Illustrated by Don Pallarito.)

WRITINGS—For children, except as noted: (Adapter) *Texas: The 28th Star* (young adult history textbook), Graphic Ideas, 1971; (with Bertha M. Cox and Joe B. Frantz) *The Texans: From Tejas to Today* (social studies supplementary reader; with teacher's guide), Graphic Ideas, 1972; *Joshua Wiggins and the King's Kids: Stories for Family Devotions* (illustrated by Chris W. Dyrud), Bethany House, 1981; *Joshua Wiggins and the Tough Challenge: More Stories about Joshua and His Friends for Family Devotions*, Bethany House, 1983; *Charlcie Arrow and the Magic Red Cape* (fiction), Baker Book, 1983.

"The Ideas Reader" series; all published by Graphic Ideas, 1973: *Imagine That!* (primer); *Think Happy!* (first grade supplementary reader); *Dream Machine!* (second grade supplementary reader); *The Very Idea!* (third grade supplementary reader).

"The Legends of Eorthe" series; both fantasy for children; both published by Thomas Nelson: *Magician's Bane* (illustrated by Don Pallarito), 1980; *Lightning in the Bottle* (illustrated by Phillip Francis), 1981.

For adults: *Mesquite Leaves: Images of the South Texas Hills* (poetry; self-illustrated), Naylor, 1967; *Human Relations: A Guideline to Programs*, Austin Writers Group, 1971; *Drug Abuse: A Problem Solving, Decision-Making Program*, Austin Writers Group, 1971; *Learning Centers: Toward Individualized Instruction*, Austin Writers Group, 1971; (contributor) Laird, *Psychology*, 5th edition (Beamer was not associated with earlier editions), Gregg Division, McGraw, 1973; *Video Fever* (nonfiction), Thomas Nelson, 1982; *Love's Majesty* (novel), Harvest House, 1983; *When the Gods Returned*, Del Rey, 1986.

Also author, photographer, and/or producer of several training programs for educators (including filmstrips, leaders' guides, and participants' manuals); contributor of articles, short stories, and over one-hundred thirty poems to various periodicals, including *Child Life, Highlights for Children, Boys' Life, proTeen, Descant Review, Foxfire,* and *Poem.*

WORK IN PROGRESS: Thirty-Three, mass market speculative fiction; *Sisters of the Light; The Sword*, Christian speculative fiction.

SIDELIGHTS: "I don't really like to talk about my writing. I've had a long and varied apprenticeship; I've written almost every kind of thing that needs a writer. My books are subject to individual interpretation independent of whatever I intend. I would like to create an American mythology, since myth is a missing substance in our lives. I would like to present God, faith in Christ, and positive living in accurate, exciting ways. I want to entertain, first and foremost, but also to help an audience understand that negative, chaotic, and/or apathetic lifestyles are not the only option."

BECHTEL, Louise Seaman   1894-1985

OBITUARY NOTICE—See sketch in *SATA* Volume 4: Born June 29, 1894, in Brooklyn, N.Y.; died April 12 (another source cites April 13), 1985, in Mount Kisco, N.Y. Editor, author, children's book critic, and lecturer. Bechtel began her publishing career in 1919 as a member of the advertising department at Macmillan. She later became editor and head of the company's juvenile department, the first of its kind in the United States. Considered a pioneer in the field of children's literature, Bechtel was instrumental in setting the standard of quality for children's books published in the last half-century. During her fifteen year association with Macmillan, she worked with noted authors and illustrators such as Rachel Field, Margery Bianco, Elizabeth Coatsworth, and Padraic Colum.

In addition to her editorial work, Bechtel wrote her own catalogs, lectured extensively, contributed reviews to periodicals, and hosted a weekly radio program on children's books. She retired from Macmillan in 1934 but continued writing and lecturing. From 1935 to 1969 she served as associate editor and director of *Horn Book*, later becoming honorary director; she was also editor of children's books for the *New York Herald Tribune* between 1949 and 1956. Among her writings are *The Brave Bantam, Mr. Peck's Pets*, and *Books in Search of Children: Speeches and Essays.*

FOR MORE INFORMATION SEE: Elinor W. Field, *Horn Book Reflections*, Horn Book, 1969; Louise Seaman Bechtel, *Books in Search of Children: Speeches and Essays*, compiled and with an introduction by Virginia Haviland, Macmillan, 1969; Barbara Bader, *American Picturebooks from "Noah's Ark" to "The Beast Within,"* Macmillan, 1976; *Contemporary Authors, Permanent Series*, Volume 2, Gale, 1978. Obituaries: *AB Bookman's Weekly*, May 6, 1985; *Horn Book*, July, 1985; *School Library Journal*, September, 1985.

BELTRAN, Alberto 1923-

PERSONAL: Born March 22, 1923, in Mexico City, Mexico. *Education:* Attended Escuela Libre de Publicidad y Arte Commercial, Mexico City, Mexico, and Escuela Nacional de Artes Plasticas, San Carlos, Mexico. *Home address:* Apartado Postal 1865, Mexico 1, D.F. 06000.

CAREER: Artist, engraver, illustrator, and political cartoonist. Founder, editor, and illustrator of satirical political magazines, *Ahi va el Golpe* and *El Coyote emplumado.* Director of popular arts of the Ministry of Public Education, Mexico, 1971-76. Work has been exhibited in Mexico, Europe, U.S.S.R. and the United States, and in Biennale of Japan, 1957, and Library of Congress, Washington, D.C., 1958; work is represented in the permanent collection of the Hermitage Museum, Leningrad, U.S.S.R. *Awards, honors:* Recipient of a prize from Art Directors Club of Chicago, 1952, for *Life in a Mexican Village: Tepoztlan Restudied;* Premio Nacional de Grabado, Mexico, 1954; first prize for engraving from first Inter-American Painting and Engraving Biennale, Mexico City, 1958.

ILLUSTRATOR: Oscar Lewis, *Life in a Mexican Village: Tepoztlan Restudied,* University of Illinois Press, 1951; Fernando Benitez, *La Ruta de Hernan Cortes,* Fondo de Cultura Economica (Mexico), 1951, translation published as *In the Footsteps of Cortes,* Pantheon, 1952; Victor W. Von Hagen, *Sun Kingdom of the Aztecs,* World Publishing, 1958; V. W. Von Hagen, *Maya: Land of the Turkey and the Deer,* World Publishing, 1960, reprinted, Collins & World, 1977; V. W. Von Hagen, *The Incas: People of the Sun,* World Publishing, 1961, reprinted, Collins & World, 1977; Elena Poniatowska, *Todo empezo el domingo* (title means "Everything Began on Sun-

ALBERTO BELTRAN

day"), Fondo de Cultura Economica, 1963; B. Traven, *The Creation of the Sun and the Moon,* Hill & Wang, 1968. Illustrator of over thirty other books, many of them printed in Spanish, including a series of Indian readers. Contributor of a Sunday political cartoon to *El Dia,* Mexico City, Mexico and weekly *Punto y aparte.*

SIDELIGHTS: Beltran lectures throughout Mexico on the topics of art, popular art, and graphic journalism.

As a muralist he did the "Quetzalcoatl" mosaic mural (4 by 20 meters) for the Anthropology Museum in Jalapa City, Veracruz, Mexico, and one stained glass window (6 by 15 meters) in the office of the Civil Registration, also in Veracruz.

(From *The Incas: People of the Sun* by Victor W. Von Hagen. Illustrated by Alberto Beltran.)

BETANCOURT, Jeanne 1941-

BRIEF ENTRY: Born October 2, 1941, in Burlington, Vt. Author of books for young adults. Betancourt has taught English and film studies at junior high and high schools in Vermont and New York and has served as a faculty member at the New School for Social Research. She has also developed workshops for librarians and educators on the topic of film programming for adolescents. Her first book, published in 1974, was an adult study of films about women entitled *Women in Focus.* Since then Betancourt has concentrated her writing efforts on books for young adults. Recalling her own past experiences, she comes to the aid of young readers who share a common adolescent problem in *SMILE! How to Cope with*

Braces (Knopf, 1982). According to *Booklist*, it contains "a veritable wealth of information . . . from the definition of malocclusion (bad bite) to kids' advice on how to kiss with braces ('Take off the rubber bands, just to be safe')."

SMILE! was followed by book adaptations of two highly-acclaimed adolescent films. *Am I Normal?*, for boys, and its companion volume, *Dear Diary* (both Avon/Flare, 1983), for girls, deal with awakening feelings of sexuality and the normal bodily changes that occur during puberty. *Voice of Youth Advocates* noted: "Diagrams and factual information are accurate, concise and up-to-date . . . , [and] boy/girl relations are particularly well handled." Betancourt continued to reveal her affinity for adolescents in her novel *The Rainbow Kid* (Avon/Camelot, 1983), an exploration of the pain and confusion endured by those who suddenly become "a joint custody kid." *Publishers Weekly* observed: "Betancourt's exhuberant style with its natural humor is very engaging while in no way making light of the problems of broken families." Her latest works are *The Edge* (Scholastic, 1985) and *Turtle Time* (Avon/Camelot, 1985). In addition to her books, Betancourt has written articles and reviews and is a contributing editor to *Channel* magazine. She has served as president of New York Women in Film as well as an advisory board member of the Media Center for Children. *Residence:* New York, N.Y.

FOR MORE INFORMATION SEE: Contemporary Authors, Volumes 49-52, Gale, 1975.

BILLINGTON, Elizabeth T(hain)

BRIEF ENTRY: Born in New York, N.Y. A naturalist and author, Billington has been a full-time writer since the publication of her first book for young readers, *Adventure with Flowers* (Warne, 1966). She received reviewers' praise for her straightforward look at the ecology problem in her second book, *Understanding Ecology* (Warne, 1968). *Times Literary Supplement* observed: "The author simplifies the whole structure of the created world so that it is easy to understand . . . why it behooves man to be pretty careful . . . about interfering without prior thought." A reviewer for *Horn Book* agreed, berating the sensationalism that occurred following the publication of Rachel Carson's *Silent Spring* and noting that Billington "makes it perfectly clear that man is just another species—a variable . . . among the other variables."

Billington has also written three novels for young readers, each of which focuses on a preadolescent who, in some manner, undergoes an emotional change. In *Part-Time Boy* (Warne, 1980), described by *Horn Book* as "a quiet, gentle story about a boy who doesn't fit in either at home or at school," ten-year-old Jamie makes friends with the young woman in charge of the natural science center at school and ends up spending the summer at her cabin in the woods. Labeled as "too quiet" and "a loner," Jamie gains new self-confidence during his stay and returns home, not a transformed boy but a changed one. Likewise, in *Getting to Know Me* (Warne, 1982), a young New York city dweller gains a deeper self-awareness after visiting a small New England town. Twelve-year-old Peter finds that he is able to defend himself against the town bully, discovers a love for animals, and decides that his interest in photography exists only to please his father. *School Library Journal* called it "a carefully plotted, pleasant and uncomplicated story of an important summer in a boy's life."

Billington again transports her characters from an urban to a more rural setting in *The Move* (Warne, 1984), this time permanently as eleven-year-old Tim and his family leave behind the violence of a New York tenement for the comparative security of the suburbs. *School Library Journal* again noted that "the psychological and emotional stress of moving is personalized . . . [as] the setting reflects the tension and attitudes of the main characters." *Booklist* added: "[Billington] carefully brings home her point that there are good and bad people everywhere and that it is up to the individual to find friendship and security in a new situation." In addition to her nonfiction and novels, Billington is the editor of *The Ralph Caldecott Treasury* (Warne, 1978). *Address:* c/o Frederick Warne & Co., Inc., 101 Fifth Ave., New York, N.Y. 10003.

FOR MORE INFORMATION SEE: Contemporary Authors, Volume 101, Gale, 1981.

BLOOM, Lloyd

BRIEF ENTRY: A graduate of Indiana University at Bloomington, Bloom has illustrated nearly twenty books for young people. These include award winners like Charlotte Towner Graeber's *Grey Cloud*, which received the Friends of American Writers Juvenile Book Merit Award in 1980, and Mavis Jukes's *No One Is Going to Nashville*, given the Irma Simonton Black Award in 1984. He also illustrated *Like Jake and Me* by Jukes, which was named a Newbery Honor Book and an honor book in the illustration category of the *Boston Globe-Horn Book* Awards, both in 1985. While working on the book, Bloom created his own technique for painting with pastels.

Critics have praised Bloom's illustrations for their effectiveness in conveying elements contained in the text. According to *Horn Book*, "full-page drawings are immensely evocative of the toil and the strain . . ." in *Fire Snake: The Railroad That Changed East Africa* by Francine Jacobs. The same magazine also praised his pictures in *No One Is Going to Nashville*, noting that "the illustrations, executed in tones of gray, depict the intense emotions only suggested by the text. . . ." Similarly, *Publishers Weekly* found that emotions expressed in Patricia MacLachlan's *Arthur, for the Very First Time* are "mirrored in Bloom's evocative, old-fashioned pictures." Bloom's other illustrated works for young people include *Bobcat* by Virginia F. Voight, *We Be Warm Till Springtime Comes* by Lillie D. Chaffin, *The Green Book* by Jill Paton Walsh, *Nadia the Willful* by Sue Alexander, and *The Elves and the Shoemaker*, retold by Eric Suben. *Residence:* Brooklyn, N.Y.

BLY, Janet Chester   1945-

PERSONAL: Born February 23, 1945, in Visalia, Calif.; daughter of Raymond Thomas Chester (a contractor) and Betty (a homemaker; maiden name, Carpenter) Hart; married Stephen A. Bly (a pastor and writer), June 14, 1963; children: Russell, Michael, Aaron. *Education:* College of Sequoias, A.A., 1977. *Home:* 736 Tighe Lane, Fillmore, Calif. 93015.

CAREER: Moore's Miniature Roses, Visalia, Calif., secretary, 1962-74; free-lance writer, 1976—; lecturer at Christian writers' seminars. *Member:* Christian Women's Club (chairman, 1969), Junior Women's Club. *Awards, honors:* Writer of the Year Award, Mount Hermon Christian Writer's Conference, 1982, for uniqueness as a husband/wife team and a volume of published works as new writers.

STEPHEN A. and JANET CHESTER BLY

WRITINGS: (With husband, Stephen A. Bly) *Devotions with a Difference* (young adult), Moody, 1982; (with S. Bly) *Questions I'd Like to Ask* (juvenile), Moody, 1982; *The Hawaiian Computer Mystery* (juvenile), David C. Cook, 1985; (with S. Bly) *Crystal's Perilous Ride* (juvenile), David C. Cook, 1986; (with S. Bly) *Crystal's Solid Gold Discovery* (juvenile), David C. Cook, 1986; (with S. Bly) *Crystal's Page in History,* David C. Cook, 1986. Contributor of over three-hundred nonfiction articles, fictional stories, and poetry to numerous religious publications.

WORK IN PROGRESS: A woman's leadership Bible study series.

SIDELIGHTS: "I find satisfaction in both editing and writing. I'm on the growing edge of creative tension through team writing efforts with my writer husband. Clear, fresh, imaginative craftsmanship that glorifies God continues to be my consuming goal.

"My husband and I both believe we are better writers together than we would have been alone. We prod and poke one another in our weak areas. He's brimming with creative ideas. I picture the developed product on the page and work through the nitty gritty of depth of treatment. Sometimes we clash, but we know enough to know we've got a long way to go. Our best work is yet to come. All that's been written before is our practice. Even so, we trust it's still beneficial and entertaining for our readers.

"Since my first writing attempts and sales in 1976 after the burst of inspiration from a writer's conference, we together have published over 300 articles, stories, and poems, and soon will see our eighth book in print. We have eight other book projects at various stages and numerous other article and story ideas waiting their turn.

"We began to write together because I could see writing potential through my husband's sermons and other speaking, and pestered him until he allowed me to edit his work and submit it to publishers. When he realized they bought everything I sent to them, he decided to join me as a serious partner.

"Most all our books center either on radical discipleship to Jesus Christ, or the best of the moral traditions of the Old West. Most of our writings reflect our spiritual commitments and our expertise in the founding of the West, 1840-1910.

"One reason our success rate in published works is fairly high for today's market is due to the fact we scout around to find out editor's needs. Then, we look into our lifestyle or experiences to see how we can match that need. That's how *Questions I'd Like to Ask* and *Devotions with a Difference* were created. We worked with youth and had teenage sons and an editor mentioned at a writer's conference, 'We haven't had a devotional for kids or teens in over fifteen years.'

"Many of our other books came about because an editor, familiar with our work through consistent contacts, asked us to do a particular project.

"Religious books are selling today because people don't buy the idea that God is dead. For one thing there's too much occult activity in the world around and in the media. They know the supernatural is real and can't be laughed away. If they can find their way to God, maybe they'll find the answers to the deep questions to the apparent meaninglessness of their own existence. Even kids sense the despair of our times and are asking unsettling questions. We're just one of many pilgrims who are digging deep, to the best of our talents and integrity, to help them find the way."

BLY, Stephen A(rthur)   1944-

PERSONAL: Born August 17, 1944, in Visalia, Calif.; son of Arthur Worthington (a farmer) and Alice (a homemaker; maiden name, Wilson) Bly; married Janet Chester (a free-lance writer), June 14, 1963; children: Russell, Michael, Aaron. *Education:* Fresno State University, B.A. (summa cum laude), 1971; Fuller Theological Seminary, M.Div., 1974. *Home:* 736 Tighe Lane, Fillmore, Calif. 93015. *Office:* Fillmore Bible Church, 461 Central Ave., Fillmore, Calif. 93015.

CAREER: Worked as ranch foreman in central California, 1965-71; ordained to Presbyterian ministry, 1974; youth pastor in Orosi, Calif., 1969-70, Los Angeles, Calif., 1971-72, Woodlake, Calif. and Fillmore, Calif., 1974—, Winchester, Idaho, 1981-82. Lecturer, Moody Bible Institute; member of teaching staff, Mount Hermon Christian Writer's Conference. *Awards, honors:* Writer of the Year Award, Mount Hermon Writer's Conference, 1982.

WRITINGS: Radical Discipleship (adult), Moody, 1981; *God's Angry Side* (adult), Moody, 1982; (with wife, Janet Bly) *Devotions with a Difference* (young adult), Moody, 1982; (with J. Bly) *Questions I'd Like to Ask* (juvenile), Moody, 1982; *The President's Stuck in the Mud and Other Wild West Escapades* (juvenile; illustrated by Scott Gustafson), David Cook, 1982; *Quality Living in a Complicated Age*, Here's Life, 1984; *Trouble in Quartz Mountain Tunnel*, David Cook, 1985; *Thompson, Mowrey, and Mud*, Tyndale, 1986; (with J. Bly) *Crystal's Perilous Ride*, David Cook, 1986; (with J. Bly) *Crystal's Solid Gold Discovery*, David Cook, 1986; (with J. Bly) *Crystal's Page in History*, David Cook, 1986; *Mowrey, Thompson*, Tyndale, 1986.

Also contributor of over 300 articles and short stories to religious publications.

WORK IN PROGRESS: Dads Do Care for Moody Press; *How Will You Answer Him* (nonfiction).

SIDELIGHTS: "My writing career is indebted to the inspiration and guidance of seminars taught at Mount Hermon Writer's Conferences. Much of my writing relates directly to Christian readers. I also have interest in nineteenth-century western historical writings."

The sight coming toward you. . . . is a fully rigged stagecoach pulled by six big horses. ■ (From *The President's Stuck in the Mud and Other Wild West Escapades* by Stephen A. Bly. Illustrated by Scott Gustafson.)

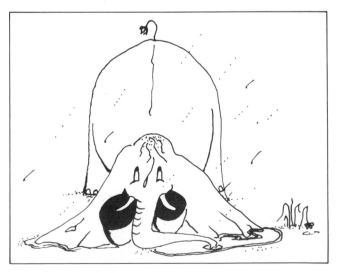

Ella hated rain. It made her hair go straight. ■ (From *Ella: An Elephant—Un Elephant* by Jan Andrews. Illustrated by Pat Bonn.)

PATRICIA CAROLYN BONN

BONN, Patricia Carolyn   1948-
(Pat Bonn)

PERSONAL: Born January 9, 1948, in Nova Scotia, Canada; daughter of Warren E. (a marine consultant) and Dorothy (Parker) Bonn. *Education:* Carelton University, Ottawa, Canada, B.S. 1969. *Home:* 177 Dahlia Ave., Ottawa, Ontario, Canada K1H 6G1.

CAREER: Government of Canada-Taxation Division, Ottawa, Canada, office clerk, 1967; Agriculture Canada, Ottawa, Canada, agricultural research technician, 1969-84.

ILLUSTRATOR: Jan Andrews, *Ella: An Elephant—Un Elephant,* Tundra Books, 1977.

SIDELIGHTS: "My favourite medium is ink or pencil, which is a residual effect from doing biological illustrations for lab reports in university."

HOBBIES AND OTHER INTERESTS: Skiing, T-shirt designs, rughooking.

BOOTH, Ernest Sheldon   1915-1984

PERSONAL: Born October 8, 1915, in Lehman, Pa.; died May, 1984; son of Sherman (a teacher) and Mary (Henkes) Booth; married Dorothy Cushman, September 5, 1938; children: Lowell Sheldon, Laurel Ann. *Education:* Pacific Union College, B.A., 1938; University of Washington, Seattle, M.S., 1940; State College of Washington (now Washington State University), Ph.D., 1947. *Home:* 1438 Rosario Rd., Anacortes, Wash. 98221. *Office address:* Outdoor Pictures, Box 277, Anacortes, Wash. 98221.

CAREER: Walla Walla College, College Place, Wash., instructor, 1938-44, assistant professor, 1944-46, associate pro-

fessor, 1946-47, professor of biology and director of biological station, 1947-58; Loma Linda University, Loma Linda, Calif., professor of biology, 1962-68; Outdoor Pictures (publishers), Anacortes, Wash., president, beginning 1968. Conducted eight scientific expeditions for students to Mexico and Central America, 1946-58. *Member:* American Society of Mammalogists, American Ornithologists' Union, Kiwanis International (past chapter president).

WRITINGS: Laboratory Anatomy of the Cat, [College Place, Wash.], 1943, 5th edition, W. C. Brown, 1973; *Birds of the West,* [College Place, Wash.], 1948, 4th edition, Outdoor Pictures, 1971; *Biology: The Story of Life,* Pacific Press, 1950, revised edition, 1954: *How to Know the Mammals,* W. C. Brown, 1950, 3rd edition, 1972; *Field Record for Birds,* Outdoor Pictures, 1960; *Birds of the East,* Outdoor Pictures, 1962; *Western Bird Guide for Youth,* Outdoor Pictures, 1963; *Eastern Bird Guide for Youth,* Outdoor Pictures, 1963; *Mammals of Southern California,* University of California Press, 1968; *Life List for Birds,* Outdoor Pictures, 1969.

Author of works published by Department of Biological Sciences, Walla Walla College, including *Field Key to the Mammals of Washington,* 1941; *Ecological Distribution of the Birds of the Blue Mountains Region of Southeastern Washington and Northeastern Oregon,* 1952; (with Chester E. Horner) *Spring Flowers of Southeastern Washington and Northeastern Oregon,* 1953. Editor or co-editor of fifteen laboratory anatomy guides for W. C. Brown. Contributed about seventy-five articles to scientific journals, 1940-60. Editor, *Outdoor World,* 1969-72.

SIDELIGHTS: Booth traveled throughout Central and South America, North America, the West Indies, Europe, Africa, and southern Asia.

ERNEST SHELDON BOOTH

In 1929 the Graf Zeppelin became the first aircraft to fly round the world. Crossing the vast unknown wilderness of Siberia on her way to Japan, the great ship caused panic among the inhabitants of the remote villages. ■ (From *Shadow in the Clouds* by Douglas Botting. Illustrated by Michael Jackson.)

DOUGLAS BOTTING

BOTTING, Douglas (Scott)   1934-

PERSONAL: Born February 22, 1934, in London, England; son of Leslie William (a civil servant) and Bessie (Cruse) Botting; married Louise Young (a financial consultant and broadcaster), August 29, 1964; children: Catherine, Anna. *Education:* St. Edmund Hall, Oxford, M.A. (honors), 1958. *Home and office:* 44 Worcester Rd., Wimbledon, London SW19 7QG, England. *Agent:* Andrew Hewson, John Johnson Authors' Agent, Ltd., 45-47 Clerkenwell Green, London EC1R OHT, England.

CAREER: British Broadcasting Corp. (BBC), London, England, writer and independent producer for television, 1958—; explorer, writer, and photographer. *Military service:* British Army, King's African Rifles, 1952-54; served in East Africa; became lieutenant. *Member:* Society of Authors, Royal Geographical Society (fellow), Royal Institute of International Affairs.

WRITINGS: Island of the Dragon's Blood (exploration in Arabia), Funk, 1958; *The Knights of Bornu* (travels in Tchad), Hodder & Stoughton, 1961; *One Chilly Siberian Morning* (travels in Siberia), Macmillan, 1965; *Humboldt and the Cosmos* (biography), Harper, 1973; *Pirates of the Spanish Main* (juvenile), Puffin, 1973; *Shadow in the Clouds* (juvenile), Puffin, 1974; *Wilderness Europe,* Time-Life, 1976; *Rio de Janeiro,* Time-Life, 1977; *The Pirates,* Time-Life, 1978; *The Second Front,* Time-Life, 1979; *The U-Boats,* Time-Life, 1980; *The Giant Airships,* Time-Life, 1980; *The Aftermath: Europe,* Time-Life, 1983; *Nazi Gold,* Congdon & Weed, 1985; *From the Ruins of the Reich: Germany 1945-1949,* Crown, 1985.

WORK IN PROGRESS: America's Secret Army; The Road to Camusfearna.

SIDELIGHTS: Douglas Botting has traveled in Siberia, the Soviet Arctic, the Amazon, Orinoco, Mato Grosso, the Sahara, Southern Arabia, and many parts of Africa. He has participated in scientific and archaeological expeditions, including a balloon flight over East Africa for a study of game migration. Botting speaks French, Portuguese, German, and Swahili.

HOBBIES AND OTHER INTERESTS: Playing classical guitar.

BRANSOM, (John) Paul   1885-1979

PERSONAL: Born July 26, 1885, in Washington, D.C.; died July 12, 1979, in Quakertown, Penn.; married Grace Bond (an actress), 1906 (died, 1963). *Education:* Educated at public schools in Washington, D.C. *Residence:* New York, N.Y. (winter); Canada Lake, Adirondack Mountains, N.Y. (summer), and Jackson Hole, Wyo. (summer).

CAREER: Free-lance artist and illustrator. Worked as a mechanical, patent, and electrical draftsman for U.S. Patent Office, Southern Railway Co., and General Electric Co., about 1899-1903; *New York Evening Journal,* New York, N.Y., illustrator of cartoon series, "The News from Bugsville," 1903-06. Co-founder, Artists' Fellowship, 1925; founder and senior instructor, Teton Artists Outdoor School, Jackson Hole, Wyo. Exhibited work at galleries, including Woodmere Art Gallery, Philadelphia, Penn., 1963. *Member:* Audubon Artists, Society of Illustrators, American Water Color Society, Society of Animal Artists (former president; honorary president), American Artists Professional League, Salmagundi Club. *Awards, honors:* D.A., Weber State College, 1974; Benjamin West Clinedinst Memorial medal, 1976, for distinguished achievement of the Artists' Fellowship; Award of Merit medal, Society of Animal Artists, 1978.

PAUL BRANSOM

(From *The Wahoo Bobcat* by Joseph Wharton Lippincott. Illustrated by Paul Bransom.)

ILLUSTRATOR: Charles G.D. Roberts, *Kings in Exile,* Macmillan, 1910; C.G.D. Roberts, *Neighbours Unknown,* Ward, Lock, 1910; Jack London, *The Call of the Wild,* Macmillan, 1912; C.G.D. Roberts, *Children of the Wild,* Macmillan, 1913; C.G.D. Roberts, *The Feet of the Furtive,* Macmillan, 1913; Kenneth Grahame, *The Wind in the Willows,* Scribner, 1913; C.G.D. Roberts, *The Secret Trails,* Macmillan, 1916; Jean M. Thompson, *Over Indian and Animal Trails,* Frederick A. Stokes, 1918; Louis Dodge, *The Sandman's Forest: A Story for Large Persons to Read to Small Persons,* Scribner, 1918.

Leo E. Miller, *The Hidden People: The Story of a Search for Incan Treasure,* Scribner, 1920; Louis Dodge, *The Sandman's Mountain: A Story for Large Persons to Read to Small Persons,* Scribner, 1920; Frederic T. Cooper, editor, *An Argosy of Fables: A Representative Selection from the Fable Literature of Every Age and Land,* Frederick A. Stokes, 1921; L. E. Miller, *In the Tiger's Lair,* Scribner, 1921; Olaf Baker, *Dusty Star,* Dodd, 1922; Emma-Lindsay Squier, *The Wild Heart,* Cosmopolitan Book Corp., 1922; Charles Alexander, *The Fang in the Forest,* Dodd, 1923; E. Squier, *On Autumn Trails, and Adventures in Captivity,* Cosmopolitan Book Corp., 1923; O. Baker, *Thunder Boy,* Dodd, 1924; Allen Chaffee, *Brownie, the Engineer of Beaver Brook,* Milton Bradley, 1925; Albert P. Terhune, *Gray Dawn,* Harper, 1927, reprinted, 1965.

(With Don Nelson) Edyth Kaigh-Eustace, *Jungle Babies,* Rand McNally, 1930; Rudyard Kipling, *Just-So Stories,* Garden City

Publishing, 1932; Helen D. Fish, *Animals of American History:/A Picture Book,* Frederick A. Stokes, 1939.

Harold McCracken, *The Last of the Sea Otters,* Frederick A. Stokes, 1942; H. McCracken, *The Biggest Bear on Earth,* Frederick A. Stokes, 1943; Joseph W. Lippincott, *Wilderness Champion: The Story of a Great Hound,* Lippincott, 1944; Archibald H. Rutledge, *Hunter's Choice,* A. S. Barnes, 1946; J. W. Lippincott, *The Wolf King,* Lippincott, 1949.

C.G.D. Roberts, *More Kindred of the Wild,* Ward, Lock, 1950; J. W. Lippincott, *The Wahoo Bobcat,* Lippincott, 1950; H. McCracken, *The Flaming Bear,* Lippincott, 1951; J. W. Lippincott, *The Phantom Deer,* Lippincott, 1954; (with Seymour Fleishman) Marlin Perkins, *Zooparade,* Rand McNally, 1954.

Contributor of illustrations to periodicals, including *Saturday Evening Post* and *Field and Stream.* Contributor of illustrations to *New International Encyclopedia.*

SIDELIGHTS: Bransom was born in Washington, D.C. on **July 26, 1885.** He loved drawing, and his earliest artistic efforts used animals and birds as subject matter. On his first day at school, six-year-old Bransom was so impressed with the large, empty blackboard that he spent his recess filling in the blackboard spaces with pictures of animals. A self-taught artist, Bransom quit school after the eighth grade. "When I reached the mature age of fourteen, I had fully determined to be an artist, so I decided to leave school and be about it at once. Any kind of drawing was associated with art in my mind, and it was not long before I was grinding India ink and learning how to push a ruling-pen in the office of a 'Patent' draughtsman.

"The next four years were spent in this office, including a short time with the Southern R. R. Company and also the General Electric Company as a patent mechanical and electrical draughtsman in turn. At this point I saw that I was on the wrong road, so at eighteen years of age I took the inevitable flight to New York to seek my fortune. There I found two Zoölogical Parks!—one of them bigger and better than anything I had dreamed of. However, I couldn't live in the Zoo and presently found employment with a free-lance artist who was engaged in the illustration of an encyclopedia which was then being published (by Dodd, Mead Company)." [Bertha E. Mahony and Elinor Whitney, compilers, *Contemporary Illustrators of Children's Books*, Bookshop for Boys and Girls, 1930.[1]]

While still a teenager, Bransom took over a syndicated comic strip originated by Gus Dirks. ". . . After a period of vicissitudes common to every struggling aspirant, I found myself engaged by the *New York Evening Journal* to carry on a daily series of comic pictures concerning the whimsical doings of insects, small animals, birds, etc., and known as 'The News from Bugville,' originated by Gus Dirks.

"This was great fun and during this stage of experience I enjoyed daily contact with many brilliant and unusual men, one of whom, Mr. T. S. Sullivan, though a caricaturist, was especially interested in animals and a wonderful draughtsman. I owe a great deal to his kind help and advice. Also, about this time I chanced to meet and form a close friendship with Walt Kuhn, who had just returned from a course of study in Munich under Heinrich Zugel, the noted painter of domestic animals. Kuhn gave me an insight into the principles of construction and organization of form, and I am glad . . . to acknowledge my indebtedness to him. I must not neglect to say that all the while I consistently applied every spare moment to work in the Zoölogical Park, endeavoring to perfect my drawings to the point where there might be acceptable to the illustrated magazines.

"*The Saturday Evening Post* gave me my first chance by accepting four cover designs from my stock of pictures offered and shortly after sent me my first animal story for illustration. This success so encouraged me that I forthwith abandoned the newspaper comic strip and launched into the field of serious magazine and book illustration.

"Shortly after leaving the *Journal* my work in the Zoo attracted the generous interest of Dr. William T. Hornaday, and through his good offices I was accorded the rare privilege and inestimable benefit of having a studio right in the New York Zoölogical Park, where I did all of my commissions for some years."[1]

Bransom's portfolio of animal art became respectable enough to impress several magazine art directors, and his career as a magazine and book illustrator was launched. At the age of twenty-one, the animal artist began a lifetime career that included illustrations for hundreds of animal stories in magazines and illustrations in more than forty books. Among the books that Bransom illustrated were Jack London's *Call of the Wild*, Kenneth Grahame's *The Wind in the Willows* and Rudyard Kipling's *Just-So Stories*. "I do aim to be an outstanding wild-

life artist some day, but at present I do not consider myself as having attained that degree of achievement.

"So far, my efforts have been devoted to the illustration of animal stories for various books and magazine publishers and I think perhaps I've been unusually fortunate in being associated with authors of great distinction and ability. Certainly such writers as Jack London, Charles G.D. Roberts, Kenneth Grahame, A. P. Terhune, Oliver Curwood, Emma Lindsay-Squier, Olaf Baker, H. R. Newell, Enos Mills, etc., should afford sufficient inspiration for any one."[1]

Bransom spent winters working in his Bronx Zoo studio, but in the summertime, he studied and painted animals at his summer homes in Wyoming and the Adirondacks. Bransom studied and painted animals in Grand Teton National Park in Jackson Hole, Wyoming for fifteen years, and was senior instructor of Teton Artist Outdoor School there. He also painted in his studio at Canada Lake in the Adirondacks. There he built a home and studio in the early 1920s in a small colony of early moviemakers, artists and writers that included such notables as James Thurber.

During his later years, Bransom's eyesight began to fail, and he turned to painting subjects that did not require the precise detail and accuracy of animals, such as towns and still lifes. He was often referred to as the "Dean of American Animal Artists."

Bransom, who was a winter resident of New York City, died at the age of ninety-four on **July 12, 1979,** in Quakertown, Pennsylvania during a visit there. In accordance with his wishes there was no funeral. "I have been to so many funerals I didn't want to go to, that I don't want anyone to have to be at mine," he wrote.

FOR MORE INFORMATION SEE: Ladies' Home Journal, March, 1926; *Pictorial Review,* May, 1936; *Saturday Evening Post,* July 29, 1944; *Field & Stream,* August, 1953. Obituaries: *New York Times,* July 22, 1979.

BRONSON, Wilfrid Swancourt   1894-1985

OBITUARY NOTICE: Born October 24, 1894, in Chicago, Ill.; died after a lengthy illness, April 23, 1985, in Milford, Pa. Artist, and author and illustrator of books for young people. After serving in the U.S. Army during World War I, Bronson was a mural painter's assistant in several studios in New York. He later worked as a staff artist on four scientific marine expeditions; paintings from these were presented to the Peabody Museum at Yale. As a result of these trips, Bronson began to produce nature books for young people. The first of the books, *Fingerfins: The Tale of a Sargasso Fish,* was published in 1930 and stemmed from his experiences on trips to tropic seas. Another work, *Paddlewings: The Penguin of Galapagos,* was written after an expedition to the Galapagos Islands. Other books written and illustrated by Bronson include *Pollwiggle's Progress, Children of the Sea, Freedom and Plenty: Ours to Save,* and *Dogs: Best Breeds for Young People.* He was also the illustrator of *Lucky Llama* and *Feathers: The Story of a Rhea* by Alice C. Desmond as well as *Wolf-Eye: The Bad One* by Will Henry.

FOR MORE INFORMATION SEE: Junior Book of Authors, 2nd edition, revised, H. W. Wilson, 1951; *Illustrators of Children's Books: 1946-1956,* Horn Book, 1958; *Story and Verse for Children,* 3rd edition, Macmillan, 1965; *Authors of Books for Young People,* 2nd edition, Scarecrow, 1971; *Contemporary Authors,* Volumes 73-76, Gale, 1978. Obituaries: *Middletown Times Herald-Record,* April 25, 1985.

BROWN, Elizabeth M(yers) 1915-

PERSONAL: Born December 31, 1915, in Brooklyn, N.Y.; daughter of Garry Cleveland (an educator, and co-founder and editor of *Highlights for Children*) and Caroline (an editor and co-founder of *Highlights for Children;* maiden name, Clark) Myers; married Kent Louis Brown (a physician, editor, and author), June 26, 1940; children: Karen Elizabeth (Mrs. Lyman Anders Johnson), Kent Louis, David Stuart, Garry Myers. *Education:* Cornell University, B.S., 1937; Case Western Reserve University, M.A., 1960. *Home:* 148 South Portage St., Westfield, N.Y. 14787. *Office:* 803 Church St., Honesdale, Pa. 18431.

CAREER: Teacher at junior and senior high schools in Walden, N.Y., 1937-38, Auburn, N.Y., 1938-39, Cleveland Heights, Ohio, 1939-40; Cornell University, Ithaca, N.Y., assistant Erie County (N.Y.) home demonstration agent, 1940-42; *Highlights for Children,* Columbus, Ohio, and Honesdale, Pa., director, 1961—, editorial assistant, 1962-64, assistant editor, 1964-66, associate editor, 1966-81, assistant secretary, 1968—, senior editor, 1981—. Zaner-Bloser Co. (publishers), Columbus, director, 1972—. Member, Metro Writers Workshop,

Cleveland, Ohio, 1970-83; trustee, New Day Press, Cleveland, 1972-79; trustee, YWCA, Westfield, N.Y., 1985—. *Member:* Women's National Book Association (director, Cleveland chapter, 1978—), Cornell Women's Club (Cleveland; president, 1953-55), Federation of Cornell Women's Clubs (board of directors, 1955-57), Women's Association of University Center for Continuing Education (treasurer, 1959-61; president, 1961-63), Nutrition Association of Greater Cleveland (board of directors, 1964-68), Women's Auxiliary of Academy of Medicine of Cleveland (president, 1969-70), Ohio State Medical Association Auxiliary (chairman of members-at-large committee, 1970-71; member of state board, 1970-71, 1975-77; district director, 1975-77).

WRITINGS—Editor; for children: (With others) *Pilgrims and Their Times,* Highlights for Children, 1960, revised edition, 1973; *A Free Nation: The Beginning of the United States,* Highlights for Children, 1975; *Successful American Women: Some Satisfying Careers,* Highlights for Children, 1976.

SIDELIGHTS: "I believe that children, especially, should encounter beauty of language. Any time someone writes by 'formula' or wordlist, the beauty and flow of language become secondary and often impossible to enjoy. Children's literature can expose children to exciting worlds and ideas. The more children read (and are read to) the more likely they will be to express themselves well. They will find more meaningful all that they encounter.

"I have become very concerned about the spread of misinformation through the printed word. In presenting nonfiction (even fiction) to any age, accuracy is a must. The old adage, 'write what you know' is imperative. It seems inexcusable to me for an author to write a biographical account without using an autobiography when one is available. If there are only biographies available, what evidence is there that the author has used dependable sources? Remember that quality of sources is far more important than quantity. There are many times in checking a story when I deliberately *avoid* reading a source which appears to have inaccuracies."

BRUNA, Dick 1927-

PERSONAL: Born August 23, 1927, in Utrecht, Netherlands; son of Albert Willem (a publisher) and Johanna Clara Charlotte (Erdbrink) Bruna; married Irene de Jongh, 1953; children: Sierk, Marc, Madelon. *Education:* Attended Art Academy, Amsterdam, Netherlands. *Religion:* Protestant. *Home:* Gabriellaan 10, Utrecht, Netherlands 3582 HC. *Office:* Jeruzalemstraat 3, Utrecht, Netherlands 3512 KW.

CAREER: Designer of book jackets, 1945—, and posters, 1947—; author and illustrator of books for children, 1953—. Also designer of postage stamps, murals, greeting cards, and picture postcards. *Exhibitions:* Central Museum, Utrecht, 1966-67; Gemeentemuseum, Arnhem, Netherlands, 1977; Rijksmuseum Van Het Boek, The Hague, Netherlands, 1985. *Member:* Authors League of America, P.E.N. International, Netherlands Graphique Internationale, Art Directors Club (Netherlands). *Awards, honors:* Recipient of various awards for the design of posters, including the Poster Prize, 1958, 1960, 1967, and the Benelux Prize, 1960; created knight in the order of Oranje Nassau.

WRITINGS—All for children; all self-illustrated; all original Dutch titles published by Bruna & Zoon (Utrecht, Nether-

ELIZABETH M. BROWN

DICK BRUNA

lands), except as indicated: *De appel,* 1953, revised edition, written with Judith Klugmann, published as *The Happy Apple,* Hart Publishing, 1959, translation by Sandra Greifenstein published as *The Apple: A Toy Box Tale,* Follett, 1963; *Toto in volendam,* 1953; *De kleine koning,* 1955, revised edition published as *De koning,* 1962, translation published as *The King,* Methuen, 1964, Follett, 1968; *De auto* (title means "The Car"), 1957; *Tijs,* 1957; *Fien en Pien,* 1959, translation published as *Tilly and Tessa,* Methuen, 1962, translation by S. Greifenstein published as *Tilly and Tess: A Toy Box Tale,* Follett, 1963; *Het vogeltje,* 1959, translation published as *The Little Bird,* Methuen, 1962, Two Continents, 1975, translation by S. Greifenstein published as *Little Bird Tweet: A Toy Box Tale,* Follett, 1963; *Poesje Nel,* 1959, translation by S. Greifenstein published as *Kitten Nell: A Toy Box Tale,* Follett, 1963 (published in England as *Pussy Nell,* Methuen, 1966).

Circus, 1962, translation by S. Greifenstein published as *The Circus: A Toy Box Tale,* Follett, 1963; *Het ei,* 1962, transla-

tion published as *The Egg,* Methuen, 1964, translation by S. Greifenstein published as *The Egg,* Follett, 1968; *De vis,* 1962, translation published as *The Fish,* Methuen, 1962, translation by S. Greifenstein published as *The Fish: A Toy Box Tale,* Follett, 1963; *Kerstmis,* 1963, translation published as *The Christmas Book,* Methuen, 1964, new edition, Two Continents, 1976, translation into verse by Eve Merriam published as *Christmas,* Doubleday, 1969; *De matroos,* 1964, translation published as *The Sailor,* Methuen, 1966, translation by S. Greifenstein published as *The Sailor,* Follett, 1968; *De school,* 1964, translation published as *The School,* Methuen, 1966, Follett, 1968; (adapter) *Klein duimpje,* 1965, translation published as *Tom Thumb,* Methuen, 1966; *Ik kan lezen,* 1965, translation published as *I Can Read,* Methuen, 1968, Two Continents, 1975; *Ik kan nog meer lezen,* 1965, translation published as *I Can Read More,* Methuen, 1969, Two Continents, 1976; (adapter) *Assepoester,* 1966, translation published as *Cinderella,* Follett, 1966; (adapter) *Sneeuwwitje,* 1966, translation published as *Snow White and the Seven Dwarfs,*

Follett, 1966; (adapter) *Roodkapje*, 1966, translation published as *Little Red Riding Hood*, Follett, 1966; *B is een beer*, 1967, translation published as *B Is for Bear: An ABC*, Methuen, 1967, 2nd edition, 1971; *Telboek*, 1968, translation published as *I Can Count*, Methuen, 1968, Two Continents, 1975; *Bolk zonder woorden*, 1968, translation published as *A Story to Tell*, Methuen, 1968, Two Continents, 1975; *Snuffie*, 1969, translation published as *Snuffy*, Methuen, 1970, Two Continents, 1975; *Snuffie en de brand*, 1969, translation published as *Snuffy and the Fire*, Methuen, 1970, Two Continents, 1975.

ABC Frieze (four foldout paper panels), Methuen, 1971, Methuen (U.S.), 1976; *Dierenboek*, 1972, translation published as *Dick Bruna's Animal Book*, Methuen, 1974, Two Continents, 1976; *Mijn hemd is wit*, 1972, translation published as *My Vest Is White*, Methuen, 1973, published as *My Shirt Is White*, Two Continents, 1975; *Telboek 2*, 1972, translation published as *I Can Count More 13-24*, Methuen, 1973, Two Continents, 1976; *Boek zonder woorden 2*, 1974, translation published as *Another Story to Tell*, Methuen, 1974; *Ik ben een clown*, 1974, translation published as *I Am a Clown*, Methuen, 1976; *Christmas Crib Print-Outs*, Methuen (U.S.), 1974; *Bloemenboek* (title means "Flower Book"), 1975; *Dick Bruna's Animal Frieze* (four foldout paper panels), Methuen, 1975; *One-Two-Three Frieze* (four foldout paper panels), Two Continents, 1976; *Ik kan moeilijke woorden lezen*, 1976, translation published as *I Can Read Difficult Words*, Methuen, 1977,

Quickly they rolled out the hose, and turned on the water. ■ (From *Snuffy and the Fire* by Dick Bruna. Illustrated by the author.)

It was a little yellow duckling with a piece of shell on its head. ■ (From *The Egg* by Dick Bruna. Illustrated by the author.)

Methuen (U.S.), 1978; *Ik kan nog veel meer lezen*, 1976, translation published as *I Can Dress Myself*, Methuen, 1977, Methuen (U.S.), 1978; *Betje Big*, 1977, translation published as *Poppy Pig*, Methuen, 1978; *De tuin van Betje Big*, 1977, translation published as *Poppy Pig's Garden*, Methuen, 1978; *The Dick Bruna Calendar 1979*, Methuen, 1978; *Dick Bruna's Nature Frieze*, Methuen, 1978, published in America as *The Nature Frieze* (four foldout paper panels), Methuen (U.S.), 1979; (written with Edith Brinkers) *Verjaardagboekje t.b.v. unicef* (title means "Birthday Book in Support of UNICEF"), 1979; *A Child's First Books* (contains *I Can Read*, *I Can Count*, *A Story to Tell*, and *My Vest Is White*), Methuen, 1979; *Eten*, 1979, translation published as *My Meals*, Methuen, 1980; *Spelen*, 1979, translation published as *My Toys*, Methuen, 1980; *Naar buiten*, 1979, translation published as *Out and About*, Methuen, 1980.

Betje big gaat naar de markt, 1980, translation published as *Poppy Pig Goes to Market*, Methuen, 1981; *Heb jij een hobbie?*, 1980, translation published as *When I'm Big?*, 1981; *Ik kan sommen maken*, 1980, translation published as *I Know about Numbers*, Methuen, 1981; *Ik kan nog meer sommen maken*, 1980, translation published as *I Know More about Numbers*, Methuen, 1981; *Dick Bruna's Word Book*, Methuen, 1982; *Jan*, De Harmonie, 1982, translation published as *Farmer John*, Price, Stern, 1984; *Rond, vierkant, driehoekig*, De Harmonie, 1982, translation published as *I Know about Shapes*, Price, Stern, 1984; *Wij hebben een orkest*, De Harmonie, 1984, translation published as *The Orchestra*, Price, Stern, 1984; *De redding*, De Harmonie, 1984, translation published as *The Rescue*, Price, Stern, 1984; *Blue Boat*, Methuen, 1984; *Sportboek* (title means "Sport Book"), De Harmonie, 1985; *Wie zijn hoed is dat?* (riddle book), De Harmonie, 1985; *Wie zijn rug is dat?* (riddle book), De Harmonie, 1985. Also author of *Children's Haemopilia Book*.

"Miffy" series; all original Dutch titles published by Bruna & Zoon, except as indicated: *Nijntje*, 1955, revised edition, 1963, translation published as *Miffy*, Methuen, 1964, Follett, 1970; *Nijntje in de dierentuin*, 1955, revised edition, 1963,

translation published as *Miffy at the Zoo*, Methuen, 1965, Follett, 1970; *Nijntje in de sneeuw*, 1963, translation published as *Miffy in the Snow*, Methuen, 1965, Follett, 1970; *Nijntje aan zee*, 1963, translation published as *Miffy at the Seaside*, Methuen, 1964, Follett, 1970, published as *Miffy at the Beach*, Methuen, 1979; *Het feest van Nijntje*, 1970, translation published as *Miffy's Birthday*, Methuen, 1971, Two Continents, 1976; *Nijntje vliegt*, 1970, translation published as *Miffy Goes Flying*, Methuen, 1971, Two Continents, 1976; *Miffy Painting Book* (activity book), Methuen, 1974; *Nijntje in de speeltuin*, 1975, translation published as *Miffy at the Playground*, Methuen, 1976; *Nijntje in het ziekenhuis*, 1975, translation published as *Miffy in Hospital*, Methuen, 1976, published as *Miffy in the Hospital*, Methuen (U.S.), 1978; *Miffy Books* (includes *Miffy*, *Miffy's Birthday*, *Miffy Goes Flying*, and *Miffy in Hospital*), Methuen (U.S.), 1978; *Nijntje's droom*, 1979, translation published as *Miffy's Dream*, Methuen, 1979, Methuen (U.S.), 1980; *Read-with-Miffy Frieze*, Methuen, 1980; *Nijntje op de fiets*, De Harmonie, 1982, translation published as *Miffy's Bicycle*, Price, Stern, 1984; *Bruna's Miffy Calendar 1980*, Methuen (U.S.), 1980; *Nijntje op school*, De Harmonie, 1984, translation published as *Miffy Goes to School*, Price, Stern, 1984.

Illustrator: Vera Cerutti, *Kind Little Joe*, Hart Publishing, 1959. Cover illustrator of adult book, *Moeder, moeder de beer is los*.

SIDELIGHTS: Bruna's great-grandfather founded a publishing company in the Netherlands, which his father later ran. When Bruna was sixteen, he produced his first book jacket for the family firm. "I was often on my own as a child, it was marvellous. I always was pretty quiet. Yes, and insecure. I played the accordian and I sang French songs. I was 15, 16 then and at secondary school. That's something I really wouldn't dare to do again."

Instead of becoming a publisher, Bruna chose graphic art, and attended the Art Academy in Amsterdam, but left after six months. From 1945 he has worked as an artist, designing book jackets and posters.

(From *I Can Count More 13-24* by Dick Bruna. Illustrated by the author.)

Bruna's success in the field of children's literature occurred after his own three children were old enough to read. His wife, Irene, played an important role in the creation of his books, providing critical comments on his designs.

His picture books appeal to young children. "I regard children as my equals, almost as adults. And that's how I approach them. If I'm making a book or whatever for children, I don't sit down and think: this is meant for children. I design a book that I like myself and if that happens to get across to children, then that's my good luck.

"Maybe I do have some kind of contact with children, but I don't experience it as such. You know, I don't feel all that

**Miffy sat at the table
next to Grandpa Rabbit
and held tight to her teddy bear
all through her dinner.**

■ (From *Miffy's Birthday* by Dick Bruna. Illustrated by the author.)

comfortable with children. Every so often I have to visit a school or a children's hospital, but I find it really difficult. I'm not sure what kind of attitude to adopt towards them.

"I never test my books out on children either. Everything happens . . . in my studio. I'll work for months on a book and when I feel it's finished, the only person I show it to is my wife. That's what I've done for more than thirty years. She doesn't draw herself, but she's very critical. She doesn't even have to say anything. I can tell from the expression on her face whether it's good or whether it should be put away in a drawer. If that happens sometimes, after a year or two, I suddenly know what was wrong with it.

"It's really strange, some of my books turn out to be suitable for four-year-olds, and others for two-year-olds. Sometimes I can understand why, but I didn't work on them with that conscious goal. And I certainly don't try to educate children one way or another. Of course, when it's a counting-book, then some kind of teaching is automatically involved. But even then, the most important thing is for the child to have nice pictures. You know, I have been asked a few times to do something on air-pollution or whatever, but I wouldn't know how to approach that sort of problem. I'm not an educator or a psychologist. In the same way, I wouldn't know how to make books for seven- or eight-year-olds. My work, which I try to do to the best of my ability, ends up in the two to six age-group, so it seems."

Bruna explained how he works: "In the first place, I think in images quite a lot. As soon as I have an image, for instance something with a sun, I start to make up a story, since I need that as a reference point when I'm drawing. But it quite often happens that I change it when I'm about halfway through, and then the story goes off in a completely different direction. For example, at a certain moment I might be quite unable to do a particular drawing. At times like that, you really feel like tearing out your hair. The whole process takes quite a long time; I always manage to get through it somehow, but I really have to push myself.

"I always work with brushes and poster paints, I never use a pen or anything. I do one drawing a day on average. If I start a second drawing the same day, my concentration suffers and I get tired. So my rule is: finish it or even start again tomorrow."

Bruna began making his extraordinarily simple children's books because he was irritated by the complexity of many of the children's books offered. "They sometimes seemed to be written for parents more than for children of a particular age. My books are definitely intended for children. I'm not the kind of person who puts in jokes meant for the fathers and mothers that go over the children's heads. A complicated children's picture is one where absolutely everything is included, like those in old books of fairy-tales where every inch of the drawing is filled up. There are some really beautiful ones around these days. . . . And there are wonderful illustrators too, like Peter Vos and Tomi Ungerer. I wish I had half their technique. But those crowded drawings—I'm just involved in a different area.

"Once I've drawn a bear or a house, I find it terribly difficult to draw another house or another bear, because it all becomes a kind of visual language. You're simplifying right down and you try to carry that through in everything, including colour. I use one red, one yellow, one blue, and only primary colours as far as possible.

"Everything starts out complicated. Then, I take out more and more that seems to me unnecessary. The same applies to the words, so that they compliment the picture. It's difficult because you sometimes overstep the mark and leave too much out and then all the intensity of the drawing is suddenly gone and you can't decide which detail it was which made the difference. I can spend hours worrying about that. If I'm doing a drawing and there's, say, a blue boat, I'll try it in red as well, and then in green, to see whether one of those is more powerful, whether it changes the mood. Another time, I'll try leaving a window out of a house—that's the sort of way I spend my time."

Bruna's designs have changed little over the years. "I don't believe that my creativity has gradually become restricted by simplification. I usually make twelve pictures and twelve pages of text for one book. When they are finished I lay them out on the table and check to make sure that every page is a good piece of work in it's own right. I really love Matisse's work, his completely direct forms. If you can make a book for children that way, with a green in it and a blue up alongside—that's fantastic."

Simplification, according to Bruna, appeals to young children. "If you make it that simple, you leave the children a lot of room for their own imagination. You can tell afterwards from their reactions that this is exactly what happens. But that doesn't mean I'm trying to draw like a child, not at all. It's definitely not a case of me consciously sitting there thinking: children will love it if I use only a few bright colours. I just draw what I think is good and I try to do that to the best of my ability. I wouldn't know how to do it any other way.

"Take Miffy, if, for instance, I only want to show her face with sad eyes. Because I draw so little, say two dots for eyes and a nose and a mouth it takes me ages to get exactly the expression I want. After all, there's very little difference between a little bit of sadness and a bit more sadness. I often do it over and over again. You try all kinds of things. If I feel there's something wrong with a drawing, it's bound to end up in the waste bin. I get through an incredible amount of paper."

Bruna consciously creates books with little or no action. "My pictures are nearly always static. The figures look straight out at you, I've done very few that you see sideways on. Even in the most dangerous moments they look straight at you, like my firemen on a fire engine. It's a matter of directness, it's there in my other work too. The book covers I once did for Simenon, Havank or whoever, I always tried to make as simple and direct as possible. It's just like talking to someone, you look straight at them, don't you? I never put in figures on those Simenon book covers, but I did try to create an atmosphere. I left the rest open. . . ."

If, at the same time, Bruna can also be of practical service to children, then, "I think that's great. . . . The books have a practical use. For instance they're used for children with all kinds of problems and handicaps. Incidentally, some good things happen along the way. Take *Miffy in Hospital*. In that book, ordinary kinds of things happen, like tonsils being taken out. At some point in the hospital, they give you a jab. I had written that it didn't hurt. I showed the book to a child psychologist, Dolf Kohnstamm. He said: 'It's all very nice, but you shouldn't say that a jab doesn't hurt.' I thought, he's right, and so I wrote: the jab only hurts a little bit. You can't shy away from these things, you must be honest."

In 1985 a Dick Bruna exhibition was held at the Dutch National Museum of Book and Typography in the Hague. His books for young children have been translated into over twenty-eight languages and have been adapted into wooden toys.

FOR MORE INFORMATION SEE: Bettina Hürlimann, *Picture-Book World,* World Publishing, 1969; Gedolph Adriaan Kohnstamm, *The Extra in the Ordinary: Children's Books by Dick Bruna,* translated by Patricia Crampton, Mercis, 1976; Lee Kingman and others, editors, *Illustrators of Children's Books: 1967-1976,* Horn Book, 1978.

BUTTERWORTH, Emma Macalik   1928-

PERSONAL: Born September 5, 1928, in Vienna, Austria; came to the United States in 1955, naturalized citizen, 1958; daughter of Josef (a designer) and Olga (Pomaisel) Macalik; married William Edmund Butterworth III (a writer), July 12, 1950; children: Patricia Olga (Mrs. Thomas Black), William Edmund IV, John Scholefield II. *Education:* Attended University of Vienna, 1945-50. *Home address:* Creek Dr., P.O. Drawer A-L, Fairhope, Ala. 36532. *Agent:* Jane Cushman, JCA Literary Agency, Inc., 242 West 27th St., Suite 4A, New York, N.Y. 10001.

I never got to tell Marcella that I was going to be in the movies. And I never would have the chance to tell Olaf. ■ (Jacket illustration by Ronald Himler from *As the Waltz Was Ending* by Emma Macalik Butterworth.)

CAREER: Vienna State Opera, Vienna, Austria, member of Corps de Ballet, 1936-44; calligrapher, engrosser, and illuminator, 1947—.

WRITINGS: The Complete Book of Calligraphy, Lippincott, 1980; *As the Waltz Was Ending* (young adult; autobiographical; ALA Notable Book), Four Winds, 1982.

WORK IN PROGRESS: A novel about a young woman who comes to the United States as the bride of an American.

SIDELIGHTS: "When I was growing up, I was convinced that writers were creatures from another planet. When I married, I was convinced that my husband's dream of becoming a writer was just that. When my husband insisted that I start writing my own first book, I thought he was dreaming again.

"Thirty-five years of marriage to, and three children with, my writer has convinced me that I had, and most people have, the wrong ideas about writing and writers.

"What it's all about is hard work. For twenty-five years of our marriage, he wrote his books (the last time someone counted, he had published 146 books) in the morning, and I typed his manuscripts in the afternoon. Our children, knowing nothing different, thought this was the way everybody lived, and showed no interest whatever in writing, or, for that matter, literature. It took months of screaming at each of them to get them to write their high school graduation speeches. The two who went to college failed freshman English.

"Our daughter Patricia's first job was as a typist in the administrative office of the Birmingham (Alabama) *News.* Eighteen months later, she was the editor of the 'Wedding and Engagements' section. After marrying a writer and having a baby, she 'retired' and is writing a book on her experiences as an editor.

"Our son Bill's first job was as a trainee in the engineering section of Dahlgren Manufacturing Company, which makes newspaper printing presses. After a year of that, he walked in the *Dallas Morning News* and talked himself into a job as an assistant editor of *Houston City Magazine.* He is now an editor of *Boy's Life* magazine, and author of a young adult novel. Our youngest son, John, writes well enough to become a writer, too.

"So it looks like everybody in the family will be writers. And the common thread between everybody has far less to do with art, or the study of 'creative writing' than it does with understanding what my husband taught, by example, to all of us: 'Published writers are people who don't talk about writing, but rather sit down at a typewriter (now, a word processor) day after day after day and stay there until they get it right, and don't let anything get in the way.'"

CAINES, Jeannette (Franklin)

BRIEF ENTRY: Born in New York, N.Y. Author of children's books. During her career, Caines has worked for a publishing company and has also been a member of the Coalition of 100 Black Women, the Council on Adoptable Children, and the Negro Business and Professional Women of Nassau County. She also received the National Black Child Development Institute's Certificate of Merit and Appreciation. Her four picturebooks all center on relationships within black families. In *Abby* (Harper, 1973), a preschooler enjoys looking through her baby book and hearing stories from her mother and big brother, Kevin, about the day that she was adopted into their family. *Publishers Weekly* called it "an endearing story," and *Bulletin of the Center for Children's Books* found it "far more effective than most [stories about adoption]."

Caines's second book, *Daddy* (Harper, 1977), describes the things that a child of separated parents does with her father on Saturdays. *School Library Journal* termed it a "gentle, evocative book about a child of separated parents." Reviewers have also been favorable toward *Window Wishing* (Harper, 1980), the story of two children who spend a vacation with their Grandma Mag. According to *Interracial Books for Children Bulletin*, "This is a lovely book that encourages children to view older people in a non-ageist way . . . [and] a refreshing portrait of African American people." Caines also wrote *Just Us Women* (Harper, 1982), in which a young girl and her aunt Martha plan a long car trip to North Carolina for just the two of them. *Residence:* Freeport, Long Island, New York.

FOR MORE INFORMATION SEE: Early Years, March, 1983.

CAULEY, Lorinda Bryan   1951-

BRIEF ENTRY: Born July 2, 1951, in Washington, D.C. Author, reteller, and illustrator of books for children. Cauley received her A.D. from Montgomery Junior College in 1971 and her B.F.A. from Rhode Island School of Design in 1974. An author and illustrator since 1976, she currently has about thirty books to her credit. Among these are several self-illustrated retellings of well-known tales, including *The Ugly Duckling: A Tale from Hans Christian Andersen. New York Times Book Review* found her version "convincingly depicted," while *Publishers Weekly* noted the book's "fresh loveliness" and "soupçon of humor." Known for her meticulous attention to detail, Cauley works in a variety of mediums such as pencils, pastels, black crayon, and oils. As *Booklist* observed: "Her characteristic warm colors and penchant for domestic detail operate . . . strongly." *School Library Journal* agreed, calling the illustrations in her retelling of *The Town Mouse and the Country Mouse* (Putnam, 1984) "glowing . . . large colorful drawings . . . [that] create a homey atmosphere."

Other books retold and illustrated by Cauley include *The Goose and the Golden Coins* (Putnam, 1981), *The Cock, the Mouse, and the Little Red Hen* (Putnam, 1982), and *Jack and the Beanstalk* (Putnam, 1983). Among her original works are *Pease Porridge Hot: A Mother Goose Cookbook* (Putnam, 1977) and *The Animals Kids* (Putnam, 1979). Cauley's illustrated works for others include *The House of Five Bears* by Cynthia Jameson, *Ants Don't Get Sunday Off* by Penny Pollock, and *Old Hippo's Easter Egg* by Jan Wahl. *Home and office:* 17 Leonard St., New York, N.Y. 10013.

FOR MORE INFORMATION SEE: Contemporary Authors, Volume 101, Gale, 1981.

Books are the treasured wealth of the world and the fit inheritance of generations and nations. . . . Their authors are a natural and irresistible aristocracy in every society, and, more than kings or emperors, exert an influence on mankind.

—Henry David Thoreau

CLEARY, Beverly (Bunn)   1916-

PERSONAL: Born in 1916, in McMinnville, Ore.; daughter of Chester Lloyd (a farmer) and Mable (a teacher; maiden name, Atlee) Bunn; married Clarence T. Cleary (an accountant), October, 1940; children: Marianne Elisabeth, Malcolm and James (twins). *Education:* Chaffee Junior College, Ontario, Calif., A.A., 1936; University of California, Berkeley, B.A., 1938; University of Washington, Seattle, B.A. in Librarianship, 1939. *Address:* c/o William Morrow & Co., 105 Madison Ave., New York, N.Y. 10016.

CAREER: Public Library, Yakima, Wash., children's librarian, 1939-40; U.S. Army Hospital, Oakland, Calif., post librarian, 1943-45; writer for young people, 1950—. *Member:* Authors Guild.

AWARDS, HONORS: Young Readers' Choice Award from Pacific Northwest Library Association, 1957, for *Henry and Ribsy*, 1960, for *Henry and the Paper Route*, 1968, for *The Mouse and the Motorcycle*, 1971, for *Ramona the Pest*, and 1980, for *Ramona and Her Father;* Dorothy Canfield Fisher Memorial Children's Book Award, 1958, for *Fifteen*, and 1966, for *Ribsy;* South Central Iowa Association of Classroom Teachers' Youth Award, 1968, for *The Mouse and the Motorcycle;* Nene Award from Hawaii Association of School Librarians and Hawaii Library Association, 1968, for *Ribsy*, 1969, for *The Mouse and the Motorcycle*, 1971, for *Ramona the Pest*, 1972, for *Runaway Ralph*, and 1979, for *Ramona and Her Father;* William Allen White Award from Kansas Association of School Libraries and Kansas Teachers' Association, 1968, for *The Mouse and the Motorcycle*, and 1976, for *Socks.*

Georgia Children's Book Award from College of Education of University of Georgia, 1970, Sequoyah Children's Book Award from Oklahoma Library Association, 1971, and Massachusetts Children's Book Award runner-up, 1977, all for *Ramona the Pest;* New England Round Table of Children's Librarians Honor Book, 1972, for *Henry Huggins*, and 1973, for *The Mouse and the Motorcycle;* Sue Hefley Award from

BEVERLY CLEARY

Mrs. Risley possessed the perfect lap, a lap rarely experienced by a cat who lived in a world of people determined to stay thin. ■ (From *Socks* by Beverly Cleary. Illustrated by Beatrice Darwin.)

Louisiana Association of School Librarians, 1972, and Surrey School Book Award from Surrey School District, 1974, both for *The Mouse and the Motorcycle;* Charlie Mae Simon Children's Book Award from Arkansas Elementary School Council, 1973, for *Runaway Ralph,* and 1984, for *Ramona Quimby, Age 8;* Distinguished Alumna Award from University of Washington, 1975; Laura Ingalls Wilder Award from American Library Association, 1975, for substantial and lasting contributions to children's literature; Golden Archer Award from University of Wisconsin, 1977, for *Socks* and *Ramona the Brave;* Children's Choice Election Award, second place, 1978; Mark Twain Award from Missouri Library Association and Missouri Association of School Librarians, 1978, for *Ramona the Brave;* Newbery Honor Book Award from American Library Association, 1978, for *Ramona and Her Father,* and 1982, for *Ramona Quimby, Age 8;* Boston Globe-Horn Book Honor Book Award, 1978, Land of Enchantment (New Mexico) Children's Book Award, 1981, and Texas Bluebonnet Award, 1981, all for *Ramona and Her Father.*

International Board on Books for Young People Honor Book Award, Tennessee Children's Book Award of Tennessee Library Association, and Utah Children's Book Award of Children's Library Association of Utah, all 1980, for *Ramona and Her Father;* Regina Medal, Catholic Library Association, 1980, for ''continued distinguished contributions to children's literature''; Garden State Children's Choice Award of New Jersey Library Association, 1980, for *Ramona and Her Father,* 1982, for *Ramona and Her Mother,* and 1984, for *Ramona Quimby, Age 8; Ramona Quimby, Age 8* was chosen one of *School Library Journal*'s ''Best Books 1981''; American Book Award, 1982, for *Ramona and Her Mother;* Silver Medallion from University of Southern Mississippi, 1982, for her distinguished contribution to children's literature; American Book Awards nominee, 1982, and Michigan Young Readers' Award, 1984, for *Ramona Quimby, Age 8; Ralph S. Mouse* received the Golden Kite Award from Society of Children's Book Writers, 1983, and was included on *School Library Journal*'s list of ''Best Books 1982''; *Dear Mr. Henshaw* was included on *School Library Journal*'s list of ''Best Books 1983''; Commonwealth Club of California Award, 1983, selected by the *New York Times* as a Notable Book of the Year, 1983, New-

bery Medal, 1984, and Christopher Award, 1984, all for *Dear Mr. Henshaw;* Hans Christian Andersen Award nominee from the United States, 1984; Iowa Children's Choice Award, 1984, for *Ralph S. Mouse;* Everychild citation for children's books, 1985.

WRITINGS—All published by Morrow, except as indicated: *Henry Huggins* (illustrated by Louis Darling; ALA Notable Book), 1950; *Ellen Tebbits* (illustrated by L. Darling), 1951; *Henry and Beezus* (illustrated by L. Darling), 1952; *Otis Spofford* (illustrated by L. Darling), 1953; *Henry and Ribsy* (illustrated by L. Darling), 1954; *Beezus and Ramona* (illustrated by L. Darling), 1955; *Fifteen* (illustrated by Beth Krush and Joe Krush), 1956; *Henry and the Paper Route* (illustrated by L. Darling), 1957; *The Luckiest Girl,* 1958; *Jean and Johnny* (illustrated by B. Krush and J. Krush; ALA Notable Book), 1959; *The Real Hole* (picture book; illustrated by Mary Stevens), 1960, reissued (illustrated by Dyann DiSalvo), 1986; *Hullabaloo ABC;* (picture book; verse; illustrated by Earl Thollander), Parnassus, 1960; *Two Dog Biscuits* (picture book; illustrated by M. Stevens), 1961, reissued (illustrated by Dyann DiSalvo), 1986; *Emily's Runaway Imagination* (illustrated by B. Krush and J. Krush), 1961; *Henry and the Clubhouse* (illustrated by L. Darling), 1962; *Sister of the Bride* (illustrated by B. Krush and J. Krush), 1963; *Ribsy* (illustrated by L. Darling), 1964; *The Mouse and the Motorcycle* (illustrated by L. Darling; ALA Notable Book), 1965; *Mitch and Amy* (illustrated by George Porter), 1967; *Ramona the Pest* (illustrated by L. Darling), 1968; *Runaway Ralph* (illustrated by L. Dar-

It poked its head out of Henry's jacket and announced its presence with a small mew. ■ (From *Henry and the Paper Route* by Beverly Cleary. Illustrated by Louis Darling.)

Ramona was poster girl for an American Library Association's reading campaign. (Poster illustrated by Alan Tiegreen.)

ling), 1970; *Socks* (illustrated by Beatrice Darwin), 1973; *The Sausage at the End of the Nose* (play), Children's Book Council, 1974; *Ramona the Brave* (illustrated by Alan Tiegreen), 1975; *Ramona and Her Father* (illustrated by A. Tiegreen; ALA Notable Book; *Horn Book* honor list), 1977; *Ramona and Her Mother* (illustrated by A. Tiegreen), 1979; *Ramona Quimby, Age 8* (illustrated by A. Tiegreen), 1981; *Ralph S. Mouse* (illustrated by Paul O. Zelinsky), 1982; *Dear Mr. Henshaw* (illustrated by P. O. Zelinsky; ALA Notable Book; *Horn Book* honor list), 1983; *Cutting Up with Ramona* (illustrated by JoAn L. Scribner), Dell, 1983; *Lucky Chuck* (illustrated by J. Winslow Higginbottom), 1984; *Ramona Forever* (illustrated by A. Tiegreen), 1984; *The Ramona Quimby Diary* (illustrated by A. Tiegreen), 1984. Contributor of adult short stories to magazines, including *Woman's Day*.

ADAPTATIONS—All produced by Miller-Brody, except as indicated: "Henry and the Clubhouse" (filmstrip with cassette), Pied Piper, 1962; "Ribsy" (filmstrip with cassette), Pied Piper, 1964; "Ramona and Her Father" (record or cassette), 1979, (filmstrip with cassette), 1980; "Beezus and Ramona" (filmstrip with cassette; listening cassette), 1980; "Henry Huggins" (filmstrip with cassette; listening cassette), 1980; "Henry and Ribsy" (listening cassette), 1980; "Ramona and Her Mother" (listening cassette), 1980; "Ramona the Brave" (filmstrip with cassette; listening cassette), 1980; "Ramona Quimby, Age 8" (listening cassette), 1981, (filmstrip with

Unfortunately, the napkins did not absorb egg very well. ■ (From *Ramona Quimby, Age 8* by Beverly Cleary. Illustrated by Alan Tiegreen.)

cassette), 1982; "Henry and Beezus" (listening cassette), 1981; "Ralph S. Mouse" (listening cassette), 1983; "Dear Mr. Henshaw" (listening cassette), 1984, (filmstrip with cassette), 1985.

WORK IN PROGRESS: Ten-part television series based on three of the Ramona books.

SIDELIGHTS: Cleary was born in **1916** in McMinnville, Oregon and spent part of her childhood on a farm in a small town called Yamhill. "My mother was an independent, determined, vivacious, intense woman, ambivalent about the life she led. She had unshakable faith in the importance of books, reading, and libraries. [Beverly Cleary, "Newbery Medal Acceptance," *Horn Book*, August, 1984.[1]]

Her mother established the first library in Yamhill, ". . . in a lodge room upstairs over a bank with a book collection from the State Library in Salem. It was in this dingy room filled with shabby leather-covered chairs and smelling of stale cigar smoke that I made the most magic of discoveries. There were books for children!" [Margaret Novinger, "Beverly Cleary: A Favorite Author of Children," *Authors and Illustrators of Children's Books*, edited by Miriam Hoffman and Eva Samuels, Bowker, 1972.[2]]

"I . . . liv[ed] with my mother and father in a thirteen-room house built by children of pioneers. There I spent my first six years playing alone on the eighty-acre farm in the Willamette Valley. My life was exceptionally happy.

"But something had gone wrong with the pioneer dream of peace and plenty. There was frightening adult talk of the World War, prices, interest rates, taxes, and mortgages. Then in the

P.S. If my dad was here, he would tell you to go climb a tree. ■ (From *Dear Mr. Henshaw* by Beverly Cleary. Illustrated by Paul O. Zelinsky.)

There was no time for Emily to run and hide. Pete Ginty sauntered over and stood watching her rub and scrub. ■ (From *Emily's Runaway Imagination* by Beverly Cleary. Illustrated by Beth and Joe Krush.)

early 1920's came a year when . . . a rich harvest did not bring in enough money to pay the debts and meet the needs of three people. . . .

"A decision was made. We would rent the farm and move to the city to seek our fortunes. . . . To a six-year-old the move meant that at last I would have what I longed for: someone to play with and a big library full of books which I would learn to read." [Beverly Cleary, "Laura Ingalls Wilder Award Acceptance," *Horn Book*, August, 1975.[3]]

"I recall my pleasure upon entering the first grade at seeing above the blackboard in room 1 a reproduction of Sir Joshua Reynolds' painting 'The Age of Innocence.' I was filled with admiration for the pretty little girl who was wearing, to my six-year-old eyes, a white party dress. I loved that little girl, but by Thanksgiving my love had changed to resentment. There she sat under a tree with nothing to do but keep her party dress clean. There I sat itching in my navy blue serge sailor dress, the shrunken elastic of my new black bloomers cutting into my legs, struggling to learn to read.

"We had no bright beckoning book covers with such words as 'fun,' 'adventure,' or 'horizon' to tempt us on. No children played, no dogs romped, no ships sailed or planes flew on the covers of our schoolbooks. Our primer looked grim. Its olive-

green cover with its austere black lettering bore the symbol of a beacon light, presumably to guide us and to warn us of the dangers that lay within.

"The sight of that book's olive-green cover still brings back the feelings of bewilderment I experienced that year when I was confined to a city classroom full of strange children after a life of freedom and isolation on a farm; it brings back the anger, guilt, and despair some of us endured that first year of school while the girl in the white party dress sat there smiling serenely above the blackboard.

"The first grade was soon sorted into three reading groups—Bluebirds, Redbirds, and Blackbirds. I was a Blackbird, the only girl Blackbird among the boy Blackbirds who had to sit in the row by the blackboard. Perhaps this was the beginning of my sympathy for the problems of boys. How I envied the bright, self-confident Bluebirds, most of the girls, who got to sit by the windows and who, unlike myself, pleased the teacher by remembering to write with their right hands—ridiculous thing to do in my six-year-old opinion. Anyone could see that both hands were alike. One should simply use the hand nearer the task.

"Even Redbirds in the center rows were better off than Blackbirds. To be a Blackbird was to be disgraced. I wanted to read, but somehow I could not. I wept at home while my puzzled mother tried to drill me on the dreaded word charts.

Ribsy pawed the air with his front feet and strained at his collar until he choked. ■ (From *Ribsy* by Beverly Cleary. Illustrated by Louis Darling.)

'But reading is fun,' insisted mother. I stamped my feet and threw the book on the floor. Reading was *not* fun.

"At school we Blackbirds struggled along, bored by our primer, baffled when our reading group gathered in the circle of little chairs in the front of the room to stumble over the phonic lists. 'Sin, sip, sit, red, rill, till, tin, tip, bib, bed.' The words meant nothing.

"Memorizing rules which we chanted in unison was easier, even though we might be too frightened or confused to apply these rules. '*E* on the end makes *a* say *ā* in cake.' At least we were anonymous. Sounding out words in chorus, *c a t*, our voices mingling with those of the Bluebirds and Redbirds, was less painful than trying to decipher, 'lad, lag, lap' when our turn came in the dreaded reading circle. When a wretched Blackbird lost his place during word drill, he was banished to the cloakroom to huddle among the muddy rubbers and lunch bags that smelled of peanut butter. Once the teacher switched my hands with a bamboo pointer with a metal tip for not paying attention. I was too ashamed to tell my parents.

"In the second grade this Blackbird, although not exactly taking wing, at least got off the ground. No serene little girl in a clean party dress made me feel inferior. The teacher was kind and gentle; crowds of children were no longer bewildering. I could tell my right hand from my left, although I was still skeptical about the necessity for doing so. We were not made anxious by bird labels, and probably the former Blackbird had reached that mysterious point in life now known as reading readiness.

Ramona's eye caught the reflection of her face distorted in a green Christmas ornament.... I can't really look like that, thought Ramona in despair. I'm really a nice person. ■ (From *Ramona and Her Father* by Beverly Cleary. Illustrated by Alan Tiegreen.)

"At any rate, I was able to plod through my reader a step or two ahead of disgrace, but here another problem presented itself. Although I could read if I wanted to, I no longer wanted to. Reading was not fun. It was boring. Most of the stories were simplified versions of folk tales that had been read aloud to me many times. There was no surprise left.

"Then in the third grade, the miracle happened. It was a dull rainy Portland Sunday afternoon when there was nothing to do but thumb through two books from the Sunday-school library. After looking at the pictures, I began out of boredom to read *The Dutch Twins* by Lucy Fitch Perkins. Here was a book with a story in which something happened. With rising elation I read on. I read all afternoon and evening and by bedtime I had read not only *The Dutch Twins* but *The Swiss Twins* as well. It was one of the most exciting days of my life. Shame and guilt dropped away from the ex-Blackbird who had at last taken wing. I could read and read with pleasure! Grown-ups were right after all. Reading was fun.

"From the third grade on, I was a reader, and when my school librarian suggested that I should write children's books when I grew up, I was ecstatic. Of course! This was exactly what I wanted to do. By now I had gone on from the twin books and was reading everything on the children's side of our branch library. I had grown critical. Why couldn't authors write about the sort of boys and girls who lived on my block? Plain, ordinary boys and girls, I called them when I was a child. Why couldn't authors skip all that tiresome description and write books in which something happened on every page? Why couldn't they make the stories funny?" [Beverly Cleary, "Low Man in the Reading Circle: Or, A Blackbird Takes Wing," *Horn Book,* June, 1969.[4]]

"... My mother had ... important wisdom to impart.... 'Reading is to the mind as exercise is to the body'.... I was constantly directed to use my imagination and my ingenuity and to stand on my own two feet.

"When a teacher required a composition, my mother said, 'Always remember, the best writing is simple writing' and produced her own high school rhetoric book to prove it."[1]

"Writing for young readers was my childhood ambition.... I had had enough of books about wealthy English children who had nannies and pony carts or books about poor children whose problems were solved by a long-lost rich relative turning up in the last chapter. I wanted to read funny stories about the sort of children I knew and I decided that someday when I grew up I would write them.

"And so, with some hardship to my parents, I was sent off to college, not to catch a husband, as was the custom for young women of that time and place, but to become independent. I became a children's librarian, the next best thing to a writer...."[1]

"During the time I was a children's librarian ... I met a variety of children—the children of migratory workers, mill hands, doctors, lawyers, and all the people who did whatever they could to survive during the depression.

"Two groups stand out in my memory. One was a band of unenthusiastic readers, who came to the library once a week from one of the parochial schools for help in selecting books that might encourage them to read. They were a lively bunch and fun to work with, but the sad truth was that there was very little in the library that they wanted to read. They wanted funny stories, and they wanted stories about the sort of children they knew. I sympathized because I had wanted funny stories about the sort of children I knew when I was their age.

"The second group vivid in my memory was a loyal story-hour audience, particularly a little girl with blond pigtails who always brought her little brother and sat in the middle of the front row. Although I told folk and fairy tales, I think I learned to write for children in those Saturday afternoon story hours. When I began Henry Huggins, I did not know how to write a book, so I mentally told the stories to that remembered audience and wrote them down as I told them. This is why my first book is a collection of stories about a group of characters rather than a novel." [Shirley Fitzgibbons, "A National Heroine and an International Favorite," *Top of the News*, winter, 1977.[5]]

"I want to play," said Ramona, riding her tricycle up to the coffee table. . . . ■ (From *Beezus and Ramona* by Beverly Cleary. Illustrated by Louis Darling.)

In 1940, after her marriage to Clarence T. Cleary, she moved to Oakland California, and for the duration of World War II served as a post librarian at the Oakland Army Hospital. "After the war, my husband and I bought a house in the Berkeley hills, and in the linen closet I found several reams of typing paper. 'Now I'll have to write a book,' I remarked to my husband. 'Why don't you?' he asked. 'Because we never have any sharp pencils,' I answered.

"The next day he brought home a pencil sharpener and I realized that if I was ever going to write a book, this was the time to do it."[2]

". . . Shortly after this I worked for three months selling children's books during the Christmas rush in a large bookstore. There I met all of the children's books published that year instead of those selected from good reviews. This gave me a new view of children's books, and I was sure I could write a better book than some I read. After the Christmas rush, I found myself for the first time in my life with free time, a quiet place in which to work and—oh joy!—confidence in myself."[5]

"I . . . began a story based on an incident that once amused me about two children who had to take their dog home on a streetcar during a heavy rain. This turned into a story about a boy who would be allowed to keep a stray dog if he could manage to take him home on a bus. When I finished that chapter I found I had ideas for another chapter and at the end of two months I had a whole book about Henry Huggins and his dog Ribsy."[2]

". . . As I wrote I discovered I had a collaborator, the child within myself—a rather odd, serious little girl, prone to colds, who sat in a child's rocking chair with her feet over the hot air outlet of the furnace, reading for hours, seeking laughter in the pages of books while her mother warned her she would ruin her eyes. That little girl, who has remained with me, prevents me from writing down to children, from poking fun at my characters, and from writing an adult reminiscence about childhood instead of a book to be enjoyed by children. And yet I do not write solely for that child; I am also writing for my adult self. We are collaborators who must agree. The feeling of being two ages at one time is delightful, one that surely must be a source of great pleasure to all writers of books enjoyed by children." [Beverly Cleary, "The Laughter of Children," *Horn Book*, October, 1982.[6]]

The mother of twins, Cleary related how her son influenced her writing in one instance. "I had written five or six books before I had children of my own. However, I probably would not have written fantasy if I had not had a fourth-grade son who was disgusted with reading, who wanted to read about motorcycles but found all the books too hard, and who happened to run a high fever in the middle of the night when we were staying in a strange hotel. *The Mouse and the Motorcycle* was the result."[5]

The most difficult part of the writing process admits Cleary is "getting started, because it's very easy to put off. It's much easier to *not* write, than to write. So I usually chew pencils for a week, and swivel around in my chair a lot, and stare out the window, hoping to see some strange new bird so I can study it with my binoculars and go look it up in the bird book. Once I do get started though, I keep at it.

"As soon as I begin to write, I know what came before that incident, and what will come after. Once I get the first draft pinned down on paper, the fun begins. Because then I can cross out and revise and shape, and I love doing that. Every

book has a trouble spot though. When that happens, I've learned to put it out of my mind and turn to something else." ["Meet the Newbery Author: Beverly Cleary," Random House/Miller Brody, n.d.[7]]

After several of the books about Henry and his friends had been published, Cleary was invited to speak at a junior high school. Several girls there asked why she didn't write similar stories for youngsters in their age group. Acting on this suggestion, she wrote *Fifteen* (Morrow, 1956), followed by *Jean and Johnny* (Morrow, 1959).

Cleary's advice for aspiring children's book authors is to: "Ignore all trends. Trends don't last. Original writers may start trends, if they write good, strong books.

"I also tell beginning writers to write as though talking to a child. An eight-year-old can understand anything you tell him. It's not necessary to have your stories look like telegrams. I have never changed a word to make it easier to read. If a child doesn't understand something, he can ask his parent, or use a dictionary. But most of the time, he can figure it out from the context of the story.

"Most of all, a writer must enjoy the work being written. If I find that I'm not having fun with what I'm writing, I stop." [Sandra Hansen, "The Writing Life," *Writer's Digest*, January, 1983.[8]]

Most rewarding about Cleary's career has been "the number of people who tell me of a child who didn't enjoy reading until my books came along. I remember the great feeling of release I got when I discovered I was reading . . . and enjoying what I read."[8]

Cleary's books have won many awards, including the prestigious Newbery Medal for *Dear Mr. Henshaw* in 1984. "*Dear Mr. Henshaw* was a most satisfying book to write. It seemed almost to write itself. Because life is humorous, sorrowful, and filled with problems that have no solutions, my intent was to write about the feelings of a lonely boy and to avoid the genre of the problem novel."[1]

Her books appear in over ten countries in a variety of languages. Television programs based on Henry Huggins have appeared in Japan, Denmark and Sweden.

HOBBIES AND OTHER INTERESTS: Travel, needlework.

FOR MORE INFORMATION SEE: Wilson Library Bulletin, October, 1961; Huck and Young, *Children's Literature in the Elementary School,* Holt, 1961; *Pacific Northwest Library Association Quarterly,* April, 1961; Muriel Fuller, editor, *More Junior Authors,* H. W. Wilson, 1963; May Hill Arbuthnot, *Children and Books,* 3rd edition, Scott, Foresman, 1964; *The Children's Bookshelf,* Child Study Association of America, Bantam, 1965; Nancy Larrick, *A Teacher's Guide to Children's Books,* Merrill, 1966; *Books for Children, 1960-1965,* American Library Association, 1966; G. Robert Carlsen, *Books and the Teen-Age Reader,* Harper, 1967; *Elementary English,* November, 1967; *Young Readers' Review,* May, 1968; *Book World,* September 8, 1968, October 9, 1977; *Horn Book,* June, 1969, August, 1970, August, 1975, October, 1982, August, 1984; Miriam Hoffman and Eva Samuels, *Authors and Illustrators of Children's Books,* Bowker, 1972; Lee Bennett Hopkins, *More Books by More People,* Citation Press, 1974; *Top of the News,* April, 1975, winter, 1977; *Bulletin of the Center for Children's Books,* July, 1975; *Publishers Weekly,* February 23, 1976; *Children's Literature Review,* Volume II, Gale, 1976;

Growing Point, January, 1976, September, 1978; *Booklist*, October 1, 1977; *Times Literary Supplement*, July 7, 1978; *Catholic Library World*, February, 1980; *The Christian Science Monitor*, May 14, 1982, June 6, 1983; *Early Years*, August-September, 1982; *Writers Digest*, January, 1983; *The Washington Post*, May 31, 1983; *St. Louis Globe-Democrat*, February 13, 1984; "Meet the Newbery Author: Beverly Cleary" (filmstrip), Random House/Miller Brody, n.d.

CLEAVER, Elizabeth (Mrazik) 1939-1985

OBITUARY NOTICE—See sketch in *SATA* Volume 23: Born November 19, 1939, in Montreal, Quebec; died of cancer, July 27, 1985, in Montreal, Quebec. Canadian illustrator of books for children. Known nationally and internationally as one of Canada's foremost children's illustrators, Cleaver was most noted for her unique torn paper collages. She was the recipient of numerous awards throughout her career, including the first Amelia Frances Howard-Gibbon medal, in 1971, for her illustrations in *The Wind Has Wings: Poems from Canada*. Seven years later she again received the medal for her work in William Toye's *The Loon's Necklace*. In l972 she represented Canada at the International Book Year Commonwealth Book Fair held in London; that same year, she was runner-up for the Hans Christian Andersen Award.

Cleaver reflected her love for folklore and legendry in her illustrations. She carefully researched her subject matter, traveling to different lands to study the history and cultures of peoples. In 1971 the National Film Board of Canada invited her to create a filmstrip of her own choosing. The result was "The Miraculous Hind: A Hungarian Legend," released in 1972. Cleaver later provided text and illustrations for a book version. She also wrote and illustrated *Petrouchka*, adapted from the work of Igor Stravinsky and Alexandre Benois. It received the 1980 Parents' Choice Award and the 1981 Canadian Children's Literature Award, both for illustration. Cleaver's work was presented at numerous international competitions and exhibitions and is part of the permanent exhibitions at McGill University and the Toronto Public Library. Among the thirteen books she illustrated are *How Summer Came to Canada* and *The Mountain Goats of Temlaham*, both retold by Stoye, and *The Witch of the North: Folk Tales of French Canada*, adapted by Mary Alice Downie.

FOR MORE INFORMATION SEE: Contemporary Authors, Volumes 97-100, Gale, 1981. Obituaries: *Horn Book*, August 23, 1985.

CLEVELAND, George 1903(?)-1985 (Bob Cleveland, Cappy Dick)

OBITUARY NOTICE: Born about 1903, in Peoria, Ill.; died of cancer, April 29, 1985, in Chicago, Ill. Creator of comic features, journalist, and businessman. Known as George "Bob," Cleveland was the creator of the popular comic feature "Cappy Dick." It was during his twenty-year association with the *Southtown Economist*, one of Chicago's daily newspapers, that he created "Cappy Dick" under the pseudonym of the same name. The feature presented contests and brain teasers through its host, sea captain Cappy Dick. Beginning in the 1960s, it was syndicated by Field Enterprises of Chicago and has since appeared in sixty-four newspapers nationwide. In 1977 Cleveland retired from producing the feature, allowing others to

continue it. He was also the creator of "Hobby Corner," another comic feature which often ran beside "Cappy Dick." Cleveland's avocational interest was magic, and he frequently inserted tricks he had learned into "Cappy Dick." In addition, Cleveland ran a mail-order magic-trick business, Vanguard Syndicate, from 1977 to 1984.

FOR MORE INFORMATION SEE—Obituaries: *Chicago Tribune*, May 3, 1985.

CLISH, (Lee) Marian 1946- (Marian Lee)

PERSONAL: Born September 27, 1946, in Madison, Wis.; daughter of Arthur John (a fireman) and Mary (a licensed practical nurse; maiden name, Hoffman) Halverson; married Raymond Francis Clish (an accountant), August 28, 1971; children: Gregory, Lori, Jeffrey. *Education:* Attended University of Wisconsin-Stevens Point and University of Wisconsin-Milwaukee.

CAREER: M. R. Business Services, Carson City, Nev., owner; author of children's books. *Member:* Society of Children's Book Writers.

WRITINGS—Under pseudonym Marian Lee; all for children; "From the Casebook of J. P. Landers, Master Detective" series; all published by Childrens Press: *Solve a Mystery: From*

MARIAN CLISH

the Casebook of J. P. Landers, Master Detective (illustrated by Steven Crombie), three books, 1982; *The Missing Room and Other Mysteries to Solve*, 1984.

WORK IN PROGRESS: A new adventure series that includes games and mystery treasures; four more ''From the Casebook of J. P. Landers, Master Detective'' books.

SIDELIGHTS: ''Owning an Apple computer has given me the idea to combine game-playing and reading. We all know kids prefer games to reading a book, so as a trademark in all my books, the reader gets involved either by answering a riddle, finding a mystery treasure, or just trying to stump the detective. My readers will always have to do more than just read.''

CONKLIN, Paul

PERSONAL: Born in Louisville, Kentucky; children: two sons. *Education:* Wayne State University, B.A., 1951; Columbia University, M.A. *Residence:* Washington, D.C.

CAREER: Photographer and author of books for children. *Awards, honors: Choctaw Boy* was chosen as a Notable Children's Trade Book in the field of Social Studies; *Touching*

Washington, D.C. was selected for the American Institute of Graphic Arts Book Show, 1976.

WRITINGS—All nonfiction for children; all self-illustrated with photographs: *Cimarron Kid*, Dodd, 1973; *Choctaw Boy*, Dodd, 1975; *Michael of Wales*, Dodd, 1977.

Illustrator; all juvenile nonfiction; all illustrated with photographs: Seymour Reit, *Child of the Navajos* (Junior Literary Guild selection), Dodd, 1971; S. Reit, *Rice Cakes and Paper Dragons*, Dodd, 1973; Grace E. Moremen, *Touching Washington, D.C.*, privately printed, (Washington, D.C.), 1976; Brent K. Ashabranner, *Morning Star, Black Sun: The Northern Cheyenne Indians and America's Energy Crisis*, Dodd, 1982; B. K. Ashabranner, *The New Americans: Changing Patterns in U.S. Immigration* (Junior Literary Guild selection), Dodd, 1983; B. K. Ashabranner, *Gavriel and Jemal: Two Boys of Jerusalem*, Dodd, 1984; B. K. Ashabranner, *Go Live in Two Worlds: American Indian Youth Today*, Dodd, 1984.

FOR MORE INFORMATION SEE: Natural History, December, 1975; *Authors of Books for Young People*, 2nd edition supplement, Scarecrow, 1979.

(From *Cimarron Kid* by Paul Conklin. Photograph by the author.)

COOMBS, Charles I(ra) 1914-
(Chick Coombs)

PERSONAL: Born June 27, 1914, in Los Angeles, Calif.; son of Daniel F(ish) (a building contractor) and Fleda (Colf) Coombs; married Eleanor Haines Evans, September 17, 1939; children: Lee Charles, Dan William, Lynn Eleanor. *Education:* Riverside City College, A.A., 1934; University of California, Los Angeles, B.A., 1939. *Politics:* Republican. *Religion:* Protestant. *Home and office:* 32114 Lake Meadow Lane, Westlake Village, Calif. 91361.

CAREER: Employed as farm hand, store clerk, and carpenter's helper, 1929-39; Sears Roebuck Co., Los Angeles, Calif., worked in merchandising department, 1939-41; Douglas Aircraft Co., El Segundo, Calif., methods analyst, 1941-46; entertainment columnist and producer of comic strips "Chip Grant" and "Tex Martin and the Twins" for *Hi Way, Catholic Boy, Catholic Miss,* and *Junior Life,* 1945-69; free-lance writer, 1946—. West Coast movie and television representative for *Boys' Life. Member:* Aviation/Space Writers of America, Santa Monica Bay Press Club. *Awards, honors:* Boys' Clubs of America Book Award, 1958, for *Rockets, Missiles, and Moons;* Southern California Council of Literature for Children and Young People Award, 1968, for "significant contributions to the field of informational books"; Outstanding Science Book for Children Award from National Science Teachers Association/Children's Book Council Joint Committee, 1980, for *Coal in the Energy Crisis.*

WRITINGS—All for young adults: *Teen Age Adventure Stories,* Lantern Press, 1948; *Teen Age Treasure Chest of Sports,* Lantern Press, 1948; *Teen Age Champion Sports Stories,* Lantern Press, 1950; *Young Pony Express Rider,* Lantern Press, 1953; *Young Circus Detective,* Lantern Press, 1954; *Young Infield Rookie,* Lantern Press, 1954; *Skyrocketing into the Unknown,* Morrow, 1954; *Sleuth at Shortstop,* Lantern Press, 1955; *The Case of the Purple Mark,* Westminster, 1955; *Celestial Space, Inc.,* Westminster, 1956; *Treasure under Coyote Hill,* Westminster, 1956; *Young Ranch Detective,* Lantern Press, 1956; *Survival in the Sky,* Morrow, 1956; *Rockets, Missiles, and Moons,* Morrow, 1957; *Wings at Sea,* Morrow, 1958; *Young Atom Detective,* Lantern Press, 1958; *Airmen and What They Do,* F. Watts, 1958; *Mystery of Satellite 7* (Junior Literary Guild selection), Westminster, 1958; *Sabre Jet Ace,* Harper, 1959.

Countdown to Danger (illustrated by Gerald McCann), Lantern Press, 1960; *Project Mercury* (illustrated by Robert G. Smith), Morrow, 1960; *Gateway to Space,* Morrow, 1960; *High Timber: The Story of American Forestry,* World Publishing, 1960; *Bush Flying in Alaska* (illustrated by Morgan Henniger), Morrow, 1961; *B-70: Monarch of the Skies* (illustrated by Lou Paleno), Morrow, 1962; *Rocketmen and What They Do,* F. Watts, 1962; *Alaska Bush Pilot,* Harper, 1963; *Lift-Off: The Story of Rocket Power* (illustrated by R. H. Foor), Morrow, 1963; *Wheels, Wings, and Water: The Story of Cargo Transport,* World Publishing, 1963; *Aerospace Pilot,* Morrow, 1964; *Project Apollo: Mission to the Moon,* Morrow, 1965; *Rocket Pioneer,* Harper, 1965; *Window on the World: The Story of Television Production,* World Publishing, 1965; *Frank Luke: Balloon Buster,* Harper, 1966; *Deep Sea World: The Story of Oceanography,* Morrow, 1966; *Aerospace Power: A Pictorial Guide,* Morrow, 1966; *Skyhooks: The Story of Helicopters,* Morrow, 1967; *Ace of the Argonne* (illustrated by Donn Albright), World Publishing, 1967; *Motorcycling,* Morrow, 1968; *Spacetrack: Watchdog of the Skies,* Morrow, 1969; *Cleared for Take-Off: Behind the Scenes at an Airport,* Morrow, 1969.

CHARLES I. COOMBS

Drag Racing, Morrow, 1970; *Auto Racing,* Morrow, 1971; *Skylab,* Morrow, 1972; *Bicycling,* Morrow, 1972; *Pipeline Across Alaska,* Morrow, 1978; *Mopeding,* Morrow, 1978; *Passage to Space: The Shuttle Transportation System,* Morrow, 1979; *Tankers: Giants of the Sea,* Morrow, 1979.

Coal in the Energy Crisis, Morrow, 1980; *Hot-Air Ballooning,* Morrow, 1981; *Gold and Other Precious Metals,* Morrow, 1981; *BMX: A Guide to Bicycle Motocross,* Morrow, 1983; *Ultralights: The Flying Featherweights* (Junior Literary Guild selection), Morrow, 1984; *Let's Rodeo!,* Holt, 1986.

"Young Readers" series; published by Lantern Press: *Young Readers Basketball Stories,* 1950; . . . *Football Stories,* 1950; . . . *Stories of the Diamond,* 1951; . . . *Mystery Stories,* 1951; . . . *Detective Stories,* 1951; . . . *Indoor Sports Stories,* 1952; . . . *Sports Treasury,* 1952; . . . *Water Sports Stories,* 1952; . . . *Railroad Stories,* 1953; . . . *Baseball Stories,* 1955.

"Be a Winner" series; published by Morrow: *Be A Winner in Baseball,* 1973; . . . *in Ice Hockey,* 1974; . . . *in Football,* 1974; . . . *in Tennis,* 1975; . . . *in Basketball,* 1975; . . . *in Track and Field,* 1976; . . . *in Horsemanship,* 1976; . . . *in Soccer,* 1977; . . . *in Skiing,* 1977; . . . *in Windsurfing,* 1982.

Also author of several books featuring Walt Disney characters. Work appears in anthologies and textbooks. Contributor of over five hundred short stories and two hundred articles to numerous publications.

SIDELIGHTS: After graduating from UCLA in 1939, Coombs worked a variety of jobs during the day, and wrote stories and articles during predawn and late night hours "until I'd fall asleep with my forehead on my typewriter."

An athlete at school and college, Coombs began his career as a writer of sports fiction. In 1946 he turned to full time free-lance writing, working, at one time, on books for five different publishers, which he refers to as his "tiger-charging years." His work space began as a card table set up in a closet.

"Half the fun of writing books for young people," says Coombs, "is having new and exciting adventures while doing research. With a good idea of what I'm looking for, I go into the field to get the first-hand experiences so essential to honest writing. I have explored the blockhouses and launch pads of Cape Canaveral, fought off frostbite on Alaska's North Slope, been on hand during exploration of the ocean deeps. I have tooled around in all sorts of wheeled vehicles, and either actively or vicariously enjoyed the excitement of many sports.

"One notable experience was a . . . round-trip winter voyage aboard the Atlantic Richfield Company's 120,000-dwt crude-oil tanker the SS *Arco Fairbanks,* up the Pacific Coast to Valdez, Alaska. In the midst of a serious energy crisis, it seemed important to me to try and find out what oil tankers are like, what they do, and why they are needed.

"After reading all I could about these behemoths of the sea, I boarded the empty *Fairbanks* in Long Beach, California. As we sailed north, I had the run of the vessel, from bilge to bridge. Keeping out of the way of officers and deckhands, I was able to observe closely everything that took place aboard the tanker.

"I peered over shoulders, peeked through hatches, and asked endless questions. The answers I received were prompt, candid, and, I have every reason to believe, honest. Tankering is good, if sometimes lonely, work. Seamen know that their ships will be around for as long as the world depends on crude oil for energy and petroleum products. Few nations are energy-independent; therefore, oil must be sent by sea to those countries that have purchased it.

"To say that I was impressed with the operation of *Arco Fairbanks* is to put it mildly. The ship was immaculate, and despite sudden changes in the delivery schedule, and what I considered a horrendous storm, which struck while we were northbound in the Gulf of Alaska, the vessel completed its mission on time and without mishap. 'What storm?' the captain asked wryly the next morning, in response to my dramatized version of the sleepless, sea-tossed night." [Charles Coombs, *Tankers: Giants of the Sea,* Morrow, 1979.[1] Amended by the author.] *Tankers: Giants of the Sea* was the result of the voyage.

Coombs on his moped, February, 1978.

A final sprint to the finish. ■ (From *BMX: A Guide to Bicycle Motocross* by Charles Coombs. Photograph by the author.)

For his book *Hot Air Ballooning,* Coombs was invited aloft a "rainbow-hued Raven AX-7 hot-air balloon. The first day we were together they invited me along . . . and from there on the adventure soared. One day we skimmed across a small lake without getting our feet wet, and then we lifted and drifted quietly over the awakening desert. Another time we joined the ground crew chasing desperately after the balloon, which was being carried seaward by an unexpected wind. The pilot did manage finally to put down before reaching the water. At other times we shared coffee and doughnuts while waiting for sunrise when the balloon could take to the air.

"The spirit of fun and excitement prevailed wherever I went in pursuit of ballooning knowledge. Don Picard, famous son of a famous ballooning family, showed me how hot-air balloon systems are made, and he patiently explained the way that they function." [Charles Coombs, *Hot-Air Ballooning,* Morrow, 1981.[2] Amended by the author.]

"Exploring any interesting subject leads a writer down diverse pathways, or in the case of [*Be a Winner in Windsurfing*] waterways. My investigation of windsurfing took me from the frigid straits along the west coast of Canada to the warmer climes of Southern California, where it all began. . . .

"Wherever there was water, I usually located some gathering of boardsailors avidly pursuing their sport. Always they were cooperative and most willing to demonstrate their skills. Unfortunately, many were fleeting acquaintances, and I regret not being able to remember their names.

"But a number of them I remember very clearly. June Everett and Kim Baldwin, for instance, invited me to their classes in which, after a few hours of instruction and simulator training, they converted hesitant beginners into confident and reasonably skilled windsurfers. Diana Gowman, Pat Study, and Kenny Thompson, three students who allowed me to focus my camera on them at all moments whether graceful or awkward, have all long since become experts." [Charles Coombs, *Be a Winner in Windsurfing*, Morrow, 1982.[3]]

Coombs, who once aspired to be a pilot, has written a number of books about aerospace subjects for young people. "The military is interested in having young people informed of aerospace plans and activities, hence, I received full cooperation within the bounds of security." For his book *Wings at Sea*, Coombs contends that "there is no substitute for firsthand witnessing of the things about which you are to write, no substitute for living with, talking with, and flying with the people who make them click.

"Starting out at the U.S. Naval Air Training Station in Pensacola, Florida, and working northward to the Pentagon, the Office of Naval Research, the Naval Research Laboratory, and other eastern naval facilities, I began to fill up my notebooks, and a rather colorful and exciting picture of naval aviation took form. Here, indeed, was an entirely different and fantastic area of flight, too little understood by the public.

"Working westward, I began to round out the material with the aid of personnel in the Bureau of Aeronautics located at El Segundo, California. Then I headed southward to the U.S. Naval Air Station in North Island, San Diego, where I boarded the combat aircraft carrier USS *Kearsarge* for maneuvers at sea and the final phase of my research." [Charles Coombs, *Wings at Sea*, Morrow, 1958.[4] Amended by the author.].

The subject matter in Coombs' books range from such diverse topics as horses, oil tankers, windsurfing, and hot-air ballooning to a 1981 publication, *Gold and Other Precious Metals*. "Preparing for and writing this book has been both fun and a real challenge. The search for gold, or other valued metal, lies somewhere deep in the Coombs' family veins. Some years ago my brother and I inherited two placer claims staked out by our adventuresome father. The claims—twenty acres each—are located near Quartzsite, deep in the hot, but beautiful Arizona desert.

"When my brother and I took over the claims, we knew very little about mining. But we tried to become miners, and we gained experience. Dad had built a dry washer according to plans undoubtedly dug out of some government publication or provided by the Bureau of Mines, United States Department of the Interior. We used it, and at times we still sweat over it.

"... We have 'gone modern' and begun to use a sensitive electronic metal detector. Although 'sweeping' forty acres with an eight-inch disk, or loop, takes a long time, we're in no hurry. The excitement and expectation of the hunt are a big part of the treasure.

'Perhaps that is fortunate. Thus far we have not been able to find enough gold (or silver, platinum, or lead, for that matter) to 'prove up.' Consequently, we have never been able to patent our claims—that is, get full title to the land by virtue of finding 'commercially valuable' minerals.

"We are still prospecting. Each year, when weather permits, we trek out to Quartzsite to do our assessment work as the Government requires. We paint the trim on the old cabin that Dad built stone by stone. We clean the well and repair the dirt road washed out by seasonal cloudburst.

"We dig, we dry wash, and we listen to the soft murmurs and promising sputters of a battery-powered detector. I would love to be able to say that we have a Mason jar full of nuggets. Not so.

"But there is always the hope. Down this arroyo, over that rise, along the desert wash, or clinging to the roots of some gnarled saguaro cactus may be our bonanza, just waiting to be discovered.

"If not, perhaps another trip to the Mother Lode—I haven't yet tried the metal detector there—may sniff out a fortune. Frankly, I'd settle for a pea-sized nugget and cherish it as fervently as a nation cherishes its crown jewels.

"In fact, when you get right down to it, the size of the nugget or, indeed, whether or not there even is a nugget has little to do with the real pleasure of prospecting. The biggest treasure is the joy and anticipation of the search itself. And the knowledge that goes with it." [Charles Coombs, *Gold and Other Precious Metals*, Morrow, 1981.[5]]

Coombs spends about two months organizing his notes. Then, "sometimes working at home, sometimes retreating to a small family cabin in the San Bernardino mountains, I spend each long and anguishing day trying to get out about 3,000 words of copy. With luck and a brisk tailwind, in about two weeks I push away from my desk or head down the hill with perhaps 150 to 200 pages of very rough copy." He then spends another month of rewriting and polishing.

He incorporates another interest into his books—photography. Photographs are taken during the research period. "Searching for appropriate photos to back up interesting and important facts helps me focus sharply on the really pertinent things I hope to say."

Coombs writes for a young audience with whom he feels an identification. "I have a teen-age mentality. The things that really interest me seem to interest the teenagers I write for. I'm not really an expert in the fields I write about, but there's an advantage to that. I look at each picket while the experts look at the whole fence.

"... Experts in their respective fields think everyone (the reader) know[s] everything to begin with, but I try not to take that for granted when I write." [Ed Klodt, "Author Sees Picket, Not Fences," *News Chronicle* (Thousand Oaks, Calif.) April 16, 1973.[6] Amended by the author.]

Author of over seventy books, Coombs hopes to continue writing "as long as young readers keep enjoying my books. The world is full of wonderful things to explore."

Coombs' works are included in the de Grummond Collection at the University of Southern Mississippi and at the Library of Congress, Washington, D.C.

FOR MORE INFORMATION SEE: Young Readers Review, November, 1968, May, 1969; Ed Klodt, "Author Sees Picket, Not Fences," *News Chronicle* (Thousand Oaks, Calif.), April 16, 1973; *Washington Post Book World*, November, 9, 1980; *Junior Literary Guild*, March, 1984.

COOPER, Lester (Irving) 1919-1985

OBITUARY NOTICE—See sketch in *SATA* Volume 32: Born January 20, 1919, in New York, N.Y.; died of cancer, June 6, 1985, in Manhattan, N.Y. Television writer and producer. Cooper began his career in 1937 as a film writer for Warner Bros. in Hollywood; following World War II, he was employed in England by J. Arthur Rank—British National Productions. Returning to the United States, Cooper worked briefly for *Esquire* magazine before forming his own film production company in 1953. That same year, he began his career in television as a writer on CBS News' "Eye on New York" series. In 1956 he joined NBC News as a member of the writing staff for the "Today" show. He next worked for Westinghouse Broadcasting as head-writer and producer of "PM," a nightly news and talk show with newscaster Mike Wallace, and then produced the highly-acclaimed "Exploring the Universe" series for PBS-TV. In 1964 Cooper began a twenty-year association with ABC News, producing and writing a number of award-winning documentaries and public affairs programs. Among these were the children's series "Make a Wish," winner of Peabody and Emmy Awards, and "Animals, Animals, Animals," honored with Emmy, Peabody, Ohio State, and ACT Awards as well as the "Award of Excellence" from Coalition on Children and Television. Beginning in 1978, he wrote a series of books based on "Animals, Animals, Animals," including *Starring Dogs and Dolphins, Starring Pelicans, Cats, and Frogs,* and *Starring Sharks.* Cooper retired from ABC-TV in 1984.

FOR MORE INFORMATION SEE: Contemporary Authors, Volume 108, Gale, 1983; *Who's Who in America,* 43rd edition, Bowker, 1984. Obituaries: *New York Times,* June 13, 1985.

CORBETT, Grahame

PERSONAL: Born in Fiji. *Education:* Studied art in New Zealand. *Residence:* London, England.

CAREER: Author and illustrator of books for children.

WRITINGS—All self-illustrated: *Front and Back,* Macdonald Educational, 1976, Grosset, 1977; *Guess Who?,* Dial, 1982; *What Number Now?,* Dial, 1982; *Who Is Hiding?,* Dial, 1982; *Who Is Next?,* Dial, 1982; *Who's Inside?,* Dial, 1982; *Who Am I?,* Methuen Children's Books, 1982; *Who Are You?,* Methuen Children's Books, 1982. Also author of *My Animal Storybook.*

Illustrator: (With James Hanson) Gordon Murray, *Gordon Murray's Trumpton Annual,* Purnell, 1972; Diana Ferguson, *Beetles,* Macdonald & Co., 1974; Jenni Orme, reteller, *The Story of Pinocchio* (based on the original story by Carlo Collodi), Robert Tyndall, 1974; (with Mike Jackson and Carol Lawson) Tilla Brading, *Pirates,* Macdonald Educational, 1976; Eileen Deacon, *Making Jewelry,* Macdonald Educational, 1975, Raintree, 1977; Sue Tarsky, *Taking a Walk in the Town,* Marshall Cavendish, 1978; S. Tarsky, *Taking a Walk in the Park,* Marshall Cavendish, 1978; (with Amanda Severne) S. Tarsky, *The Window Box Book,* Methuen/Walker, 1980; (with Will Giles) S. Tarsky, *The Prickly Plant Book,* Walker, 1980, Little, Brown, 1981; Margaret Lane, *The Frog,* Dial, 1981.

WORK IN PROGRESS: Another series of books.

(From *Who Is Hiding?* by Grahame Corbett. Illustrated by the author.)

COSNER, Shaaron 1940-

PERSONAL: Born February 10, 1940, in Albuquerque, N.M.; daughter of Roy F. (a U.S. Air Force officer) and Louise (a housewife; maiden name, Brian) Bigelow; married Ron Cosner (a teacher), March 3, 1962; children: Bob, Vikki. *Education:* Arizona State University, B.A., 1965, M.A., 1982. *Religion:* Catholic. *Home:* 1116 East Watson Dr., Tempe, Ariz. 85283. *Agent:* Ruth Cantor, 156 Fifth Ave., New York, N.Y. 10010. *Office:* Corona del Sol High School, 1101 Knox Rd., Tempe, Ariz. 85283.

CAREER: Arizona State University, Tempe, Ariz., teaching assistant, 1979-82; Corona del Sol High School, Tempe, teacher, 1982—.

WRITINGS—Juvenile: American Windmills: Harnessers of Energy (diagrams by Marie Ostberg and Nils Ostberg), McKay, 1977; *American Cowgirls: Yesterday and Today,* McKay, 1978; *Masks Around the World and How to Make Them* (drawings by Ann George), McKay, 1979; *Be Your Own Weather Forecaster,* Messner, 1981; *The Light Bulb: Inventions That Changed Our Lives,* Walker & Co., 1983; *Paper Through the Ages* (illustrated by Priscilla Kiedrowski), Carolrhoda, 1984; *Special Effects in Movies and TV,* Messner, 1985.

Also contributor of over fifty articles to numerous periodicals including *Arizona, Arizona Highways,* and *Americana.*

WORK IN PROGRESS: American Monasteries and *New Uses for Everyday Products,* for adults; *Clans; Lunar Bases; Submarines; Rubber.*

SIDELIGHTS: "I was the type of person who always did everyone's term papers in high school and college. Then I took a course at Arizona State University from Ken Donelson, an expert in children's literature. I wrote a paper on Nancy Drew for him and he wrote, 'This deserves publication.' Until then, it never dawned on me that I could get paid for doing something I loved. I took a few courses at a local junior college and was soon on my way to becoming a paid writer. Some of the things I learned very quickly were not to expect undue attention from friends, family and relatives, not to think because one piece was not edited, the next piece will be perfect too. It just isn't so.

"I have become a writer of science topics by accident. My first book was on windmills after I had done an article on them for a magazine. I sold it to the first person I sent it to, which, I soon learned, also doesn't happen very often. After that the topics that kept popping up all seemed to be somewhat scientific. I'm most fascinated by inventors. I think, like writers, they are very special people who are way unappreciated.

"I spent my childhood traveling around the world since my father was in the Air Force. I went to elementary schools in the Philippines and Germany and high school was spent in Vicenza, Italy. I think always being new in school gave me the skills I need now to get to know and evaluate people quickly in interviews although I would much rather be in the library researching.

"I think the most important thing a writer can learn, besides the limitations of the job already mentioned, is what he or she does best. I know I am good at research and putting in lay-

Blizzards have been known to dump drifts up to thirty or forty feet on the Earth, enough to cover a house three stories high. ■ (From *Be Your Own Weather Forecaster* by Shaaron Cosner. Photograph courtesy of the National Oceanic and Atmospheric Administration.)

SHAARON COSNER

man's language some of the more difficult or confusing descriptions of scientific terms. Yet, people are always asking, 'Why don't you try fiction? That's where the money is.' I would love to try fiction and maybe someday when I'm really established I will, but right now I think I should stick with what I know I do best. Since I think in outlines and 3 x 5 cards, it would be very difficult to make the transition to creative make-believe.''

CRARY, Elizabeth (Ann) 1942-

BRIEF ENTRY: Born May 18, 1942, in New Orleans, La. Publisher, educator, author, and consultant. Crary has accumulated over ten years of experience in the field of parent education. An instructor in that subject at North Seattle Community College since 1977, she was formerly founder and director of Parenthood Education Programs in Madison, Wis. She is also co-director of Parent Education Associates and founder of Parenting Press, established in 1976. Her publishing company focuses on the subjects of child development, child guidance, and children's books, all of which are reflected in Crary's own writings. She has produced two books for parents, *Without Spanking or Spoiling: A Practical Approach to Toddler and Preschool Guidance* (1979) and *Kids Can Cooperate* (1984). In her ''Children's Problem Solving'' series for preschoolers and early primary graders, Crary presents the variables that exist in interpersonal relationships and provides alternative behavior for a variety of situations. The titles are *I Can't Wait* (1982), *I Want It* (1982), *I Want to Play* (1982), *My Name Is Not Dummy* (1983), and *I'm Lost* (1985). *Office:* Parenting Press, 7750 31st Ave. N.E., Seattle, Wash. 98115.

FOR MORE INFORMATION SEE: Who's Who in the West, 19th edition, Marquis, 1983.

DENNY, Norman (George) 1901-1982 (Norman Dale)

PERSONAL: Born May 26, 1901, in Catford, Kent, England; died in 1982; son of Henry Samuel (a mining engineer) Denny; married Gillian Margaret Watts, 1935; children: two sons, one daughter. *Education:* Attended Radley College; studied in Vienna and Paris. *Residence:* Hove, Sussex, England.

CAREER: Author and translator. The Bodley Head (book publishers), London, England, chief reader and literary advisor, 1939-55. *Member:* Translators' Association. *Awards, honors:* Runner-up, Carnegie Medal, 1967, for *The Bayeux Tapestry: The Story of the Norman Conquest, 1066.*

WRITINGS: The Serpent and the Dove, John Lane, 1938; *Sweet Confusion,* John Lane, 1947, reprinted, M. Joseph, 1975; (compiler) *The Yellow Book: A Selection,* Bodley Head, 1949; *Arrival in Wycherly,* Dodd, 1951; *Story in a Half-Light,* Cresset, 1954; (with Josephine Filmer-Sankey) *The Bayeux Tapestry: The Story of the Norman Conquest, 1066* (ALA Notable Book; *Horn Book* Honor List), Atheneum, 1966; (editor, with J. Filmer-Sankey) John Mandeville, *The Travels of Sir John Mandeville,* Collins, 1973.

Under pseudonym Norman Dale; for children: *Secret Service!* (illustrated by Gertrude Elias), John Lane, 1943, new edition, 1953; *Dangerous Treasure* (illustrated by Diana John), John Lane, 1944; *The Best Adventure* (illustrated by D. John), John Lane, 1945, revised edition, Hamish Hamilton, 1961; *The Exciting Journey* (illustrated by Ley Kenyon), Bodley Head, 1947, revised edition, John Lane, 1954; *Mystery Christmas* (illustrated by L. Kenyon), Bodley Head, 1948; *Skeleton Island* (illustrated by L. Kenyon), Bodley Head, 1949.

Clockwork Castle: A Novel for Boys and Girls (illustrated by Barbara Bradley), Bodley Head, 1952; *The Valley of the Snake,* Bodley Head, 1953; *The Secret Motor Car* (illustrated by Shirley Hughes), Bodley Head, 1954, (illustrated by Edward Shenton), Harper, 1957; *The Casket and the Sword* (illustrated by Biro), James Barrie, 1955, (illustrated by Irv Docktor), Harper, 1956; *The Clock That Struck Fifteen* (illustrated by Prudence Seward), Hamish Hamilton, 1956; *Johnnie-by-the-River* (illustrated by Zelide Teague), Hamish Hamilton, 1957; *The Medenham Carnival* (illustrated by P. Seward), Hamish Hamilton, 1957; *The House Where Nobody Lived* (illustrated by Christopher Brooker), Hamish Hamilton, 1958; *All Change for Medenham* (illustrated by Jean Harper), Hamish Hamilton, 1959; *The Game That Really Happened* (illustrated by C. Brooker), Hamish Hamilton, 1959; *The Pied Piper of Medenham* (illustrated by J. Harper), Hamish Hamilton, 1959.

The Six Stone Faces (illustrated by D. John), Barnes & Noble, 1960; *Look at Farms* (illustrated by Thomas Godfrey), Hamish Hamilton, 1960, school edition with workbook, 1963; *A Medenham Secret* (illustrated by P. Theobalds), Hamish Hamilton, 1962; *The House in Cobble Lane* (illustrated by Biro), Hamish Hamilton, 1964.

Translator: Alma S. Wittlin, *Abdul Hamid, the Shadow of God,* John Lane, 1940; André Maurois, *Fattypuffs and Thinifers* (illustrated by Jean Bruller), John Lane, 1941, new edition (illustrated by Fritz Wegner), Penguin, 1972; Marcel Aymé, *Barkeep of Blémont,* Harper, 1950; Charles Perrault, *The Fairy Tales of Charles Perrault* (illustrated by Philippe Jullian), Bodley Head, 1950; M. Aymé, *Fanfare in Blémont,* Bodley Head, 1950; M. Aymé, *The Second Face,* Bodley Head, 1951, Harper, 1952; M. Aymé, *The Wonderful Farm* (illustrated by

Maurice Sendak), Harper, 1951; M. Aymé, *Clérambard: A Play in Four Acts*, Bodley Head, 1952; M. Aymé, *The House of Men*, Bodley Head, 1952; Rene Masson, *Green Oranges*, Knopf, 1953; M. Aymé, *The Secret Stream*, Harper, 1953; M. Aymé, *Magic Pictures: More about the Wonderful Farm* (illustrated by M. Sendak), Harper, 1954; M. Aymé, *Return to the Wonderful Farm* (illustrated by Geoffrey Fletcher), John Lane, 1954; A. Maurois, *The Women of Paris* (illustrated with photographs by Nico Jesse), Bodley Head, 1954.

Georges Simenon, *The Hitchhiker* (Part I of *Destinations: Two Novels*), Doubleday, 1955; M. Aymé, *The Green Mare*, Bodley Head, 1955, Atheneum, 1963; G. Simenon, *Danger Ahead* (includes *Red Lights* and *The Watchmaker of Everton;* also see below), Hamish Hamilton, 1955; G. Simenon, *The Watchmaker of Everton*, Doubleday, 1956; M. Aymé, *Across Paris, and Other Stories*, Bodley Head, 1957, Harper, 1959; Herbert Zand, *The Well of Hope*, Collins, 1957; Jean Gamo, *Héresmédan*, Bodley Head, 1958, published as *The Golden Chain*, McKay, 1958; Hedda Adlon, *Hotel Adlon: The Life and Death of a Great Hotel*, Barrie & Rockliff, 1958, Horizon Press, 1960; Christine de Rivoyre, *The Tangerine*, Hart-Davis, 1958, Dutton, 1959; Gustav Regler, *The Owl of Minerva*, Hart-Davis, 1959, Farrar, Straus, 1960.

She and Jeremy hugged one another in rapture. ■
(From *The Casket and the Sword* by Norman Dale. Illustrated by Irv Docktor.)

Heinrich Schirmbeck, *The Blinding Light*, Collins, 1960; Edzard H. Schaper, *The Dancing Bear*, Bodley Head, 1960, John Day, 1961; Kurt Frischler, *Ayesha*, Barrie & Rockliff, 1961; Petru Dumitriu, *The Prodigals* (Part II of *The Boyars*), Collins, 1961; M. Aymé, *The Proverb, and Other Stories*, Bodley Head, 1961; Michael Horbach, *The Reckoning*, Bodley Head, 1961; M. Aymé, *The Conscience of Love*, Bodley Head, 1962; P. Dumitriu, *Incognito*, Collins, 1964; Pierre Teilhard de Chardin, *The Future of Man*, Harper, 1964.

P. Teilhard de Chardin, *Building the Earth*, Geoffry Chapman, 1965; A. Maurois, *Prometheus: The Life of Balzac*, Harper, 1965; Jean Renoir, *The Notebooks of Captain Georges*, Collins, 1966; Jacques Borel, *The Bond*, Collins, 1968; J. Renoir, *Grand Illusion*, Simon & Schuster, 1968; Michel Tournier, *Friday; or, The Other Island*, Collins, 1969; Gabriel Veralsi, *Spies in Good Intent*, Deutsch, 1969.

Pierre Joffroy, *A Spy for God: The Ordeal of Kurt Gerstein*, Collins, 1970; M. Aymé, *The Walker-through-Walls, and Other Stories*, Bodley Head, 1972; André Gorz, *Socialism and Revolution*, Anchor Books, 1973; Jean Renoir, *My Life and My Films*, Atheneum, 1974; Victor Hugo, *Les Misérables* (illustrated by Charles Keeping), two volumes, Folio Press, 1976; G. Simenon, *The White Horse Inn*, Harcourt, 1980.

Translator; under pseudonym Norman Dale: Georges Arnaud, *The Wages of Fear*, Bodley Head, 1952, Viking, 1956; H. G. Girard (pseudonym of G. Arnaud), *Journey Past Repentance*, Bodley Head, 1953; Rene Guillot, *The Wind of Chance* (illustrated by Pierre Collot), Oxford University Press, 1955, S. G. Phillips, 1958; R. Guillot, *The Sea Rover*, Oxford University Press, 1956; Mira Lobe, *The Zoo Breaks Out* (illustrated by Suzanne Weigel), Bodley Head, 1958, A. S. Barnes, 1960; Colette Richard, *Climbing Blind*, Hodder & Stoughton, 1966, Dutton, 1967; Francis Ryck, *Loaded Gun*, Collins, 1971.

HOBBIES AND OTHER INTERESTS: Beekeeping.

FOR MORE INFORMATION SEE: W.O.G. Lofts and D. J. Adley, *The Men Behind Boys' Fiction*, Howard Baker, 1970.

DOBIE, J(ames) Frank   1888-1964

PERSONAL: Born September 26, 1888, in Live Oak County, Tex.; died September 18, 1964, in Austin, Texas; buried in Texas State Cemetery, Austin; son of Richard Jonathan and Ella (Byler) Dobie; married Bertha McKee, September 20, 1916. *Education:* Southwestern University, B.A., 1910; Columbia University, M.A., 1914. *Residence:* Austin, Tex.

CAREER: Writer. Started writing as summer reporter on Texas newspapers; high school and preparatory school teacher, 1910-13; University of Texas, Main University (now University of Texas at Austin), instructor in English, 1914-17, 1919-20, 1921-23, assistant professor, 1925-26, associate professor, 1926-33, professor of English, 1933-47; manager of half-million-acre ranch, Texas, 1920-21; Oklahoma A & M College (now Oklahoma State University), Stillwater, head of English department, 1923-25. Visiting professor of American history, Cambridge University, 1943-44. *Military service:* U.S. Army, Field Artillery, 1917-19; became first lieutenant. U.S. Army, Information and Education, 1945-46; lecturer at Shrivenham American University and to troops in Austria and Germany.

MEMBER: Texas Folklore Society (secretary, 1922-43), Texas Institute of Letters, Town and Gown Club (Austin). *Awards,*

He could hear the Indians above him. . . . ■ (From *Tales of Old-Time Texas,* edited by J. Frank Dobie. Illustrated by Barbara Latham.)

honors: Rockefeller Foundation grants, 1930-31, 1934-35; Literary Guild Award, 1931, for *Coronado's Children: Tales of Lost Mines and Buried Treasures of the Southwest;* Guggenheim fellowship in literature, 1932-33; Huntington Library research grant, 1948-49; Boys' Club of America Junior Book Award, 1951, for *The Ben Lilly Legend;* Carr P. Collins Award of Texas Institute of Letters, 1952, for *The Mustangs;* Presidential Medal of Freedom, 1964; M.A. from Cambridge University, 1944; D.Litt. from Southern Methodist University, Texas Christian University, and Southwestern University.

WRITINGS: A Vaquero of the Brush Country (illustrated by Justin C. Gruelle), Southwest Press, 1929, reprinted, Little, Brown, 1960; *Coronado's Children: Tales of Lost Mines and Buried Treasures of the Southwest* (illustrated by Ben Carlton Mead), Southwest Press, 1930, reprinted, University of Texas Press, 1978 (published in England as *Lost Mines of the Old West,* Hammond, 1960); (author of introduction) N. A. Jennings, *A Texas Ranger,* Southwest Press, 1930, reprinted, Turner, 1965; *On the Open Range* (illustrated by B. C. Mead), Southwest Press, 1931; *Tongues of the Monte,* Doubleday, 1935, published as *The Mexico I Like,* Southern Methodist University Press, 1942; *The Flavor of Texas* (illustrated by Alexandre Hogue), Dealey & Lowe, 1936, reprinted, Jenkins, 1975; *Tales of the Mustang* (illustrated by Jerry Bywaters), Book Club of Texas, 1936; *John C. Duval: First Texas Man of Letters* (illustrated by Tom Lea), Southwest Review, 1939,

2nd edition, Southern Methodist University Press, 1965; *Apache Gold and Yaqui Silver* (illustrated by T. Lea), Little, Brown, 1939, reprinted, University of New Mexico Press, 1976.

The Longhorns (illustrated by T. Lea), Little, Brown, 1941, reprinted, 1972; *Guide to Life and Literature of the Southwest,* University of Texas Press, 1943, revised edition, Southern Methodist University Press, 1952; *A Texan in England,* Little, Brown, 1945; *The Voice of the Coyote* (illustrated by Olaus T. Murie), Little, Brown, 1949; *The Ben Lilly Legend,* Little, Brown, 1950; (contributor) Charles Russell, *Seven Drawings,* Hertzog, 1950; *Sancho and Other Returners: John Latham's Lonesome Longhorn,* Westminster, 1951; *The Mustangs* (illustrated by Charles Banks Wilson), Little, Brown, 1952; (author of introduction) T. Lea, *A Portfolio of Six Paintings,* University of Texas Press, 1953; *Stories of Christmas* [and] *The Bowie Knife,* Steck, 1953; (compiler) *Up the Trail from Texas* (anthology; illustrated by John C. Wonsetler), Random House, 1955.

(With Isabel Gaddis) *I'll Tell You a Tale* (illustrated by B. C. Mead), Little, Brown, 1960; *Cow People* (illustrated by Will Crawford), Little, Brown, 1964; *Rattlesnakes,* Little, Brown, 1965; *Some Part of Myself,* edited by wife, Bertha M. Dobie, Little, Brown, 1967; *Out of the Old Rock* (character sketches), Little, Brown, 1972; (with Ruth Goddard) *Ralph Ogden* [and] *The Seven Mustangs,* Jenkins, 1973; *Prefaces,* Little, Brown, 1975.

Editor; all originally published by Texas Folklore Society; all reprinted by Southern Methodist University Press: *Coffee in the Gourd,* 1923, reprinted, 1969; *Legends of Texas,* 1924, reprinted, 1976; *Rainbow in the Morning,* 1926, reprinted, 1975; *Texas and Southwestern Lore,* 1927, reprinted, 1967; *Follow de Drinkin' Gou'd,* 1928, reprinted, 1965; *Man, Bird, and Beast,* 1930, reprinted, 1965; *Southwestern Lore,* 1931, reprinted, 1965; *Tone the Bell Easy,* 1932, reprinted, 1965; *Spur-of-the-Cock,* 1933, reprinted, 1965; *Puro Mexicano,* 1935, reprinted, 1969; (with Mody C. Boatwright) *Straight Texas,*

J. FRANK DOBIE

It consisted of five dead men, several dead horses, castaway packsaddles, a whipsaw, flour scattered over the rocks, and other evidences of a surprise attack by Indians. ■ (From *Apache Gold and Yaqui Silver* by J. Frank Dobie. Illustrated by Tom Lea.)

1937, reprinted, 1966; (with Mody C. Boatwright) *Straight Texas*, 1937, reprinted, 1966; (with M. C. Boatwright and Harry H. Ransom), *Coyote Wisdom*, 1938, reprinted, 1965; (with M. C. Boatwright and H. R. Ransom) *In the Shadow of History*, 1939, reprinted, 1971; (with M. C. Boatwright and H. R. Ransom) *Mustangs and Cow Horses*, 1940, reprinted, 1965; (with M. C. Boatwright and H. R. Ransom) *Texian Stomping Grounds*, 1941, reprinted, 1967.

Editor: *Happy Hunting Ground*, Texas Folklore Society, 1926, published with L. W. Payne's *When the Woods Were Burnt*, Folklore Associates, 1964; Solomon Wright, *My Rambles as East Texas Cowboy, Hunter, Fisherman, Tie-Cutter*, Texas Folklore Society, 1942; Charles Siringo, *Texas Cowboy*, Sloane, 1950; *Tales of Old-Time Texas* (illustrated by Barbara Latham), Little, Brown, 1955. Contributor to *Atlantic Monthly, Harper's, Saturday Evening Post, Holiday, Yale Review*, and other magazines. Author of Sunday newspaper column for various newspapers including, *Dallas Morning News, Houston Post, San Antonio Light, Austin American-Statesman*, 1939-64.

SIDELIGHTS: "On the twenty-sixth day of **September, 1888**, I was born in a three-room whitewashed rock house on the ranch of my parents in southern Live Oak County, Texas, in the Brush Country west of the Nueces River. Ramirenia Creek

and Long Hollow coursed through the ranch. My father owned the land before he and my mother were married. They added to it and added to the house while rearing six children, I being the oldest. As ranches went at the beginning of this century, it was small, approximately seven thousand acres. . . .

"My mother had some sort of help a good part of the time but often none. With or without help, she was too busy cooking, sewing, raising children and keeping house to garden. My father tended the flowers as well as the vegetables. He set out orange trees, which never bore. He laid out a croquet ground in the shade of oaks. He could do anything from repairing a windmill to making a coffin for a Mexican child that died on the ranch and lining it with the bleached domestic my mother kept on hand. He was *patrón* for some Mexicans who did not live on the ranch, sometimes going security for them at the store where they bought food and other supplies. He hoped his eldest son would choose a career better than ranching—that of a clean-collared banker perhaps. He paid eight and ten per cent to his banker and liked him.

"Back of the house was a rock smokehouse, long ago crumbled down, for the rock was caliche, not true stone. Every winter my father, aided by Mexicans, killed hogs and cut them up for curing. Occasionally he killed a calf. The meat he butchered was all the meat we had. It was ample. The Mexicans cut the long, strong-fibered leaves of bear grass (a yucca), heated them lightly over a fire to make them more pliable, and then used them to tie the hams, shoulders, and side bacon to poles across the smokehouse. The meats were cured by smoke from a fire of corncobs kept smoldering for days on the dirt floor. We had no hickory, needed none. Bear grass will always for me mean homemade hemp, also thatches for Mexican huts.'' [J. Frank Dobie, *Some Part of Myself*, Little, Brown, 1967.[1]]

Dobie's childhood was spent on the frontier—he grew up with the pioneer's feeling for the land. "When I was a child and papa was gone, Mama always had the old .44 Winchester right at her head when she went to bed. At times she lit lanterns and kerosene lamps, putting them in the rooms of the house when papa was late getting home from a long ride; then she would go out under one of the live oaks a little distance from the house and sit, waiting. There she could see, unseen, any intruder." [Winston Bode, *A Portrait of Pancho: The Life of a Great Texan, J. Frank Dobie*, Pemberton Press, 1965.[2]]

Ranch life before the turn of the century was a difficult life—men and women labored long and hard for it. Dobie shared his mother's enthusiasm for nature and a zest for the life of the ranch. "I grew up among men who had spent their lives on the ground, often sleeping upon it, eating upon it, riding horseback over it, gazing beyond it. They could squat upon it comfortably. They read little and many of them talked sparingly. The women were busy from the time they got up until they went to bed, but the men usually had an hour or two of free time after supper. Typically, my father enjoyed silences. In warm weather, after dark, he would sit for long while in a chair on the front gallery saying nothing, hearing, I suppose, the wind in the tops of the liveoak trees, or if there were no wind, hoping it would rise to make the windmills pump. I doubt that he became bored with his own company. He liked people from whom he could learn something and loved deeply his wife and children, but he did not seem to hunger after company, as my mother often hungered.

"Both my father and my mother often used maxims, sayings, fables, and folk rhymes to instruct us children. . . . As we boys grew older, Papa advised, 'Make all you can, save all you can, give all you can.'"[7]

1896. Formally entered school. Dobie's early education came from his mother who had been a school teacher. She read to him from a carefully chosen group of books, ranging from *Ivanhoe* to *Plutarch's Lives*. "One year after my sister Fannie and I were old enough to be in school we had a governess. The next year . . . my father, Mr. Tol McNeill, 'a sinner,' and my cousin Dick Dobie, who improved his mind by reading law and begot a child annually, built a schoolhouse about a mile from us on our land. The teacher always boarded with us.

"Our schoolhouse, on a patch of open land against blackbrush and guajillo hills to the west, overlooked liveoak slopes to the south and east. One day a flock of wild turkeys that came feeding near the schoolhouse while we were inside disrupted study. Another day just as we children burst out of the building to go home a big buck jumped a pasture fence in front of us. One evening while John Dobie and I were walking to his home from school, a coyote followed us. Ours was still wild country, we children thought.

"In time the schoolhouse was moved to another site on the ranch, a little farther away for us but located so that four more families to the northwest could attend it. We and Cousin Dick's children walked, as we had only a mile or so to go. The other pupils came horseback or in hacks. One winter my sister Fannie and I rode horseback for a few months to a one-teacher school five or six miles east of our ranch. It was taught by a man. One of the subjects was general history. The teacher dramatized Caesar's crossing of the Rubicon. After that day ancient history was something else to me than it had been.

"So far as book education is concerned, the only specific pieces of learning I can recall from ranch schooling are how to spell the word *irksome,* on which I was turned down in a spelling match, and knowledge that a branch of science called physical geography existed. I remember the green binding of a textbook on the subject but don't remember a single detail of the contents. I remember in a reader the ballad of 'Markos Bozzaris,' which I memorized, and also the thrilling recitation of 'Lasca' by a young lady older than our teacher who had studied elocution somewhere.''[1]

1904. Sent to a high school in Alice, a town that was several miles from the family ranch. "Long before I was sixteen years old, my parents had determined that I should have a college education. I was indifferent to the idea; at that time, in our environment, college was as remote as the pyramids of Egypt. I had not raised a thirst for knowledge commensurate with the ambitions of my parents for me and their other five children, or with their willingness for self-denial in order to fulfill those ambitions. To enter college I had to know more than I knew, or, at least, to have graduated from a high school. That meant leaving the ranch and Live Oak County. Grandma Dubose, with Grandpa, lived at Alice. In September . . . I went to live with them and enroll[ed] in the high school.

"Forty miles away, Alice was more distant in travel time from our ranch than New York now is from San Antonio. I had been there on several visits with Mama and the children. Papa went once or twice maybe; ranch affairs held him, perhaps he didn't want to go. It was an all-day drive in the hack. Meeting any other travelers was a rarity; on some trips we saw nobody at all. There were no mileposts—those indicators of distance erected by a man driving a wagon with a rawhide thong tied around the tire of the front wheel next to his seat. He kept his eye on that wheel, counting the revolutions, and when the number measuring off a mile had been made, he called 'Whoa!' got out, dug a posthole beside the road, took from the wagon

bed a short post into which had been chiseled a mile number, and drove it in. Speedless travel needed no speedometers.''[1]

1906. Family moved twenty-seven miles away from the ranch, to a town called Beeville, although they continued to manage the ranch as absentee owners. Dobie entered Southwestern University at Georgetown, Texas. ". . . That fall I left for college, never to reside again in the region. Nevertheless, for years after I left, I spent summers on the ranch, and have never ceased returning to it with eagerness. It has been a place where I belonged both in imagination and in reality, a place on which I felt free in the way that one can feel only on his own piece of earth. It has said more to me than any person I have known or any writer I have read, though only through association with fine minds and spirits have I come to realize its sayings.

"I was eighteen years old and could not have been greener. I had bought a pair of patent leather shoes as a part of my equipment; they were at that date several notches in style above celluloid collars, which I would never have worn. These shoes pinched my feet. While waiting to be registered as a freshman, I sat down by a table in one of the rooms of the Main Building. I looked out of a big window and wished that, unconscious of feet, I were riding Buck [Dobie's horse] over a Live Oak County pasture. Presently a man of quick movement, quick

Every herd-stallion had to combat constantly against other leaders as well as against the ever-hungering outcasts. ■ (From *The Mustangs* by J. Frank Dobie. Illustrated by Charles Banks Wilson.)

He was stubby, round-shouldered, his chest built like a panther's. ■ (From *The Longhorns* by J. Frank Dobie. Illustrated by Tom Lea.)

speech, and countenance quickened by intelligence introduced himself to me as R. S. Hyer, president of the college, and sat down. He asked if I liked to read. I doubt if he said 'read good books,' for at that time people out in the country who read books at all read good ones—mostly. Drugstore literature was as unknown as drugstore cowboys.

"I told Dr. Hyer that I very much liked to read. He then said something that made a profound and enduring impression on my mind. He said that he had long made it a practice to read one book a week. Right there I determined to read a book a week myself, and in the more than 2600 weeks that have passed since Dr. Hyer spoke, I have, without being methodical, been absorbed by that many books, not to speak of many thousands glanced through or searched into for something I could use.

"I was very young when some of Benjamin Franklin's maxims from *Poor Richard's Almanack* sank into me. One became a kind of star to follow. 'Dost thou love life? Then do not squander time, for that is the stuff life is made of.' Yet I wasted far more time in college than I studied. . . .''[1]

During his four years at Southwestern, he learned a great deal about writing and English literature. "Before entering college I had had no particular course in English composition, though I had studied grammar. However, words, their sound more than their meaning, fascinated me. While riding horseback alone on the ranch I used to compose phrases and say them over and over aloud with variations. From that exercise and from my reading of literature and from my father's nightly reading out of the Bible, I went to college with some sense of the architecture of sentences and with a consciousness of the harmonies in the prose of master writers. During college years and for several years afterward I used to make lists of new words learned from Robert Louis Stevenson, Charles Lamb, Hazlitt, Sir Thomas Browne and some other writers. I would write out the definitions of newly acquired words—veritable riches they seemed then—and devise occasions for using them in talk or writing. I was delighted when I learned that to Oliver Wendell Holmes the dictionary was the most romantic book in the world and that it was O. Henry's favorite reading.

"I did not set out immediately giving my days and my nights to trying to learn to write, but I became increasingly conscious of the craft and found pleasure in the practice of it. I still have pleasure in a writer's craft and still have to work at it. A long time ago now I thought that by the time I had written a million words all I would have to do would be to open the gate and the words would file out in decent, exact order. I have written several million words; yet words remain as stubborn, as elusive and also as effusive as they ever were.''[1]

1910. "After four years . . . at Southwestern University, I was soon to graduate with an A.B. degree. I had not yet settled on a career, had not resolutely applied myself to anything, had merely drifted, reading what I wanted to read, neglecting courses that required application of will, wasting much time that I did not want to waste on 'bull sessions.' I had found the drifting so pleasant that I did not want to leave college, college town, and college friends. Had I announced that I was going to be a preacher, my mother would have been equally surprised and pleased. My father never advised me beyond the simple injunction to live an upright life and to 'be a man, or a mouse or a bob-tailed rat.'

"When, in my senior year, I enrolled for a course in Education, I must have had some notion of teaching—teaching English. Without any consideration of a professional career, I

The James gang robbed not to live; they lived to rob. . . . ▪ (From *Coronado's Children: Tales of Lost Mines and Buried Treasures of the Southwest* by J. Frank Dobie. Illustrated by Ben Carlton Mead.)

drifted into teaching solely because I had fallen in love with English poetry and wanted to continue and communicate that love. The course in Education spurred nothing in me and added not a whit to my fitness to teach anything or anybody. Many collegians took it as a crip. Everything I took was a crip: if I liked it, it was easy; if I didn't like it, I took it easy.''[1]

Taught English in a school in Alpine, Texas for a year. "When I left Alpine in the summer of **1911** my career as teacher in public schools ended, though I was still fumbling around in the dark. I threw away a year and a half as teacher (for a few months) in the Preparatory School—long since dropped—of Southwestern University at Georgetown, then as secretary to the president. The next time I got back to Alpine, along in the 20s, I was teaching English at the University of Texas and was writing—for joy and for money.''[1]

Spring, 1914. Earned a master's degree in English literature from Columbia University. "I had decided to teach English beyond high school level, and with this purpose in mind . . . set out for Columbia University in New York to take a Master's degree. Actually, I wasn't much concerned with my career. I had only a vague, dim conception of what was involved in university or college teaching. I knew that it took a whole year to get a Master's degree. I planned to use at least a year and a half. I was young enough not to have any idea that time would ever run out. . . . New York gave me more than the university gave me. For a while I kept a kind of diary, but after looking it over a few years ago, I was so disgusted with the sentimentality in it that I destroyed it.''[1]

Fall, 1914. "I came to the University of Texas as instructor in English. . . . I was twenty-six years old. . . . The University of Texas seemed as fresh to me, as I look back now, as Southwestern University at Georgetown seemed when I entered it as a freshman in 1906. The enrollment was around twenty-two hundred. It wasn't hard for an instructor to come to know most of the teaching staff; he almost had to know all the instructing force in his own department.

"There was no journalism department in 1914. Then as now the best newspaper writers depended for effect on natural intelligence, cultivation of the art of composing words, and knowledge gained outside of all journalism classes. A big university has to have big buildings, of course. I believe the best teaching I did at the University of Texas was during the post-World War I days when the campus was dotted with frame shacks heated by iron stoves. I taught several classes in those shacks. I doubt that the intellectual content of any journalism instructor has been advanced by moving into a million-dollar building that often makes me think of the old saying about a forty-dollar saddle on a twenty-dollar horse. Journalism, as an agent of learning, is on a par with Education spelled with a capital E. It prevents students, by taking up their time, from studying economics, history, biology, anthropology, languages, English literature, and other subjects that fortify the mind.''¹

September 20, 1916. Married his college sweetheart, Bertha McKee.

1917. ''When the United States finally declared war on Germany . . .—after we had grown richer selling to England and she and France were almost bled to death—I hastened to try to join the army. The army wouldn't take me on account of varicose veins. I had them cut out and got into the second officers' training camp at Leon Springs, Texas. The captain who passed on my application asked what branch of the army I wanted to join.

'' 'The cavalry,' I answered.

'' 'Why?'

'' 'Because I want to ride.'

'' 'The cavalry is already afoot,' he said. 'If you want to ride, join the field artillery.'

''I joined it—and it was on the verge of being mechanized.

''My career in the training camp marked the second distinct loss of personality, lapse of power, lack of self-confidence that I had suffered. The first occurred when I entered Columbia University 'in the City of New York'—pitiless, to me personless. The condition endured for almost a year until I came to be a powerful figure in a little coterie of unpowerful men. At Leon Springs, in a military life new to me, in which competition was keen, I was pavid and puerile. A certain refined sensibility kept me apart from my fellows. I could not understand the drill regulations, however assiduously I studied them. I had too long soaked myself in poetry and novels. Subsequently, the natural robustness of my nature asserted itself and without losing sensibility I became a match for the hardiest soldier. By degrees the drill regulations became models of lucidity. I began to enjoy the problems of artillery as much as I had formerly enjoyed a novel. With knowledge came power and self-confidence.''¹

1919. ''After the war, I went back to my old job as instructor in the University of Texas. Long before this I had ascertained that the love of literature and the ability to impart that love bore no relation whatsoever to the advancement of English teachers in the 'scholarly' colleges and universities of America. I'd been overseas and learned a lot. Life at the University seemed pretty tame, but that wasn't the worst. My wife and I were doing worse than starving to death on a government claim. My salary was meager, as all University of Texas salaries were at the time, but I was at the bottom of the ladder with very little prospect of getting higher up until I got a Ph.D. degree, and I did not intend to get one.''¹

1920. Managed a Texas ranch. ''Uncle Jim (J. M.) Dobie had been after me several times to go back into the cow business. He was willing to back me. . . . He owned 56,000 acres in La Salle County and leased land in La Salle, McMullen, Duval,

and Webb counties, altogether a big spread. He had a ranch down in Mexico. He had business interests in San Antonio and elsewhere. He said he wanted a kind of segundo to go around and look after his affairs. I agreed to go with him.

''When spring came I resigned my job at the University of Texas and we moved to San Antonio. By this time the cattle market had begun to go down and before long, instead of traipsing over the country looking after varied affairs, I was managing the Olmos ranch in La Salle County. It straddles the Nueces River. We grew about ten acres of sorghum, and that was all the farming we did. We had a cow outfit and another outfit to build tanks and repair fences. Generally I was the only 'white' man on the ranch; the hands were all Mexicans. I had never been entirely weaned from ranch life, for I habitually spent several weeks out of each year in the saddle. But as the majordomo of the Rancho de Los Olmos (The Elms), I knew that I had just about reached paradise. On many a half-day's ride I have counted between fifty and one hundred white-tailed deer on the ranch.

''During the year I spent on Los Olmos ranch, while Santos talked, while Uncle Jim Dobie and other cowmen talked or stayed silent, while the coyotes sang their songs, and the sand-hill cranes honked their lonely music, I seemed to be seeing a great painting of something I'd known all my life. I seemed to be listening to a great epic of something that had been commonplace in my youth but now took on meanings. . . .

''If it had not been for Uncle Jim and Los Olmos, if it hadn't been for Santos Cortez, the taleteller, I don't know in what direction I might have gone. It was certainly lucky for me that I left the University in 1920 and learned something.''¹

1921. ''Uncle Jim went broke. The sharp decline of cattle prices beginning in 1920 broke cattlemen as the 1929 plummet broke stockholders. He and I agreed that I should go back to my old job at the University of Texas. There I helped reorganize the Texas Folklore Society, became editor of its publications, and have, since that time, been gathering, sorting and setting down the lore of Texas and the Southwest. My academic work has been erratic and disrupted; the other has not.

''I soon became as much interested in the history and legends of the longhorn and mustang as in the traditions of old Sublett's gold in the Guadalupe Mountains. The coyote, the rattlesnake, the mesquite tree and the headless horseman of the Nueces are as interesting to me as the forty-nine jack loads of Spanish silver buried on the Colorado River just a few miles above Austin, where I live. If people are to enjoy their own lives, they must be aware of the significances of their own environments. . . . We in the Southwest shall be civilized when the roadrunner as well as the nightingale has connotations. Above all, I want to capture with their flavor, their metaphor, and their very genius the people who rode mustangs, trailed longhorns, stuck Spanish daggers (yucca spines) in their flesh to cure rattlesnake bites, and who yet hunt for the Lost Bowie Mine on the San Saba and prospect for Breyfogle's gold in Death Valley.

''The qualities most lacking in American literature are flavor and gusto. Flavor and a gusto for life are, nevertheless, dominating qualities in the pioneer stock of America where freed from Puritanical restraint, and the pioneer stock of the Southwest was and yet is pretty free of that restraint. I can't understand why American realists think that in order to be faithful to life they must forever deal with the dull and banal.''¹

"He never stood when he could sit or sat when he could lie down." ■ (From _Cow People_ by J. Frank Dobie. Illustrated by Will Crawford.)

In **1924** Dobie compiled and edited for the Texas Folklore Society a volume of legends entitled _Legends of Texas_. By the time this book was published, Dobie was head of the English Department at Oklahoma A & M, where he stayed until 1925. During his two years there, Dobie became a professional author, writing stories on cowboy songs and legends for the _Country Gentleman_. He returned to the University of Texas, and began writing regularly for magazines and periodicals.

1929. First book, _A Vaquero of the Brush Country_ was published. Began teaching a course in the literature of the Southwest called "Life and Literature of the Southwest." The course's popularity made Dobie famous as a teacher. "Good writing about any region is good only to the extent that it has universal appeal. Texans are the only 'race of people' known to anthropologists who do not depend upon breeding for population.

Like princes and lords, they can be made by 'breath,' plus a big white hat—which comparatively few Texans wear. A beef stew by a cook in San Antonio, Texas, may have a different flavor from that of a beef stew cooked in Pittsburgh, Pennsylvania, but the essential substances of potatoes and onions, with some suggestion of beef, are about the same, and geography has no effect on their digestibility."[2]

1931. Second book, _Coronado's Children: Tales of Lost Mines and Buried Treasures of the Southwest_, won the Literary Guild Award.

1932-1933. Received a Guggenheim grant to travel and collect stories in Mexico. The result was _Tongues of the Monte_, first published in 1935 and reissued in 1942 as _The Mexico I Like_.

1943-1944. Visiting professor of American history at Cambridge University. "During World War II while the patriots of what is now West Germany and also East Germany bombed London almost nightly, I was living with the dons in Emmanuel College, Cambridge, as visiting professor of American history. There's nothing in America like the colleges of the old English universities. Every night, almost, some man from far away who had been at Emmanuel came to High Table for dinner. After dinner we always repaired to the Common Room for talk with wine and then with coffee and tobacco. A man might linger there a good while or he might rush away to work or to some other pleasure."[1]

1947. Ended his affiliation with the University of Texas. "I have tried to give significance to the natural things of the Southwest and to emphasize its cultural inheritance. Yet I combat provincial-mindedness. After teaching 'Life and Literature of the Southwest' for years, I came to the conclusion that the Southwest needs perspective on itself and the rest of the world, as much as it needs knowledge of its own past."[1]

Dobie published three books about Southwestern animals after he left the University: *The Voice of the Coyote* (1949); *The Mustangs* (1952); *Rattlesnakes* (published posthumously in 1965).

1955. Compiled an anthology for young people entitled *Up the Trail from Texas,* which was one of the Landmark Books of general histories published by Random House.

1957. Hospitalized for six weeks with pneumonia. Subsequent damage to his heart left him forever bereft of his usual exuberant energy. "I feel hungry for something to put juice into me lots of times. I don't know what it is. The earth won't tell me. I *do* know the chemical apparatus in my body doesn't translate raw stuff into energy as it once did. What the world needs is more doctors who know more chemistry." [Lon Tinkle, *An American Original,* Little, Brown, 1978.[3]]

1963. Unable to withstand the extreme heat of Austin, Texas in the summertime, Dobie went to San Francisco to complete a book he was currently writing about "cow people." "[Robert] Frost said that what does not add to writing subtracts from it. The older I grow, the more I value economy. The art of omission applies to facts as much as it applies to style. Yet I like some narrative, etc., too much to delete."[3]

July, 1964. In his Sunday newspaper column, Dobie reflected: "I have for years known that my writing considerably on Southwestern and Western subjects has in certain quarters lowered my reputation for literary achievement. That regard has never bothered me. I have written the best I could on what I wanted to write about. In my own judgment, I have in several books written with more power, precision of diction, vividness and continually cultivated use of the English language than quite a few of the literati have achieved."[3]

September 18, 1964. Died in Austin, Texas, eight days before his seventy-sixth birthday. "What is the spirit, the tempo, the rhythm of this plot of earth to which we belong and as writers endeavor to express? Often it seems that the essential spirit has been run over and killed. But nature is as inexorable, as passionless, and as patient in revenge as she is in fidelity to 'the heart that loves her.' In the long run, she cannot be betrayed by man; in the long run, man can betray only himself by not harmonizing with her."[3]

HOBBIES AND OTHER INTERESTS: Book collecting, hunting, swimming, riding.

FOR MORE INFORMATION SEE: John William Rogers, *Finding Literature on the Texas Plain,* Southwest Press, 1931; *Time,* September 25, 1964; *Publishers Weekly,* September 28, 1964; *Newsweek,* September 28, 1964; Winston Bode, *A Portrait of Pancho: The Life of a Great Texan,* J. Frank Dobie, Pemberton Press, 1965; *Christian Science Monitor,* December 14, 1967; F. E. Abernethy, *J. Frank Dobie,* Steck-Vaughn, 1967; J. Frank Dobie, *Some Part of Myself,* Little, Brown, 1967; Mary Louise McVicker, *The Writings of J. Frank Dobie: A Bibliography,* Museum of the Great Plains, 1968; *Virginia Quarterly Review,* spring, 1968; William A. Owens, *Three Friends,* Doubleday, 1969; Lon Tinkle, *An American Original,* Little, Brown, 1978.

EINZIG, Susan   1922-

PERSONAL: Born in 1922, in Berlin, Germany. *Education:* Attended the Central School of Art, London, England, 1939.

CAREER: Illustrator and painter. Taught at Camberwell School of Art and Crafts and St. Martin's School of Art for eight years after World War II. *Awards, honors:* Carnegie Medal from the British Library Association, 1958, for *Tom's Midnight Garden.*

ILLUSTRATOR: Philippa Pearce, *Tom's Midnight Garden* (ALA Notable Book), Oxford University Press, 1958, Lippincott, 1959, reprinted, Puffin, 1976; Gillian Avery, editor, *In the Window Seat,* Oxford University Press, 1960, Van Nostrand, 1965; Eleanor Spence, *Lillipilly Hill,* Oxford University Press, 1960, Roy, 1963, reprinted, Oxford University Press, 1974; Elizabeth Poston, *The Children's Song Book,* Bodley Head, 1961, Dufour, 1963, reprinted, Merrimack Book Service, 1979; Robert Gittings and Jo Manton, *Story of John Keats,* Dutton,

Go to sleepy, little baby. . . . ■ (From "The Little Horses," in *The Children's Song Book* by Elizabeth Poston. Illustrated by Susan Einzig.)

1963; Edith Nesbit, *The Bastables,* Nonesuch, 1965, F. Watts, 1966; Margaret Love, *Explorer for an Aunt,* Follett, 1967. Contributor to *Radio Times.*

FARLEY, Walter 1920-

PERSONAL: Born June 26, 1920, in Syracuse, N.Y.; son of Walter and Isabelle (Vermilyea) Farley; married Rosemary Lutz, May 26, 1945; children: Pamela, Alice, Steve, Tim. *Education:* Attended Columbia University. *Residence:* Pennsylvania and Florida. *Address:* c/o Random House, Inc., 201 E. 50th St., New York, N.Y. 10022.

CAREER: Writer. *Military service:* U.S. Army, 1942-46; reporter for *Yank,* an army publication. *Awards, honors:* Pacific Northwest Library Association's Young Reader's Choice Award, 1944, for *The Black Stallion,* and 1948, for *The Black Stallion Returns;* Boys Club Junior Book Award, 1948, for *The Black Stallion Returns.*

WRITINGS—Published by Random House, except as indicated: *The Black Stallion* (illustrated by Keith Ward; Junior Literary Guild selection; also see below), 1941 (adapted as *Big Black Horse* under supervision of Josette Frank [illustrated by James Schucker], 1953); *Larry and the Underseas Raider* (illustrated by P. K. Jackson), 1942; *The Black Stallion Returns* (illustrated by Harold Eldridge; Junior Literary Guild selection; also see below), 1945, new edition, 1982; *Son of*

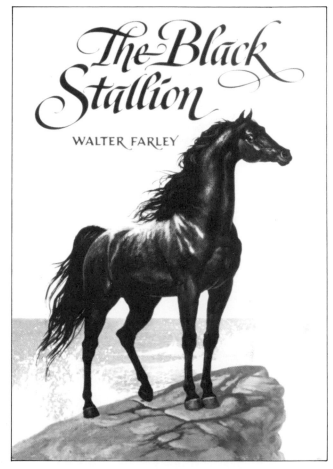

He was a giant of a horse, glistening black . . . a stallion born wild. ■ (Jacket illustration by Ruth Sanderson from *The Black Stallion* by Walter Farley.)

the Black Stallion (illustrated by Milton Menasco; Junior Literary Guild selection), 1947; *The Island Stallion* (illustrated by K. Ward; Junior Literary Guild selection), 1948; *The Black Stallion and Satan* (illustrated by M. Menasco; Junior Literary Guild selection; also see below), 1949; *The Blood Bay Colt* (illustrated by M. Menasco), 1950; *The Island Stallion's Fury* (illustrated by H. Eldridge), 1951; *The Black Stallion's Filly* (illustrated by M. Menasco), 1952; *The Black Stallion Revolts* (illustrated by H. Eldridge; Junior Literary Guild selection), 1953; *The Black Stallion's Sulky Colt* (illustrated by H. Eldridge), 1954; *The Black Stallion Races* (illustrated by H. Eldridge), 1955; *The Black Stallion's Courage* (illustrated by Allen F. Brewer, Jr.; Junior Literary Guild selection), 1956; *The Black Stallion Mystery* (illustrated by Mal Singer; also see below), 1957; *The Horse-tamer* (illustrated by J. Schucker), 1959.

The Black Stallion and Flame (illustrated by H. Eldridge), 1960; *Little Black, a Pony* (illustrated by J. Schucker), 1961; *Man o' War* (illustrated by Angie Draper), 1962; *Little Black Goes to the Circus* (illustrated by J. Schucker), 1963; *The Black Stallion Challenged!* (illustrated by A. Draper), 1964; *The Horse That Swam Away* (illustrated by Leo Summers), 1965; *The Great Dane, Thor* (illustrated by Joseph Cellini), 1966; *The Little Black Pony Races* (illustrated by J. Schucker), 1968; *The Black Stallion's Ghost* (illustrated by A. Draper), 1969; *The Black Stallion and the Girl* (illustrated by A. Draper), 1971; *The Black Stallion Picture Book* (illustrated with photographs from the motion picture), 1979; *Walter Farley's Black*

WALTER FARLEY

Stallion Books, four volumes (contains *The Back Stallion, The Black Stallion Returns, The Black Stallion and Satan,* and *The Black Stallion Mystery*), 1979; *How to Stay Out of Trouble with Your Horse: Some Basic Safety Rules to Help You Enjoy Riding* (illustrated with photographs by Tim Farley), Doubleday, 1981; *The Black Stallion Returns: A Storybook Based on the Movie* (photos by T. Farley), edited by Stephanie Spinner, 1982; *The Black Stallion: A Comic Book Album* (illustrated by Michel Faure), adapted by Robert Genin, 1983; *The Black Stallion Legend,* 1983; *The Black Stallion Returns: A Comic Book Album* (illustrated by M. Faure), adapted by R. Genin, 1984.

A triumphant Alec Ramsay, astride The Black, gives a victory salute. ■ (From the movie "The Black Stallion Returns," starring Kelly Reno. Copyright © 1983 by United Artists Corp.)

ADAPTATIONS: "The Black Stallion" (motion picture), starring Kelly Reno and Mickey Rooney, United Artists, 1979; "The Black Stallion" (filmstrip with cassette), Media Basics, 1982; "The Black Stallion Returns" (motion picture), starring Kelly Reno and Vincent Spano, United Artists, 1983.

WORK IN PROGRESS: Another Black Stallion adventure.

SIDELIGHTS: Farley was born in Syracuse, New York, and grew up in New York City. "I lived in midtown Manhattan at the Hotel Roosevelt where my father worked as an assistant manager. I commuted by subway to Erasmus Hall High School in Brooklyn, because the school had a good track team. I loved New York City for all its year-round opportunities for sports and other activities; it was a great place for a kid in those days and perhaps still is, providing kids take advantage of what is there. Like most kids, I was very interested in sports and was able to play tennis, ride, run, and ice skate most of the year. And there were plenty of horses—in Central Park, Squadron A with its indoor polo, Long Island, Connecticut, and Westchester trails, and the race tracks at Belmont, Jamaica, and Aqueduct where I spent many, many days. Later I moved to Flushing where several of my friends had horses stabled in lots now occupied by apartment buildings. And it was there I set the locale for *The Black Stallion* as I rode on trails through Kissena Park and along the Long Island Expressway.

"I enjoyed writing as much as I did reading or participating in sports or anything else. I enjoyed writing stories on the typewriter, any kind of story at all, at the ages of fourteen, fifteen, and sixteen. I read a great deal, but there were few books about horses—at least only a couple that I knew of. There was Anna Sewell's *Black Beauty* and Will James' *Smoky, the Cow Horse,* but these were not enough to satisfy me; I honestly thought, even at that age, about the thousands of horse lovers like me who wanted more books about horses. So I had fun writing my story for them and for myself. I became absorbed in *The Black Stallion* by becoming Alec, of course, a boy from New York City who brought a horse like The Black to my Flushing barn. I remember well devoting two and three nights a week writing it." [Lee Bennett Hopkins, *More Books by More People,* Citation, 1974.[1]]

Farley attended Mercersburg Academy in Pennsylvania, where he participated in track. At school he was to continue to write stories for boys and girls as he had done since the age of eleven. After graduating in 1935, Farley attended Columbia University. Under the guidance of an English professor, Farley

. . .Alec tried to make The Black understand what he wanted him to do. ■ (From *The Black Stallion* by Walter Farley. Photograph from the movie adaptation starring Kelly Reno. Copyright © 1978 by United Artists Corp.)

(From the movie "The Black Stallion," starring Kelly Reno. Copyright © 1978 by United Artists Corp.)

wrote the final draft of *The Black Stallion*, which was published in 1951.

From 1942 to 1946, Farley served in the United States Army. Most of the time he was assigned to *Yank*, an army weekly magazine, although he continued to write stories for children during his army service. In a letter to Louise Bonino, editor of children's books at Random House, he wrote about his books and the army life at Fort Knox, Kentucky. "If someone had asked me what I wouldn't like in this man's army previous to my induction I would have said, 'To be put in a tank!' But that is precisely where I am, and will soon be driving one! Somehow, though, as the days go on, and I become more and more a soldier, and the heaven of a civilian life I left behind is slowly forced to the back of my mind. I find that I'm beginning to take great pride in being part of the Armed Forces and all that it is being trained to do. It certainly is a funny world!

"But enough of that—now about the book. Remember, on *The Black Stallion* I gave you a list of names of people that I knew would help publicize the book? If you can, I wish you'd send them copies of *The Undersea Raider*. . . .

"I do hope the book goes over with a bang! As yet I haven't seen a copy of it—but am eagerly looking forward to it." [Walter Farley to Louise Bonino, March 19, 1942. Taken from a personal collection in the Rare Book and Manuscript Department of the Columbia University Libraries.[2]]

After his Army discharge, Farley and his wife travelled widely, and established a farm in Pennsylvania, where they could raise their own horses. Farley devoted his life to writing about horses and raising them. "Stallions, in most cases, should be purchased only by breeding farms and professionals. I realize this seems near heresy after all the books I've written on the close relationship between Alec Ramsay and the Black Stallion, as well as Steve Duncan and Flame, the Island Stallion. But Alec and Steve had no choice and they lived under unusual circumstances in stories of adventure.

". . . As it is with any animal, much depends on the temperament of the stallion. I have seen and owned some as docile and tractable as any gelding. I know many horse people who will have nothing but stallions in their barns. However, more often than not, stallions are far more of a handful and a responsibility than mares or geldings, especially if you are stabled in a mixed barn and want to ride in mixed company. . . .

"Mares are sometimes moody and unpredictable, especially when they're 'in season.' But if you understand her moods, a mare can be your favorite (this is so for me, even though I have stallions and write about them). . . .

"Geldings are a very pleasant and serviceable type of horse. Some people say, 'You can't beat a good gelding for all-around usefulness and as a friend.' They are far less trouble than stallions or mares in most respects and their attitudes, temperaments, and dispositions are the same every day; good or bad as they may be, they will change very little, if at all. Don't underestimate the courage and ability of geldings when comparing them to stallions, for some of the greatest American racehorses have been geldings—Kelso and Forego, as examples.

". . . There is no way to explain the *magic* that some people have with horses. It is almost a mystical gift. It may be that horses sense that these people truly care about them. It may be a handler's sensitivity that accounts for his or her uncannily

precise timing and coordination that creates a oneness between horse and rider. Or it may be none of these, but a form of art itself, as creative as any art can be and just as unexplainable and rewarding.

"I've learned that one thing is certain. You cannot cultivate this magic, any more than you can any other art form. You have it or you don't have it. But it *is* possible to become a competent horse person without it—as it is for many riders, amateurs and professionals alike. . . ." [Walter Farley, *How to Stay Out of Trouble with Your Horse: Some Basic Safety Rules to Help You Enjoy Riding*, Doubleday, 1981.[3]]

In 1955 *The Island Stallion Races* was published. Farley wrote to his Random House editor: "I must confess that I was terribly disappointed in your reaction to *The Island Stallion Races* for, as you know, I've been very excited about this book and have worked hard for well over a year, trying to get the most out of what I thought was an unusual idea. But often that's the way it's been between us—I go booming skyward and you pull me down to Earth with a 'See here, Private Farley!' But

Gripping the hypodermic firmly, the prowler advanced again, more cautiously this time. ■ (From *The Black Stallion Returns* by Walter Farley. Illustrated by Harold Eldridge.)

He buried the colt in the lower pasture where Black Sand had spent so many hours with Pam. ∎
(From *The Black Stallion and the Girl* by Walter Farley. Illlustrated by Angie Draper.)

I do wish you'd found a few things to praise, Louise, for when I stop going boom there won't be any more books.

"The big thing here is that I cannot do away with the Epilogue as you have suggested, for it together with Chapter 20 are what, in my opinion, make this a good, strong book. I would rather not have the book published at all than to leave the reader with the knowledge that Jay and Flick and the race itself were *definitely, positively* and *absolutely* nothing but a dream! What a disappointing, heartbreaking way of ending this story! There are far too many of us who have accepted Jay and Flick, and welcome with all our hearts the Epilogue which tells us that regardless of the conclusion *Steve* came to in Chapter 20 (that it was all a dream), he and Flame *actually did race,* for Pitch recognizes Flame in the news picture and is sure the rider is Steve! Of course, we're not at all surprised that it wasn't a dream, just pleased because that was a pretty hard wallop for anyone to hand us as late as Chapter 20. Our only regret now is that Steve didn't learn to fly when he had the chance!

"I don't believe the Epilogue will confuse any of the kids either—as you've suggested—even those with the oldest, coldest eyes and hearts. They'll just naturally have the adult reaction mentioned in your letter—that of having to decide for themselves 'whether the whole thing was a dream or whether

it actually happened'—and I know darn well which they'll choose. But the very worst the Epilogue has done to them is to make them *think* about what they've read, maybe even stretched their imaginations a bit.

"I do hope you're taking all this in the friendliness in which it is being written. I'm making no bones about being very keen on this story complete with Epilogue, but there's no reason in the world why you have to agree with me and publish. To me the book doesn't move into the 'realm of science fiction,' to compete with all such titles being published. There's nothing scientific about it. Instead, it's a horse story with a touch of, if I *must* say it, easy-to-take fantasy (but I won't say it too loud for fear Jay and Flick will overhear!). And that's why I thought we had an off-beat, exciting book to offer our readers, even those who intend to be jockies when they grow up.

"Let me know where we go from here, if anywhere. I like your suggestion for the Chapter 1 change, and I'll clarify anything in Chapter 20 and the Epilogue that you feel is confusing. But I cannot make the ending to this story something that I never intended it to be.

"The only book the Junior Literary Guild didn't take was *The Island Stallion's Fury*. It's a pretty good record and I'm most proud. So if you decide to take this latest story, I'd appreciate your sending it to the Guild.'' [Walter Farley to Louise Bonino, September 20, 1954. Taken from a personal collection in the Rare Book and Manuscript Department of the Columbia University Libraries.[4]]

A book about horse-tamers under the same title was published in 1959. Farley instructed his editor to carefully choose an illustrator for the book. ''I've had this book done for several weeks but put it to one side while working on the next. During that time I've had several people read it, and they've all liked it.

''The story represents a lot more work and copy than will be evident. I found that once I forgot that part of it and read what I'd done as a novella rather than a novel I wanted to see it published. It may be the kind of story I'll be doing from time to time, and perhaps after some fourteen books it's not to be unexpected.

''Good illustrations are most necessary and will do much for this story. For this reason I've included stats illustrating various scenes or as aids for the illustrator—and for you too! Let me know when you've had a chance to read it, and I do hope you'll find time to read it at one sitting, for it's that kind of a story.'' [Walter Farley to Louise Bonino, January 8, 1958.

Taken from a personal collection in the Rare Book and Manuscript Department of the Columbia University Libraries.[5]]

Besides a farm in Pennsylvania, Farley and his family also spent a part of each year in Florida, where the author wrote his books from a small office that overlooked the water. ''It's good for my eyes to look up from the typewriter to the horizon. There's been lots of close work through the years. And I love water. We have a small Boston whaler and a thirty-four-foot Rhodes-designed sloop. We sail a lot, race a little, and skin dive as much as possible. There are beautiful islands to the south of us. I also do lots of riding, mostly on Arabians.''[1]

About his work habits, Farley commented: ''I get up very early, usually just before dawn. When in Florida I jog on the beach; at the Pennsylvania farm I jog around the pond, always accompanied by a great dane—I've always had one. . . . We swim after running, then I work at my writing until about 1:00 p.m. After that I'm off riding, sailing, swimming, or doing some other outdoor activity; I truly need the exercise after a long stint at the typewriter.

''. . . I always make a point of encouraging kids to develop the talent that comes easy and naturally. You ought to pursue

(From *Son of the Black Stallion* by Walter Farley. Illustrated by Milton Menasco.)

your hobby—not become a lawyer so you can spend your spare time pursuing your hobby. If you can't make a living water skiing, then take up something related to it—sell the equipment or edit a magazine about it.''

''I have no occupation other than writing. The only income I've ever had has come from writing books. I do raise race horses and Arabians occasionally and sell them, but there's really little money in it. Writing for me is fun. All my books are completely different from one another; otherwise I could never have stayed with the same characters who are used as springboards into whatever it is I want to write about. Kids know how different my books are; most adults don't. I've

written fantasy and science fiction, *The Black Stallion's Ghost* is a horror story of the supernatural; *Man o' War*, the story of one of America's mightiest thoroughbred racing horses, is a fictional biography—authentic but seen through the eyes of a fictitious stableboy.''[1]

Farley first met the famous racehorse, Man o' War, when he was a young boy. ''. . . Like many boys and girls, I wanted to visit the well-known horse farms in Kentucky, and one summer my father took me there. I saw many fine stallions, for all horse lovers are welcome in that country and no one who behaves himself is ever turned away. When we reached Faraway Farm, there were many visitors swarming through

Walter Farley and his Black Stallion.

the gates. For my father this was the highlight of our tour since he had seen Man o' War race and 'the flame-colored stallion was the greatest horse that ever lived.' To someone like myself, who had not been around long enough to see Man o' War race, he was a legendary horse, a monument, a part of the history I had read on American racing. I was excited, too, but not prepared at all for the moment to come.

"I recall adding my name to a guest book, which according to my father already totaled over half a million visitors. I followed the large group into the stallion barn, thinking that if Man o' War had belonged to the public in his racing days, things hadn't changed much for him.

"We approached his big stall, and Will Harbut, the Negro groom who took care of him, looked us over, rather critically, I thought, as if deciding for himself how much we knew about horses and Man o' War in particular. Like others in the throng, I had read many stories in magazines about Will Harbut's love and care for Man o' War in these—his later years—at Faraway Farm. I was prepared to listen to his well-publicized and very complete monologue on Man o' War's record and the accomplishments of his foals. But at that moment my father's hand tightened on my arm, directing my attention to the stall itself.

"The door had been swung open and Man o' War stood there. I was prepared to see a great champion and sire. But, suddenly, I knew that while I had never seen him race it made no difference at all. I felt as my father did. I was lucky to be there, close enough to touch him if that had been allowed.

"Man o' War stood in the doorway, statuesque and magnificent. There was a lordly lift to his head and his sharp eyes were bright. He didn't look *at* us, but far out over our heads. If his red coat and mane and tail had faded with time, as my father said later, I was not aware of it. Nor did I notice the dip of his back, deepening too with age. I could not even have said whether his massive body was red or gold or yellow. I was aware only of one thing, that for the first and perhaps the only time in my life I was standing in the presence of a horse which was *truly* great, and it would be a moment always to be remembered.

"What accounted for this stirring of the heart? For that is what it was. If one attributes it to the emotions of youth, what about my father's adulation for Man o' War? And all the others of his generation who had seen this horse and felt no differently? Was the look in Man o' War's eyes responsible for it? His gaze, I recall, shifted occasionally to look at us. They were deep, intelligent eyes and very bright. More often than not, however, he seemed not to know we were there at all, his gaze fixed and far away, so intent that I could have sworn he was watching something far beyond our vision.

"Or was it the regal lift of his head, the giant sweep of his body, or the dignity with which he held himself up for our inspection? Or, perhaps, a combination of everything, for there was nothing about him that did not seem right to me. Whatever accounted for it, I stood in his presence in quiet reverence, unmindful of anything but Man o' War. I heard only snatches of the eloquent recital that rolled from Will Harbut's tongue. 'He's got everything a hoss ought to have and he's got it where a hoss ought to have it. He is de mostest hoss. Stand still, Red.'

"It has also been said of Man o' War that 'He touched the imagination of men and they saw different things in him. But one they all remember was that he brought exaltation into their hearts.' Whatever else may be written or said of Man o' War

I know this to be true from my one visit to an aged but majestic stallion. It was with the hope that I could impart something of what I felt . . . that I wrote this book.

"Many years have passed since Man o' War raced. The few who remember him on the track will tell you that all the great champions that have raced since—Equipoise, War Admiral, Whirlaway, Assault, Citation, Native Dancer, Nashau, to name a few—were only 'the best since Man o' War.' To them Man o' War is *the* one to be remembered. He alone is their yardstick of time." [Walter Farley, *Man o' War,* Random House, 1962.[6]]

Farley's most famous book, *The Black Stallion,* was made into a movie in 1979, which was a commercial success. Another movie, "The Black Stallion Returns," has also been adapted from his book. His books have sold over twelve million copies in the United States and in fifteen other countries, including Saudi Arabia, Czechoslovakia, India, and Malaya. "Children's letters are very, very important to me. I don't really know how many hundreds of thousands of letters I've received over the years, but I've read them all between books. And . . . I've saved them all; they're in an appropriate place, stored in my tack room at the farm above stalls and horses. I can't destroy them and sometimes wonder if there isn't someone who would like to make a study of them for they span such a long period of time. And how different are kids in their love for horses now than they were in the 1940s? I think little. Many kids would rather ride on the back of a horse at twenty to twenty-five miles per hour than pilot a spaceship to the moon!"[1]

Farley's manuscripts and papers are in the Special Collections at Columbia University, New York City.

HOBBIES AND OTHER INTERESTS: Besides riding, writing and traveling, Farley enjoys sailing. He sometimes races his 35-foot auxiliary sloop "Circe."

FOR MORE INFORMATION SEE: Young Wings, September, 1945; *New York Times Book Review,* November 2, 1947, November 6, 1966; Earl F. Wallbridge, "Walter Farley," *Wilson Library Bulletin,* February, 1949; *Current Biography Yearbook: 1949,* H. W. Wilson, 1950; Stanley Kunitz and Howard Haycraft, editors, *Junior Book of Authors,* H. W. Wilson, 1951; Huck and Young, *Children's Literature in the Elementary School,* Holt, 1961; *The Children's Bookshelf,* Child Study Association of America, Bantam, 1965; Nancy Larrick, *A Teacher's Guide to Children's Books,* Merrill, 1966; G. Robert Carlsen, *Books and the Teen-Age Reader,* Harper, 1967; *Book Week,* April 30, 1967; *Atlantic Monthly,* December, 1969; Richard Brunner, "In a Field of Seasonal Authors, a Perennial Phenomenon," *Christian Science Monitor,* February 1, 1971; *Authors of Books for Young People,* 2nd edition, Scarecrow, 1971; P. Close, "Walter Farley and the Black Stallion," *Western Horseman,* December, 1973; Lee Bennett Hopkins, *More Books by More People,* Citation Press, 1974; D. L. Kirkpatrick, *Twentieth-Century Children's Writers,* St. Martin's Press, 1978; *Contemporary Literary Criticism,* Volume XVII, Gale, 1981; *Dictionary of Literary Biography,* Volume 22, "American Writers for Children, 1900-1960," Gale, 1983.

Grown-ups never understand anything for themselves, and it is tiresome for children to be always and forever explaining things to them.

—Antoine de Saint-Exupéry

FERRY, Charles   1927-

PERSONAL: Born October 8, 1927, in Chicago, Ill.; son of Ignatius Loyola (a postal clerk) and Madelyn Anne (Bartholemew) Ferry; married Ruth Louise Merz (an executive travel coordinator), September 26, 1958; children: Ronald Edmund Richardson (stepson). *Education:* Attended University of Illinois, 1952. *Politics:* Republican. *Religion:* Episcopalian. *Address:* c/o Houghton Mifflin Co., 2 Park St., Boston, Mass. 02108.

CAREER: Journalist, 1949-71; writer, 1971—. *Military service:* U.S. Navy, 1944-49. *Awards, honors: Raspberry One* was named Best Children's Book of 1983 by the Friends of American Writers, one of the Best Books of the Year by *School Library Journal,* and one of American Library Association's Best Books for Young Adults, both 1983.

WRITINGS—All juvenile; all published by Houghton: *Up in Sister Bay,* 1975; *O Zebron Falls!,* 1977; *Raspberry One,* 1983; *One More Time!,* 1985.

WORK IN PROGRESS: Binge, a novel about a teenage alcoholic.

SIDELIGHTS: "I kind of eased into the role of author. I had pursued a career in journalism and related fields. Then when I was in my forties, I began writing vignettes about my boyhood summers in northern Wisconsin. The vignettes grew into the manuscript of my first novel, *Up in Sister Bay.* I found an agent who was impressed with my work, and she found a publisher who was also impressed—Houghton Mifflin Company.

"Houghton felt that my books had a particular suitability for young people. I'm glad it turned out that way. I have no interest in writing for adults. In general, I think the best writing is being done in the children's field. Authors have the freedom to give of themselves and to dream a little.

"I believe that to one degree or another, all good fiction involves truth. As William Faulkner put it, 'Truth is what a person holds to his or her heart.' What do my books offer that young people can hold to their hearts? It's not for me to say, really. My strong suit appears to be evoking mood and atmosphere. I tell stories of young people coming of age, and I tend to focus on life's sweet moments. My books come from deep inside of me, and they are slow to develop. I am not a paneled-den, mahogany-desk kind of writer. My wife and I live very modestly. I have a typewriter stand in a corner of the living room, and I use an A & P grocery bag for a wastebasket.''

''. . . During the writing of *Raspberry One*—I learned how Stephen Crane, without having experienced combat, was able to write *The Red Badge of Courage.* Had he been a combat veteran, he would have unavoidably been limited by his own experience, wanting to write the demons out of his system. Good reporting; not necessarily good art. However, without that limitation, he was able to immerse himself in research of the Civil War and write a representative combat engagement, one that would stand for all such engagements.

(Jacket illustration by Diane de Groat from *O Zebron Falls!* by Charles Ferry.)

CHARLES FERRY

"I never experienced combat. . . . Hence, without any personal demons to exorcise, I too was able to strive for the representative. An enormous amount of work went into the novel. For two years, through research, I relived the war, in all of its theaters. God, what a horror! . . . *Raspberry One* is my little prayer that it will never happen again." [From an article by Charles Ferry in *Horn Book,* December, 1983.[1]]

"Thus far, all of my books have dealt with young people coming of age in the 1930s and 1940s, the period of my youth. My future books will deal with contemporary themes and settings. One of them will be the most personally important book I will ever write. For much of my life, I was plagued by the ravages of alcohol. I could fill a large volume, recounting the horrors it caused in my life. Fifteen years ago, I finally whipped the problem. Still, hardly a night goes by that some bad memory of that period doesn't return to haunt me. I want to write it out of my system. And so I am at work on a novel that will be titled simply *Binge.* It will be the story of a boy with a drinking problem, a boy in his late teens, and will follow him on a colossal binge that has disasterous consequences.

"If the book spares one young person the ravages of alcohol, I will consider it the greatest achievement of my life.

"My wife, Ruth, and I have lived in Rochester Hills, Michigan, for the past twenty-six years. We have a married son who lives in Dixon, New Mexico, and a black, eight-year-old Belgian sheepdog ("Darling Girl") who rules our household. When I'm not writing, I cook, bake bread, garden—and pray for peace."

FOR MORE INFORMATION SEE: New York Times Book Review, November 2, 1975, March 5, 1978; *Christian Science Monitor,* November 5, 1975; *School Library Journal,* October, 1977, September, 1983; *Horn Book,* September/October, 1985.

All that mankind has done, thought, gained or been: it is lying as in magic preservation in the pages of books.
—Thomas Carlyle

FILSTRUP, E(dward) Christian   1942-
(Chris Filstrup)

PERSONAL: Born May 9, 1942, in Hollywood, Calif.; son of Edward C. (an inventor) and Elizabeth (an artist; maiden name, Merritt) Filstrup; married Jane Merrill (a writer), August 10, 1968 (divorced, 1984); married Laurie Smith, August 17, 1985; children: (first marriage) Emma Nilufar and Burton Thomas (twins). *Education:* Haverford College, B.A. (with honors), 1965; Harvard University, M.A., 1967, doctoral study, 1967-72; Columbia University, M.L.S., 1974. *Religion:* Baha'i. *Home:* 76 Chatfield Rd., Bronxville, N.Y. 10708. *Office:* Overseas Operation Division, Library of Congress, Washington, D.C. 20540.

CAREER: Teacher of Western civilization and comparative religion at private secondary school in Tehran, Iran, 1969-71; New York Hospital, Payne Whitney Clinic, New York City, assistant librarian, 1973-74, head librarian, 1974-75; New York Public Library, New York City, first assistant for Oriental Division of Research Libraries, 1957-78, chief of division, 1978-86; Library of Congress, Washington D.C., assistant chief of overseas operations, 1986—. Consultant to Manhattan Center for Advanced Psychoanalytic Studies.

MEMBER: American Library Association (Middle East chairperson of International Relations Round Table, 1981—), Middle East Librarians Association (member of executive board, 1978-81; chairman of committee on machine-readable Arabic data, 1980-81), Middle East Studies Association, Association for Asian Studies, Association of College and Research Libraries (member of board of directors, 1979-81; vice-chairman

E. CHRISTIAN FILSTRUP

of Asian and African section, 1979-80; chairman of section, 1980-81), Phi Beta Kappa, Beta Phi Mu.

WRITINGS—Under name Chris Filstrup: (Contributor) *American Book World Geography,* American Book Co., 1979; *Japanese Technology: Yesterday and Today,* New York Public Library, 1979; (with Janie Filstrup) *Beadazzled: The Story of Beads* (juvenile nonfiction; illustrated by Loren Bloom), Warne, 1982; (with J. Filstrup) *China: From Emperors to Communes* (juvenile nonfiction), Dillon, 1983; (contributor) *Japanese Scientific and Technical Information in the United States,* National Technical Information Service, 1983. Contributor to magazines, including *World Order, Armchair Detective, New York,* and *Garden.* Editor of *Leads,* summer, 1983; bibliography editor of *Journal of the History of the Behavioral Sciences,* 1975.

WORK IN PROGRESS: (With J. Filstrup) *Carp Kites on Main Street: Ethnic Holidays in America* for Dodd.

SIDELIGHTS: "I was born in Hollywood, California. Weekends, my father wore his pajamas until well into the afternoon. Even when he mowed the lawn. This was during World War II and caused *talk.* Since he designed airplanes for Lockheed, the eccentricity led to a security check. During these early years, my mother sculpted. I was distinguished from other babies by clay-red diapers.

"When I was four we bucked the demographic tide and moved to a small town in Michigan. Here my dad donned weekend clothes by late morning. My mother now bought her clay instead of mining it in the Mohave Desert. Here I grew up.

"I left home to go to college near Philadelphia—Haverford College. Then Harvard graduate school. It was really too much education. I OD'd on classes, credits, papers, exams, and Bailey's ice cream sundaes. I dropped out of academia and moved with my wife to New York to work.

"For me writing marked a volte-face from a long—too long—academic career. To write, in a way I have to put blinders on. Instead of surveying the horizons of the world I now try to look at a small bit and discover what lies within. This approach is inspired by the Mahayana Buddhist notion that every atom mirrors the universe. It also requires leaving the middle of the stream and grabbing hold of a stone or tree root that is firm. It is the holding on that I find difficult, and rewarding.

"The subject of my first book was beads. While researching the abacus—beads as counters—I discovered the difference between analog and digital computers. Along with the slide rule and conventional speedometer, the abacus does its work so that the user can see physical relationships. Digital computers solve problems but mask the process. I began to think about the uroborus in Erich Neumann's *Origin and History of*

Most Chinese schools are old, plain-looking, and crowded. ■ (From *China: From Emperors to Communes* by Chris and Janie Filstrup. Photograph by Ann Newman.)

Consciousness and the Sioux Indians' sacred hoop. I gave our digital clock away and repaired an old banjo pendulum that had hung silent for years.

"Considering how hard it is to write intelligible prose, there is a marvelous passiveness in this kind of discovery. The sentences, written, fall together to reveal a truth one can't ignore. The abacus message was 'Count on your fingers and mark time by round clocks.'"

FINLEY, Martha 1828-1909
(Martha Farquharson)

PERSONAL: Born April 26, 1828, in Chillicothe, Ohio; died of bronchopneumonia, January 30, 1909, in Elkton, Md.; daughter of James Brown (a doctor) and Maria Theresa (Brown) Finley. *Education:* Educated in private schools in South Bend, Ind., and Philadelphia, Pa. *Religion:* Presbyterian. *Residence:* Elkton, Md.

CAREER: Author of children's books, most notably of series of books about Elsie Dinsmore. School teacher in Indiana, 1851-53, and in Phoenixville, Pa., 1853; began writing stories for periodicals about 1854, and Sunday school books for Presbyterian Publication Board, Philadelphia, Pa., beginning about 1855, with early stories and books written under name Martha Farquharson; *Elsie Dinsmore* published, 1867.

WRITINGS—All for children; "Elsie Dinsmore" series; published by Dodd, except as indicated: *Elsie Dinsmore,* 1867, reprinted, Harmony & Co., 1980 [other editions include those illustrated by E. M. Fenn, Griffith, Farran, 1886; Howard C. Christy, Dodd, 1897; Henry Muheim, Saalfield Publishing, 1943]; *Elsie's Holidays at Roselands,* 1868, reissued as *Holidays at Roselands,* 1898 [another edition illustrated by E. M. Fenn, Griffith, Farran, 1886]; *Elsie's Girlhood,* 1872, reprinted, Buccaneer, 1981 [another edition illustrated by E. M. Fenn, Griffith, Farran, 1886]; *Elsie's Womanhood,* 1875; *Elsie's Motherhood,* 1876, reprinted, Buccaneer, 1981; *Elsie's Children,* 1877, reprinted, Buccaneer, 1981; *Elsie's Widowhood,* 1880; *Grandmother Elsie,* 1882; *Elsie New Relations: What They Did and How They Fared at Ion,* 1883; *Elsie at Nantucket,* 1884, reprinted, Buccaneer, 1981; *The Two Elsies,* 1885; *Elsie's Kith and Kin,* 1886; *Elsie's Friends at Woodburn,* 1887; *Christmas with Grandma Elsie,* 1888; *Elsie and the Raymonds,* 1889; *Elsie Yachting with the Raymonds,* 1890; *Elsie's Vacation and After Events,* 1891; *Elsie at Viamede,* 1892; *Elsie at Ion,* 1893; *Elsie at the World's Fair,* 1894; *Elsie's Journey on Inland Waters,* 1895; *Elsie at Home,* 1897; *Elsie on the Hudson and Elsewhere,* 1898; *Elsie in the South,* 1899; *Elsie's Young Folks in Peace and War,* 1900; *Elsie's Winter Trip,* 1902; *Elsie and Her Loved Ones,* 1903; *Elsie and Her Namesakes,* 1905.

Other works; all published by Presbyterian Board of Publication, except as indicated: *Ella Clinton; or, "By Their Fruits Ye Shall Know Them",* 1856; *Marion Harvie: A Tale of Persecution in the Seventeenth Century* (novel), 1857; *Clouds and Sunshine; or, The Faith Brightened Pathway,* 1859; *Willie Elton, the Little Boy Who Loved Jesus* (novel), 1864; *Mysie's Work, and How She Did It,* 1864; *Black Steve; or, The Strange Warning,* Presbyterian Publication Committee, 1865; *Brookside Farm-House from January to December* (novel), Presbyterian Publication Committee, 1865; *Hugo and Franz* (novel), 1865; *Allan's Fault* (novel), Presbyterian Publication Committee, 1866; *A Week in Lilly's Life* (novel), 1866; *Eva Merton; or, The Blue Morocco Shoes* (novel), 1866; *The Shan-*

MARTHA FINLEY

nons; or, From Darkness to Light (novel), Presbyterian Publication Committee, 1868; *Annandale: A Story of the Times of the Convenanters* (novel), Blackwood, 1868; *Casella; or, The Children of the Valleys* (novel), Lippincott, 1869; *Rufus the Unready,* Presbyterian Publication Committee, 1870; *Lillian; or, Did She Do Right?,* W. B. Evans, 1871; *Wanted—A Pedigree* (novel), W. B. Evans, 1871; *An Old-Fashioned Boy* (novel), Evans, Stoddart, 1871; *Our Fred; or, Seminary Life at Thurston* (novel), [New York], 1874; *Signing the Contract, and What It Cost* (novel), Dodd, 1879; *The Thorn in the Nest* (novel), Dodd, 1886; *The Tragedy of Wild River Valley* (novel), Dodd, 1893; *Twiddletwit: A Fairy Tale* (novel), Dodd, 1898.

"Do Good Library" series; published by the Presbyterian Publication Committee, 1868: *Anna Hand, the Meddlesome Girl; Grandma Foster's Sunbeam; Little Patience; Little Helper; Little Dick Positive; Loitering Linus; Maud's Two Homes; Milly, the Little Girl Who Tried to Help Others; Stupid Sally, the Poor House Girl.*

"Little Books for Little Readers" series; published by Presbyterian Publication Committee, 1870: *Amy and Her Kitten; Bertie Page and Tom Cross; Jamie by the Lake; Jane Hart; The Broken Basket; The White Dress.*

"Pewit's Nest" series; published by Presbyterian Board of Publication, 1876: *Pewit's Nest; Harry's Fourth of July; Harry's Ride; Harry's Walks; Harry's Little Sister; Harry's Christmas; Harry and His Chickens; Aunt Kitty's Fowls; Harry's Grandma; Rose and Robbie; Harry at Aunt Jane's; Harry and His Cousins.*

(From *Elsie's Friends at Woodburn* by Martha Finley.)

"Mildred" series; published by Dodd: *Mildred Keith,* 1878; *Mildred at Roselands,* 1879; *Mildred and Elsie,* 1881; *Mildred's Married Life, and a Winter with Elsie Dinsmore,* 1882; *Mildred at Home, with Something about Her Relatives and Friends,* 1884; *Mildred's Boys and Girls,* 1886; *Mildred's New Daughter,* 1894.

Also author of numerous books for Presbyterian Board of Publication, including *Cares and Comforts, Lame Letty; or, Bear Ye One Another's Burdens, Nursery Tales for Her Little Friends,* and *Try: Better Do It than Wish It Done;* of "Finley" series (for adults), seven volumes; and of "Honest Jim" series (for adults), six volumes.

SIDELIGHTS: **April 26, 1828.** Born in Chillicothe, Ohio, Finley was the daughter of first cousins, Dr. James Brown Finley and Maria Theresa (Brown) Finley. The family was of substantial middle-class stock, strongly Presbyterian, boasting two famous ancestors, a grandfather who had been a general in the Revolutionary War, the War of 1812, and who had been a personal friend of George Washington, and a great-uncle, Samuel Finley, who had been president of Princeton Theological Seminary. Of Scotch-Irish descent, the name of the ancestral clan was Farquharson, the Gaelic of Finley.

At the age of eight Finley moved with her family to South Bend, Ind. where she received her education in the form of private schooling. She lived in Indiana until she was twenty-five, when her parents died. She then moved on to New York,

Philadelphia and eventually to Phoenixville, Penn., where she taught school.

In **1853** Finley began her literary career by writing a newspaper story and a small book published by the Presbyterian Board of Publication. At first they were published anonymously, later under the name of Farquharson as her family was said to have objected to the use of her real name. She spent most of her life in the service of the church, writing Sunday school material and about one hundred highly moralistic volumes for young girls.

1867. Finley was an invalid and living in genteel poverty when she wrote her first "Elsie" book. She used her nieces as models to create her fictionalized account of a beautiful, motherless Southern heiress named Elsie Dinsmore. She submitted the manuscript to Dodd Publishing Company, who cut the book in half, publishing the first volume as *Elsie Dinsmore* [1867] and the second volume as *Elsie's Holiday* [1868].

About her first publications, Finley remarked in the preface to *Elsie's Girlhood:* "[Elsie] was sent out with many an anxious thought regarding the reception that might await her there. But she was kindly welcomed, and such has been the favor shown her ever since that Publishers and Author have felt encouraged to prepare a new volume in which will be found the story of those years that have carried Elsie on from childhood to womanhood—the years in which her character was developing, the

Elsie spent the morning in Mrs. Travilla's room. . . . ■
(From *Elsie Dinsmore* by Martha Finley.)

(From *Mildred Keith* by Martha Finley.)

mind and body were growing and strengthening for the real work and battle of life.

"May my readers who have admired and loved her as a child find her still more charming in her fresh young girlhood; may she prove to all a pleasant companion and friend; and to those of them now treading the same portion of life's pathway a useful example also, particularly in her filial love and obedience." [Martha Finley, Preface to *Elsie's Girlhood*, Dodd, 1879.¹]

Finley introduced some strong statements into her books—strong in the light of the times during which they were written. She regarded slavery as unforgivable; war as evil; and women as oppressed in the business and political arenas. The only salvation to Finley's reasoning was fundamental application of the Protestant faith.

In **1875,** she wrote in the preface to *Elsie's Womanhood:* "The call for a sequel to *Elsie's Girlhood* having become too loud and importunate to be resisted, the pleasant task of writing it was undertaken.

"Dates compelled the bringing in of the late war: and it has been the earnest desire and effort of the author to so treat the subject as to wound the feelings of none; to be as impartial as if writing history; and, by drawing a true, though alas, but faint picture, of the great losses and sufferings on both sides, to make the very thought of a renewal of the awful strife *utterly*

abhorrent to every lover of humanity, and especially of this, our own dear native land.

"Are we not one people: speaking the same language; worshipping the one true and living God; having a common history, a common ancestry; and united by the tenderest ties of blood? And is not this great grand, glorious old Union—known and respected all over the world—our common country, our joy and pride? O! let us forget all bitterness, and live henceforth in love, harmony, and mutual helpfulness.

"The description of Andersonville, and the life led by the prisoners there, was supplied by one who shared it for six months. An effort was made to obtain a sketch of a Northern prison also, but without success.

"Yet what need to balance accounts in respect to these matters? The unnatural strife is over, and we are again one united people." [Martha Finley, Preface to *Elsie's Womanhood,* Dodd, 1875.²]

These were the first books in a series of twenty-eight. For the most part, Finley was ignored by contemporary critics and by such popular children's magazines as *St. Nicholas* and *Youth's Companion.* She was extremely popular and successful among her readership, however. Each of her Elsie Dinsmore books was bound in blue or red and had a pansy embossed on the cover. At the peak of her popularity, her books are estimated to have been read by twenty-five million readers on both sides of the Atlantic and to have earned her close to a quarter of a million dollars.

"It will not hurt you *now,*" he said, "it is dead; the men killed it this morning in the meadow. Now do you see why I forbid you to go there?" ■ (From *Elsie Dinsmore* by Martha Farquharson. Illustrated by Fay and Cox.)

Enjoying such financial success, Finley moved to Elkton, Cecil County, Md. She had built a cottage in a pleasant section of that town near her half brother, Charles Finley, of whom she was particularly fond. The rest of her family harrassed her continuously about what they considered the frivolity of writing fiction. Perhaps, as a consequence, Finley became a recluse in her home. Recalled Joseph Grant, who as a young boy helped to deliver milk to the Finley home, "Whenever you went to her house you never saw her. A servant always came to the door instead." [Claudine Wirths, "'Ms.' Elsie Dinsmore," *Maryland Magazine,* winter, 1979.[3]]

In **1893** the *Ladies' Home Journal* wrote: "She has kept her personality so completely hidden from a curious public that it is almost as an entire stranger to her readers that the *Ladies' Home Journal* is able to present Miss Martha Finley." The magazine went on, praising her "bright and cheerful disposition, her simple womanliness and Christianity . . . a type of the best in American spinsterhood."

In retrospect, however, Finley has not fared well. In 1972 the *Encyclopedia Americana* noted: "By far the most popular [of Finley's works] were the 28 'Elsie' books, published between 1867 and 1905. The obedient, pious, self-satisfied heroine, Elsie, was held up as a paragon of virtue by parents of the Victorian era. However, by modern standards, she would be considered an impossible prig." Changing times and standards have banished "Elsie Dinsmore" into obscurity. They could, however, be of extreme interest to the student of American culture.

She was an advocate of education for women. Her character "Elsie" announced that she was "not bringing up daughters to consider marriage as the chief end of woman."[3] Another of her characters is quoted as saying, "I'm the most unfortunate woman—the poorest in the whole country—I wasn't brought up to support myself."[3]

Initially her publisher refused to grant Finley the copyright to her "Elsie" books, forcing her to go to court to claim them.

January 30, 1909. Died of bronchopneumonia at her home in Elkton, Md. According to the Presbyterian Church record in Elkton, Martha Finley "fell sweetly asleep in Jesus."[3] She is buried in the Finley family plot in the town cemetery, her grave marked by an imposing monument.

Besides her books, one of the most revealing documents on Finley is her will, filed in the Country Court House in Elkton. Under the terms of the will she left most of her money and possessions (considerable by the time of her death), to Charles and many of her female relatives—remembering especially her maid and friend, Mary White. She cancelled old family debts to her and even left her gardening tools to her sister-in-law. The list of contents of her home and possessions showed that she held ownership in a women's bakery in Chicago. It also reflected her blunt rejection of several members—perhaps the ones who disapproved of her writing.

The Elkton Library in Maryland has a small section dedicated to Martha Finley and her works.

FOR MORE INFORMATION SEE: Bookman, March, 1909, January, 1926, October, 1927; William A. Newman Dorland, *The Sum of Feminine Achievement,* Stratford, 1917; Josie Turner, *Elsie Dinsmore on the Loose,* J. Cape and H. Smith, 1930; *Publishers Weekly,* December 31, 1932; *New Yorker,* March 14, 1936; Edward M. Dodd, Jr., *The First Hundred Years,* Dodd, 1939; *University of Buffalo Studies,* Volume XVII, number 3, 1945; Stanley Kunitz and Howard Haycraft, *American Authors, 1600-1900,* H. W. Wilson, 1938; Helen Waite Papashvily, *All the Happy Endings,* Harper, 1956; Edward T. James, and others, editors, *Notable American Women: 1607-1950,* Volume I, A-F, Belknap Press, 1971. Obituaries: *Baltimore Sun,* January 31, 1909; *New York Times,* January 31, 1909; *Cecil Democrat* (Maryland), February 6, 1909.

FRIEDMAN, Frieda 1905-

PERSONAL: Born in 1905, in Syracuse, New York. *Education:* New York University, B.S.; graduate study at Columbia University and New York University. *Home:* New York City.

CAREER: Author of books for children. Worked for several magazines and newspapers, including the New York *American.* Wrote greeting-card verse for Norcross, beginning 1930, and has since become editor. *Awards, honors: Dot for Short, A Sundae with Judy,* and *The Janitor's Girl* received honorable mention in the *New York Herald Tribune* Spring Book Festivals, 1947, 1949, and 1956.

WRITINGS: Peppy, the Lonely Little Puppy (illustrated by Vivienne Blake), Rand McNally, 1947; *Dot for Short* (illustrated by Carolyn Haywood), Morrow, 1947, reprinted, Buccaneer Books, 1981; *Make Believe* (illustrated by Valeria Patterson), J. Martin, 1948; *A Sundae with Judy* (illustrated by C. Haywood), Morrow, 1949; *Carol from the Country* (illustrated by Mary Barton), Morrow, 1950; *Pat and Her Policeman* (illustrated by M. Barton), Morrow, 1953; *The Janitor's Girl* (illustrated by Mary Stevens), Morrow, 1956; *Bobbie Had a Nickel,* S. Lowe, 1959; *Ellen and the Gang* (illustrated by Jacqueline Tomes), Morrow, 1963; *Now That You Are 10* (illustrated by Leonard Shortall), Association Press, 1963.

FRIEDA FRIEDMAN

She had better turn right around and go home before they saw her. Everyone, it seemed, had someone to talk to except herself. ■ (From *The Janitor's Girl* by Frieda Friedman. Illustrated by Mary Stevens.)

FOR MORE INFORMATION SEE: Muriel Fullcr, editor, *More Junior Authors,* H. W. Wilson, 1963.

FUCHSHUBER, Annegert   1940-

PERSONAL: Surname is pronounced "fooks-hoober"; born May 5, 1940, in Magdeburg, Germany; daughter of Friedrich (an architect) and Marianne (Bindseil) Weber; married Dieter Fuchshuber (a city administrator), May 27, 1963; children: Gregor, Markus, Kathrin. *Education:* Attended School of Arts, Augsburg, Germany. *Religion:* Catholic. *Home:* Breitwiesenstrasse 40A, D-8900, Augsburg 21, Germany.

CAREER: Dorland (advertising agency), Munich, Germany, designer, 1962-64; free-lance author and illustrator of books for children, 1965—. *Awards, honors: Fidibus* was selected as one of the fifty most beautiful books in Germany, 1981; *Mäusemärchen* was selected as one of the fifty most beautiful books in Germany, 1983, and received the Deutsches Jugendliteraturpreis, 1984.

WRITINGS—Selected works; all for children; all self-illustrated: *Der allerschönste Stern der Welt,* Annette Betz, 1969, translation published as *Most Beautiful Star in the World,* Merry Thoughts, 19(?); *Miezekatze,* Kaufman, 1970, translation published as *Pussy Cat, Pussy Cat* (nursery rhymes), Methuen (London), 1973; (with Lene Hille-Brandt) *Das boeckchen im roeckchen* (title means "The Fawn in the Skirt"), A. Betz, 1972; *Das land in der seifenblase* (title means "The Land in the Soap Bubble"), A. Betz, 1974; *Tiere der urwelt,* Sellier, 1974, translation published as *From Dinosaurs to Fossils,* Carolrhoda, 1981; *Korbinian mit dem wunschhut,* Thienemanns, 1976, translation by Elizabeth D. Crawford published as *The Wishing Hat,* Morrow, 1977; *Vom bombarden,* Thienemanns, 1977, translation by Gwen Marsh published as *Henry and the Bombardon,* Dent, 1977; *Fidibus,* Thienemanns, 1980, translation by G. Marsh published as *The Joker and the Lion,* Dent, 1981; *Mäusemärchen: Riesengeschichte,* Thienemanns, 1983, translation by G. Marsh published as *A Mouse Tale: A Giant Story,* Dent, 1984.

Illustrator; selected works; all for children: Michael Ende, *Das Traumfresserchen,* Thienemanns, 1978, translation by G. Marsh published as *The Dream-Eater,* Dent, 1978; Hans Baumann, *Ein stern fuer alle* (title means "A Star for Everyone"), Deutscher Taschenbuch Verlag, 1978; Josef Guggenmos, *Das und dies* (title means "This and That"), Georg Bitter, 1980; Gertrud Fussenegger, *Die Arche Noah,* Annette Betz, 1982, translation by Anthea Bell published as *Noah's Ark,* Hodder & Stoughton, 1983; Barbara Bartos-Höppner, *Der Rattenfänger von Hameln,* Annette Betz, 1984, translation by A. Bell published as *The Pied Piper of Hamlin,* Hodder & Stoughton, 1985; Beatrice Schenk deRegniers, *Ich habe einen freund* (title

ANNEGERT FUCHSHUBER

When Korbinian got dressed on Tuesday morning, he saw to his great annoyance that his left sock had a hole in it again. ■ (From *The Wishing Hat* by Annegert Fuchshuber. Illustrated by the author.)

means ''I Have a Friend''), Otto Maier, 1985. Author and/or illustrator of over seventy additional books for children in German.

WORK IN PROGRESS: Several books for children.

SIDELIGHTS: Fuchshuber's daily discipline is to spend time at her desk writing or illustrating every morning, again in the evening, but only if household chores and her family life permit. ''My family will not suffer because of my career.'' She feels strongly that ''children have a right to good books.''

GARDNER, Robert   1929-

BRIEF ENTRY: Born in 1929. As an author of nonfiction for middle-grade and high-school readers, Gardner brings to his writing a science teaching background. He has written nearly a dozen books that explore facets of the scientific world, from the phenomenon of shadows to the mechanisms of machinery to different species of whales. Several of these books are interspersed with experiments, puzzles, and games, designed not only to spark reader interest but reader participation as well. *Shadow Science* (Doubleday, 1976) contains over one hundred black-and-white photographs through which Gardner and co-author David Webster explore the cause and effect of shadows. Readers are asked to identify the object casting the shadow or pinpoint the time of day. *Horn Book* called it "a beautiful combination of photographic problems . . . and suggested activities." Likewise, in *Kitchen Chemistry: Science Experiments to Do at Home* (Messner, 1982), familiar objects become part of methodology as readers are led through a series of experiments that reveal basic scientific principles. "An excellent choice," stated *School Library Journal*, "for children who want to find out 'why' or 'how'—and then do it themselves."

Other books by Gardner involving "reader participation" include *Moving Right Along: A Book of Science Experiments and Puzzlers about Motion* (Doubleday, 1978), also written with Webster; *Magic Through Science* (Doubleday, 1978), an exploration of optical illusions and the science of light; *Save That Energy* (Messner, 1981), filled with ideas on how to conserve electricity, heat, and gas; and *Water: The Life Sustaining Resource* (Messner, 1982), a thorough look at one of life's most necessary elements. Gardner does not always require active response from his readers. His other books are also clear, concise studies of their particular topics, such as *This Is the Way It Works: A Collection of Machines* (Doubleday, 1980), *Space: Frontier of the Future* (Doubleday, 1981), and *The Whale Watchers' Guide* (Messner, 1984).

FOR MORE INFORMATION SEE: Authors of Books for Young People, supplement to the second edition, Scarecrow, 1979.

GORSLINE, Douglas (Warner)   1913-1985

OBITUARY NOTICE—See sketch in *SATA* Volume 11: Born May 24, 1913, in Rochester, N.Y.; died of a stroke, June 25 (another source cites June 26), 1985, in Dijon, France. Artist, illustrator, and writer. Interested in art from childhood, Gorsline studied at the Yale School of Fine Arts and the Art Students League. About 1944 he began working in commercial art and illustrating books for a number of publishers. He wrote and illustrated two books: *Farm Boy*, a young adult novel that was chosen a Spring Book Festival honor book in 1950, and a history of costume entitled *What People Wore*. Among the more than two dozen books Gorsline illustrated were Florence W. Rowland's *Jade Dragons*, Clyde R. Bulla's *Viking Adventure*, and Ferdinand Monjo's *Me and Willie and Pa: A Story of Abraham Lincoln and His Son Tad*. His work has also appeared in periodicals like the *New Yorker, Sports Illustrated, American Heritage*, and *Horizon*. In 1973 Gorsline became the first American artist to receive an invitation from the People's Republic of China to visit that country and paint whatever he wished. He received numerous awards throughout his career, and his oil and watercolor works are represented in many private and public collections.

FOR MORE INFORMATION SEE: American Artist, May, 1966; *Contemporary Authors, New Revision Series,* Volume 9, Gale, 1983; *Who's Who in American Art,* 16th edition, Bowker, 1984. Obituaries: *Rochester (New York) Democrat and Chronicle,* June 28, 1985; *New York Times,* July 10, 1985.

GOULD, Chester   1900-1985

OBITUARY NOTICE: Born November 20, 1900, in Pawnee, Okla.; died of congestive heart failure, May 11, 1985, in Woodstock, Ill. Cartoonist and creator of the comic strip "Dick Tracy." Gould's hard-nosed detective made his first appearance in the October 4, 1931 edition of the now-defunct *Detroit Daily Mirror*. The comic strip grew in popularity until, by the late 1950s, it was syndicated in over 500 newspapers worldwide. Tracy was the result of Gould's fascination with J. Edgar Hoover's G-men and Prohibition-era gangsters like Al Capone. The cartoonist conceived and drew the strip until his retirement in 1977, when the task was taken over by other artists. Through the years, Gould became known for his use of graphic violence as the plainclothes detective brought to justice villains like Flattop, the Mole, Pruneface, and the Brow.

Gould also gained a reputation for the extensive research and innovativeness that went into his stories. His strip often featured technology not yet in public use, such as the two-way wrist radio and closed circuit television to monitor criminals, both of which were used by Tracy in the late 1940s. Gould received numerous awards throughout his career, including two Reuben Awards from the National Cartoonists Society, an Edgar Award from Mystery Writers of America, and accolades from law enforcement agencies and police departments. In addition to the strip, Tracy appeared in book form under titles like *Dick Tracy and Dick Tracy, Jr., and How They Captured "Stooge" Viller, Dick Tracy Meets the Night Crawler*, and *The Celebrated Cases of Dick Tracy, 1931-1951*.

FOR MORE INFORMATION SEE: Current Biography Yearbook, H. W. Wilson, 1972; *The World Encyclopedia of Comics,* Volume 1, Chelsea House, 1976; *Contemporary Authors,* Volumes 77-80, Gale, 1979; *Who's Who in America,* 43rd edition, Bowker, 1984. Obituaries: *Chicago Tribune,* May 12, 1985, May 13, 1985; *Los Angeles Times,* May 12, 1985; *New York Times,* May 12, 1985; *Times* (London), May 14, 1985; *Facts on File,* May 17, 1985; *Newsweek,* May 20, 1985; *Time,* May 20, 1985; *Current Biography,* July, 1985.

GREENBERG, Polly   1932-

BRIEF ENTRY: Born April 21, 1932, in Milwaukee, Wis. An author of books for children and adults, Greenberg graduated from Sarah Lawrence College and received her M.Ed. from the University of Delaware in 1957. In the mid-1960s she founded the Child Development Group of Mississippi, a Head Start program that became the topic of her book entitled *The Devil Has Slippery Shoes* (Macmillan, 1969). During the 1970s she held positions with the General Learning Corp. as well as Human Service Group; in 1977 she became a staff member of the U.S. Department of Health, Education, and Welfare. Greenberg's first book for children, *Oh Lord, I Wish I Was a Buzzard* (Macmillan, 1968), has remained in print for over fifteen years. Accompanied with illustrations by Aliki, this simple story of a small Black girl picking cotton was described by *Bulletin of the Center for Children's Books* as having "warmth" and "rhythmic appeal." Her more recent children's works include *I Know I'm Myself Because . . .* (Human Services Press, 1981), a book on self-perception, and *Birds of the World* (Platt & Munk, 1983). Throughout her writing career, Greenberg has produced several books of special interest to parents. These include *Day Care Do-It-Yourself Staff Growth Program* (Kaplan Press, 1975), *How to Convert the Kids from What They Eat to What They Oughta* (Kaplan Press, 1978), and *Changes and Challenges: Our Children's Future* (Pergamon, 1979). *Home:* 4914 Ashby St., Washington, D.C. 20007.

FOR MORE INFORMATION SEE: Authors of Books for Young People, supplement to the second edition, Scarecrow, 1979; *Contemporary Authors,* Volumes 85-88, Gale, 1980.

GRIMM, Cherry Barbara Lockett 1930-
(Cherry Wilder)

BRIEF ENTRY: Born September 3, 1930, in Auckland, New Zealand. Author of science fiction for young adults. From 1954 to 1976 Grimm lived in Australia where she worked variously as a theater director, high school teacher, editorial assistant, and film librarian; in 1976 she and her husband moved to West Germany. Critics agree that Grimm's novels, all written under the pseudonym Cherry Wilder, are for "confirmed fantasy readers," describing her work as "demanding but rewarding" and "difficult but worth exploring." With the publication of her first novel, *The Luck of Brin's Five* (Atheneum, 1977), she was welcomed by *Publishers Weekly* as "a newcomer to SF, [who] writes gracefully. . . . [and] handles a large cast and strange locales expertly, to deliver a suspenseful entertainment." The fantasy is set on the planet Torin and features marsupial humanoids known as Moruians who, aside from the fact that they nurture their young in pouches, very much resemble their Earthling counterparts. Action centers around Scott Gale, a human whose vessel crashes on Torin. *Horn Book* observed that, more so than the plot, "it is the extraordinary intricacy of the society which gives the novel its fascination." *The Luck of Brin's Five* was followed by two sequels, *The Nearest Fire* (Atheneum, 1980) and *The Tapestry Warriors* (Atheneum, 1983).

Prior to the publication of the third book in her "Torin" trilogy, Grimm wrote *Second Nature* (Pocket/Timescape, 1982), in which the descendants of a shipwrecked expedition anticipate the arrival of other humans after two centuries in isolation. *Booklist* called it "a little gem . . . with a wealth of convincing detail and good characterization." Grimm has completed two volumes of a planned second trilogy, "The Rulers of Hylor." Comparing this series with her earlier "Torin" trilogy, *Horn Book* observed: "Although nomenclature and linguistic form echo those of medieval European legend, the political and social institutions of the diverse peoples are realized with the [same] extraordinary richness of invention." The two books, set in the same world, differ from each other in tone. *Booklist* called *A Princess of the Chameln* (Atheneum, 1984) an "enthralling and romantic" story, while *School Library Journal* viewed *Yorath the Wolf* (Atheneum, 1984) as "earthy" with a "vivid and gutsy quality." *Home:* 16-B Egelsbacherstrasse, Langen 6070, Hessen, West Germany.

FOR MORE INFORMATION SEE: Contemporary Authors, Volume 101, Gale, 1981; *The Writers Directory: 1984-1986,* St. James Press, 1983.

GROSS, Alan 1947-

BRIEF ENTRY: Born June 29, 1947, in Chicago, Ill. Playwright and author of books for children. From 1969 to 1977 Gross was employed as a writer and creative director in advertising; he later worked as a teacher and actor. His three books for children, all published by Children's Press, deal with fears inherent in many preschool and primary-grade readers. *Sometimes I Worry* (1978) contains, according to *School Library Journal,* "all sorts of conceivable ('What if nobody picks me for their team?') and inconceivable ('What if I swallow my gum and a great big gum tree grows in my stomach?') happenings." Likewise, *What If the Teacher Calls on Me?* (1980) offers comfort to children who panic at the thought of answering in class. For those children who believe that staying home is preferable to going to school, Gross provides an idea of what they would be missing in *The I Don't Want to Go to School Book* (1982). Gross was the recipient of two Joseph Jefferson Awards in 1978 for his play "Lunching," produced on Broadway in 1979. He also wrote "Phone Room," a 1978 finalist in the O'Neill Festival National Playwrights Conference, and "The Man in 605." *Agent:* William Morris Agency, 1350 Avenue of the Americas, New York, N.Y. 10019.

FOR MORE INFORMATION SEE: Contemporary Authors, Volumes 89-92, Gale, 1980.

GUTMAN, Bill

BRIEF ENTRY: Born in New York, N.Y. Author of nonfiction for young adults. Although Gutman entered Washington College with intentions of becoming a dentist, he graduated in 1965 with a B.A. in English literature. After a year of graduate study at the University of Bridgeport, he joined the staff of the *Greenwich Time* in Connecticut as a reporter and feature writer, and eventually became the newspaper's sports editor. Following a brief stint in advertising, Gutman decided to devote all his time to writing. A prolific writer, he has produced over fifty books on the subject of sports. These books include overviews of a variety of sports (baseball, football, basketball, soccer) as well as individual looks at the players (Aaron, Csonka, Maravich, Pelé).

Due to the high young adult interest in his subject matter, many of Gutman's works are useful aids in dealing with reluctant readers of that age group. As a reviewer for *School Library Journal* observed: "Gutman knows his audience, and his straight-forward, no-nonsense prose coupled with an abundance of game action and statistics is sure to prove popular." Among his titles are *Pistol Pete Maravich: The Making of a Basketball Superstar* (Grosset, 1972), *New Breed Heroes of Pro Football* (Messner, 1973), *O. J.* (Grosset, 1974), *Modern Hockey Superstars* (Dodd, 1976), *Modern Women Superstars* (Dodd, 1977), and *The Signal Callers: Sipe, Jaworski, Ferguson, Bartkowski* (Grosset, 1981). Several of Gutman's books digress from the sports genre. These include the biography *Duke: The Musical Life of Duke Ellington* (Random House, 1977) and *Women Who Work with Animals* (Dodd, 1982), profiles of six women in animal-related, male-dominated fields of work.

FOR MORE INFORMATION SEE: Authors of Books for Young People, supplement to the second edition, Scarecrow, 1979.

Children are the keys of Paradise.
—Richard Henry Stoddard

CAROLYN BUHAI HAAS

HAAS, Carolyn Buhai 1926-

PERSONAL: Born January 1, 1926, in Chicago, Ill.; daughter of Michael (a manufacturer) and Tillie (a social worker; maiden name, Weiss) Buhai; married Robert G. Haas (an advertising executive), June 29, 1947; children: Andrew, Mari, Betsy, Thomas, Karen. *Education:* Smith College, B.Ed., 1947; graduate study at National College of Education, Art Institute of Chicago, and Froebl Teachers College, 1957-59. *Politics:* Democrat. *Religion:* Jewish. *Home:* 400 East Ohio St., Chicago, Ill. 60011. *Agent:* Marilyn Marlow, Curtis Brown Ltd., 575 Madison Ave., New York, N.Y. 10022. *Office:* CBH Publishing, Inc., Box 236, Glencoe, Ill. 60022.

CAREER: Francis W. Parker School, Chicago, Ill., elementary school teacher, 1947-49; Glencoe Public Schools, Glencoe, Ill., art teacher, 1968-69; Parents As Resources Project, Northfield, Ill., co-founder and partner, 1970-82. Member of LWV of Glencoe, Glencoe PTA (West School, chairman, 1957-59), board of directors of Glencoe Family Counseling Service, Glencoe Human Relations Committee, Friends of Glencoe Public Library (president, 1981-83), Illinois Committee for Child Abuse, and Glencoe Patriotic Days Committee. Co-founder of Glencoe Art Fair. *Member:* American Jewish Committee (member of national board), Scholarship and Guidance Association (Chicago), Children's Reading Roundtable, Society of Children's Authors and Artists, Smith College Club of Chicago (president, 1972-74; member of board).

WRITINGS: (With Ann Cole and Betty Kiralfy Weinberger) *Recipes for Fun* (juvenile), seven volumes, Parents As Resources Project, 1970-78, revised edition published as *Recipes for Fun and Learning: Creative Learning Activities for Young Children* (illustrated by Jane B. Phillips), CBH Publishing, 1982; (with Faith Bushnell, A. Cole, and B. K. Weinberger) *I Saw a Purple Cow and One Hundred Other Recipes for Learning* (juvenile; illustrated by True Kelley), Little, Brown, 1972; (with Elizabeth Heller, A. Cole, and B. K. Weinberger) *A Pumpkin in a Pear Tree: Creative Ideas for Twelve Months of Holiday Fun* (juvenile), Little, Brown, 1976; (with A. Cole, E. Heller, and B. K. Weinberger) *Children Are Children Are*

Children: An Activity Approach to Exploring Brazil, France, Iran, Japan, Nigeria, and the U.S.S.R., Little, Brown, 1978.

(With A. Cole and Barbara Naftzger) *Backyard Vacation: Outdoor Fun in Your Own Neighborhood,* (juvenile; illustrated by Roland Rodegast), Little, Brown, 1980; *The Big Book of Recipes for Fun: Creative Learning Activities for Home and School* (illustrated by Jane B. Phillips), CBH Publishing, 1980; (with A. Cole, B. K. Weinberger, and F. Bushnell) *Purple Cow to the Rescue* (activities manual; illustrated by True Kelley), Little, Brown, 1982; *Look at Me: Activities for Babies and Toddlers,* CBH Publishing, 1985.

Co-author of "Recipes for Fun," a newspaper column, syndicated by the *Des Moines Register and Tribune,* 1972-77. Contributor to education journals and magazines for parents, including *McCall's, Parenting, Parents' Magazine, Day Care and Early Education, Teacher,* and *Instructor Magazine.* Consultant to WTTW-TV's series "Look at Me!," 1974-76, and 1978-79. Member of editorial board, *My Own Magazine,* 1985.

WORK IN PROGRESS: Parents and Reading in collaboration with Ellen De Franco.

SIDELIGHTS: "I think I have been writing and illustrating books all of my life. Perhaps my earliest recollections are: making up stories to tell to my younger sister; passing notes to my friends when I was bored in school; drawing paper doll outfits; and during one entire year, making hundreds of chalk faces.

"My writing 'career' really started in sixth grade when I was chosen to be editor of the school newspaper. Later, I served as secretary of my eighth grade student council and had to learn to take minutes. In college, I worked (for money!) for the Press Board (first as a file clerk at *50 cents* an hour), and later as college correspondent to a nearby newspaper.

"English was always one of my best subjects: In fact, since I attended a progressive school in Winnetka, Illinois, where we were allowed to proceed individually at our own pace through a series of 'goals,' I had completed seventh grade grammar before ever entering junior high and was thereby allowed to take an 'elective' instead of the regular English course. This turned out to be puppetry, a skill that has stood me in good stead ever since. I also took an art course that year where I learned all about mixing colors, light and shadow, and drawing well-spaced alphabet letters (for headlines, and so forth). I never did learn cursive writing, but taught myself to do it out of a third grade workbook.

"During the two years following college when I taught elementary school, I had many opportunities to help children write. My rule was, 'be as positive as you can, don't put too many red marks on the papers—be critical, but always helpful.' Even back then, I drew smiley faces on the papers!

"For many years while I was raising my own children, my writing consisted of doing publicity for various groups. I seem to have a knack for writing a clear, concise news story. That still is my greatest writing strength—rewriting and editing what others write.

"The business of writing takes a lot of thinking, organizing and rewriting (sometimes five and six times) and patience. The real joy comes in those rare moments of spontaneity when one can sit down and scrawl out some thoughts—or better still, type reams of them. (Which *sometimes* happens, but not often.)

An outdoor fashion show featuring outfits from bygone days is another great way to get the generation together.... ■ (From *Backyard Vacation: Outdoor Fun in Your Own Neighborhood* by Carolyn Haas, Ann Cole, and Barbara Naftzger. Illustrated by Roland Rodegast.)

Since 1984 I have been lucky enough to own a word processor, which really is a tremendous asset.

"I have a large 'failure,' and that is being a very slow reader. But, perhaps that's why I can proofread and catch mistakes.

"Up until several years ago I worked with co-authors which involved lots of ideas and brainstorming. Four heads are usually better than one, but everyone must compromise. *The Big Book of Recipes For Fun,* which I wrote and published myself, was *my* responsibility and I must admit, I enjoyed not having to ask other people's advice and doing my *own* thing.

"With the Little, Brown books, there was much less control. After the first draft of the manuscript is sent off to them, four or five months elapse before an 'edited' copy is sent back, full of red pencilled spelling, punctuation and grammar changes, as well as cryptic notes from our editor, saying things like 'clarify this,' 'I would delete that,' 'Too sweet-ugh!' 'What is your source?' 'I never heard of that game,' and so forth. Then follows several feverish days (and nights) of rewriting, deleting, adding new information, etc., retyping of some parts, and finally a finished manuscript. Then working with an illustrator, followed by checking galley proofs. Finally the big day—a real book! The final copy is always full of surprises and looks different than you had imagined—usually better, but not always.

"I am always asked where I get my ideas. The answer is simple: *everywhere.* From my childhood memories of games, projects, art activities, trips, and so forth; from my children and their friends; fellow teachers, magazine and newspaper articles and other books and resources. I like to take bits and pieces of ideas, expand them, build on themes and write them in my own particular style.

"It's rather a challenge to take a commonplace activity, like play dough, and turn it into a 'Fun Dough Restaurant.' Or make up a math game from boxes, egg carton cups and marking pens (Lady Bug House).

"And food recipes—there are so many new, healthier items on the market now. Finding simple, yet nutritious recipes is a special pleasure (even though I myself am not a very inventive cook).

"Perhaps the most satisfying moments of all are when perfect strangers come up to you and start raving about your books and ask for your autograph! When mom's books are assigned to your own child, who's studying early childhood—that's the biggest thrill of all!"

HOBBIES AND OTHER INTERESTS: Art, sports, reading, old books, theater, music, travel, and especially "my grandchildren."

FOR MORE INFORMATION SEE: Small Publishers of the Chicago Area, Chicago Review Press, revised edition, 1984.

If we work upon marble, it will perish; if we work upon brass, time will efface it; if we rear temples, they will crumble into dust; but if we work upon immortal minds, if we imbue them with principles, with the just fear of God and love of our fellowmen, we engrave on those tablets something which will brighten to all eternity.

—Daniel Webster

HAAS, Dorothy F.
(Dee Francis)

BRIEF ENTRY: Born June 17, in Racine, Wis. Editor and author of books for children, and lecturer. Currently senior editor of books for children and young adults at Rand McNally in Skokie, Ill., Haas began her publishing career in 1955 at the Whitman Publishing Division of Western Publishing in Racine. She later worked for Worldbook Childcraft before joining the staff of Rand McNally in 1970. Haas is the editor of the series "Tween-Age Books," "Tell-a-Tale Books," "Big Tell-a-Tale Books," and "Tiny Tot Tales" as well as the author of more than twenty-five stories for children. Among her titles (all published by Whitman) are *Little Joe's Puppy* (1957), *Oh, Look!* (1961), *Grandpapa and Me* (1966), *Poppy and the Outdoors Cat* (1980), and *Tink in a Tangle* (1985).

Several of Haas's books are original stories based on television or movie series, such as *Captain Kangaroo and the Too-Small House* (1958), *Quick Draw McGraw: Badmen Beware* (1960), and *Tom and Jerry: Goody Go-Round* (1967). Under the pseudonym Dee Francis, she has also written book adaptations of movie scripts like *Pinocchio, Babes in Toyland,* and *The Sword in the Stone.* Although her stories are intended for primary-grade readers, Haas produced a novel for older children entitled *The Bears Upstairs* (Greenwillow, 1978). *Publishers Weekly* called it "an enchanting fantasy . . . a perfect balance of excitement, suspense, pathos, [and] comedy." In recognition of her long-term commitment to children's books, Haas was the recipient of the 1979 Children's Reading Round Table Award. *Home:* 336 West Wellington Ave., Chicago, Ill. 60657.

FOR MORE INFORMATION SEE: Contemporary Authors, New Revision Series, Volume 3, Gale, 1981; *Who's Who of American Women,* 13th edition, Marquis, 1983.

HALEY, Gail E(inhart)   1939-

PERSONAL: Born November 4, 1939, in Charlotte, N.C.; daughter of George C. (an advertising manager and artist) and P. Louise (an artist; maiden name, Bell) Einhart; married Joseph A. Haley (a mathematician), August 15, 1959; married second husband, Arnold F. Arnold (a designer, writer, and artist), February 14, 1966; married third husband, David Considine (a professor of mass media), September 3, 1983; children: Marguerite Madeline, Geoffrey David. *Education:* Attended Richmond Professional Institute, 1957-59, and University of Virginia, 1960-64. *Agent:* Curtis Brown Ltd., 575 Madison Ave., New York, N.Y. 10022. *Office:* Edwin Duncan Hall, Appalachian State University, Boone, N.C. 28608.

CAREER: Manuscript Press, New York, N.Y., vice-president, beginning 1965; Appalachian State University, Boone, N.C., currently writer-in-residence and curator of Gail Hailey Collection of the Culture of Childhood. Artist, author and illustrator of children's books and educational material, and designer of toys and fashion items. Graphics and illustrations exhibited at libraries and museums in southern states and New York. Work included in permanent collections at the University of Minnesota, Jacksonville (Fla.) Children's Museum, University of Southern Mississippi, and Appalachian State University. Toured Great Britain in one-woman multimedia show "Get into a Book."

AWARDS, HONORS: Boston Globe-Horn Book honor award for illustration, 1970, and Caldecott Medal, American Library

Association, 1971, both for *A Story, a Story;* Czechoslovak Children's Film Festival Award for best animated children's film of the year, 1974; Kate Greenaway Medal for illustration, British Library Association, 1977, and Kadai Tosho award (Japan), both for *The Post Office Cat;* Parents Choice Award for illustration, 1980, for *The Green Man; Birdsong* was a children's choice selection by The Children's Book Council, 1984.

WRITINGS—All self-illustrated: *My Kingdom for a Dragon,* Crozet Print Shop, 1962; *The Wonderful Magical World of Marguerite: With the Entire Cast of Characters Including Rocks, Roses, Mushrooms, Daisies, Violets, Snails, Butterflies, Breezes, and Above All—the Sun,* McGraw, 1964; *Round Stories about Things That Live on Land,* Follett, 1966; *Round Stories about Things That Live in Water,* Follett, 1966; *Round Stories about Things That Grow,* Follett, 1966; *Round Stories about Our World,* Follett, 1966.

(Reteller) *A Story, a Story: An African Tale* (ALA Notable Book), Atheneum, 1970; *Noah's Ark* (Junior Literary Guild selection), Atheneum, 1971; *Jack Jouett's Ride,* Viking, 1973; *The Abominable Swampman,* Viking, 1975; *The Post Office Cat,* Scribner, 1976; *Go Away, Stay Away!,* Scribner, 1977; *Costumes for Plays and Playing,* Methuen, 1978; *A Story, a Day,* Methuen, 1979; *Gail Haley's Costume Book,* Magnet Books, Volume I: *Dress Up and Have Fun,* 1979, Volume II: *Dress Up and Play,* 1980; *The Green Man,* Scribner, 1980; *Birdsong,* Crown, 1984. Contributor of children's stories to magazines.

Filmstrip: (Author and narrator) "Wood and Linoleum Illustration," Weston Woods, 1978.

Illustrator: Francelia Butler, editor, *The Skip Rope Book,* Dial, 1962; *One, Two, Buckle My Shoe: A Book of Counting Rhymes,* Doubleday, 1964; James Holding, *The Three Wishes of Hu,* Putnam, 1965; Bernice Kohn, *Koalas,* Prentice-Hall, 1965; Solveig Russell, *Which Is Which?* (Junior Literary Guild selection), Prentice-Hall, 1966; Lois Wyse, *P.S., Happy Anniversary,* World Publishing, 1966; Hannah Rush, *The Peek-A-Boo Book of Puppies and Kittens,* T. Nelson, 1966; (with

GAIL E. HALEY

others) E. L. Konigsburg, *All Together, One at a Time,* Atheneum, 1971. Also illustrator of syndicated column, "Parents and Children," written by Arnold F. Arnold.

ADAPTATIONS: "A Story, a Story" (filmstrip), Weston Woods, 1972; "A Story, a Story" (animated film), Weston Woods, 1973; "Jack Jouett's Ride" (filmstrip), Weston Woods, 1975; "Jack Jouett's Ride" (animated filmstrip), Weston

"Oh, Father," Maria sobbed, **"a whole pail of milk has been spilled, and I have no idea how it happened. I only turned my back for a second."** ■ (From *Go Away, Stay Away!* by Gail E. Haley. Illustrated by the author.)

Woods, 1975; ''Taleb and His Lamb'' (film; based on *A Story, a Story*), Arthur Barr Productions, 1975; ''Go Away, Stay Away'' (filmstrip), Weston Woods, 1978.

WORK IN PROGRESS: Jack and the Beantree, for Crown; slide/tape program documenting the creation of *Jack and the Beantree; Our Circus* in collaboration with husband, David Considine.

SIDELIGHTS: **November 4, 1939.** Born in Charlotte, North Carolina, and raised in the old rural village of Shuffletown. ''I grew up, a barefoot child, in rural North Carolina. A mere twenty years ago I could meet raccoons, field mice, opossums, chipmunks, and other furry creatures on my rambles through woods and fields. I tamed lizards, befriended beetles, cared for farm animals—and watched them give birth, and rear and protect their young. I experienced daily the marvels and the balance of nature and felt myself a part of them.''

Haley has had a fascination with the written word ever since childhood. Her father was art director of the Charlotte *Observer,* and she used to visit him at the newspaper. Much of her time was spent writing and drawing, even during class time.

1960-1964. After attending Richmond Professional Institute, Haley studied graphics and painting at the University of Virginia. There artist-teacher Charles Smith encouraged her to write and illustrate a children's book, *My Kingdom for a Dragon.* Haley bound and sold most of the limited edition herself. ''More than a personal catharsis, my work is an effort designed to stimulate verbal and visual responses, and a preparation for literacy. My books are for children. They are also frames of reference for the story-reader who needs to dramatize, explain, and discuss the ideas I express, the pictures I draw, and the words I use. My object is to involve adult and child. Both are my collaborators. Telling stories and illustrating them is my invitation to children to join me in a world of fantasy I envision and to elaborate on what I present to them. My aim is not to manipulate children, but to encourage them to be active, imaginative, whimsical, and curious. These, more than fact gathering or rote memorization, are the specific appetites that lead to learning which is essential for human survival. Chief among such appetites is the hunger to read.'' [Gail E. Haley, ''Caldecott Award Acceptance,'' *Horn Book,* August, 1971.[1]]

1966. Married second husband, Arnold F. Arnold. Following their marriage, the couple spent a year in the Caribbean. Their Caribbean experiences led to Haley's research into the origins

There seemed to be something with glittering eyes and sharp horns near the mouth of the cave. ■
(From *The Green Man* by Gail E. Haley. Illustrated by the author.)

He crept through the tall grasses, sora, sora, sora, till he came to the nest of Mmboro, the hornets-who-sting-like-fire. ■ (From *A Story, a Story: An African Tale,* retold and illustrated by Gail E. Haley.)

of Caribbean folklore, which became the foundation for *A Story, a Story: An African Folktale.* "My interest in African folk tales stems in large part from the role they play in the education of children. The African storyteller, like the live reader of children's books, invites questions and he answers them. He adapts his tales to the understanding and experience of his audience, and he repeats or explains what is difficult. He is an imitable example. He is marvelously well informed and he has a prodigious memory. He recalls heroic deeds of whole dynasties of chiefs, back through three or more centuries. He is the keeper of the tribe's traditions, conscience, and identity. He is the poser of riddles and conundrums. He is the spontaneous teacher of the young. He chronicles the exploits of his contemporaries and he adds them to the stories that are memorized by his successors. He plays with the sound of language, and he weaves witticisms, sly barbs, and criticism of tribal members and chiefs into the fabric of the classic stories he tells. No two renditions of the same story are ever alike. Each evokes new contributions from his audience. The African folk tale and the modern children's book are very closely related."[1]

1970. Wrote and illustrated *A Story, a Story,* which won the Caldecott Medal the following year. "One of the frequent questions asked by librarians, teachers, and children . . . has been: 'What is it like to be a Caldecott winner?' They might as well ask: 'What is it like to become Miss America, a Nobel Laureate, or a winner of the Irish Sweepstakes?' Any of these are wildly happy surprises—frosting on the cake of life; but they also raise certain problems.

"The first reaction of a partner of the publishing house that produced *A Story, a Story* on learning that this book had won the award was: 'Now you know what it's like to be famous. Next you'll have to learn what it means not to be famous any more.' He set the tone for the emotional seesaw on which most award winners find themselves—feeling exhilarated and like a target in a shooting gallery.

"The most gratifying experiences resulting from winning this medal are purely professional. You know that your work will reach the largest possible audience of children; that you will be published and read and that you have the chance to remain productive for the rest of your life. You receive immediate feedback from large numbers of librarians, teachers, parents and children. Authorship and illustration are solitary occupations. The Caldecott Medal gives an artist many opportunities to be in direct contact with his or her audience.

"The celebration at the annual ALA meeting is a unique event in the life of an award-winning author. Aside from the weeks of preparation and speech writing, there's the dinner, an audience of more than two thousand eager faces, the long line of people who want their books autographed, and the publisher's breakfasts, lunches and suppers. It's a week-long 'high' without benefit of drugs. Then there's the inevitable anticlimax.

"It must be kept in mind that parallel to the hooplah run the mundane concerns of everyday life—husband, children, paying the bills, and doing your work. And so the many gratifications, obligations, and responsibilities connected with winning these awards must be viewed in context with the normal stresses of an author's life, especially if he or she has a family. Mine survived, but only just; and after considerable turmoil and heartache. This is due in no small measure to my husband's love and firm convictions that helped see us through the worst personal crises. There were also librarians and children whose faith and steadfast confidence gave me the courage to carry on.

"Professionally, there can be problems with academic sharpshooters who want the free right to include your work in their text books and to convert it to videotape. Winning the Caldecott Medal, especially in this day of reduced library budgets, rising production costs and a shrinking children's book market, is not the way to get rich. It does provide a small steady income after the first rush of sales and it gives you the opportunity to stay in print. But authorship is always speculative and risky. The initial and main investment is the author's own, and perhaps it is larger in proportion to the publisher's part, since he can spread his financial risk over many authors and books.

"Finally, there are the book critics, and I wonder whether all Caldecott winners have been subjected to a similar amount of carping.

"You survive this kind of thing—or you don't. I have survived. . . . Winning the Caldecott Medal is a beginning and not an end. I look back on it as a high point in my life, on a par with giving birth to my two beautiful children and to my books. I savor the experience and relive it every time I receive the first copy of each new book I write and illustrate."[1]

1971. *Noah's Ark* became a Junior Literary Guild selection. Haley wrote and illustrated the book to make children aware of the need to conserve natural resources. "The woods where the animals once lived have disappeared. The rivers no longer

support any life, and the countryside I knew is covered with shopping centers, developments, used-car lots, and garbage dumps. . . . I fear for . . . all our children, for the possibility that they may lose contact with themselves, with one another, and with nature. *Noah's Ark* is designed to make children conscious of what the continued despoliation may bring about.

"The Biblical tale of Noah, that certainly commemorates the ice age, is an ecological survival tale that recurs in almost every culture. Noah is everyman who, driven by his vision of what is to come, saves all he can and what he considers most valuable. My book shows children, in terms they can understand, that it is possible to foresee the probable, to cope with it, to act and to be active in the face of great odds. I hope that my rendition of Noah will encourage children to ask: What does extinct mean? Why didn't people listen to Noah? Why is the river brown and lifeless? And that parents, teachers, and children will be moved by this book to act on behalf of life in all its forms."

1974. The film version of *A Story, a Story* won the Czechoslovak Children's Film Festival Award.

Only the man who rode next to Edwardina was sad. He had two faces. One pointed forward; the other back. ■ (From *The Abominable Swamp Man* by Gail E. Haley. Illustrated by the author.)

1977. Awarded the Kate Greenaway Medal for *The Post Office Cat,* which brought Haley the distinction of being the only illustrator to win both the Caldecott and Greenaway Medals. "The leisurely daydreams of childhood, stimulated by stories and picture books, are not mere pastimes for children. Children expect, from babyhood onward, human and humane responses from everything with which they come into contact. And they need to be able to respond, actively and spontaneously, to people, animals, objects, and ideas. Seen in this light it becomes obvious that children need anthropomorphic fantasies for proper development. They make it possible for the child to interact with his world. Children live in a world in which they are 'so small, so small'—the smallest in the family. Most of their choices are made for them: what they will eat and wear and when they have to go to bed. Their earliest independence is gained only in fantasy. At first, these fantasies may be merely rebellious. But they help children learn to cope. Children's dreams allow them to come to terms with the necessary limitations on their freedom and impulses. Eventually, this sheer resistance to authority is displaced by idealized heroic yearnings. And these permit a child to try out who and what he would like to become. No one who learned to enjoy a rich, imaginative life in childhood need ever lose this faculty. As children mature, their fantasies are converted into ideals and into goals. Such children stand a good chance to turn longings into reality—at least in part. The exercise of a child's fantasies give him foresight and prepare him for a fearless and hopeful future.

"Yet, we seem determined to choke learning that is 'species specific' to human beings. Laughter, imaginative play, curiosity, self-expression, and language are among the skills that are peculiar to our kind. They cannot flourish unless our young practice them actively. And so the picture book, among other essential early learning experiences, is pitted against the lavishness of the motion, color, imagery, and sound of television—a presentation that makes no demand on the audience. But the picture book's esthetic economy is much more valuable for the child. It demands that he fill in the void between the peaks represented by succeeding spreads. He is required to make his own contribution."[1]

1984. Presentation of Haley's puppetry and children's theater at the Smithsonian Institute.

Gail Haley Collection of the Culture of Childhood established at Appalachian State University in Boone, N.C. The culture of childhood refers to the entire process by which children are socialized into adult society through both formal education and the informal education that they get through the games they play, the toys they are given, the books they read and the mass media that they are exposed to. Haley has been interested in this process for more than twenty years and has established a research collection that will enable people interested in children, their history, sociology and education, to further understand the impact of popular culture upon the young.

Haley teaches courses in puppetry, writing and illustrating for children, and related areas at Appalachian State University. Her works are included in the de Grummond Collection at the University of Southern Mississippi and the Kerlan Collection at the University of Minnesota.

FOR MORE INFORMATION SEE: New York Times Book Review, April 12, 1970, November 8, 1970; *Publishers Weekly,* February 22, 1971, September 6, 1971; *Top of the News,* April, 1971; *Horn Book,* August, 1971; Doris de Montreville and Donna Hill, editors, *Third Book of Junior Authors,* H. W. Wilson, 1973; *Charlotte* (N.C.) *Observer,* July 29, 1973; Lee

Kingman, editor, *Newbery and Caldecott Medal Books: 1966-1975,* Horn Book, 1975; Lee Kingman and others, compilers, *Illustrators of Children's Books: 1967-1976,* Horn Book, 1978; D. L. Kirkpatrick, *Twentieth-Century Children's Writers,* St. Martin's Press, 1978; *Language Arts,* November, 1984; *New York Times Book Review,* January, 1985.

HALL, Douglas　1931-

PERSONAL: Born July 23, 1931, in Doncaster, Yorkshire, England; son of Vincent and Louisa (Thorpe) Hall; married Dorothea Taylor (a textile designer and journalist), 1953; children: Jonathan, Alexander. *Education:* Attended Doncaster School of Art, 1946-49, Leeds College of Art, National Diploma in Design, 1949-51, and Royal College of Art, A.R.C.A. (Associate of the Royal College of Art), 1953-56. *Residence:* Tunbridge Wells, Kent, England. *Studio:* Waterside Workshops, 99 Rotherhithe St., London SE16 4NF, England.

CAREER: Illustrator of books for children and adults. *Awards, honors:* Book World's Spring Book Festival Honor Award, 1968, for *The Pit.*

WRITINGS: (Compiler) *Animal Nursery Rhymes* (self-illustrated), Hamlyn, 1983.

Illustrator: Lillian Beckwith, *The Sea for Breakfast,* Hutchinson, 1961; Doris Rybot, *My Kingdom for a Donkey,* Hutchinson, 1963; Barbara Willard, *Storm from the West* (*Horn Book* honor list), Harcourt, 1964; B. Willard, *Three and One to Carry,* Harcourt, 1965; John R. Townsend, *Widdershins Crescent,* Hutchinson, 1965; B. Willard, *Charity at Home,* Har-

Douglas Hall, self-portrait.

He smiled—at least he stretched his mouth in a gap-toothed grimace. ■ (From *Storm from the West* by Barbara Willard. Illustrated by Douglas Hall.)

court, 1966; Ronald Rideout, *English Workbooks for the Caribbean*, Ginn, 1966; (with wife, Dorothea Hall) Delia Huddy, *How Edward Saved St. George*, Delacorte, 1966; Margaret M. MacPherson, *The Rough Road* (ALA Notable Book; *Horn Book* honor list), Harcourt, 1966; J. R. Townsend, *Pirate's Island*, Oxford University Press, 1968; Reginald Maddock, *The Pit*, Little, Brown, 1968; L. Beckwith, *A Rope—In Case*, Hutchinson, 1968; Maurice Wiggen, *A Cottage Idyll*, T. Nelson, 1969; Winte, *The Fursedown Comet*, Hutchinson, 1970; L. Beckwith, *The Loud Halo*, F. A. Thorpe, 1970; L. Beckwith, *About My Father's Business*, Hutchinson, 1971; Stefanie Harwood, *The Country Mouse and the Town Mouse*, Hamlyn, 1971; Irene Makin, *Cry Wolf!*, Hutchinson, 1972; L. Beckwith, *Lightly Poached*, Hutchinson, 1973; Monica Vincent, *Musoke the Musician*, Oxford University Press, 1973; Ian Serraillier, *Pop Festival*, Longman, 1973.

L. Beckwith, *Beautiful Just!*, Hutchinson, 1975; Bette Meyrick, *Behind the Light*, Hutchinson, 1975; Clifford Carver, *The Broken Bridge*, Oxford University Press, 1975; Rosemary Haughton, *Moses*, Oxford University Press, 1975; Jane Carruth, *My Big Book of Animals*, Hamlyn, 1975; C. Carver, *The Raft*, Oxford University Press, 1975; C. Carver, *The Snake*, Oxford University Press, 1975; John Escott, *The Young Reporters*, Hamilton, 1975; Janet McNeill, *Just Turn the Key, and Other Stories*, Hamilton, 1976; L. Beckwith, *Lillian Beckwith's Hebridean Cookbook*, Hutchinson, 1976; Jean Wills, *Who Wants a Job?*, Hamilton, 1976; (with Gwen Green, Terry Rogers, and Meg Rutherford) Johnny Morris, *Goodnight Tales*, Hamlyn, 1977; Evelyn Prentis, *A Nurse in Time*, Hutchinson, 1977; J. Wills, *The Hope and Glory Band*, Hamilton, 1978; Helen Griffiths, *Grip: A Dog Story*, Holiday House, 1978; L. Beckwith, *Bruach Blend*, Hutchinson, 1978; E. Prentis, *A Nurse in Action*, Hutchinson, 1978; H. Griffiths, *The Kershaw Dogs*, Hutchinson, 1978; *Douglas Hall's Nursery Rhymes*, Hamlyn, 1979; Elizabeth Chapman, *Marmaduke Goes to Morocco*, Hodder & Stoughton, 1979; E. Prentis, *A Nurse in Parts*, Hutchinson, 1980; E. Prentis, *A Nurse Near By*, Hutchinson, 1981; George MacBeth, *The Rectory Mice*, Hutchinson, 1982; E. Prentis, *A Turn for the Nurse*, Hutchinson, 1982; L. Beckwith, *A Shine of Rainbows*, Hutchinson, 1983; British Broadcasting Corporation, *The Listening Corner Storybook*, Hutch-

inson, 1984; A. R. Lloyd, *The Last Otter*, Hutchinson, 1984; Zenka and Ian Woodward, *One Hundred Favourite Poems*, Hutchinson, 1985; Elizabeth Chapman, *Marmaduke in Scotland*, Hodder & Stoughton, 1986; Kenneth Graham, *Wind in the Willows*, Orbis, 1986.

Also illustrator of textbooks, adult fiction, and book jackets.

WORK IN PROGRESS: A book on painting, drawing and techniques.

SIDELIGHTS: "I think the reason I illustrate stories and ideas is because books fascinate me and I enjoy playing a part in them.

Besides illustrating children's books, Hall illustrates adult fiction books, textbooks and book jackets. "*The Sea for Breakfast,* a humorous and semi-documentary adult book, was one of the most interesting for me because I went 'on location' to the highlands of Scotland for material and discovered, as it were, a new world. Much of the information I acquired was later used for illustrating *Storm from the West.*" [Lee Kingman and others, compilers, *Illustrators of Children's Books: 1957-1966,* Horn Book, 1968. Amended by Hall.]

FOR MORE INFORMATION SEE: Lee Kingman and others, compilers, *Illustrators of Children's Books: 1957-1966,* Horn Book, 1968.

HALLMAN, Ruth 1929-

PERSONAL: Born June 30, 1929, in Hertford, N.C.; daughter of Edgar E. (a school superintendent) and Mattie (Reid) Bundy; married Robert E. Hallman (a consultant), July 9, 1952; children: Bob, David, Robin, Lynn. *Education:* Winthrop College, B.A., 1951. *Politics:* Republican. *Religion:* Methodist. *Home:* 9602 Sudley Manor Dr., Manassas, Va. 22110. *Agent:* Janet D. Chenery, Chenery Associates Literary Agency, 440 East 23rd St., New York, N.Y. 10010.

CAREER: Elementary school teacher in Spartanburg, S.C., 1951-52, and Columbus, Ga., 1952-53; personnel secretary in Atlanta, Ga., 1953-55; remedial reading tutor in Atlanta, 1955-56; Wilson Memorial Hospital, Johnson City, N.Y., pediatrics program organizer, 1956-57; substitute teacher in Endicott, N.Y., 1957-58; Jennie F. Snapp School, Endicott, elementary school teacher, 1958-60; writer, 1971—; secretary in law firm, 1983-84; executive secretary in international investment firm, 1984. Presently a part-time legal secretary. Volunteer teacher at hospitals and prisons; creative writing instructor; public speaker through the Virginia Center for Creative Arts.

WRITINGS—All juvenile; all published by Westminster, except as noted: *Secrets of a Silent Stranger,* 1976; *I Gotta Be Free,* 1977; *Gimme Something, Mister!,* 1978; *Midnight Wheels,* 1979; *Rescue Chopper,* 1980; *Breakaway,* 1981; *Tough Is Not Enough,* 1982; *Panic Five,* Dodd, in press.

Also author of church school curriculum material. Contributor to *Childcraft's Best Loved Bible Stories* and *Childcraft's Holidays,* for World Book.

WORK IN PROGRESS: "*Some Things Are Forever* is basically a book of love between grandmother/grandson and between the grandson and the girl he meets through his grand-

RUTH HALLMAN

mother. I feel this book could answer some of the feelings a young man would have about himself and the influences of his grandmother and the girl he meets. The young man has to accept his grandmother's death, but at the same time finds this young woman.''

SIDELIGHTS: "In everything I do—writing, teaching, speaking—there is the basic concern for children [and] people who either have difficulty reading or who have never developed an interest in reading. I have spent my entire adult life working for such disadvantaged people.

"I am fortunate now to be working on a project of high interest/low vocabulary books for reluctant readers. These books have a very specific goal: to encourage, excite, and intrigue such readers to turn the next page, and the next, and the next. As a teacher and the mother of four children I say, with no reservation at all, that books of this type meet a very vital need for such reluctant readers as I have taught.

"In my books I deliberately use mysteries or adventures as my stories, having found that these will keep moving quickly enough to satisfy the shorter attention spans of reluctant readers. I have lived in many places in the United States, and different locations provide first-hand settings for my books. I try to incorporate interesting factual comments about the settings. If one child reads with more interest because of anything I write, I have achieved my goal.''

Since Hallman's children have passed into their late teens and early twenties, the focus of her writing has also shifted to include contemporary concerns.

Hallman's works are included in the de Grummond Collection at the University of Southern Mississippi.

FOR MORE INFORMATION SEE: Florida United Methodist, August 15, 1975; *Today,* August 23, 1975, August 31, 1976; *Binghamton Press,* October 21, 1977; *Raleigh News & Observer,* November 27, 1977; *Journal-Messenger* (Manassas, Va.), February 23, 1979.

HASSALL, Joan   1906-

PERSONAL: Born March 3, 1906, in London, England; daughter of John (an artist and art school proprietor) and Constance (Brooke-Webb) Hassall. *Education:* Attended Froebel Educational Institute, Royal Academy Schools, 1927-33, and London County Council School of Photo-Engraving and Lithography, 1931. *Home:* 88 Kensington Park Rd., London W. 11, England.

CAREER: Early in career worked as a secretary in father's art studio and taught book production at Edinburgh College of Art; has worked primarily as a wood engraver and book illustrator since 1945. Work appears in numerous institutions, including British Museum, Victoria and Albert Museum, National Gallery of Canada, and National Gallery of Victoria (Melbourne). *Member:* Art Workers Guild (master). *Awards, honors:* Design selected for the invitation card used for the coronation of Queen Elizabeth II, 1953; bronze medal from Paris Salon, 1973.

ILLUSTRATOR: Francis Brett Young, *Portrait of a Village,* Heinemann, 1937, Reynal, 1938; Richard Church, *Calling for a Spade* (essays), Dent, 1939; Elizabeth Gaskell, *Cranford,* Harrap, 1940; J. W. Oliver, *Sixteenth-Century Poems,* Saltire Society, 1943; J. W. Oliver, *Mally Lee,* Saltire Society, 1944;

Three young rats with black felt hats,
Three young ducks with white straw flats, . . .

■ (From "Three Young Rats" in *The Oxford Nursery Rhyme Book,* compiled by Iona and Peter Opie. Illustrated by Joan Hassall.)

"Is any thing the matter with her?" cried Mrs. Dashwood as she entered—"is she ill?" ■ (From *Sense and Sensibility* by Jane Austen. Wood engraving by Joan Hassall.)

W. Dunbar, *Seasonal Poems,* Saltire Society, 1944; G. Scott-Moncrieff, *The Marriage of Robin Redbreast and the Wren,* Saltire Society, 1945; Robert Louis Stevenson, *A Child's Garden of Verses,* Hopetoun Press, 1946, reprinted, Blackie & Son, 1974; Mary Webb, *Fifty-One Poems,* Cape, 1946, Dutton, 1947; J. W. Oliver, *Whuppity Stoorie,* Saltire Society, 1946; Anthony Trollope, *Christmas Day at Kirkby Cottage,* Sampson, Low, 1947; A. Mure MacKenzie, *Old Scottish Christmas Hymns,* Saltire Society, 1947; Mary Russell Mitford, *Our Village,* Harrap, c. 1947; Eric Robert Linklater, *Sealskin Trousers, and Other Stories,* Hart-Davis, 1947; *Scottish Children's Rhymes and Lullabies* (traditional), Saltire Society, 1948; A. Trollope, *Parsons Daughter, and Other Stories,* selected and introduced by John Hampden, Cassell, 1949; S. Sitwell, *Theatrical Figures in Porcelain,* Curtain Press, 1949.

Andrew John Young, *Collected Poems of Andrew Young,* Cape, 1950; J. M. Reid, *The Fause Knight,* Saltire Society, 1950; Christopher Vernon Hassall, *Notes on Verse Drama,* Curtain Press, c. 1950; Bernard Gooch, *The Strange World of Nature,* Lutterworth, 1950; A. Trollope, *Mary Gresley, and Other Stories,* edited and introduced by J. Hampden, Folio, 1951; *Rashie Coat* (traditional), Saltire Society, 1951; Leonard Alfred George Strong, *Sixteen Portraits,* Naldrett Press, 1951; M. Lane, *The Brontë Story,* Heinemann, 1953; P. Whitlock, *All Day Long,* Oxford University Press, 1954; Iona Opie and Peter Opie, editors, *Oxford Nursery Rhyme Book,* Oxford University Press, 1955; L. Russell, *The Saturday Book,* Hutchinson, 1955; Jane Austen, *Pride and Prejudice,* Folio, 1957; Richard Church, *Small Moments,* Hutchinson, 1957; J. Austen, *Sense and Sensibility,* Folio, 1958; J. Austen, *Mansfield Park,* Folio, 1959; J. Austen, *Northanger Abbey* (based on the definitive text of R. W. Chapman), Folio, 1960; *The Wood Engravings of Joan Hassall,* Oxford University Press, 1960; J. Austen, *Persuasion,* Folio, 1961; J. Austen, *Emma* (based on the definitive text of R. W. Chapman), Folio, 1962; Robert Burns, *The Poems of Robert Burns,* selected and introduced by De Lancey Ferguson (limited edition), Oxford University Press, 1965; John Schroder, editor, *Catalogue of Books and Manuscripts by Rupert Brooke, Edward Marsh, and Christopher Hassall,* Rampart Lions Press, 1971; J. Austen, *The Folio Jane Austen,* Folio, 1975.

FOR MORE INFORMATION SEE: Bertha M. Miller, *Illustrators of Children's Books: 1946-1956,* Horn Book, 1958; *The Wood Engravings of Joan Hassall,* Oxford University Press, 1960.

Dear little child, this little book
  Is less a primer than a key
To sunder gates where wonder waits
  Your "Open Sesame!"

—Rupert Hughes
(From *With a First Reader*)

KEVIN HENKES

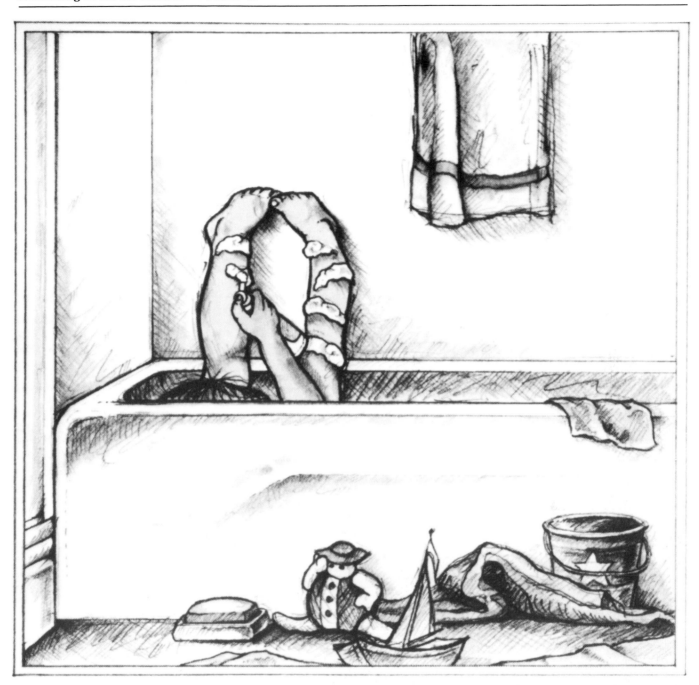

Once I took my father's shaving cream and made foamy stripes on my arms and legs. ■ (From *Clean Enough* by Kevin Henkes. Illustrated by the author.)

HENKES, Kevin   1960-

PERSONAL: Born November 27, 1960, in Racine, Wis.; son of Bernard Edward (a mailman) and Beatrice (a clerk; maiden name, Sieger) Henkes; married Laura Dronzek (a research specialist), May 18, 1985. *Education:* Attended University of Wisconsin-Madison. *Address:* c/o Greenwillow Books, 105 Madison Ave., New York, N.Y. 10016.

CAREER: Writer and illustrator.

WRITINGS—All self-illustrated; picture books, except as indicated; all published by Greenwillow: *All Alone,* 1981; *Clean Enough,* 1982; *Margaret and Taylor,* 1983; *Return to Sender*

(novel), 1984; *Bailey Goes Camping,* 1985; *Grandpa and Bo,* 1986.

SIDELIGHTS: In a review of Henkes's first book, *All Alone, Publishers Weekly* observed that "muted colors, delicate lines reflect the sensitivity in the text" as a little boy walks through the woods and muses about spending time alone. Henkes successfully employs the simple concept of taking a bath in his second book, *Clean Enough. School Library Journal* praised it as a "highly successful picture book," noting its "affectionate drawings . . . [and] equally affectionate narrative." In *Margaret and Taylor,* seven short episodes show Margaret bossing and teasing her younger brother, Taylor. *Bulletin of the Center for Children's Books* found "a clear understanding of sibling relations'' in the text, while *School Library Journal* noted that ''sensitive pencil drawings . . . provide insight into the personalities.'' Henkes digresses from the picture book format with his children's novel *Return to Sender*, the amusing story of a young boy who writes a letter to his favorite television superhero, with unexpected results.

FOR MORE INFORMATION SEE: Publishers Weekly, December 18, 1981; *School Library Journal,* October, 1982, February, 1984; *Bulletin of the Center for Children's Books,* March, 1984.

HENSON, James Maury 1936-
(Jim Henson)

PERSONAL: Born September 24, 1936, in Greenville, Miss.; son of Paul Ransom (an agronomist) and Elizabeth Marcella (Brown) Henson; married Jane Anne Nebel (his business partner), May 28, 1959; children: Lisa Marie, Cheryl Lee, Brian David, John Paul, Heather Beth. *Education:* University of Maryland, B.A., 1960. *Office:* 117 East 69th St., New York, N.Y. 10021.

CAREER: Creator of the ''Muppets,'' television and film producer and director. WRC-TV, Washington, D.C., producer of ''Sam and Friends,'' 1955-61; producer of television commercials and industrial and experimental films; Henson Associates, New York, N.Y. and London, England, co-founder and president, 1957—; creator of the Muppets for the ''Sesame Street'' series, beginning in 1968; creator and producer of the television series ''The Muppet Show,'' 1976-81, and ''Fraggle Rock,'' 1983—. Producer and/or director of motion pictures, including ''The Muppet Movie,'' 1979, ''The Great Muppet Caper,'' 1981, ''The Dark Crystal,'' 1982, ''The Muppets Take Manhattan,'' 1984, and ''Sesame Street Presents: Follow That Bird,'' 1985. President of board of directors, American Center of Union Internationale de la Marionette, 1974—. *Member:* Puppeteers of America (president, 1962-63), American Federation TV and Radio Artists (AFTRA), Directors Guild of America, Writers Guild, National Academy of Television Arts and Sciences, Screen Actors Guild.

AWARDS, HONORS: Emmy Award from National Academy of Television Arts and Sciences for best local entertainment program, 1958, for ''Sam and Friends,'' for outstanding individual achievement in children's programming, 1974, 1976, and 1978, for ''The Muppets of Sesame Street,'' for outstanding international achievement in children's programming, 1977, for ''The Muppets of Sesame Street,'' for Muppet costumes and props, 1978, for ''Sesame Street,'' for outstanding comedy and variety series, 1978, for ''The Muppet Show,'' for outstanding children's special, 1978, for ''Christmas Eve on Sesame Street,'' for outstanding writing in a variety, music, or comedy program, 1981, for ''The Muppet Show'' with Carol Burnett, for outstanding children's programming, tele-

JAMES MAURY HENSON

Singer Elton John was a guest star on "The Muppet Show" during its second television season, 1977.

vision special, 1982, for "Big Bird in China," and for film sound editing and outstanding animated program categories, 1985, for "Jim Henson's Muppet Babies."

Academy Award nomination from Academy of Motion Picture Arts and Sciences, 1965, for "Time Piece"; NET award from National Educational Television for best educational TV show, 1968, for "Muppets on Puppets"; Grammy Award, National Academy of Recording Arts and Sciences for best album for children, 1973, for "Sesame Street Live," 1977, for "Aren't You Glad You're You?", 1978, for "Sesame Street Fever Album," 1979, for "The Muppet Movie," 1980, for "In Harmony," for best recording for children, 1978, for "The Muppet Show Album," 1980, for "Sesame Country Album"; Silver Mermaid award from the First Fairytale Film Festival (Odense, Denmark), 1974, for "The Frog Prince" television special.

Broadcast Press Guild award for best comedy or light entertainment program, 1976, for "The Muppet Show"; Advertising Club of Baltimore, Outstanding Television Personality, 1976, to Jim Henson; Georgie Award from the American Guild of Variety Artists, 1976, for special attraction of the year, for "Jim Henson's Muppets"; Entertainer of the Year Award from the American Guild of Variety Artists, 1976; Pye Colour television award, 1976, for most promising newcomer, Kermit the Frog; BAFTA (British "Oscar") from the British Acad-

emy of Film and Television Arts for best light entertainment program, 1976, for "The Muppet Show," for most original program/series, 1977, for "The Muppet Show"; Variety Club of Great Britain award, joint ITV personalities of 1977, to Jim Henson and Frank Oz; Luminary award from the Advertising Club of Washington, D.C., 1977; Golden Rose of Montreux International Festival award for best light entertainment, 1977, for "The Muppet Show," for individual contribution to television entertainment, 1985, to Jim Henson; Decca Trophy from Radio Industries Club for ITV program of the year, 1977, for "The Muppet Show"; citation of distinguished service in television from the National Association for Better Broadcasting, 1977, for Jim Henson and "The Muppet Show."

Television Award of Merit from Mary Washington Colonial Chapter, National Society Daughters of the American Revolution, 1978, for "The Muppet Show"; Die Goldene Kamera (The Golden Camera) award, 1978, Outstanding Script of the Year, television variety category, from the Writer's Guild of America, 1978, for "The Muppet Show" with Maria Berenson, and "The Muppet Show" with Liza Minelli; George Foster Peabody Award from the University of Georgia, 1979, for excellence in television programming, and for "maintaining a consistently high standard for family viewing on American television" for "The Muppet Show"; Gabriel award from the Catholic Broadcasting Association of the United States for excellence in youth oriented programming, 1979, for "Emmett Otter's Jug-Band Christmas," 1981, for personal achievement; ACE award from National Cable Television Association for excellence in pay-cable programming, 1979, for "Emmett Otter's Jug-Band Christmas," for best children's or family series, 1983, for excellence in pay-cable programming, 1984, both for "Fraggle Rock"; Blue Ribbon award from *Box*

Office magazine, National Screen Council, 1979, for "The Muppet Movie"; Saturn Award from the Academy of Science Fiction, Fantasy and Horror Films for best fantasy film, 1979, for "The Muppet Movie."

First Founder's award from the International Council of National Academy of Television Arts and Sciences, 1980; Cer-

Jim Henson and "Associates."

(From the ABC-TV Children's Special "Emmet Otter's Jug-Band Christmas," starring Jim Henson's Muppets. Adapted from the book by Russell and Lillian Hoban. First aired on December 15, 1980.)

tificate of Appreciation from Common Cause, Washington, D.C., 1980; annual award from the Motion Picture Hall of Fame for best family picture, 1981, for "The Great Muppet Caper"; plaque from the Academy of Television Arts and Sciences for an outstanding children's program, 1981, for "Emmett Otter's Jug-Band Christmas"; Best Fantasy Film award from the Academy of Science Fiction, Fantasy and Horror Films, 1982, for "The Dark Crystal"; Athena award from the Rhode Island School of Design for excellence in design, 1982; "Big Apple" award from the City of New York, certificate of appreciation to Jim Henson, 1982, March of Dimes Jack Benny award for outstanding and original contributions to the world of entertainment, 1982.

Banff International Television Awards Festival, best children's programming, 1983, for "Big Bird in China"; Writer's Guild of America Award for outstanding achievement in children's programming, 1983, for "Big Bird in China"; Monitor award from Videotape Production Association for best broadcasting programming overall, 1983, for "Big Bird in China"; certificate, National Daytime Emmy Award from National Academy of Television Arts and Sciences for outstanding children's entertainment/instructional series, 1983, for "Sesame Street"; Grand Prix award from Avoriaz Fantasy Film Festival for best fantasy film, 1983, for "The Dark Crystal"; Madrid Film Festival, best film, 1983, for "The Dark Crystal"; ACT (Action for Children's Television) award for best children's program series, 1983, for significant contribution towards improving service to children on broadcast television, cable, and radio, 1985, both for "Fraggle Rock"; special achievement award for music in a series, Chicago Film Festival, 1983, for "Fraggle Rock"; Silver Medal, International Film and Television Festival of New York, 1983, for "Fraggle Rock"; International Emmy Award from the National Academy of Television Arts and Sciences, 1983, for outstanding children's programming, for "Fraggle Rock"; Career Achievement Award from the National Council for Children's Television, 1983.

On Cable Award from *On Cable* magazine for outstanding children's program, 1984, 1985, both for "Fraggle Rock"; Award of Excellence from Film Advisory Board, children's television category, 1984, for "Fraggle Rock"; Monitor award, Video Tape Production Association, best achievement in cable entertainment/original children's programming, 1984, 1985, both for "Fraggle Rock," and 1986, for best lighting director Jim Tetlow, for "Jim Henson's Muppets Babies"; special award to Jim Henson from the Massachusetts Society for the Prevention of Cruelty to Children, 1984; Vira award from *Video Review*, magazine, best kid-vid category, 1984, for *The Frog Prince;* ACTRA award from the Academy of Canadian Television and Radio Artists, best writer television variety program, 1985, for "Fraggle Rock"; Children's Television award, Children's Broadcast Institute, for best series, 1985, for "Fraggle Rock." Received an honorary degree of Doctor of Fine Arts from the University of Maryland, 1977, and from Fordham University, 1982.

SPECIAL MENTION: Many writers, producers, directors, and puppeteers have contributed to the success of the Muppets and Henson Associates. These include Jane Henson, Dave Goelz, Richard Hunt, Jerry Juhl, Don Salin, David Lazer, Jerry Nelson, Frank Oz, and Jon Stone.

TELEVISION: (Producer) "Sam and Friends," 1955-61, WRC-TV, daily late-night, five-minute series; (producer) "Youth '68," 1968, NBC-TV, one-hour documentary featured on "Experiment in Television" series; (co-writer, producer, and director) "The Cube," 1969, NBC-TV, one-hour drama fea-

(From the weekly television series "Fraggle Rock," which premiered on HBO, January 10, 1983.)

The Great Gonzo introduces opera star Beverly Sills to one of the more esoteric aspects of his art during the fourth season of "The Muppet Show," 1979.

tured on "Experiment in Television" series; (producer) "Muppets on Puppets," 1970, NET-TV, one-hour special; (producer and director) "Hey, Cinderella," April 10, 1970, ABC-TV, one-hour Muppet special; "Muppet Valentine Special," 1974, ABC-TV, one-hour special; "Out to Lunch," 1974, produced by Children's Television Workshop (CTW), ABC-TV, one-hour Muppet special; (creator, producer, and director) "The Muppet Show," 1976-81, produced by Independent Television Corp. (ITC) in association with Henson Associates, CBS-TV, weekly half-hour musical/comedy series; "The Muppets Go Hollywood," May 16, 1979, CBS-TV, one-hour special; (producer and director) "Emmett Otter's Jug Band Christmas," based on the book by Russell Hoban, December 15, 1980, ABC-TV, one-hour Muppet special; (producer) "The Muppets Go to the Movies," May 20, 1981, produced by ITC, ABC-TV, one-hour special; (creator, producer, and director) "Fraggle Rock," 1983—, produced by ITC in association with Henson Associates, HBO, weekly half-hour series; "Big Bird in China," 1983, NBC-TV, ninety-minute Muppet special. Also the Muppet specials "The Frog Prince," 1971, "Julie on Sesame Street," 1973, "Christmas on Sesame Street," 1978, "John Denver and the Muppets," 1979, "Don't Eat the Pictures," 1983, and "Bells of Fraggle Rock Christmas Special," 1984.

FILMS: (Writer, producer, and director) "Time Piece" (short), starring Henson, Contemporary Films, 1965; "Run, Run" (short), Henson Associates, 1967; "Organized Brain" (short), Henson Associates, 1968; "Final Speech" (Muppet Meeting Films series), Henson Associates, 1975; (producer) "The Muppet Movie," starring the Muppets, Associated Film, 1979;

(director) "The Great Muppet Caper," starring Charles Grodin, Diana Rigg, and the Muppets, Associated Film, 1981; (co-director and co-producer) "The Dark Crystal," Universal Pictures and Associated Film, 1982; "The Muppets Take Manhattan," Tri Star, 1984; "Sesame Street Presents: Follow That Bird," Warner Brothers, 1985.

ADAPTATIONS—A selection of books derived from the characters on the television series "Sesame Street" and "The Muppet Show": *The Sesame Street Book of Letters*, Little, Brown, 1970; *The Sesame Street Book of Numbers*, Little, Brown, 1970; *The Sesame Street Book of People and Things*, Little, Brown, 1970; *The Sesame Street Book of Puzzlers*, Little, Brown, 1970; *The Sesame Street Book of Shapes*, Little, Brown, 1970; *The Alphabet Book*, Random House, 1971; Jeffrey Moss, *People in My Family* (illustrations by Leon Jason Studios), Golden Press, 1971; *The Sesame Street Storybook* (verse adapted by Albert G. Miller; illustrated by Kelly Oechsli and others), Random House, 1971; *What Happens Next?*, Random House, 1971; *The King on a Swing*, Random House, 1972; *More Muppets from Sesame Street: Jim Henson's Big Bird and Oscar the Grouch*, Random House, 1972; Emily Perl Kingsley and others, *The Sesame Street One, Two, Three Storybook* (illustrated by Joseph Mathieu and others), Random House, 1973; *The Sesame Street Poster Pad*, Random House, 1973; *Can You Find What's Missing?* (pop-up book; illustrated by Carol Nicklaus), Random House, 1974; Jeffrey Moss and others, *The Sesame Street ABC Storybook* (illustrated by Peter Cross and others), Random House, 1974; George Mendoza, *Sesame Street Book of Opposites with Zero Mostel* (illustrated with photographs by Sheldon Secunda), Platt & Munk, 1974;

Who Are the People in Your Neighborhood?, Random House, 1974.

Sharon Lerner, editor, *Big Bird's Busy Book* (illustrated by Dave Gantz and others), Random House, 1975; *More Posters from Sesame Street* (illustrated with photographs by Charles Rowan), Random House, 1975; E. P. Kingsley and others, *The Sesame Street Book of Fairy Tales* (illustrated by J. Mathieu), Random House, 1975; *Cookie Monster, Where Are You?* (illustrated by Randy Jones), Random House, 1976; *I Am a Monster* (illustrated by J. Mathieu), Golden Press, 1976; *The Sesame Street Mother Goose* (illustrated by R. Jones), Random House, 1976; *The Sesame Street Postcard Book*, Random House, 1976; Jon Stone, *Would You Like to Play Hide-and-Seek in This Book with Lovable, Furry Old Grover?* (illustrated by Michael Smollin), Random House, 1976; David Korr, *The Day the Count Stopped Counting* (illustrated by M. Smollin), Golden Press, 1977; *Ernie and Bert's Toy Book*, Random House, 1977; E. P. Kingsley and others, *The Great Cookie Thief* (illustrated by M. Smollin), Golden Press, 1977; J. Stone, *The Monster at the End of This Book* (illustrated by M. Smollin), Golden Press, 1977; *Muppets in My Neighborhood* (illustrated by Harry McNaught), Random House, 1977; *The Sesame Street Mix or Match Storybook* (illustrated by J. Mathieu), Random House, 1977; *Sesame Street Pop-Up Riddle Book* (illustrated by David Sutherland), Random House, 1977; Ruthanna Long, *Tales of Sesame Gulch* (illustrated by Tom Cooke), Golden Press, 1977.

Grover's Super Surprise (illustrated by T. Cooke), Random House, 1978; Jack Burns and others, *The Muppet Show Book* (illustrated by Tudor Banus), Abrams, 1978; Tony Geiss and others, *The Sesame Street Bedtime Storybook* (illustrated by T. Cooke and others), Random House, 1978; Pat Tornborg, *The Sesame Street Cookbook* (illustrated by Robert Dennis), Platt & Munk, 1978; Michael Frith and others, *The Sesame Street Library* (illustrated by Mel Crawford and others), Funk & Wagnalls, 1978; *The Sesame Street Song Book* (words and music by Joe Raposo and Jeffrey Moss; arranged by Sy Oliver; illustrated by Loretta Trezzo), Simon & Schuster, 1978; *Sherlock Hemlock: Great Twiddlebug Mystery*, Golden Press, 1978; *Who Am I?*, Golden Press, 1978; *Big Bird's Rhyming Book* (pop-up; illustrated by Normand Chartier), Random House, 1979; D. Korr, *Cookie Monster and the Cookie Tree* (illustrated by J. Mathieu), Golden Press, 1979; *Cookie Monster's Book of Cookie Shapes* (illustrated by Rick Brown), Golden Press, 1979; E. P. Kingsley, *The Cookie Monster Storybook* (illustrated by T. Cooke), Random House, 1979; T. Geiss, *The Four Seasons* (illustrated by T. Cooke), Golden Press, 1979; Steven Crist, adapter, *The Muppet Movie*, Collins, 1979; *Your Friends from Sesame Street* (illustrated by M. Smollin), Random House, 1979.

Jocelyn Stevenson, *The Amazing Mumford Presents All about Bones* (illustrated by N. Chartier), Golden Press, 1980; Jocelyn Stevenson, *Anybody Can Play* (illustrated by Beverly Phillips), Golden Press, 1980; *Big Bird's Color Game* (illus-

"The Muppet Show" contribution to the world of rock and roll, Dr. Teeth and The Electric Mayhem.

LEONARDO DA VINCI. Mona Moi. Acrylic on fiberboard. Around 1503. Acquired by cash purchase from a mysterious and reclusive private collector's hoard of fine art in a locker at the Port Authority Bus Terminal. ■ (From *Miss Piggy's Treasury of Art Masterpieces from the Kermitage Collection,* edited by Henry Beard. Photograph by John E. Barrett.)

trated by T. Cooke), Golden Press, 1980; Linda Hayward, *The Case of the Missing Duckie* (illustrated by Maggie Swanson), Golden Press, 1980; Judy Freudberg and T. Geiss, *The Count Counts a Party* (illustrated by T. Cooke), Random House, 1980; B. G. Ford, *Don't Forget the Oatmeal! A Supermarket Word Book,* Golden Press, 1980; L. Hayward, *Early Bird on Sesame Street* (illustrated by Tom Leigh), Golden Press, 1980; E. P. Kingsley, *Farley Goes to the Doctor* (illustrated by M. Swanson), Golden Press, 1980; L. Hayward, *Going Up! The Elevator Counting Book* (illustrated by T. Leigh), Golden Press, 1980; Dan Elliott, *Grover Goes to School* (illustrated by N. Chartier), Random House, 1980; *Grover's Monster Album,* Random House, 1980; Janet Campbell, *The House That Biff Built* (illustrated by T. Cooke), Golden Press, 1980; E. P. Kingsley, *I Can Do It Myself* (illustrated by Richard Brown), Golden Press, 1980; Michaela Muntean, *I Like School* (illustrated by Tom Herbert), Golden Press, 1980; M. Muntean, *If I Lived Alone* (illustrated by Carol Nicklaus), Golden Press, 1980; *Muppet Madness,* Henson Associates, 1980; Jocelyn Stevenson, *Robin Hood: A High-Spirited Tale of Adventure* (illustrated by Bruce McNally), Muppet Press, 1980; L. Hayward, *The Sesame Street Dictionary* (illustrated by J. Mathieu), Random House, 1980; E. P. Kingsley, *The Sesame Street Pet Show* (illustrated by N. Chartier), Golden Press, 1980; *Sesame Street Sign Language Fun, with Linda Bove,* Random House, 1980; Patricia Relf, *Show and Tell* (illustrated by T. Cooke), Golden Press, 1980; Valjean McLenighan, *Special Delivery* (illustrated by Richard Brown), Golden Press, 1980; Pat Tornborg, *Spring Cleaning* (illustrated by Nancy W. Stevenson), Golden Press, 1980; *That New Baby!* (illustrated by DyAnne DiSalvo), Golden Press, 1980; L. Hayward, *Twiddlebugs at Work* (illustrated by Irene Trivas), Golden Press, 1980; J. Freudberg and T. Geiss, *Vegetable Soup* (illustrated by T. Cooke), Golden Press, 1980; Daisy Ellsworth, *What Did You Bring?* (illustrated by N. W. Stevenson), Golden Press, 1980.

David Korr, *ABC Toy Chest* (illustrated by N. W. Stevenson), Golden Press, 1981; Jocelyn Stevenson, *The Amazing Mumford Presents the Magic Weather Show* (illustrated by Bill Davis), Golden Press, 1981; *Big Bird's Farm* (illustrated with photographs by John E. Barrett), Random House, 1981; *Bert and Ernie on the Go* (pop-up book; illustrated by T. Cooke), Random House, 1981; Jon Stone, adapter, *Christmas Eve on Sesame Street* (from the television special written by Stone and Joseph A. Bailey; illustrated by J. Mathieu), Random House, 1981; L. Hayward, *A Day in the Life of Oscar the Grouch* (illustrated by Bill Davis), Golden Press, 1981; Sarah Roberts, *Don't Cry, Big Bird* (illustrated by T. Leigh), Random House, 1981; S. Roberts, *Ernie's Big Mess* (illustrated by J. Mathieu), Random House, 1981; Sandy Damashek, *Follow the Leader* (illustrated by T. Cooke), Golden Press, 1981; *Grover's New Kitten* (illustrated with photographs by J. E. Barrett), Random House, 1981; M. Muntean, *I Have a Friend* (illustrated by Marsha Winborn), Golden Press, 1981; M. Muntean, *Look What I Found!* (illustrated by John Constanza), Golden Press, 1981; P. Relf, *Muppet Manners; or, The Night Gonzo Gave a Party* (illustrated by T. Leigh), Random House, 1981; Jocelyn Stevenson, *The Muppets Go Camping* (illustrated by B. McNally), Random House, 1981; D. Elliot, *Oscar's Rotten Birthday* (illustrated by N. Chartier), Random House, 1981; L. Hayward, *A Phonic Dictionary* (illustrated by C. Nicklaus), Platt & Munk, 1981; D. Korr, *Prairie Dawn's Upside-Down Poem, and Other Nonsense from Sesame Street* (illustrated by T. Cooke), Golden Press, 1981; E. P. Kingsley, *The Sesame Street Circus of Opposites* (illustrated by N. W. Stevenson), Golden Press, 1981; L. Hayward, *Sesame Seasons* (illustrated by Rick Brown), Golden Press, 1981; L. Hayward, *The Sesame Street Sun* (illustrated by Tom Kirk), Golden Press, 1981;

Greg Williams, *Show and Tell* (illustrated by Sue Venning), Random House, 1981; John Stevenson, *The Whale Tale* (illustrated by the author), Muppet Press, 1981; Jocelyn Stevenson, *When I'm as Big as Freddie* (illustrated by B. Phillips), Golden Press, 1981; L. Hayward, *Which One Doesn't Belong?, and Other Puzzles from Sesame Street* (illustrated by Kimberly A. McSparran), Golden Press, 1981; E. P. Kingsley, *What Do You Do? Jobs in Your Neighborhood* (illustrated by Bill Williams), Golden Press, 1981.

Michaela Muntean, *Big and Little Stories* (illustrated by M. Swanson), Golden Press, 1982; Jocelyn Stevenson, *Bo Saves the Show* (illustrated by Richard Walz), Random House, 1982; Gregory Williams, *The Case of the Missing Hat* (illustrated by Rosekrans Hoffman), Random House, 1982; *Ernie and Bert Can . . . Can You?* (illustrated by M. Smollin), Random House, 1982; *Ernie's Bath Book* (illustrated by M. Smollin), Random House, 1982; *Ernie's Rainy Day Book* (illustrated by M. Smollin), Random House, 1982; Sheilah B. Bruce, *Gonzo and the Giant Chicken* (illustrated by R. Walz), Random House, 1982; *Good Time to Eat!* (illustrated by Richard Brown), Golden Press, 1982; Jocelyn Stevenson, adapter, *The Great Muppet Caper* (based on the movie), Random House, 1982; *In and Out, Up and Down* (illustrated by M. Smollin), Random House, 1982; *Jim Henson's Muppet Show Bill* (illustrated by S. Venning), Random House, 1982; S. Roberts, *Nobody Cares about Me!* (illustrated by J. Mathieu), Random House, 1982; *One Rubber Duckie* (illustrated with photographs by J. E. Barrett), Random House, 1982; Jill Wagner Schimpff, *Open Sesame Picture Dictionary* (illustrated by T. Cooke), Oxford University Press, 1982; *The Sesame Street Players Present Mother Goose* (illustrated by M. Smollin), Random House, 1982; *Sesame Street Playtime Book* (pop-up; illustrated by T. Cooke), Random House, 1982; Horace B. T. Calhoun, *Two for the Show* (illustrated by S. Venning), Random House, 1982; Henry Beard, editor, *Miss Piggy's Treasury of Art Masterpieces,* Holt, 1982.

Bathtime on Sesame Street, Random House, 1983; James Howe, *The Case of the Missing Mother* (illustrated by William Cleaver), Random House, 1983; *Ernie and Bert's Delivery Service,* Random House, 1983; *Sweet Dreams on Sesame Street* (pop-up book; illustrated by M. Swanson), Random House, 1983; Tom Dunsmuir, *There's No Place Like Home* (illustrated by Sammis McLean), Golden Press, 1983; D. Elliott, *A Visit to the Sesame Street Firehouse* (illustrated by J. Mathieu), Random House, 1983; Ellen Weiss, *You Are the Star of a Muppet Adventure* (illustrated by Benjamin Alexander), Random House, 1983; Norman Stiles, *I'll Miss You, Mr. Hooper* (illustrated by J. Mathieu), Random House, 1984; Jon Stone, *Lovable Furry Old Grover's Resting Places* (illustrated by M. Smollin), Random House, 1984; J. Howe, *The Muppet Guide to Magnificent Manners* (illustrated by Peter Elwell), Random House, 1984; D. Elliott, *Two Wheels for Grover* (illustrated by J. Mathieu), Random House, 1984; *Jim Henson's Muppet Show Pop-Up Book* (illustrated by Manhar Chauhan and S. Venning), Random House, 1984; Louise Gigow, *Muppet Babies at the Circus,* Random House, 1985; *Muppet Babies Playtime Book,* Random House, 1985; *Muppet Babies Take a Bath,* Random House, in press.

Numerous recordings have been made featuring the Muppets, including "The Muppet Musicians of Bremen," "Ernie and Bert," and "Rubber Duckie," all released by Columbia Records during the 1970s; "Sesame Street," Columbia Records, 1970; "Sesame Street 2," Warner Brothers, 1971; "Sesame Street Live," Columbia Records, 1973; "The Muppet Show 2," Arista, 1978; and "A Christmas Together," RCA Victor, 1979.

Big Bird and some of his "Sesame Street" friends occupy a PBS-TV fund-raising booth during a membership drive.

Computer software: "Muppet Learning Keys," Koala Technologies, 1985, Sunburst Communications, 1985; "Welcome Aboard!" (Muppets), Broderbund, 1985; "Dark Crystal" (Muppets), Sierra On-Line, 1985; "Gelfling Adventure" (Muppets), Sierra On-Line, 1985; "Sesame St. Letter," CBS Software, 1985; "Go-Round Big Bird's Funhouse" (Sesame Street), CBS Software, 1985; "Astro-Grover" (Sesame Street), CBS Software, 1985.

SIDELIGHTS: **September 24, 1936.** Born in Greenville, Mississippi. "I was a Mississippi Tom Sawyer, rarely wore shoes. It was an idyllic time. I rode my horse through the cotton fields. We had a beautiful big barn and we had a creek running in front of the house for fishing. I had a BB gun and I'd shoot at the water moccasins in the swamps just to wake 'em up." [Don Freeman, "Muppets on His Hands," *Saturday Evening Post,* November, 1979.[1]]

Father, Paul Henson, was an agronomist. "My dad was doing research with the Department of Agriculture—pasture crops like bird's-foot trefoil. I have memorialized that crop in a Muppet named Herbert Bird's Foot—a very dry lecturer." [John Culhane, "The Magical Madcap Muppets," *Reader's Digest,* September, 1977.[2]]

1944. When he was eight, Henson listened to the late puppeteer, Edgar Bergen, and his characters, Charlie McCarthy, Mortimer Snerd, and Effie Klinker on the radio. "I tried to imagine how they all looked as they made their jokes, but I don't remember ever thinking of them as one man and his puppets. To me, they were all human."[1]

When Bergen died, Henson was asked to bring Kermit the Frog, one of Henson's Muppet creations, to the funeral. "There seems to be something strange about having a puppet in this situation. But the family asked me if I would bring Kermit. . . .

"I think of all these guys as part of puppetry. The frog here— and Charlie and Mortimer—Punch and Judy—Kukla and Ollie. It's interesting to note that there have been puppets as long as we have had records of mankind. Some of the early puppets were used by witch doctors—or for religious purposes. In any case, puppets have often been connected with magic.

"Certainly, Edgar Bergen's work with Charlie and Mortimer was magic. Magic in the real sense. Something happened when Edgar spoke through Charlie—things were said that couldn't by ordinary people. . . . We of the Muppets, as well as many others, are continuing in his footsteps. We're part of the cycle. We take up where he left off—and we thank him for leaving this delightful legacy of love and humor and whimsy." [John Culhane, *New York Times Magazine,* June 10, 1979.[3]]

"Edgar considered our work as taking up where he left off. Edgar once said something to me that I'll never forget. He said, 'Kermit the Frog is Charlie McCarthy's first cousin.' Were nicer, warmer words ever spoken?"[1]

(From the stage production "Sesame Street Live," starring Jim Henson's Muppets. First presented at Madison Square Garden, December, 1984.)

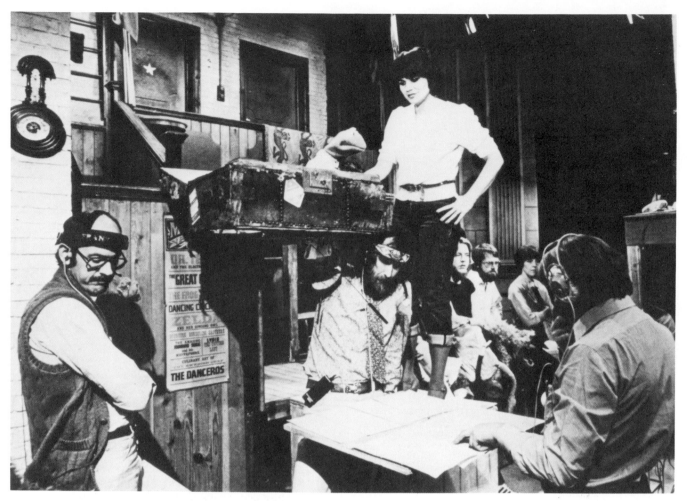

On the backstage set of "The Muppet Show," Frank Oz and Linda Ronstadt stand by as Jim Henson, with Kermit up, consults the script. ■ (From *Of Muppets and Men: The Making of the Muppet Show* by Christopher Finch.)

"We're dedicating 'The Muppet Movie' to Edgar . . . who worked with us on it."[3]

1949. "My mother told me I drove 'em all crazy until they bought a television set. That was in seventh or eighth grade, when I was 13 or 14—about 1949. Burr Tillstrom's 'Kukla, Fran and Ollie' were on when we got our set. They were on half an hour every night about dinner time. They made an impression on me. So did Bil and Cora Baird's 'Life with Snarky Parker.'

"Burr Tillstrom and the Bairds had more to do with the beginning of puppets on television than we did. But they had developed their art and style to a certain extent before hitting television. Baird had done marionette shows long before he came to television. Burr Tillstrom's puppets were basically the standard hand puppet characters that went back to Punch and Judy. But from the beginning [of the Muppets], we worked watching a television monitor, which is very different from working in a puppet theater."[3]

Henson's family moved to Hyattsville, Maryland, where at the high school, "they had a puppet club and I joined one day." [Robert Higgins, "The Muppet Family and How It Grew," *TV Guide*, May 16, 1970.[4]]

Henson's parents were supportive of his early puppeteering efforts. "My mother had a very good sense of humor and my father was excellent at carpentry. I was a quiet kid, introspective, articulate, always involved with art, a fairly good student but a terrible athlete—always the last one chosen in a ballgame and always put, protesting, in right field."[1]

When a local Washington, D.C. TV station announced an audition for young puppeteers, Henson made a puppet from his mother's old green spring coat and entered the contest. He won the audition and went on the air with "The Junior Morning Show." From there, he went on to appear on other local TV shows and then, during his freshman year at the University of Maryland, he was offered a five-minute, late evening time slot at WRC-TV in Washington, D.C.

His new program, "Sam and Friends," gave Henson a chance to develop a working style that allowed him to create his own puppetry style, as well as experiment with the technical wizardry the TV medium made possible. It also enabled him to try out a variety of whimsical story formats, since the show ran at an hour (11:25 p.m.) when "nobody important" was supposedly watching. Instead, "Sam and Friends" acquired a devoted following, lasted for eight years, and won a local Emmy in 1959 for Outstanding Television Entertainment.

It was Rowlf the Dog who made the breakthrough as a regular on network television, on the "Jimmy Dean Show." ■ (From *Of Muppets and Men: The Making of the Muppet Show* by Christopher Finch.)

Henson performed the show with a fellow student from the university's Art Education Department, Jane Nebel. The two married four years later and had five children—Lisa, Cheryl, Brian, John, and Heather.

"We tried some really way-out things, and since nobody threatened censorship or complained, I was convinced that no one else at the station ever watched the program."[1]

Despite his success with "Sam and Friends," Henson still had not decided to make puppetry his career. He realized, however, that puppetry gave him the opportunity to combine his varied interests in visual arts, theater, and scenic design, as well as writing and performing for television. "Puppetry is putting a mirror up to yourself. Just like theater, that's what it's all about. Puppetry gives us the ability to look at ourselves through different perspectives, especially the perspective of humor."

Henson and Kermit got their major network debut on Steve Allen's "Tonight Show." Wearing a blond wig, Kermit sang "I've Grown Accustomed to Your Face" to a purple skull-like monster, Yorick, operated by Jane. Henson also did commercials for television. "I rather enjoyed having money in my jeans. I drove to my college graduation in a $10,000, but old, Rolls-Royce. But I wasn't really a Rolls-Royce kind of person and I sold it. Still, it was a nice way to graduate."[1]

The summer of 1958, Henson went to Europe where he became convinced that puppeteering could be a serious form of entertainment. "I saw that puppetry was truly an art form in Europe. It was something that could be done artistically, with creativity. Back home, there weren't all that many puppeteers, but in Europe they are everywhere and everybody goes to puppet shows. It's an integral part of their lives and that was nice to see."[1]

After graduating from the University of Maryland, Henson made many commercials, notably with Rowlf the Dog, one of the first Muppet characters. For three seasons, Rowlf the Dog was a regular on the "Jimmy Dean Show."

1965-1969. Henson produced, directed and even acted in several non-puppet short films.

November, 1969. "Sesame Street," produced by The Children's Television Workshop, premiered on 160 educational television stations. The Muppets were an important part of the show.

"Sesame Street" made Henson aware of the power and influence of TV on education and the need to use it responsibly. "Right about the time 'Sesame Street' came out, people started being aware of what we were doing with violence. I've seen enough research about violence on TV to believe it doesn't belong there at all. Keep it off TV as much as possible. It does affect kids. Kids will model their behavior after the violence."

Henson's solution was simple. He constructed the "Sesame Street" puppet segment as if his own children were watching. "As a parent around your children, you behave a certain way. You use positive things that you want them to reflect in their own lives. I feel myself a positive person. I think life is basically good. People are basically good. That's the message I would like to express through the Muppets."

Henson did several television specials with the Muppets in the early 1970s. "Some of the people over at 'Sesame Street' thought it would be nice to use some of those characters and put together a prime-time commercial show.

"We combined the cast of 'The Electric Company' with the Muppets from 'Sesame Street,' and added some guest stars. We [had] Elliott Gould and Barbara Eden, and Rita Moreno [do] a segment.

"The basic idea of 'Out to Lunch' is that the entire staff of ABC-TV goes out to lunch, and all these wild people break into the studio and take over. It's really a parody of commercial TV. We do a version of the 'Johnny Carson Show,' with Cookie Monster playing Carson.

"A singer comes out to plug his record. Cookie Monster eats the record. An author comes out to plug his book. Cookie Monster eats the book.

"We do a dog-food commercial. Dog-food dessert, coconut cream pie. Of course, the dog hits the guy in the face with it at the end.

"'The Electric Company' does a game show where people bet things they already have. It's called 'Give It Back.' One guy loses his wife and job.

"In situations like this we hope to get everybody. The adults like the humor, and the kids watch the Muppets." [Mike Sahn, "Muppet Man," *Cue*, December 9, 1974.[5]]

1973. Henson and the Muppets did a special called "Keep U.S. Beautiful." The characters were made of trash. ". . . You could call the dance a Tin Can Can-Can.

"The whole world is interested in ecology. I'm not an ecology nut, but I do have my own personal cause. People are messing up the cities something awful.

"The segment I did for the NBC special, which, incidentally, features Raymond Burr as the host, and guests Ruth Buzzi, Tim Conway, Sandy Duncan, Lena Horne and Don Knotts, is on garbage taking over the world. It's what you might call a humorous contribution to making a serious statement about our ecological problems.

Kira, the Gelfling. ■ (From the movie "The Dark Crystal." Copyright © 1982 by ITC Entertainment.)

"The aim of the program is not to tell people what to do but to bring the problem out into the open so that hopefully they will think twice before they dirty up the streets and the roads again." [George Masian, "Jim Henson Fights Trash with Trash," *New York Sunday News,* March 18, 1973.[6]]

September, 1976. Premiere of Henson's own show, "The Muppet Show." It was produced in England by Lord Lew Grade at Lord Grade Studios because American networks didn't consider it family viewing, but strictly for children. "'The Flintsones' were a big breakthrough for animation. Now animation has crossed over into the adult area. But when you try to sell anyone on puppets, it's the old problem. They automatically say, 'Puppets are for kids.'" [Gerald Nachman, "How the Muppets Got That Way," *New York Post,* January 24, 1965.[7]]

"It's something I've always faced, this slight condescension toward puppets. . . . Edgar Bergen . . . always worked to an adult audience—in theaters, vaudeville, nightclubs, radio, movies, TV. But it's always been practically impossible to talk the networks into any kind of puppet show for adults. We're never thought of for prime time. It's always a vehicle for kids."[1]

"They always said the Muppets were child-oriented and adults wouldn't watch."[3] But, insists Henson, "They transcend all age groups. Their satiric comments on society seems to delight all ages."[3]

"[But I tried to . . . design each puppet] specifically for television. They're very simple. I've tried to get away from the mechanical things, because I think it's distracting, especially on TV where everything is concentrated into such a small area. Who was it that said, 'The ear is the enemy of the eye?'

"The TV screen is right there, three inches away from you, so I've tried to get as much expression into each face as possible. A painted expression on a doll is OK in a show when the audience is 15 feet away, but on TV you have to put life and sensitivity into a face."[7]

"You have to learn what works with puppets, and you have to learn what works with puppets on television, specifically. With puppets, we're dealing with a very limited form. While an actor has an enormous range of expressions on his face, most of the Muppets can only open their mouths. Thus, the angle that the head is held, how it's moved, or where the puppet is looking creates the expression. Five degrees of tilt can convey a different emotion."[2]

"When you do puppets you can create the whole show yourself—write it, perform it, direct it, design it. Everything. It's a whole thing, a mood. It's a way of saying something, I guess, and a lot of people want to say something. But I don't start out to say things. I try to keep it, first of all, entertaining, and then humorous."[7]

Introducing "The Muppet Babies." ■ (From the movie "The Muppets Take Manhattan." Copyright © 1984 by Tri-Star Pictures.)

Spoof of a famous Alfred Hitchcock chase scene. ■ (From the movie "Sesame Street Presents: Follow That Bird." Copyright © 1985 by Warner Bros. Inc. Muppet characters copyright © 1985 by Muppets Inc.)

"The characters are never based on people we know. They're based on a personality type of an attitude more than anything.

"Kermit is the closest one to me. He's the easiest to work with. He's the only one who can't be worked by anybody else. . . . See, Kermit is just a piece of cloth with a mouthpiece in it. The character is literally my hand." [Tom Shales, "Ta-Dahhh! It's Jim Henson, Creator of Kermit the Frog and King of the Muppets," *Washington Post,* January 25, 1977.[8]]

"Kermit is the oldest character I'm still using. He's sort of a comfortable middle-of-the roader—very much what I am. I have the feeling he's desperately trying to keep things rolling. And he's surrounded by all these crazies." [Don Kowet, "Behind Every Great Muppet . . . Stands Jim Henson, Who Has Crafted a Multimillion-Dollar Empire Out of Bulbous Noses, Floppy Ears and Shaggy Humor," *TV Guide,* August 6, 1977.[9]]

"Kermit the Frog has this function—he's an Everyman trying to get through life whole. He has a sense of sanity and there he is, surrounded by crazies. Kermit is the character through whose eyes the audience is viewing the show. He is the solid thing in the middle—flip, snarky, which is to say a bit smart alecky in his own way, but he's a nice guy. He operates from a point of consideration. There is a lot of warmth in Kermit."[1]

"I suppose that he's an alter ego, but he's a little snarkier than I am—slightly wise. Kermit says things I hold myself back from saying."[3]

"Kermit the Frog is not really a frog. He's called Kermit the Frog but he's really just Kermit. He became something of a frog when he did a TV special back in 1967. I changed his body and made him a bit rounder, more froglike. As a parallel, Mickey Mouse looks nothing like a mouse but he fits into that category. I mean, if nobody ever said Mickey Mouse was a mouse, we wouldn't know what he was, would we?"[1]

"We operate the Muppet's mouth with one hand. For Muppets like Kermit, who cannot grasp things with their hands, the right arms are moved with thin rods attached to their hands. We paint the rods to match the background so that they are hard to see. It's surprising how many people never notice them.

"A Muppet who can hold things takes two people to operate. One puppeteer will do his mouth and one hand with *his* two hands, and a second puppeteer will do his other hand. Other characters have electronic remote control eyes and ears, and the large ones—like Big Bird—even have television monitor sets built in.

''Often, on 'The Muppet Show,' we'll have all five-puppeteers on a single number. We're surrounded by television monitors so we can see what the audience is seeing. We do bump into each other occasionally. But the audience shouldn't be aware of your problems or they'll lose the thread of the story.''[3]

The Muppet performers include Dave Goelz, Caroll Spinney, Jerry Nelson, Richard Hunt, Steve Whitmire, Kathy Mullen, Karen Prell, and Frank Oz, one of the creators of Miss Piggy, whom Henson calls, ''absolutely the greatest puppeteer in the world.''[9] ''Frank Oz is probably the one person most responsible for the wild humor of the Muppets.''[1]

''Basically it all begins with those little sketches of characters that I or one of my associates make on people we know. They're based on a personality type or an attitude more than anything else. I look at the sketches until one seems to have whole quality of the personality. Then we begin building. I like creating different worlds of puppet characters.''[3]

''You can humanize almost anything, even furniture. If you wanted to, you could have [a] chair talk to [a] sofa. People do it all the time without knowing it. They use objects as a personality and make them come alive just as we do.''[6]

Henson underlines the importance of matching puppet to puppeteer. ''Dave Goelz did a character called Zoot on 'The Muppet Show.' Sort of an aging hippie musician. And Dave couldn't relate to Zoot, he couldn't ad-lib within the role. On the other hand I could have done Zoot easily. I used to play the piano. On 'The Muppet Show,' one of the things I do best is arranging the musical numbers. I can identify very easily with an aging hippie musician.''[9]

Concerning the Muppet character Miss Piggy, Henson remarked: ''The design has changed a little bit—little tiny things in the corners of Miss Piggy's mouth.

''They are small things. But the result, if you look at photographs of the old and new Miss Piggy side by side, is a self-satisfied smirk more in keeping with Miss Piggy's oversize ego.''[3]

1979. The Muppets' first feature-length movie, ''The Muppet Movie,'' was made at a cost of eight million dollars. It included such stars as Mel Brooks, who stated: ''I love the Muppets. Their comedy and what they mean stand for one thing—the meek shall inherit the Earth.''[1]

Others who shared the screen with the Muppets were: Bob Hope, Milton Berle, Richard Pryor, Steve Martin, Telly Savalas, Elliot Gould, Carol Kane, and Orson Welles.

''The Muppet Movie'' employed more mechanics than usual, to make the Muppets more life-like. ''Still, every time we use mechanics we try to keep them very, uh, unmechanical. As

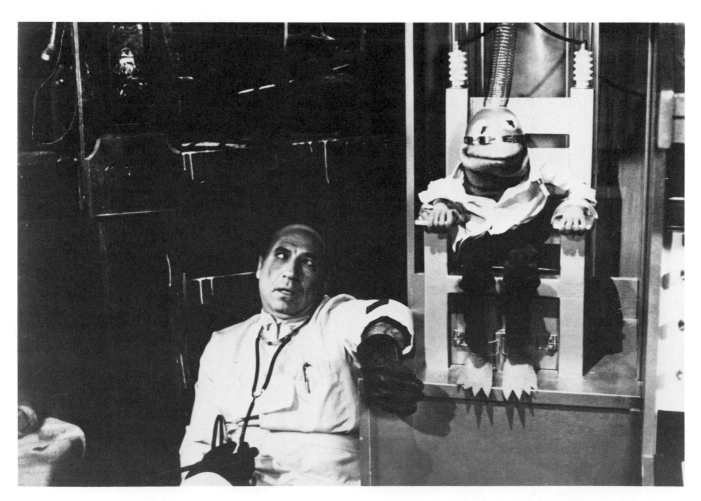

Mel Brooks attempts to brainwash Kermit. ■ (From "The Muppet Movie." Copyright © 1979 by Associated Film Distribution [AFD].)

soon as the audience starts thinking about the cleverness of it all, then they're not thinking about the performances. When the Muppets are on the screen, I want the audience to believe in the moment. The audience can see that most of the characters end at the waist most of the time, and they can know who talks for them—none of that seems to kill the moment. But when they're watching us perform, believing the moment is everything."[3]

Said Michael K. Frith, art director of Henson Associates: "The Muppets bring a certain optimism into what is not necessarily an optimistic age. Besides being magical and humorous, the show is actually reassuring for many people.

"I became involved with the Sesame Street people, which led to Jim Henson and the Muppets. As the Muppets began to go more heavily into publishing, Jim asked me to look over things for him.

"All I do is doodle something on an envelope on the subway while coming to work. It's the puppet builders who are true geniuses in coming up with personalities. Working with them is an experience you can't begin to describe. Every artist is fascinated by the Pygmalion dream—to carve Galateas and get living, breathing creatures. Part of the excitement is a sense of collaboration. Every conceivable background in the fine arts and elsewhere is represented—sculptors, painters, theater people—even electrical engineers.

"The creations are so lifelike—extraordinarily alive. The magic of inanimate objects that are alive reaches an atavistic place in our hearts; you know, stones that can speak and trees that have voices." [Hank Nuwer, "Muppets on the Move," *Saturday Evening Post*, December, 1980.[10]]

Said Henson realistically: "I treat [the Muppets] with gentility, but I never forget that they are made of a fabric with polyfoam and a little wood. The soft materials are for easy handling. I don't want to break them because they're difficult to make, but I'm not at all sentimental about them. I'm fond of them as characters but not necessarily as puppets. My emotional attachment is to the people they've become. To me, the Muppets are a medium of expression. They are, in a sense, my palette.

"They definitely aren't alive, but they do have a life of their own, much like characters in a book. They are fictional characters."[10]

Certainly success is due in great part to hard work, for as Henson admits, he and his puppeteers rehearse an act, "from two weeks to a full month."[4]

"When we're doing 'The Muppet Show' we spend two and a half days in the studio taping each show. I don't think there's another show on the air that spends that much time. We spent three full weeks doing the Emmet Otter special."[9]

Miss Piggy lends her charm and grace to a water-ballet line. ■ (From the movie "The Great Muppet Caper." Copyright © 1981 by Henson Associates, Inc.)

The success of the Muppets has earned a great deal of money for Henson Associates (letterhead: HA!). As Henson modestly put it: "We've been overdrawn at the bank now and then, but things have never been really tight."[4]

However, Henson stressed that "it's important to me that the audience doesn't think of us in terms of figures. I don't want people looking at the Muppets and thinking, 'How much are they worth?' It's just not us. It could be destructive to the show." [John Skow, "The Man behind the Frog," *Time,* December 25, 1978.[11]]

December, 1982. "The Dark Crystal," Henson's third movie, evolved from characters that appeared on "Saturday Night Live." Henson noted that the "Saturday Night Live" sequences were not very successful for his characters. "It's not an easy thing to analyze. I still like the show. But they'd write lovely, far-out things for [human performers] and square, dull nothingness for our characters."[8]

"They were puppets, but they were unlike the Muppets and because the show was on late at night, we were able to do some questionable material.

"For the first time we used taxidermist's eyes in the puppets, making them seem like living creatures. Then it became a challenge to take them a step further. Could we create another world in which there were no people?

"If ['The Dark Crystal' is] a success, I think the subject can be explored further.... But I never knew it was going to take five years." [Bob Thomas (AP), "'Dark Crystal': Mix of 'Muppets' and 'Star Wars,'" *The Day* (New London, Conn.), November 22, 1982.[12]] The film was made at a cost of twenty million dollars.

Next came "Fraggle Rock," a family-oriented half-hour program currently seen on Home Box Office (HBO) and distributed to more than 90 countries. "Fraggle Rock" has already won three Awards for Cable Excellence (ACE) since its debut in 1983. In the Henson tradition, the show is intended as entertainment, with an underlying theme fostering international understanding and tolerance for others.

"Muppet Babies," aired Saturday mornings on CBS-TV, is another Henson production. An animated children's program, it features the well-known Muppet characters in their nursery days. The format of the show is designed to encourage youngsters to use their imagination and creativity. Introduced in 1984, the show became the most popular program in its time-slot, winning two Emmy awards.

Henson is at times compared to Walt Disney. "I'm slightly uncomfortable with all the people who want to say things like that about me, 'cause I like Disney but I don't ever particularly want to do what he did. He built this great, huge empire. I'm not particularly inclined to do that. You get that large a thing going and I'm not sure that the quality of the work can be maintained. It seems that I'm bigger now than I thought I would be."[3]

Henson has maintained his creative work with his many films. "The Muppets Take Manhattan" was released in 1984. While Kermit and Piggy were the best known couple in front of the Muppet cameras, an equally influential husband-wife team worked behind the scenes. Muppet costume designer, Calista Hendrickson, and her production/designer husband, Stephen, were a key combination on this movie. In collaboration with

Frank Oz, it was the Hendricksons who largely determined the overall look of the film and its stars.

Henson is also working on a new film, "Labyrinth," for which he has teamed up with another legendary fantasy filmmaker, George Lucas. Henson created the idea for the film and will direct the production. Lucas will serve as executive producer. For "Labyrinth," they will create a new fantasy world in which humans coexist with incredible creatures.

Henson's interest in computers as an educational tool has resulted in the development of a series of software programs aimed at young people as well as the creation of a product, the Muppet Learning Keys, which enables youngsters to easily understand and master computer use.

Through Henson Associates, he is also involved in publishing a range of books aimed at both children and adults, as well as the licensing of products featuring characters from "The Muppet Show," "Fraggle Rock," and "Muppet Babies." He produces business meeting films that are used by most of the Fortune 500 companies.

Henson also has traveling arena productions, "The Muppet Show on Tour," and "Sesame Live," which have been playing major cities throughout the country.

"The Art of the Muppets," an exhibit of Muppet memorabilia, artifacts and fantasy creations from Henson's films, has appeared at a number of museums nationwide and is scheduled for future appearances in other countries around the world.

"Follow your enthusiasm," Henson advises. "It's something I've always believed in. Find those parts of your life you enjoy the most. Do what you enjoy doing."

"Jim Henson's Creature Shop" formally offered its services to the film industry for the design, construction and performance of puppets or special-effects creatures in selected motion picture properties.

FOR MORE INFORMATION SEE: Books: *Current Biography Yearbook,* H. W. Wilson, 1977; Staff of Henson Associates, *The Art of the Muppets: A Retrospective Look at Twenty-Five Years of Muppet Magic,* Bantam, 1980; Patricia Dendtler Frevert, *Muppet Magic* (juvenile), Creative Education, 1980; Christopher Finch, *Of Muppets and Men: The Making of the Muppet Show,* Knopf, 1981.

Periodicals: Gerald Nachman, "How the Muppets Got That Way," *New York Post,* January 24, 1965; *TV Guide,* May 16, 1970, August 6, 1977, April 6, 1985; George Masian, "Jim Henson Fights Trash," *New York Sunday News,* March 18, 1973; Mike Sahn, "Muppet Man," *Cue,* December 9, 1974; Tom Shales, "Ta-Dahhh! It's Jim Henson, Creator of Kermit the Frog and King of the Muppets," *Washington Post,* January 25, 1977; J. Culhane, "The Magical, Madcap Muppets," *Reader's Digest,* September, 1977; John Skow, "Man behind the Frog," *Time,* December 25, 1978; J. Culhane, "The Muppets in Movieland," *New York Times Magazine,* June 10, 1979; *New York Times Biographical Service,* June 1979; "Meet the Muppets," *National Geographic World,* August, 1979; D. Freeman, "Muppets on His Hands," *Saturday Evening Post,* November, 1979; Hank Nuwer, "Muppets on the Move," *Saturday Evening Post,* December, 1980; L. B. Frumkes, "Muppets, Gelflings and Fraggles," *Harpers Bazaar,* November, 1982; Bob Thomas (AP), "'Dark Crystal': Mix of 'Muppets' and 'Star Wars,'" *The Day* (New London, Conn.), November 22, 1982; C. Krista, "Jim Henson," *Films in Re-*

view, January, 1983; *People Weekly,* January 17, 1983; J. P. Forkan, "Henson Nurtures His New Baby," *Advertising Age,* October 17, 1983; Carol A. Emmens, "Jim Henson and the People behind Muppet Mania," *School Library Journal,* September, 1984.

HINTON, Sam   1917-

PERSONAL: Born March 21, 1917, in Tulsa, Okla.; son of Allan Francis (a civil engineer) and Nellie (a pianist; maiden name, MacDuffie); married Leslie Forster (a musician, potter, and weaver), 1940; children: Leanne, Matthew. *Education:* Attended Texas A. & M. University, 1934-36; graduated from the University of California at Los Angeles, 1940.

CAREER: Educator, marine biologist, and folksinger. Early jobs included singing, sign painting, and selling snake venom; director of Desert Museum, Palm Springs, Calif., 1940-43; curator of aquarium and museum at University of California's Scripp's Institution of Oceanography, beginning 1943, director of the Office of School Relations, University of California, beginning 1964. Teacher of college extension courses in biology and folklore, beginning 1948; singer at campus folk song concerts; performer and discussion leader at Berkeley Folk Festival, beginning 1957; taught folk music courses on educational television, 1962, 1967; featured singer on eight LP's; board of directors, *Sing Out!* magazine.

WRITINGS: Exploring Under the Sea (illustrated by Rudolph Freund), Garden City Books, 1957; *Seashore Life of Southern California: An Introduction to the Animal Life of California Beaches South of Santa Barbara,* University of California Press, 1969. Authored a newspaper feature, "The Ocean World," for the *San Diego Union,* beginning 1958.

Illustrator: Joel Hedgpeth, *Common Seashore Life of Southern California,* edited by Vinson Brown, Naturegraph, 1961.

SIDELIGHTS: Although Hinton once remarked that he has always sung, his "career" as a folksinger began in 1936 when he won a Major Bowes Amateur contest. At that time, he left school to travel with one of the Bowes troupes, and for the next two years sang throughout the United States and Canada. When he tired of traveling, he returned to college, but his singing helped to pay tuition. Hinton's first recording was an album of Anglo-Irish ballads and songs, "Buffalo Boy American Folk Songs," released in 1947. His first commercial recording was "Old Man Atom" in 1950 for Columbia Records. In the early 1950s, Hinton recorded several songs for Decca Records' Children's Series which included "The Barnyard Song," "Country Critters," "The Frog Song," and "The Greatest Sound Around."

"Folk Songs of California and the Old West," was Hinton's first LP, recorded for Bowmar Records in 1952. With Alan Lomax and Si Rady, he worked on the selection and arrangement of material for an RCA album, "How the West Was Won," on which he sang nine songs. He recorded several albums for Decca in the mid-1950s, including "Singing Across the Land," "A Family Tree of Folk Songs," and "The Real McCoy." In the 1960s, he was featured on such albums as "American Folk Songs and Balladeers" for the Classics Record Library, "Newport Folk Festival, 1963," for Vanguard, and "The Songs of Men," "Whoever Shall Have Some Peanuts," and "The Wandering Folksong," for Folkway Records.

About Hinton's book, *Exploring Under the Sea,* a reviewer noted: "A beautiful book for the child to take along on his next trip to the seashore, where it will help him identify strange creatures of the ocean and help him understand how the waves and currents affect the lives of all of us."

Hinton also appeared in the musical comedy, "Meet the People," in Los Angeles, which featured Nanette Fabray and Jack Gilford.

FOR MORE INFORMATION SEE: San Francisco Chronicle, November 10, 1957; *New York Times,* December 8, 1957.

HODGETTS, Blake Christopher   1967-

PERSONAL: Born July 7, 1967, in New York, N.Y.; son of Craig Edward (an architect) and Victoria (an artist and writer; maiden name, Kahn) Hodgetts. *Education:* Attending University of Oregon, 1985—. *Address:* P.O. Box 827, Bandon, Ore. 97411.

WRITINGS: Dream of the Dinosaurs (illustrated by mother, Victoria Hodgetts), Doubleday, 1978.

WORK IN PROGRESS: Science fiction short stories.

SIDELIGHTS: "*Dream of the Dinosaurs* is a special book in that it was a dream that I had at the age of six. It is probably the only dream ever to be published verbatim as a book in its own right. It was published largely through the efforts of my mother, Victoria, who spent nearly two years doing the magnificent illustrations which, unfortunately, were not done justice by the printing job. The great pity is that it was not feasible to do the book in color. Victoria and I had originally planned it that way, and she actually completed three or four illustrations in full color, which later could not be used because of the expense. They had to be done over in black and white, which has seemed rather sere to us ever since. Some of the original color drawings were later sold as artwork, and it is pleasing to know that they presently decorate someone's living room wall.

"I was born in New York in 1967, where I lived for only two years before moving to Los Angeles. There my father worked as a designer and architect and my mother wrote articles for *The Village Voice* and *New West.* As my father got more involved with his work, the marriage gradually dissolved and my parents eventually separated; I was five years old at the time. After that I lived with Victoria in a house on Whitley Avenue in Hollywood. We had been there for six years when she met her present husband, Mark Tierney, and decided to move to Oregon. She left first, and I lived with my father in West Hollywood for a time. I finally came to Oregon in 1977, and I have lived here ever since. I like the countryside very much—it would be difficult to find a more beautiful place to live—and the people here are quite different from the people in a big city. However, Bandon is a rather depressed area economically, and I doubt I will live here after I finish college.

"I have always been very involved with the arts. Most of my family is artistic. My mother's mother, Helen Beling, is a respected sculptor; Victoria herself is an excellent artist in several media and a very good writer; my father is a highly skilled architect and a former virtuoso trumpet player; and his brother, Kent, directs films and is generally creative. With all this talent running rampant, it is no wonder that I aspired from

But suddenly . . .

(From *Dream of the Dinosaurs* by Blake Christopher Hodgetts. Illustrated by Victoria Hodgetts.)

Blake Christopher Hodgetts with his mother, Victoria.

an early age to excel in the arts. I have always drawn, ever since I can remember, gaining skill through nothing but practice and repetition. I have always enjoyed reading and writing fiction. When I was nine years old, I landed a role as a regular in a children's television series, and over the last two years I have been a very active member of the Bandon Playhouse, our community theatre, being presently engaged as the musical director for our production of 'Fiddler on the Roof.'

"Actually, my chosen career is not writing, but music. I have been increasingly involved with music over the last four years, taking piano lessons, singing in various choirs, and playing synthesizers in a local rock group, which (unfortunately) disbanded last December. I have written a lot of original music, and am always writing more, and I have been accepted at the University of Oregon School of Music, where I would like to study piano, voice, and composition.

"Writing is still a hobby for me, to be indulged in when I have time for it. My favorite genre is science fiction, both to read and to write; science fiction probably makes up more than half of everything I read. I love it because it makes you think, and it makes you wonder. It is the final answer to the question, 'What if . . . ?' That is the way to write science fiction. You take a proposition, and work a story around it. Each science fiction writer does it in his own way, and I find them all to be wonderful. My own writing tends to be rather undisciplined, but I have a few good first-drafts, and if I ever find the

time to carefully edit and rewrite them, I will send them in to some of the better science fiction magazines; it would be fun to see my wild ideas actually in *print*. I don't see myself as a serious author, though; that's not really my field. Take a look at the music world five years from now; that's where you'll find me."

HOLMES, Marjorie 1910-

PERSONAL: Born September 22, 1910, in Storm Lake, Iowa; daughter of Samuel Arthur (a salesman) and Rosa (Griffith) Holmes; married Lynn Burton Mighell, 1932 (deceased), married George P. Schmieler (a physician), July 4, 1981; children: (first marriage) Marjorie Mighell Croner, Mark, Mallory, Melanie. *Education:* Attended Buena Vista College, 1927-29; Cornell College, B.A., 1931. *Home and office:* 637 E. McMurray Rd., McMurray, Pa. 15317. *Agent:* Edward J. Acton, 928 Broadway, New York, N.Y. 10010.

CAREER: Freelance writer, columnist, and teacher. Author of weekly column, "Love and Laughter," in Washington, D.C. *Star,* 1959-73, also appeared in syndication; author of monthly column, "A Woman's Conversation with God," 1971-77. Teacher of writing, Georgetown University Summer Writers Conference, 1959-79, Catholic University, 1964-65, Univer-

MARJORIE HOLMES

WRITINGS: World by the Tail, Lippincott, 1943; *Ten O'Clock Scholar,* Lippincott, 1947; *Saturday Night* (Junior Literary Guild selection), Westminster, 1959; *Cherry Blossom Princess,* Westminster, 1960; *Follow Your Dream,* Westminster, 1961; *Senior Trip,* Westminster, 1962; *Love Is a Hopscotch Thing,* Westminster, 1963, published as *Sunday Morning,* Dell, 1982; *Love and Laughter,* Doubleday, 1967; *I've Got to Talk to Somebody, God: A Woman's Conversation with God* (illustrated by Betty Fraser), Doubleday, 1969; *Writing the Creative Article,* Writer, Inc., 1969.

Who Am I, God?, Doubleday, 1971; *To Treasure Our Days,* Hallmark, 1971; *Two from Galilee: A Love Story of Mary and Joseph,* Revell, 1972; *Nobody Else Will Listen,* Doubleday, 1973; *You and I and Yesterday* (illustrated by Bob Brunson), Morrow, 1973; *As Tall as My Heart,* EPM Publications, 1974; *How Can I Find You, God?,* Doubleday, 1975; *Beauty in Your Own Back Yard,* EPM Publications, 1976; *Hold Me Up a Little Longer, Lord* (illustrated by Patricia Mighell), Doubleday, 1977; *Lord, Let Me Love,* Doubleday, 1978; *God and Vitamins,* Doubleday, 1980; *To Help You Through the Hurting,* Doubleday, 1983; *Three from Galilee: The Young Man from Nazareth,* Harper, 1985.

Help me to give my children good roots.... ■ (From *Hold Me Up a Little Longer, Lord* by Marjorie Holmes. Illustrated by Patricia Mighell.)

sity of Maryland, 1967-68, Philadelphia Writers Conference, and Cape Cod Writers Conference. Member of board of directors, Foundation for Christian Living, 1975—. Served as writer and commentator for radio shows, including "Alexander's Mediation Board" for the Mutual Network. Lecturer at universities. *Member:* Children's Book Guild, American Newspaper Women's Club, Washington National Press Club, Virginia Press Women, Delta Phi Beta. *Awards, honors:* Alumni Achievement Award, Cornell College, 1963; Award for Literature, American Association for Social Psychiatry, 1964; Honor Iowans Award, Buena Vista College, 1966; Woman of Achievement, National Federation of Press Women, 1972; Scholarship Celebrity Award, Ft. Worth Women in Communications, 1975; Woman of Achievement, McLean, Va., Business and Professional Women, 1976; D. Litt., Buena Vista College, 1976; Freedom Foundation of Valley Forge award, 1977; Distinguished Service Award from Buena Vista College, 1978; Certificate of Merit from Catholic Library Association for contribution to high school libraries, 1983.

All our favorite games involved hiding and mystery and pursuit, culminating in a violent chase. But the one that really sent us was Run, Sheep, Run. ■ (From *You and I and Yesterday* by Marjorie Holmes. Illustrated by Bob Brunson.)

Author of filmscript for "The General Comes Home," produced by Metro-Goldwyn-Mayer, and a film adaptation of her book *Two from Galilee: A Love Story of Mary and Joseph*. Contributor of short stories, articles, and poetry to magazines, including *Ladies' Home Journal, McCall's, Reader's Digest,* and *Family Circle*.

WORK IN PROGRESS: Three from Galilee: The Messiah, a sequel to *Three from Galilee: The Young Man from Nazareth*, to be published by Harper.

SIDELIGHTS: "I was born in Storm Lake, Iowa and spent most of my waking hours in the water or on its shore. I learned to swim almost as soon as I could walk, and I still swim three times a day all summer.

"An understanding English teacher encouraged my childhood dream of becoming a writer. She once wrote on my notebook,

'You can write beautiful things for those who crave beautiful things,' and 'There is a duty.' These words sustained me through many rejections during my early career.

"After two years at Storm Lake's Buena Vista College—with a scholarship and one good dress—I left for Cornell College at Mount Vernon, Iowa. [I went there] primarily because of its literary magazine, *The Husk*, edited by Toppy Tull, patron saint of many writers. While there I began to sell my poems, the first to a pulp magazine, *Weird Tales,* for seven dollars.

"After graduating in 1931, I met and married, within two months, a senior engineer at Iowa University, Lynn Mighell. We tried to beat the Depression by buying an old car for thirty-five dollars and rattling off to the Rio Grande Valley to raise cabbage. Floods, hurricanes and aphids ruined the cabbage but didn't deter my writing. A week before my first baby was born, at the age of twenty-two, I helped pay the stork by selling my first two stories.

"Frequent moves followed as my husband got his start in air conditioning. During this period, in addition to free lancing I did radio work, including a stint as a disc jockey. One day, realizing my daughter was being raised by a maid instead of me, I went back to the typewriter for good. My writing and my family—they were the really important things.

"Despite raising four children I was able to sell short stories and articles to the popular magazines and to produce my first novel, *World by the Tail*. It received excellent reviews but modest sales. Revived as a Bantam paperback years later, it has sold nearly a million copies. Six other novels followed, five of them young love novels.

"In 1952 I began writing a column 'Love and Laughter' for the Washington, D.C. *Star* which later was syndicated. A collection of these columns, together with pieces from magazine articles I've written were published in a book entitled *Love and Laughter*. Two years later *I've Got to Talk to Somebody, God* was published.

"It was the title, I'm sure, that grabbed people. We all have said it or felt it so many times. 'I've *got* to talk to somebody!' Yet the title, and the lead prayer in the book came to me the very last day, as I was about to deliver the manuscript to the publisher. Something made me sit down and write one more prayer; and as I did so, I realized that's what the book was all about: loneliness, how hard it is to communicate what we really feel—our fears and joys and secret dreams—except to God.

"To my absolute amazement, the mail poured in from men as well as women, and even from young girls. Over and over they said, 'You're writing about *me*! How did you know I felt that way?' And some, 'Now I don't feel so guilty.' And oh, so many—which was the greatest reward of all: 'You've helped me!'

". . . The last thing I expected or wanted to do was write a book of prayers for girls. Yet one day some prayers in the voice of a teen-age girl began to sing themselves in my head. This is ridiculous, I thought; but I wrote a few dozen anyway, mainly because I couldn't resist their cadences. I actually hid them away and forgot about them. Until one day Ann Guy, a friend who writes for young people, called to urge a project upon me. 'A book that's really needed, Marjorie, and only you can do it—a book of prayers for girls!'

"At her insistence, I got those first prayers out and reread them. They sounded better than I remembered. And suddenly new prayers began to dominate my thinking, giving me no rest. It was as if some power beyond my own was compelling me to put them down, to write this book. When I took my samples to my editor, however, she was *not* enthusiastic, 'I doubt if kids today pray any more,' she said. 'I really doubt if they would read this book.'

"Since I'd already written so many—about sixteen, I decided to find out. I typed them up and tried them out, anonymously, on two different groups: Future Homemakers of America, a wonderful group of girls for whom I had spoken in West Virginia. And a more sophisticated bunch of kids, Young Life, of McLean, near Washington, D.C. The sponsors sent me their written responses—bundles of letters all pleading for more: 'Where can I get them? My sister is mean to me, nobody understands me, I love this boy—.' That kind of thing, along

with some very real problems. It was then I knew I *had* to finish *Nobody Else Will Listen*. Ann had been right, it was needed.

"*Nobody Else Will Listen* . . . sold 130,000 copies by the first year. That said something very significant to me: Young people today are hurting, they are confused, they really want discipline and spiritual guidance. They need somebody to talk to who will care enough to listen and not condemn. And they are very grateful when they begin to realize how easy it is to talk to God. They feel better about themselves, they not only get help with their problems, through prayer they discover a source of help and comfort that will sustain them all their lives.

"So, as a Christian writer, I think we should listen to these strong compelling impulses that come to us. We'd better heed; I think it's God moving us to use the talent He gave us to help the people who need us." [Marjorie Holmes, "Writing for Young Adults," *Catholic Library World,* July/August, 1983.[1]]

"*You and I and Yesterday* is a nostalgic look at my Iowa childhood; and *God and Vitamins* is based on my own experience with exercise, supplements and natural foods. Writing is very hard work, and so are lectures and promotion tours. When people ask, 'Where do you get your energy?' I tell them 'God and vitamins. I pray a lot and take a lot of vitamins!'

"I have been writing ever since I could first hold a pencil; for me to write is to live. Since I write mostly for women, I am particularly pleased that not only my books of prayers, but my adult novels, have become favorites with high school girls. Their response to *Two from Galilee: A Love Story of Mary and Joseph* was a great joy. They could identify with Mary, who was herself a teenager, and the fact that Joseph too was young, not much more than twenty.

"My other five romances, written primarily for girls, were recently reissued by Dell after almost twenty years! All were

Help me to equip my children to live decent happy lives in a world where it is so hard to be good. ■ (From *I've Got to Talk to Somebody, God: A Woman's Conversation with God* by Marjorie Holmes. Illustrated by Betty Fraser.)

very successful when first published, all very popular with girls and their mothers, too, for I wrote them with the same skill I would use in writing for *Ladies' Home Journal*. All are filled with love, laughter, dates, dreams and romantic suspense. All of them are entertaining, funny, filled with humor as well as emotion, but all are very pure—no sex, no swear words, not even an innocent 'darn it!' Girls adored them when they first came out and still do today in their latest edition. I'm getting as many warm, wonderful letters about these books today as I did twenty years ago.

"But nothing I have ever written has brought in more mail than *Two from Galilee: A Love Story of Mary and Joseph*. From the very first, letters have poured in from readers of all ages, begging for a sequel. They just couldn't bear to part with that little family; they urged me to tell the rest of the story of Jesus' life in the human terms I had brought to the love story of Mary and Joseph. At last I have done so. *Three from Galilee: The Young Man from Nazareth* deals with Jesus' childhood and youth (those so-called 'missing years' not even mentioned in the Bible). A second and final volume *The Messiah* will follow.

"I give about five lectures a year and have taught writing at numerous conferences and universities. My book *Writing the Creative Article* is based on my writing classes at Georgetown University.

"I have four children and four grandchildren. My husband, Lynn Mighell, died in 1979. Two years later I married a Pittsburgh physician, Dr. George Schmieler, who found *I've Got to Talk to Somebody, God* among his late wife's things and was so comforted he set out to find the author. I tell of the miracles that brought us together in my book *To Help You Through the Hurting*."

FOR MORE INFORMATION SEE: Ladies' Home Journal, December, 1969; Martha E. Ward and Dorothy A. Marquardt, *Authors of Books for Young Poeple,* Scarecrow Press, 1971; Barbara Nykoruk, editor, *Authors in the News,* Volume I, Gale, 1976; Marjorie Holmes, "Off the Cuff: The Little Brown Duck," *The Writer,* December, 1979; M. Holmes, "Writing for Young Adults," *Catholic Library World,* July/August, 1983.

HUMMEL, Berta   1909-1946
(Sister Maria Innocentia Hummel)

PERSONAL: Born May 21, 1909, in Massing am der Rott, Lower Bavaria, Germany; died of tuberculosis, November 6, 1946 at the Siessen Convent, in Württemberg, Germany (now West Germany); daughter of Adolf (a department store owner) and Viktoria (Anglsperger) Hummel. *Education:* Academy of Applied Arts, Munich, graduate (first in class), 1931, graduate study, 1935-36. *Religion:* Catholic.

CAREER: Sister of The Third Order of Saint Francis, Siessen Convent, Württemberg, Germany, 1933-46. Teacher of art to young children at institutions administered by the convent. *Exhibitions:* Convent of Franciscan Sisters at Siessen, Württemberg, 1933; Leipzig Trade Fair, Germany, 1937; Saulgau, Germany, 1946; Memorial Exhibit, Massing, Germany, 1947; "Formation of an Artist: The Early Works of Berta Hummel," traveling exhibition, United States, 1980.

ILLUSTRATOR: Margarete Seemann, *Das Hummel-Buch,* Emil Fink Verlag, 1934, published as *The Hummel-Book,* translated

by Lola C. Eytel, 1950, 16th edition, Emil Fink Verlag, 1972; *Hui!, Die Hummel!* (title means "Whee! the Bumblebee!"), Ars Sacra/Josef Muller Verlag, 1939, translation published as *The Hummel: Drawings by Berta Hummel with Light Verse,* Verlag Ars Sacra, 1972.

SIDELIGHTS: Hummel was born at Massing am der Rott in Lower Bavaria, about thirty miles southeast of Munich, on **May 21, 1909.** She was the third of six children born to Adolf and Viktoria Hummel. Her father ran the family dry goods business, although he had always wanted to be an artist.

Like her father, Berta showed an early inclination toward drawing. Her mother recalled her earliest artistic endeavors: "If she wasn't using wastepaper from the store downstairs to make her drawings, she would be looking for old scraps of cloth to make dolls clothes. Often Lisa, our cook, would help her sew little costumes for the dolls. They were simple, but very colorful. When they finished Berta would go out into the garden or into the kitchen or wherever her two sisters happened to be busy and put on a little show with the dolls to entertain them." [Eric Ehrmann, *Hummel: The Complete Collector's Guide and Illustrated Reference,* Portfolio Press, 1976.[1]]

World War I erupted when Hummel was five years old, and her father was sent to fight in the German army. According to her mother, Berta suffered from her father's absence during those war years. In school, she was difficult to discipline. Her mother recalled: "Gradually we noticed that this child of promise was destined to be a problem child and would cause untold anxiety to loved ones. Her teachers did not understand the temperamental character of their charge. Her usually sunny

Hummel, self-portrait as a young girl.

**"What a sad and mournful tune
You are playing
Little fiddler!"**

■ (From *The Hummel-Book,* poems and preface by
Margarete Seeman. Translated by Lola C. Eytel.
Illustrated by Berta Hummel.)

disposition suffered visibly under the treatment of a teacher
who, while well-meaning, was unaware of the psychic condition of the child. When complaints of insubordination reached
our home, we attempted to assist the teacher by bringing force
and greater vigilance to bear upon a spirit that was already
bending under the strain of maladjustment. I can see her yet
today, when coming upon her unawares, I caught her in the
act of erasing from her slate the report meant for us to censure.
Berta trembled visibly when she was discovered, and only then
did I realize that her teacher did not understand her. My heart
ached for the child and I visited the school pleading that the
teacher substitute kindness for severity. Some time later, Berta
came to the fourth class. Here native ingenuity and her sunny
disposition were again in evidence. The sister praised her talents, and yet we never saw her study at home." [Sister M.
Gonsalva Wiegand, O.S.F., *Sketch Me, Berta Hummel! Biography of Sister Maria Innocentia,* Grail, 1951.[2]]

Hummel's teacher appointed her to decorate the blackboards
and to do illustrations for the classroom. She spent five years
at the Vjolksschule in Massing, and then joined the Girls'
Finishing School in Simback at the age of twelve. At school,
Hummel's artistic talents flourished. She designed scenery and
costumes for school plays, painted landscapes in watercolors,
and, by her fourth year at Simbach (1925), was sculpting with
terra cotta clay. According to her mother: "Berta would bring

her work home when she came for a weekend or a holiday.
She was painting still lifes, nature scenes, and of course continuing her little sketches on postcards. My husband began
noticing refinement in her style, a self-confidence that let him
know Berta really wanted to fulfill his ambition by becoming
the family artist."[1]

On **March 25, 1926,** Hummel graduated from Simbach. She
continued her art education in Munich, at the Academy of
Applied Arts. Some of the finest art teachers and successful
artists were in Munich during the late 1920s, so that Hummel
was greatly inspired. She developed and refined her artistic
talent. Later, one of her art teachers wrote about her: "With
most of my students, when I recognized them as sincere and
earnest, I entertained a social friendship. Berta was very close
to me, but because of her intensive program, we had little time
to talk about anything other than that pertained to her work.
Highly intelligent and gifted with extraordinary talent, the young
girl felt obligated to work more zealously and more intensively
than the rest. She showed great joy and enthusiasm for all
things beautiful.

"On several occasions she accompanied us when the class in
aquarelles visited Lindau and Salzburg. She sketched and worked
continuously during such tours, and I regret that so little time
was left for intimate conversation, since correcting and advis-
ing took up all our allotted time.

Thy praise swells with the voice of every living being. ■
(From *The Hummel-Book,* poems and preface by
Margarete Seemann. Translated by Lola C. Eytel.
Illustrated by Berta Hummel.)

**I'd love to bring you the whole world,
If I could!
And you'd give me a dime for it.
You sure would!**

■ (From *The Hummel-Book,* poems and preface by
Margarete Seeman. Translated by Lola C. Eytel.
Illustrated by Berta Hummel.)

"On our way to and from the place of studies we were again
occupied in observing nature, so personal references were at
a minimum. Thus I came to know little about my favorite
student beyond our mutual interests.

"After she had successfully and brilliantly passed her exam-
inations as teacher of art, I, with the rest of the faculty, cherished the hope of her returning to the Academy.

"But one day she visited my home to inform me that other
plans were preventing her returning to Munich. Thus ended
for a time all personal contact; even our correspondence was
of necessity limited."[2]

At the art academy Hummel became friends with two Franciscan Sisters from the Convent at Siessen. As their friendship
became more intimate, Hummel began to entertain thoughts
of becoming a member of the religious order. As a member
of the convent of the Franciscan Sisters at Siessen, Hummel
knew that she would be treated equally, asked to renounce her
worldly possessions, and, above all, be allowed to continue
her art within the framework of prayer and shared responsibilities of the convent.

Upon graduation from the Academy, on **March 15, 1931,**
Hummel formally announced her decision to enter the convent
to her parents and teacher. Five weeks later, on April 22, she
entered the convent, where she began teaching art while a

postulant. After two years, Hummel was given her habit of
the Sister of the Third Order of Saint Francis. On August 22,
1933, she became Sister Maria Innocentia, thus renouncing
her given name, Berta Hummel.

The convent encouraged her to continue her artwork. She designed religious vestments and banners, postcards and greeting
cards. As a result of her work for children, a series of amusing
drawings, Hummel collaborated with author Margarete Seemann on a children's book entitled *The Hummel Book* in 1934.
That same year, on August 30th, Hummel took her formal
religious vows, thus completing her novitiate.

It was in 1934 that Hummel's work first came to the attention
of Franz Goebel, the head of W. Goebel Porzellanfabrik in
Oeslau. He persuaded the convent to let him transform Hummel's sketches into ceramic figurines for the export market.
Thus, in 1935, the first seven figurines were displayed at the
Leipzig Trade Fair, bearing the mark of "M. I. Hummel."
Almost immediately, they became popular as collectibles. Since
1935, the Goebel firm, now located in Rodental, West Germany, has initiated a series of changes in trademarks, which
has subsequently increased the value of the pieces.

In the years that followed, Hummel made the sketches for the
"Hummel cards" and "Hummel figures." She was, however,
repeatedly suffering from a flu or a cold, so that her time was
spent mostly working in her studio. In 1937, the Nazi government closed all parochial and private schools and raised
taxes on all convents. During this period of severe economic
burden, the convent was supported by the manufacture of "M.
I. Hummel" figurines.

. . .With the Seven Dwarfs and Snow White. . . . ■
(From *The Hummel-Book,* poems and preface by
Margarete Seeman. Translated by Lola C. Eytel.
Illustrated by Berta Hummel.)

As the war brought more hardships and restrictions, Hummel's health suffered under its austere conditions. She developed complications to a cold, which was diagnosed first as pleurisy, and then as a lung infection. In the fall of 1944, her condition was more correctly diagnosed as chronic tuberculosis. By November, 1945, Hummel was sent to a sanatorium, but her condition continued to deteriorate, becoming complicated by dropsy. At her own request, Hummel was returned to her convent at Siessen where she died at the age of thirty-seven on **November 6, 1946.**

Although Hummel left no written messages to her numerous admirers, her art is a testimony to her faith, her love of children, goodness, and her love of life. She once remarked: "Man must have a light heart (or, translated in another manner, man must be light-hearted) to live beyond his difficulties."[1]

FOR MORE INFORMATION SEE: Hobbies, December, 1947, July, 1981, April, 1984; Sister M. Gonsalva Wiegand, O.S.F., *Sketch Me, Berta Hummel! Biography of Sister Maria Innocentia,* Grail, 1951; *Catholic World,* May, 1953; *Acquire,* July, 1975; Eric Ehrmann, *Hummel: The Complete Collector's Guide and Illustrated Reference,* Portfolio Press, 1976; John F. Hotchkiss, *Hummel Art,* Wallace-Homestead, 1978; *People Weekly,* December 15, 1980; Carl F. Luckey, *A Collectors Identification and Value Guide: Hummel Figurines and Plates,* 4th edition, Books Americana, 1982. Obituaries: *Hobbies,* March, 1947; *Das Munster* (Germany), spring-fall, 1947.

An "M. I. Hummel" figurine may consist of as many as thirty-nine singly molded parts—as in "Adventure Bound," shown above. ■ (From *Hummel: The Complete Collector's Guide and Illustrated Reference* by Eric Ehrmann. Photograph by Seymour Linden.)

Berta Hummel, also known as Sister Maria Innocentia.

JACOBS, Francine   1935-

PERSONAL: Born May 11, 1935, in New York, N.Y.; daughter of Louis (a glove manufacturer) and Ida (Schrag) Kaufman; married Jerome L. Jacobs (a psychiatrist), June 10, 1956, children: Laurie, Larry. *Education:* Queens College (now Queens College of the City University of New York), B.A., 1956. *Home:* 93 Old Farm Rd., Pleasantville, N.Y. 10570.

CAREER: Elementary school teacher in Rye, N.Y., 1956-58, and Chappaqua, N.Y., 1967-68; writer, 1967—. *Member:* Authors Guild. *Awards, honors: A Secret Language of Animals: Communication by Pheromones* was selected as one of the children's books of the year, 1976, by the Children's Book Committee of the Child Study Association; Outstanding Science Book for Children Award from the National Science Teachers Association and Children's Book Council, 1975, for *The Sargasso Sea: An Ocean Desert,* 1980, for *Coral,* 1981, for *Bermuda Petrel: The Bird That Would Not Die,* 1982, for *Supersaurus,* and 1983, for *Cosmic Countdown: What Astronomers Have Learned about the Life of the Universe.*

WRITINGS—Juvenile; published by Morrow, except as indicated: *The Wisher's Handbook,* Funk, 1968; *The Legs of the Moon,* Coward, 1971; *The King's Ditch,* Coward, 1971; *Sea Turtles,* 1972; *The Freshwater Eel,* 1973; *Nature's Light: The Story of Bioluminescence,* 1974; *The Sargasso Sea: An Ocean Desert,* 1975; *A Secret Language of Animals: Communication by Pheromones* (illustrated by Jean D. Zallinger), 1976; *Sounds in the Sea* (illustrated by J. D. Zallinger), 1977; *The Red Sea* (illustrated by Elsie Wrigley), 1978; *Africa's Flamingo Lake*

(illustrated with photographs by Jerome Jacobs), 1979; *Sewer Sam: The Sea Cow* (illustrated by Harriet Springer), Walker & Co., 1979.

Coral, Putnam, 1980; *Fire Snake: The Railroad That Changed East Africa* (illustrated by Lloyd Bloom), 1980; *Bermuda Petrel: The Bird That Would Not Die* (illustrated by Ted Lewin), 1981; *Barracuda: Tiger of the Sea* (illustrated by H. Springer), Walker & Co., 1981; *Supersaurus* (illustrated by D. D. Taylor), Putnam, 1982; *Cosmic Countdown: What Astronomers Have Learned about the Life of the Universe,* Evans, 1983; *Breakthrough: The True Story of Penicillin,* Dodd, 1985.

SIDELIGHTS: Jacobs grew up in the small, oceanside community of Long Beach on Long Island, New York. ''My favorite pastime was searching along the shore to discover treasures that the tides swept in. I came to recognize the different kinds of seashells, to collect beach glass and best of all, to know the marvelous shore creatures: the clams, crabs, starfish, and seabirds.''

Jacobs studied elementary education and child psychology at Queens College. After graduation she began teaching elementary school and married Jerome Jacobs. ''When my children started school I began a new career, writing for young readers. Writing is work that is done alone in quiet. It stirs one's memories. I found myself thinking about the sea, hearing the screech of gulls, smelling the salt air, and wishing I were back at the shore, exploring tidal pools and poking through clumps of seaweed. I and my husband and children have spent much time together camping in wilderness and shore areas. I am not only a beachcomber today but a snorkeler and a certified scuba diver. I also enjoy hiking and fishing. Ideas for my books sometimes come from experiences on my travels. A visit to a turtle farm on a Caribbean island led me to write *Sea Turtles. Coral* developed while I explored the beautiful reefs in the Caribbean Sea.

''*Bermuda Petrel* began as a result of a child's question: 'If so many animals are in danger of dying out, is there anything

FRANCINE JACOBS

They toss what remains in the cup over their left shoulders. ■ (From *The Wisher's Handbook* by Francine Jacobs. Illustrated by Ingrid Fetz.)

we can do to help them?' Soon after that, a piece in the newspaper caught my attention. It was about a bird, the Bermuda petrel, and how it is being saved. I started to learn more about this small seabird and discovered an exciting story. Much is written about animals that are dying out, but here was an animal that was making a comeback—and largely through the efforts of one man. I decided to write a book about the Bermuda petrel to answer the child who had asked what can be done to help animals in danger.

"The idea for my latest book, *Breakthrough: The True Story of Penicillin*, came from my daughter. Laurie had been fascinated by the development of penicillin in a lecture given by a chemist-professor who had taken part in it. The subject sounded so interesting that I had to learn more. So I visited Professor Max Tishler at Wesleyan University myself and thus began this exciting project.

"I enjoy writing nonfiction. Each of my books is a story—a true one!"

HOBBIES AND OTHER INTERESTS: Travel, hiking, fishing, beachcombing, reading, cooking, gardening.

FOR MORE INFORMATION SEE: Washington Post Book World, January 13, 1980.

The hills are dearest which our childish feet
Have climbed the earliest; and the streams most sweet
Are those at which our young lips drank.
—John Greenleaf Whittier

JONES, Geraldine 1951-
(Geraldine McCaughrean)

PERSONAL: Born June 6, 1951, in Enfield, London, England; daughter of Leslie Arthur (a fireman) and Ethel (a teacher; maiden name, Thomas) Jones. *Education:* Christ Church College, B.A. (honors), 1977. *Religion:* Catholic ("almost"). *Home and office:* 3 Melton Dr., Didcot, Oxfordshire OX11 FJP, England. *Agent:* Giles Gordon, Anthony Sheil Assoc. Ltd., 43 Doughty St., London WC1N 2LF, England.

CAREER: Thames Television, London, England, secretary, 1970-73; Marshall Cavendish Ltd., London, assistant editor, 1977-80, staff writer, 1982—; Carreras-Rothman Ltd., Aylesbury, England, editorial assistant, 1980-81, writer, 1981—. *Member:* National Union of Journalists, Journalists against Nuclear Extermination. *Awards, honors:* Winner of All-London Literary Competition in the short story category, sponsored by Wandsworth Borough Council, 1979, for "The Pike."

WRITINGS—For children; all published by Oxford University Press; all under name Geraldine McCaughrean, except where indicated: (Under name Geraldine Jones) *Adventure in New York* (illustrated by Cynthia Back), 1981; (adapter) *One Thousand and One Arabian Nights* (illustrated by Stephen Lavis), 1982; *Stories from Chaucer* (illustrated by Victor Ambrus), 1984; *Saint George and the Dragon*, 1986; *The Bedtime Story Book* (illustrated by Brian Wildsmith), 1986. Editor of *Banbury Focus*, 1981-82; sub-editor and staff writer of stories to *Storyteller* and *Great Composers*.

WORK IN PROGRESS: New versions of the Greek myths: the Odyssey, the Iliad, Theseus, Perseus, Jason; press series of world myths and legends.

SIDELIGHTS: "Having struggled with several unsuccessful and unpublished novels, I have now found that my true talent lies in writing for children. In doing so, I have cleaned up a previously elaborate and overwritten style into one that is both more valid and of more use to publishers. The pure luck of being in the right place at the right time has led to the remarkable good fortune of making a living from the thing I like doing best."

GERALDINE JONES

The story of Sinbad the Sailor. . . . An adventure drawn up from the liquid mountains of the sea.
■ (From *One Thousand and One Arabian Nights,* adapted by Geraldine McCaughrean. Illustrated by Stephen Lavis.)

HOBBIES AND OTHER INTERESTS: "I have a delapidated cabin cruiser on the River Thames, play the concertina, and write unpublished novels."

JUKES, Mavis

BRIEF ENTRY: Author of children's books. A former schoolteacher and lawyer, Jukes is now a full-time writer. She received several awards for her first two books, both illustrated by Lloyd Bloom. *No One Is Going to Nashville* (Knopf, 1983) won the Irma Simonton Black Award in 1984, and *Like Jake and Me* (Knopf, 1984) was named a Newbery Honor Book in 1985. According to *New York Times Book Review,* the two stories are similar in that they both stress "the positive potential of a stepfamily." In *No One Is Going to Nashville,* young Sonia, an aspiring veterinarian, finds a stray dog and names him Max. When her father objects to her keeping her new pet, they both write ads to find the dog a home. In the end, Max remains when Sonia's stepmother decides to take her side. "The story has an appealing childlike conflict," noted *Horn Book,* "and likable characters developed as distinct personalities."

Like Jake and Me relates the story of Alex and his stepfather, Jake, who seem to have little in common until a fuzzy spider helps to reveal some similarities. "It is the story of a child coming to terms with a stepparent," stated *New York Times Book Review,* "written with humor and insight. . . ." *Horn Book* agreed, observing that "the story combines integrity in characterization and speech with earthy humor and great joy in the flowering of Jake's and Alex's affection." Jukes is also the author of a short story for children, "Make a Wish," that appeared in *Ms.* Her latest work is entitled *Blackberries in the Dark* (Knopf, 1985). *Residence:* Sonoma County, Calif.

I was eleven years old when they came and fourteen when they left. Dad said I was lucky—*he'd* gone from forty to fifty in three short years! ■ (Jacket illustration by Robert Andrew Parker from *The Great Toozy Takeover* by Rosalie Kelly.)

Rosalie Kelly with her grandson.

KELLY, Rosalie (Ruth)

PERSONAL: Born in Grand Rapids, Mich.; daughter of Charles (a building contractor) and Emmiline (Barth) Schley; married Gleason Kelly (a business manager), May 18, 1944; children: Nancy, Meredith (Mrs. Philip Lewis), William. *Education:* Attended Oregon State University, 1939-40. *Religion:* Protestant. *Home:* 246 Orchard Rd., Orinda, Calif. 94563.

CAREER: Has worked as secretary and clerk in private industry, 1936-42, and for U.S. Department of the Interior, 1950-52. Creative writing teacher, Acalanes Adult Education Department, Walnut Creek, Calif., 1976—.

*WRITINGS—*Juvenile fiction: *The Great Toozy Takeover,* Putnam, 1975; *Addie's Year,* Beaufort Books, 1981. Contributor of short stories to small literary magazines.

WORK IN PROGRESS: Love Jane, a fantasy; *The Robins of Kirkleigh,* a fantasy about Robin Hood.

SIDELIGHTS: "I once read somewhere that all writers seem to have had memorable childhoods. I'm not sure this is true; it may be only that writers retain more vivid memories of that period than others do. My own midwestern childhood is still a joy to remember, one of creeks and violets and meadows, books, kittens, daydreams. Later we moved to Southern California and then on to Oregon, but the security of a warm family circle remained unchanged.

"At nineteen I published my first story in what was then called a 'Sunday school paper,' receiving ten dollars for it. The check was promptly cashed for these were hard times. I stopped writing when I finally got a job and it wasn't until much had intervened—college, a war, marriage and children—that I finally returned to it. We had by then moved to the San Francisco Bay area where I enrolled in a writing class taught by Sonia Levitin. Such classes have taken a good many verbal hard knocks, but for anyone who is truly serious about writing I think they are invaluable: They keep you working. It was during this time of apprenticeship that the Toozy book was begun and completed.

"Particular joys just now center around two grandsons, occasional foreign travel, and of course those hours spent each day at the typewriter."

CARL KIDWELL

It wasn't fear—at least he hoped it wasn't—but just an awareness of danger, and the suspense of uncertainty. ■ (Jacket illustration by Carl Kidwell from *Granada, Surrender!* by Carl Kidwell.)

KIDWELL, Carl 1910-

PERSONAL: Born August 8, 1910, in Washington, Ind.; son of William and Martha Kidwell.

CAREER: Author and illustrator of juvenile adventure fiction. Prior to World War II, held a number of jobs, including bell-hop, railway coach painter, and drugstore clerk. *Military service:* U.S. Navy, World War II; served as a radioman.

WRITINGS—All self-illustrated; all for children: *Arrow in the Sun,* Viking, 1961; *The Angry Earth,* Viking, 1964; *Granada, Surrender!,* Viking, 1968.

Illustrator; all for children: Marion Brown, *Swamp Fox,* Westminster, 1950; Manuel Komroff, *True Adventures of Spies,* Little, Brown, 1954; Ernie Rydberg, *The Dark of the Cave,* McKay, 1965; C. L. Murphy, *Buffalo Grass,* Dial, 1966; Gertrude E. Finney, *To Survive We Must Be Clever,* McKay, 1966; Marjorie A. Zapf, *The Mystery of the Great Swamp,* Atheneum, 1967; Dorothy Heiderstadt, *Stolen by the Indians,* McKay, 1968; Janet Randall, *Island Ghost* (Junior Literary Guild selection), McKay, 1970; Martha C. King, *Smugglers' Island,* Ives Washburn, 1970.

KIMMEL, Margaret Mary 1938-

PERSONAL: Born May 12, 1938, in Gary, Ind. *Education:* Rosary College, B.A., 1960, M.L.S., 1963.

CAREER: Has worked as a children's librarian in the Gary Public Library, Gary, Ind. and at the Enoch Pratt Free Library, Baltimore, Md., and has taught at the College of Librarianship Wales, and at Simmons College Boston, Mass. Free-lance writer, Science Research Associates, 1961-62.

WRITINGS: Magic in the Mist (juvenile fiction; illustrated by Trina Schart Hyman), McElderry Book, 1975; (editor with Thomas J. Galvin and Brenda H. White) *Excellence in School Media Programs,* American Library Association, 1980; (with Elizabeth Segel) *For Reading Out Loud! A Guide to Sharing Books with Children* (*Horn Book* honor list; illustrated by Trina Schart Hyman), foreword by Betsy Byars, Delacorte, 1983.

(From *For Reading Out Loud! A Guide to Sharing Books with Children* by Margaret Mary Kimmel and Elizabeth Segel. Illustrated by Trina Schart Hyman.)

KUH, Charlotte 1892(?)-1985

OBITUARY NOTICE: Born about 1892; died March 4, 1985, in Cambridge, Mass. Educator and author. Kuh taught at Chicago's Francis Parker School from 1914 to 1919 and served as a trustee of the private school from 1945 to 1957. Her teaching experiences prompted a concern for the welfare of children and adolescents that led her eventually into the fields of social work and social reform. Kuh's early concerns were for the rights of small children who worked at menial jobs. She served as president of the Juvenile Protection Association in the early 1950s and campaigned in Illinois for laws to regulate safety, working conditions, and working hours for children.

Later the educator turned her attention to adolescents with social and behavioral problems and young people in trouble with the law. She reorganized the Juvenile Court Committee in her community and succeeded in her attempt to provide professional guidance for troubled youth. Kuh also found time to write children's books such as Macmillan's "Happy Hour Books" series published in 1929, with illustrations by Kurt Wiese. The series served as an introduction to community helpers, including *The Deliverymen, The Engineer, The Fireman,* and *The Postman,* among others. She also wrote *A School, a Train, and a Ship* and *A Train, a Boat, and an Island.*

FOR MORE INFORMATION SEE: Barbara Bader, *American Picturebooks from "Noah's Ark" to "The Beast Within,"* Macmillan, 1976. Obituaries: *Chicago Tribune,* March 8, 1985.

LASH, Joseph P. 1909-

PERSONAL: Born December 2, 1909, in New York, N.Y.; son of Samuel (a storekeeper) and Mary (Avchin) Lash; married Trude Wenzel (a director of Citizens Committee for Children), November 8, 1944; children: Jonathan. *Education:* City College (now City College of the City University of New York), A.B., 1931; Columbia University, M.A., 1932. *Politics:* Democrat. *Religion:* Jewish. *Home:* Skyline Dr., Oakland, N.J. 07436.

CAREER: Americans for Democratic Action, New York, N.Y., director, 1946-49; *New York Post,* New York, N.Y., United Nations correspondent, 1950-61, assistant editor of editorial page, 1961-66; free-lance writer, 1966—. *Military service:* U.S. Army, World War II; became second lieutenant; received Air Medal. *Awards, honors:* Pulitzer Prize and National Book Award for biography, both 1972, for *Eleanor and Franklin.*

WRITINGS: Dag Hammarskjold: Custodian of the Brushfire Peace, Doubleday, 1961; *Eleanor Roosevelt: A Friend's Memoir,* Doubleday, 1965; *Eleanor and Franklin: The Story of Their Relationship Based on Eleanor Roosevelt's Private Papers,* Norton, 1971; *Eleanor: The Years Alone,* Norton, 1972; (editor) *From the Diaries of Felix Frankfurter,* Norton, 1975; *Roosevelt and Churchill—1939-1941: The Partnership That Saved the West,* Norton, 1976; *Helen and Teacher: The Story of Helen Keller and Anne Sullivan Macy,* Delacorte, 1980; (with Franklin D. Roosevelt, Jr.) *Love, Eleanor: Eleanor Roosevelt and Her Friends,* Doubleday, 1982; *A World of Love: Eleanor Roosevelt and Her Friends 1943-1962,* Volume II, Doubleday, 1984; *Life Was Meant to Be Lived: A Centenary Portrait of Eleanor Roosevelt,* Norton, 1984.

JOSEPH P. LASH

WORK IN PROGRESS: A book about Thomas Corcoran and Benjamin Cohen, the two principal architects of Franklin Roosevelt's New Deal.

SIDELIGHTS: Lash has written six books about Eleanor Roosevelt. "Time has . . . confirmed her insights—which reflected her temperament, her disposition, her great love and concern for people—instead of making her appear to be the fool, or, as some suggested at the time, simple-minded. Hers were the great causes of our time."

Lash made a biographer's comparison: "FDR was a very great person and a very great leader, but people get more out of studying Mrs. Roosevelt's life because she spoke so frankly about the difficulties she confronted and how she surmounted them. With FDR, you know it's hard to put yourself in his shoes and make him a personal model. But as both men and women study her approach to life, to the problems of bringing up a family, of marriage, not to mention things like politics and the movements she embraced, they say, 'If she can do it, I can do it, or I can *try* to do it.' That certainly was borne in on me as time has passed." [Charles Trueheart, "PW Interviews: Joseph Lash," *Publishers Weekly,* October 19, 1984.]

FOR MORE INFORMATION SEE: New York Post, March 31, 1966; *Publishers Weekly,* October 19, 1984.

Children know,
Instinctive taught, the friend and foe.
—Sir Walter Scott

LEVINE, David 1926-

PERSONAL: Born December 20, 1926, in Brooklyn, N.Y.; son of Harry L. (a garment pattern-maker) and Lena (maiden name, Isaacman) Levine; married Mildred Eisenberg (divorced); children: Matthew, Eve. *Education:* Temple University, B.F.A., 1949, B.S., 1949; Hans Hoffman School of Painting, 1950. *Mailing address:* 161 Henry St., Brooklyn, N.Y. 11201. *Agent:* Forum Gallery, 1018 Madison Ave., New York, N.Y. 10021.

CAREER: Oil and watercolor painter; caricaturist, draughtsman. Drawings have appeared in numerous periodicals, including *Horizon, Esquire, McCall's, New York Magazine, Washington Post, Sunday Times* (London), *Observer* (London), and on the covers of *Time, Newsweek,* and others; regular contributor of drawings to *New York Review of Books,* 1963—. Has also been an instructor in drawing at Brooklyn Museum Art School, and the School of Visual Arts. Member, Board of Trustees, Brooklyn Museum. One-man shows include those held at Davis Galleries, New York, N.Y., 1953-63; Forum Gallery, New York City, 1967—; California Palace Legion of Honor, San Francisco, 1968-69, 1971-72; Wesleyan University, Middletown, Conn., 1970; Galerie Yves Lambert, Paris, France, 1972; "Artists, Authors, and Others: Drawings

He loved the sea, and there was always the chance of meeting a new child friend. ■ (From *The Snark Was a Boojum: A Life of Lewis Carroll* by James Playsted Wood. Illustrated by David Levine.)

DAVID LEVINE

by David Levine," Hirshhorn Museum and Sculpture Garden, Washington, D.C., 1976; Galerie Claude Bernard, Paris, 1979, 1982, 1984; Phillips Gallery, Washington, D.C., 1980; "Caricatures of English Nineteenth-Century Authors," Pierpont Morgan Library, New York City, 1981. Several group exhibitions include "David Levine and Aaron Shikler," Brooklyn Museum, Brooklyn, N.Y., 1971; and "Satirical Drawings," Hirshhorn Museum and Sculpture Garden, Washington, D.C., 1976. Work is represented in numerous permanent and private collections, including those of the Cleveland Museum, Cleveland, Ohio, National Portrait Collection, Washington, D.C., Fogg Art Museum, Cambridge, Mass., and National Portrait Gallery, London, England. *Military service:* U.S. Army, 1945-46; served in infantry, special services (near Cairo, Egypt), and in Europe.

MEMBER: Association of American Editorial Cartoonists, Century Association. *Awards, honors:* Recipient of numerous awards for art work, including the Tiffany Foundation Award, 1955, and the Benjamin Altman Prize from National Academy

of Design, 1973; commendation from Society of Illustrators for *The Fables of Aesop,* about 1964; *The Heart of Stone* was included in the Children's Book Exhibit of the American Institute of Graphic Arts, 1963-64, and in the Society of Illustrators Annual Show, about 1964; Guggenheim fellow.

WRITINGS: (Compiler) Abraham Aesop (pseudonym of John Newbery), *The Fables of Aesop* (juvenile; self-illustrated), translated by Patrick Gregory and Justina Gregory, Gambit, 1975.

Illustrator; all for children, except as indicated: Elizabeth Kirtland, *Buttons in the Back* (young adult), Vanguard Press, 1958; Washington Irving, *Rip Van Winkle [and] The Legend of Sleepy Hollow,* with an afterword by Clifton Fadiman, Macmillan, 1963; Wilhelm Hauff, *The Heart of Stone: A Fairy Tale,* retold by Doris Orgel, Macmillan, 1964; Aesop, *The Fables of Aesop,* Macmillan, 1964; James Playsted Wood, *The Snark Was a Boojum: A Life of Lewis Carroll,* Pantheon, 1966; Joseph Moses, *The Great Rain Robbery,* Houghton, 1975; (with Al-

The Beatles. ■ (From *Pens and Needles: Literary Caricatures*, selected and introduced by John Updike. Illustrated by David Levine.)

mada Negreiros) *The Man Who Never Was,* introduction by George Monteiro, Gavea-Brown, 1982.

Illustrator, all for adults: *A Summer Sketchbook,* with a foreword by Peter A. Wick, Mitchell Press, 1963; *The Man from M.A.L.I.C.E.: Movies, Art, Literature, and International Conmen's Establishment,* introduced by Malcolm Muggeridge, Dutton, 1966; Albert E. Kahn, *Smetana and the Beetles: A Fairy Tale for Adults* (based on the career of Svetlana Allilueva), Random House, 1967; *Caricatures,* Stock (Paris), 1969; *Pens and Needles: Literary Caricatures,* compiled and introduced by John Updike, Gambit, 1969; *No Known Survivors: David Levine's Political Plank,* introduced by John K. Galbraith, Gambit, 1970; *David Levine's Gallery* (portfolio), New York Review of Books, 1974; Maryellen Spencer, editor, *The More or Less Cookbooks: Two Closely Matched Volumes of Selected Recipes for Lovers of Good Cooking, Both the Cautious and the Care Free,* Van Nostrand, 1976; *Words and Music: Caricatures of Writers, Composers, and Performers from ''The New York Review of Books''* (portfolio), 1977(?); *The Arts of David Levine,* Knopf, 1978; *The Watercolors of David Levine,* University of Washington Press, 1981. Contributing editor to *Esquire* and *New York Magazine.*

WORK IN PROGRESS: Preparing for an exhibition at Ashmolean Museum in England.

SIDELIGHTS: Levine was born in Brooklyn, New York on December 20, 1926. Early in life, he aspired to be a cartoonist, and attended art classes at the Pratt Institute and the Brooklyn Museum Art School. ''I grew up in a garment shop in Brooklyn. I tried to ghost-draw some comic strips but failed. I started a Christmas card business with a friend, but that failed, too. I never had any real luck hustling my portfolio, and by the time I reached my late twenties my career as a professional caricaturist and illustrator consisted of occasional drawings in *Gasoline Retailer* and *Atlas* magazines.

''Then I illustrated a 'promo' for an art show at the Davis Galleries and Clay Felker, who was then an editor at *Esquire,*

saw it and immediately commissioned me to do a caricature of Stan Freberg.'' [W. H. Masters, ''Grand Master of Pen and Ink,'' *More,* March, 1977.¹]

Levine had his first one-man show at the Davis Galleries in 1953. In the next ten years, he continued to exhibit there, and had seven additional one-man shows. Although his professional interest had switched from cartooning to serious painting, Levine began to get more offers for his caricatures after his *Esquire* commission.

During the politically troubled 1960s Levine's satirical drawings filled numerous pages and covers of a wide variety of magazines, such as *New York Review of Books, Look, Newsweek, Esquire* and *Time.* Caricature drawing, which had once been a hobby, became his successful profession. ''In the satirical drawings I have an outlet for things that bother me— things I wouldn't put in my paintings. In them, I'm after pretty much what any moralist or preacher wants, social reform. I've come to see power as a devastating thing, and I'm against its abusive exercise. Besides, any time I can bring a god down to human scale, so people can say, 'Gee, [Lyndon] Johnson has big ears, just like my kid,' I'm delighted.'' [Grace Glueck, ''A Rapier Named Levine,'' *New York Times,* December 18, 1966.²]

In 1975 Levine was elected to the National Academy of Art, thus gaining recognition as a serious artist regardless of his popularity in magazines.

Levine approached his cartooning with a very definite method, using pencil to outline. ''I try to bring to my drawings an awareness of the draftsmanship of the traditional artists. . . . These artists were great draftsmen to begin with. . . . That is something forgotten by many of the aspiring young artists doing illustrations today. I always direct them to art history and allegorical references instead of merely copying modern cariacaturists. There is so much to learn from different cultures and traditions—Japanese prints, for example, with their wonderful silhouettes. I don't try to emulate others in the field of

He is the master. . . . ■ (From *The Heart of Stone: A Fairy Tale* by Wilhelm Hauff, retold by Doris Orgel. Detail of illustration by David Levine.)

"Not long ago," said the Mouse, "you laughed at the thought of my returning your favor...." ■
(From *The Fables of Aesop,* selected and illustrated by David Levine.)

caricature. My ambition is to get something drawn that can stand next to an Ingres rather than a Nast. On a straight comparison to Nast, I would fall short. For my own interests, I'm always trying to angle upward....

''I always work on 11 by 14 paper, which permits me to keep enough open spaces between my lines to take care of reduction. I outline in pencil first—not fully, though, because I want to leave myself enough play. Pencil is a fine medium. It has more touch, more suggestion, so I lose something in the process of ink translation later. But if I did finished work in pencil, I would lose 30 to 40 percent when translated to screen dots. Then I do the finished drawing with a metal point—a

crow quill, which got its name because it originally used to be a crow feather—and good black India ink, not blue-black. This way at least 90 percent of what I draw is retained in reproduction.

''I've learned a great deal from Rembrandt's work. When I drew him, I put a bunch of hats at his feet, not in homage but because I think he had a hat fetish. Of course, the real thing is his brilliant technique, all his lines counting. In my drawings, I don't only think of sculptural outlines but shades of monocolor. Working with a pen or pencil, it isn't enough to draw in just one tone. You achieve certain effects as you apply different weights of your hand. The cross-hatching in my drawing helps to get different shadings. I'm not just hatching squares evenly—I move my lines in different angles to give life to the drawing. You can get another kind of tone by diminishing the white spaces between the lines. So you try to achieve tones from light gray to dark black, not simply for mechanical variety but to help convey the essence of a personality or idea.

"We're in a day when a good editorial cartoonist is valued for his ideas—Robert Osborn, Bill Mauldin, Herblock, all have strong views that they put across. And all are good draftsmen in their own ways. On the other hand, I don't get any feeling of a statement being made in the art work that appears on the opinion page of some newspapers. They seem to have a premium on ambiguity and decoration. With some exceptions, the opinion page art is contrary to the intelligent and independent work being done by many editorial cartoonists today. . . .

"I come well-armed with a bias. I've been called a bed-wetting Commie and bleeding heart. But, if you notice, there are no good Right-wing cartoonists. I saw things in *The New York Review of Books* that were close to my way of thinking right from the start. On the stupidity of the Vietnam war, for ex-

ample. But I also had my own ideas. I'm against government oppression, no matter who's in power. Left or Right have to be called to question by the artist. Social issues and causes still count." [Herbert Mitgang, "Reducing the Gods to Scale," *Artnews,* March, 1976.[3]]

Active in both cartooning and painting, Levine has had much success with his oils and watercolors, exhibiting in such museums as the Whitney, the Corcoran Gallery, the National Portrait Gallery, and in private collections from Hirshhorn's to Jacqueline Onassis'. "Watercolor is more immediate in its relationship to draftsmanship. I tend to *draw* more in watercolor. Watercolor is harder when done in the Cézanneist or American academic traditions, where white paper has to be preserved and, therefore, every brushstroke is sudden death. I approach it as a free mix. There are no rules, and white is only relative as a color. Then, playfulness on the surface becomes an element." [Amanda Urban, "On the Other Side of David Levine," *Esquire,* October 24, 1978.[4]]

Levine has also illustrated several children's books, among them, *The Heart of Stone,* a fairy tale by Wilhelm Hauff, *The Fables of Aesop,* and *The Snark Was a Boojum,* a biography of Lewis Carroll.

FOR MORE INFORMATION SEE: Newsweek, January 24, 1955, May 3, 1971, February 14, 1977; Grace Glueuk, "A Rapier Named Levine," *New York Times,* December 18, 1966; *The Man from M.A.L.I.C.E.: Movies, Art, Literature, and International Conmen's Establishment,* introduced by Malcolm Muggeridge, Dutton, 1966; Lee Kingman and others, compilers, *Illustrators of Children's Books: 1957-1966,* Horn Book, 1968; *Time,* November 15, 1968; *Vogue,* June, 1969; *Pens and Needles: Literary Caricatures,* edited by John Updike, Gambit, 1969; *No Known Survivors: David Levine's Political Plank,* introduced by John K. Galbraith, Gambit, 1970; *Graphis,* 152, 1970/71; *Esquire,* February, 1971, October 24, 1978; *American Artist,* November, 1971.

Artists, Authors, and Others: Drawings by David Levine (exhibition catalogue), introduced by Daniel P. Moynihan, catalogue by Frank Gettings, Smithsonian Institution Press, 1976; David Levine, "Reducing the Gods to Scale," *Art News,* March, 1976; *New Republic,* March 20, 1976; Christopher P. Anderson, "Speaking Softly but Wielding a Poison Pen, David Levine Is the Reigning King of Caricature," *People,* April 12, 1976; W. H. Masters, "Grand Master of Pen and Ink," *More,* March, 1977; *The Arts of David Levine,* Knopf, 1978; *David Levine: Aquarelles: Galerie Claude Bernard, Paris* (exhibition catalogue), catalogue and introduction by John Canaday, Galerie Claude Bernard, 1979; William Feaver, *Masters of Caricature,* Knopf, 1981; *Atlantic Monthly,* January, 1982.

(From "The Legend of Sleepy Hollow," in *Rip Van Winkle [and] The Legend of Sleepy Hollow* by Washington Irving. Illustrated by David Levine.)

LIM, John 1932-

PERSONAL: Born August 13, 1932, in Singapore; son of Yang Chua (a businessman) and Ah Lin (a housewife; maiden name, Quek) Lim. *Education:* University of Pennsylvania, B.Sc., 1959. *Home:* Acorn Cottages, Roseneath, Ontario, Canada KOK 2XO.

CAREER: Turner's Cement and Asbestos Co., Manchester, England, cost accountant, 1962-64; painter, sculptor, and author and illustrator of children's books, beginning 1963. *Exhibitions:* Works have been included in exhibitions in Montreal, Canada; San Francisco, Calif.; Miami, Fla.; Toronto,

"The Beautician." ■ (From *Merchants of the Mysterious East* by John Lim. Illustrated by the author.)

Canada; New York; Chicago, Ill.; and Washington, D.C. *Awards, honors:* Kiwanis Award, 1968, and Ontario Society of Artists Award, 1970, for sculpture; Certificate of Excellence, Art Directors Club, 1978, for *At Grandmother's House,* and 1982, for *Merchants of the Mysterious East;* Amelia Frances Howard-Gibson Illustrators' Award for *Merchants of the Mysterious East.*

WRITINGS—Both for children; both self-illustrated: *At Grandmother's House,* Tundra Books, 1977; *Merchants of the Mysterious East,* Tundra Books, 1981.

Other: *Lovers* (adult), Tundra Books, 1983.

WORK IN PROGRESS: A book on the theme, "My father's three wives," for Tundra Books.

FOR MORE INFORMATION SEE: The Gazette (Montreal), December 3, 1982; *Canadian Children's Literature,* number, 27/28, 1982.

A boy's will is the wind's will,
And the thoughts of youth are long, long thoughts.
—Henry Wadsworth Longfellow

JOHN LIM

LINDMAN, Maj (Jan) 1886-1972

PERSONAL: Born August 17, 1886, in Örebro, Sweden; died August 6, 1972; married; children: one son, two daughters. *Education:* Attended the Royal Academy of Fine Arts, Stockholm, Sweden.

CAREER: Author and illustrator of books for children. *Awards, honors:* Lewis Carroll Shelf Award, 1959, for *Snipp, Snapp, Snurr and the Red Shoes.*

WRITINGS—"Snipp, Snapp, Snurr" series; published in America by A. Whitman; for children; all self-illustrated: *Snipp, Snapp, Snurr and the Gingerbread*, 1932; . . . *and the Red Shoes*, 1932, reprinted, 1968; . . . *and the Magic Horse*, 1933; . . . *and the Buttered Bread*, 1934; . . . *and the Yellow Sled*, 1936; . . . *and the Big Surprise*, 1937; . . . *and the Big Farm*, 1946; . . . *Learn to Swim*, 1954; . . . *and the Reindeer*, 1957; . . . *and the Seven Dogs*, 1959.

"Flicka, Ricka, Dicka" series; published in America by A. Whitman; for children; all self-illustrated: *Flicka, Ricka, Dicka and the New Dotted Dresses*, 1939, reprinted, 1968; . . . *and the Girl Next Door*, 1940; . . . *and the Three Kittens*, 1941; . . . *and Their New Friend*, 1942; . . . *and the Strawberries*, 1944; . . . *and a Little Dog*, 1946; . . . *and Their New Skates*, 1950; . . . *Bake a Cake*, 1955; . . . *Go to Market*, 1958; . . . *and the Big Red Hen*, 1960.

Other works for children; all self-illustrated; all published in America by A. Whitman: *Fire Eye: The Story of a Boy and His Horse*, 1948; *Little Folks' Life of Jesus*, 1948; *Snowboot, Son of Fire Eye*, 1950; *Sailboat Time*, 1951; *Holiday Time*, 1952; *Dear Little Deer*, 1953.

She even used a big scrubbing brush. ■ (From *Snipp, Snapp, Snurr and the Gingerbread* by Maj Lindman. Illustrated by the author.)

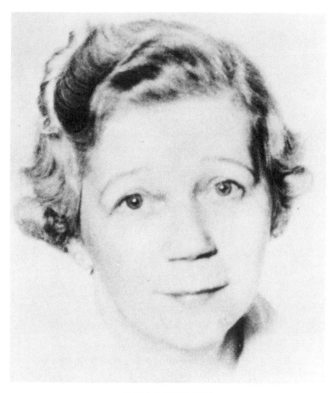

MAJ LINDMAN

Illustrator: Lois Donaldson, *Greta in Weather Land* (juvenile), A. Whitman, 1932.

SIDELIGHTS: Lindman, whose Christian name was Mary, was called Maj "for the sake of brevity." She grew up in Orebro, Sweden where she spent a happy childhood. When not in school she enjoyed skiing and skating in the winter, dances, going to the theater, and visiting relatives.

At nineteen, Lindman began painting seriously. She studied at the Royal Academy of Art until she married.

While her children were growing up, Lindman returned to her art work doing book illustration, book cover illustration, Christmas cards and painted portraits in oil.

In 1922 Lindman wrote her first book, which was the first of the "Snipp, Snapp, Snurr" series—story-picture books about three little Swedish boys. Many of her books, including ten in this series as well as ten in her "Flicka, Ricka, Dicka" series (about three Swedish sisters), have been published in the United States.

FOR MORE INFORMATION SEE: Stanley J. Kunitz and Howard Haycraft, editors, *Junior Book of Authors,* H. W. Wilson, 1951; Martha E. Ward and Dorothy A. Marquardt, *Authors of Books for Young People,* Scarecrow, 1964.

Child! do not throw this book about;
Refrain from the unholy pleasure
Of cutting all the pictures out!
Preserve it as your chiefest treasure.

—Hilaire Belloc

LONETTE, Reisie (Dominee) 1924-

PERSONAL: Born February 13, 1924, in New York, N.Y.; daughter of Daniel G. and Mary (Bott) Lonette; married Vincent Nucera (an artist), October 19, 1952 (died, 1964); children: Marc, Marisa. *Education:* Graduated from Pratt Institute; attended Art Students League, 1944-52, New School for Social Research, 1949-51, and New York School of Interior Design, 1951.

CAREER: Doubleday & Co., New York, N.Y., staff artist, 1945-53; free-lance illustrator, beginning in 1953.

ILLUSTRATOR—All for children: Edward Fenton, *Hidden Trapezes,* Doubleday, 1950; Paul Gallico, *Small Miracle,* Doubleday, 1952; Margarethe Erdahl Shank, *Coffee Train,* Doubleday, 1953; Helen Rushmore, *Ghost Cat,* Harcourt, 1954; Dorothy Sterling, *Brownie Scout Mystery,* Doubleday, 1955; Robert R. Harry, *Island Boy,* Lothrop, 1956; Louisa May Alcott, *Little Women,* Doubleday, 1956; Jean Bothwell, *Search for a Golden Bird,* Harcourt, 1956; Andrew Lang, editor, *The Blue Fairy Book,* Looking Glass Library, 1959.

A. Lang, editor, *The Red Fairy Book,* Looking Glass Library, 1960; A. Lang, *The Green Fairy Book,* Looking Glass Library, 1960; Eleanor Ratigan, *Deep Water,* Lothrop, 1961; Caroline D. Snedeker, *Lysis Goes to the Play,* Lothrop, 1961;

It suddenly struck her . . . that she was actually in Paris. ■ (From *Libby's Step-Family* by Shirley Simon. Illustrated by Reisie Lonette.)

Helen Hoyt, *Aloha Susan*, Doubleday, 1961; Ella Gibson, *Martha's Secret Wish*, Lothrop, 1961; Shirley Simon, *Cousins at Camm Corners*, Lothrop, 1962; Ruth L. Holberg, *What Happened to Virgilia?*, Doubleday, 1963; S. Simon, *Best Friend*, Lothrop, 1964; L. M. Alcott, *Eight Cousins*, Albert Whitman, 1965; Marguerite Vance, *Jared's Gift: A Christmas Story*, Dutton, 1965; Marisa Nucera, *One Day Means a Lot*, Bobbs-Merrill, 1965; Charlene J. Talbot, *Tomas Takes Charge*, Lothrop, 1966; S. Simon, *Libby's Step-Family*, Lothrop, 1966; Mary Ellen Chase, *A Walk on an Iceberg*, Norton, 1966; Alice R. Viklund, *Moving Away*, McGraw, 1967; Eugenie C. Reid, *The Mystery of the Second Treasure*, Lothrop, 1967.

Flora G. Jacobs, *The Haunted Birdhouse*, Coward, 1970; Dorothy Clewes, *The Library*, Coward, 1970; Mary Adrian (pseudonym of Mary Eleanor Venn), *The Ghost Town Mystery*, Hastings House, 1971; Carol B. York, *The Tree House Mystery*, Coward, 1973; Shirley Algieri, *Events That Shook the World*, edited by Thomas J. Mooney, Xerox Education Publications, 1974; Anne Hawkes, *Rose Kennedy*, Putnam, 1975; Child Study Association of America, *Courage to Adventure: Stories of Boys and Girls Growing Up with America*, Crowell, 1976; Mary Adrian, *The Fireball Mystery*, Hastings House, 1977; Alberta Eiseman, *The Sunday Whirligig*, Atheneum, 1977.

SIDELIGHTS: "I have always wanted to draw or paint or try to create something. There has never been anything else for me. It is my way to exist. I am happy to be able to work with books.

"I have two children, Marc and Marisa. When she was not yet five, my daughter wrote a little book of poems, *One Day Means a Lot*. I did the drawings and designed the book and it was published by Bobbs-Merrill." [Lee Kingman and others, compilers, *Illustrators of Children's Books: 1957-1966*, Horn Book, 1968.[1]]

Except for books jackets, Lonette worked in black-and-white and two colors, using pencil and wash, and characterized her work as "representational with some whimsy." When designing a book jacket, she said: "I usually do hand-lettering. It seems to integrate more with the illustration."[1]

HOBBIES AND OTHER INTERESTS: Collecting antiques.

FOR MORE INFORMATION SEE: Bertha E. Miller and others, compilers, *Illustrators of Children's Books: 1946-1956*, Horn Book, 1958; Lee Kingman and others, compilers, *Illustrators of Children's Books: 1957-1966*, Horn Book, 1968.

LOWREY, Janette Sebring 1892-

PERSONAL: Born March 2, 1892, in Orange, Tex.; daughter of Ruluph R. (a teacher and school superintendent) and Janette (Scurry) Sebring; married Fred Vestal Lowrey (an attorney), August 3, 1922 (died, 1962); children: Alfred Sebring. *Education:* University of Texas, B.A., 1929. *Politics:* Democrat. *Religion:* Episcopalian. *Agent:* McIntosh & Otis, Inc., 18 East 41st St., New York, N.Y. 10017.

CAREER: Teacher of English in Texas high schools, 1913-18; advertising manager of Houston Land & Trust Co., Houston, Tex., 1918-22; author of books and short stories for young people, 1938—. *Member:* San Antonio Art League, San Antonio Conservation Society, Theta Sigma Phi. *Awards, honors:* Theta Sigma Phi Headliner Award, 1953; Communicating

Arts Award, Bexar County (Tex.) Library Committee, 1963; Steck-Vaughn Award from Texas Institute of Letters Award for best youth book of the year, for *Love, Bid Me Welcome*, 1965.

WRITINGS: Annunciata and the Shepherds, Gentry, 1938; *The Silver Dollar*, Harper, 1940; *Rings on Her Fingers*, Harper, 1941; *Tap-a-tan*, Harper, 1942; *The Poky Little Puppy*, Golden Books, 1942; *Baby's Book*, Golden Books, 1942; *Bible Stories*, Golden Books, 1943; *A Day in the Jungle*, Golden Books, 1943; *The Lavender Cat*, Harper, 1944; *In the Morning of the World*, Harper, 1944; *The Bird*, Harper, 1947; *Margaret* (Junior Literary Guild selection), Harper, 1950; *Mr. Heff and Mr. Ho*, Harper, 1952; *Where Is the Poky Little Puppy?*, Golden Books, 1962; *Love, Bid Me Welcome*, Harper, 1964; *Six Silver Spoons* (illustrated by Robert Quackenbush), Harper, 1971. Contributor of short stories to children's magazines.

ADAPTATIONS: "Annette" (serialized on the "Mickey Mouse Club" television show; based on book *Margaret*), starring Annette Funicello, Walt Disney, 1955.

WORK IN PROGRESS: A juvenile book and an adult novel, both still untitled.

SIDELIGHTS: "I was born in Orange, a small town in East Texas. There were five girls in our family; Margaret and Kate and the twins, Eddie and Claire, and I. How well I remember that Christmas when we had twenty-five dollars to display to our admiring friends in the sleepy little town! Along with our five *new* dolls were twenty old ones that had disappeared a few weeks before. Now they were back, all repaired and newly dressed and as charming as ever.

"I remember, too, the set of Dickens, bound in green, which stood on the bottom shelf of the bookcase. The summer when Margaret was eleven and I was twelve, we fell in love with Dickens. We were supposed to help with the housework during the summer, but Margaret and I somehow managed to disappear with our favorites: *Our Mutual Friend, Barnaby Rudge*, and *David Copperfield*—and dear Pip. We always said Margaret could read in the dark!

"Kate was our musician. She was only three when our mother took her to Beaumont to buy a new piano. At a recital there Kate, as small as a doll, became quite a celebrity for a day by playing an arrangement of 'The Kiss Waltz.'

"After graduating from the University of Texas, I taught school for a while. I can never forget the funny little place where I first taught. It is described in *Margaret* as Nichols Station, but that is not its real name. Walking back to Bonnie's house—only she was not called Bonnie—I used to think how much I'd like to write a book about it all.

"*Margaret* is not the story of my sister, though I named both the book and the heroine for her. The book Margaret is an entirely different person from my sister.

"My home is now in San Antonio."

FOR MORE INFORMATION SEE: Horn Book, February, 1947; *San Antonio Light*, San Antonio, Tex., April 17, 1963; Martha E. Ward and Dorothy A. Marquardt, *Authors of Books for Young People*, second edition, Scarecrow, 1971.

Sunlight runs a race with rain,
All the world grows young again.

—Mathilde Blind

The sun was not up yet. ■ (From *Six Silver Spoons* by Janette Sebring Lowrey. Illustrated by Robert Quackenbush.)

MAIORANO, Robert   1946-

PERSONAL: Surname is pronounced My-o-ra-nō; born August 29, 1946, in Brooklyn, N.Y.; son of Robert and Elizabeth Hope (Hawthorne) Maiorano; married Rachel Isadora (a ballet dancer, author, and illustrator), September 7, 1977 (divorced, May, 1982). *Education:* Attended American School of Ballet, 1954-62. *Residence:* New York. *Agent:* Richard Boehm Literary Agency, 737 Park Ave., New York, N.Y. 10021.

CAREER: Joined New York City Ballet Company, New York, N.Y., 1962, soloist, 1969-84; free-lance author of children's books, 1978—. *Awards, honors:* Professional Children's School Alumni Award for Outstanding Contribution to the Performing Arts, 1969; *Worlds Apart: The Autobiography of a Dancer from Brooklyn* was chosen as a "Best Book for Young Adults" by the American Library Association, 1980.

WRITINGS—All for children; all fiction, except as indicated: (With Rachel Isadora) *Backstage* (illustrated by R. Isadora), Greenwillow, 1978; *Francisco* (illustrated by R. Isadora), Macmillan, 1978; *A Little Interlude* (illustrated by R. Isadora), Coward, 1980; *Worlds Apart: The Autobiography of a Dancer from Brooklyn* (young adult), Coward, 1980; *Balanchine's Mozartiana: The Making of a Masterpiece* (adult; edited by Valerie Brooks), Freundich Books, 1985.

WORK IN PROGRESS: A novel for adults.

ROBERT MAIORANO

around the trunks,

(From *Backstage* by Robert Maiorano and Rachel Isadora. Illustrated by Rachel Isadora.)

SIDELIGHTS: Maiorano was born into a poor family in a tough section of Brooklyn, New York. His mother supported his older sister and him as a welfare recipient with a break or two of odd jobs. "At home we never had parties and no friends ever came to visit. Our coldwater flat was constantly in a shambles and we could never find anything in the disorder. The ceiling leaked, and eventually came down, and one of the walls was soggy and bulging from the weight of water behind it. There was always laundry dripping from the clotheslines strung across the kitchen. The bathtub was under a broken skylight, and the soot from the foundry across the street fell on us whenever we took a bath. We had to wait an hour for the hot-water tank to heat up. . . . We had one small kerosene burner to heat the entire five-room flat, and in the winter we slept under old coats because we did not have enough blankets.

"There was still an icebox in the hallway outside our apartment. Twice a week, in the summer, I bought a block of ice from the iceman and lugged it home on my wagon to use in the icebox. My friends with electric refrigerators didn't even know what an icebox was.

"We had no roaches but we did have plagues of . . . mice and bedbugs. Pounding Paws, our cat, didn't have much of a taste

for mice. After he died, we accumulated eighteen cats. They finally got rid of the vermin, but their stench almost got rid of us.

"Every other month the welfare social worker paid us a visit. . . ." [Robert Maiorano, *Worlds Apart: The Autobiography of a Dancer from Brooklyn,* Coward, 1980.[1]]

Using their meager income, Maiorano and his sister were given private lessons in music and dance. Their mother encouraged them to pursue a more cultural background than their environment offered.

Maiorano was sent to ballet school at a very early age. A disciplined, serious, and talented dancer, Maiorano first performed with the New York City Ballet at the age of nine. "My mother . . . had written notes to the Board of Education and my principal, and had gotten permission for me to leave school early on Tuesdays and Thursdays, to attend ballet class at the School of American Ballet. How lucky I thought I was, to be going to the greatest ballet school in America. All of the teachers had been great dancers with famous ballet companies throughout Europe and Russia.

"Performing in the Nutcracker and studying at the School of American Ballet indirectly resulted in new opportunities, and I leaped at any chance that was offered me."[1]

At the age of twelve, Maiorano left New York City public schools, and attended the Professional Children's School (PCS). "The kids who went to the PCS were models and TV and Broadway stars, singers, ice skaters, musicians and dancers, as well as the sons and daughters of famous performers, and most of them were spoiled. They were very different from my Brooklyn friends, Anselmo, Tito, Butch, Junior, Steve, Lonnie and Gary. At PCS I was teased and taunted almost every day. The kids in my school in Brooklyn were tough and cut with knives, but the kids in PCS were mean and cut with their tongues. I knew I could beat up any one of them but it wouldn't do me any good. I didn't want to give in to them by getting myself expelled. Every day I escaped to ballet, where I could spin and leap into the air."[1]

At the age of fifteen, Maiorano held the distinction of being the youngest full member of the New York City Ballet. "The New York City Ballet was a world unto itself, and it was a long while before I felt that I belonged there. At the age of fifteen I was the 'baby' of the company. There were a few girls a couple of years older than I was, who had been taken in at the same time, but the youngest man was seven years older. I had studied ballet for a long time, yet I had so much more to learn.

"Everyone looked at me strangely during the first classes and rehearsals. 'Are you an apprentice or a member?' a few of them questioned. When I answered that I was a full member of the Corps de Ballet, they looked surprised. I sensed that they doubted my ability. But no matter what they felt about me, I respected and admired them.

"On August 29, 1962, the New York City Ballet left on the tour that marked the return of its creator, George Balanchine, to his native Russia. But this day was also my sixteenth birthday, and the company gave me a surprise birthday party on the KLM charter flight across the Atlantic. It was only the second birthday party I had ever had. The company manager, Betty Cage, even presented me with a small gift from the airline. Deeply touched, I finally felt like a true member of

(Jacket design by Rachel Isadora and photograph by Martha Swope from *Worlds Apart: The Autobiography of a Dancer from Brooklyn* by Robert Maiorano.)

this family of sixty. I celebrated with them throughout the entire overnight flight and waited for the dawn.

"It took me a few days to realize that I was truly in Europe. The antiquity of the buildings and their unusual architecture, the unfamiliar social habits, the cleanliness and lack of waste, the style and charm and sense of quality that I found everywhere had me wandering wide-eyed for days, though I was afraid to approach people and ask questions in a foreign language.

". . . There were many grand receptions and dinners in our honor, either in American embassies, theaters or luxurious homes of patrons of the arts. I wore my fifty-dollar Robert Hall tuxedo proudly to all these functions, but it wasn't until halfway through the tour that I began feeling comfortable handling the silverware, much less able to get up enough courage to shake hands with and talk to foreign heads of state, cultural administrators, ambassadors, famous artists and members of royal families.

"We landed in Berlin, and it wasn't long before I ventured out to the curious and newly constructed Berlin Wall. I was shocked at how low the eerie gray barrier was in places and how easy it looked to climb, but the long coils of barbed wire were ominous. . . .

"We flew to Moscow on the [sixth] anniversary of the first Sputnik launching. Electric bulbs were strung across Gorky Avenue, forming rockets, satellites and stars. But our arrival was not overshadowed in the least. Mr. B, who had left Russia in 1924, was now returning with his own company. This was the culmination of his creativity and of Mr. Kirstein's philanthropic nurturing and cultural sensitivity.

"We stepped out of the plane to be overwhelmed by floodlights and interviewers, cultural affairs officials, interpreters and State Department delegates. The midnight air was moonless.

"The rigid officialdom and depressing atmosphere of Moscow were offset by the audience's spontaneous and warm enthusiasm at our opening-night performance at the famous Bolshoi Theater. There was more than one-half hour of rhythmic applause and stamping after the final curtain. This wonderful reception followed us for eight weeks, all the way to Baku!

"A week after our opening, we were transferred to an enormous modern theater called the Kremlin Palace of Congress, situated behind the foreboding red stone of the Kremlin walls. I had very queer feelings whenever I showed my pass and walked by the Russian soldiers guarding the gates to the austere heart of Russian Communism. The luminous red stars atop the monstrous towers seemed to watch the city.

"It was the height of the Cuban crisis.

"On the very day of our opening at the new theater, President John F. Kennedy had warned Premier Khrushchev to 'Get out of Cuba or else!' All that day, couriers from the American Embassy kept the company posted with any new developments, direct from Washington. There were rumors that we would be sent home immediately while it was still possible. We all had visions of being annihilated by American missiles. A barrage of rocks was hurled at the American Embassy by a demonstrating mob, and that night it seemed almost certain that there would be a riot at the theater. Preparations were being made to wheel in the heavy steel fire curtain in order to

hold back a surging mass of six thousand people. The attention of all humanity was focused on Cuba, and the control of the world's fate rested within the Kremlin. To be an American behind the Kremlin walls at a time like this seemed suicidal, and yet I felt, what could anyone have against a ballet dancer? But this was the eve of nuclear warfare, and the force of a tension that could pull the globe apart was felt everywhere. I wondered which would be destroyed first, me or my homeland. How futile it all seemed.

"That night, clinging to tradition, both National Anthems were played before the first curtain. The audience seemed tensely silent. Onstage the dancers paced back and forth like condemned prisoners. Those of us who were backstage huddled together, ready for anything. The curtain slowly rose. Those onstage stood frozen; a few forced a smile. Robert Irving, the conductor, cautiously raised his baton. Suddenly the entire audience of over six thousand rose, then cheered. The music sang and we danced joyously, bursting with the release of our fear. After the people's tremendous reception, I felt sure there could be no war between our two countries. By the end of the performance I felt like a genuine cultural ambassador of goodwill.

"Our last stop was Baku, the capital of Azerbaijan, on the Caspian Sea. The company couldn't wait to escape home from this Asian city and spoke of nothing else all week, but I, on the other hand, was dreaming of the day I might return to dance in Russia. On the last night of the tour I sat alone by the edge of the Caspian Sea. The black-jeweled sky gently turned to topaz.

"We returned to America in triumph! After a twenty-four-hour flight we touched down to Mayor Robert Wagner's official New York welcome. We were presented with the key to the city. Then we were bused to the theater, and from there I took the subway home to Brooklyn. I got out at Flushing Avenue. The smell of Pfizer filled the air. I walked past the Marcy Houses and Gorman's Grocery."[1]

At the age of twenty-five, Maiorano begin writing—poetry, at first. After he married Rachel Isadora, a dancer and author, he began to write children's books. Together they wrote a children's book, *Backstage*. Isadora also illustrated two of Maiorano's books. The marriage ended in 1982.

Maiorano claims to have lived life backwards, having had one job for twenty-two years and is now happily searching for work, albeit with much experience. He is pursuing an acting career, teaching ballet when financially necessary, and is formulating a new novel.

FOR MORE INFORMATION SEE: Dance Magazine, June, 1971; Robert Maiorano, *Worlds Apart: The Autobiography of a Dancer from Brooklyn,* Coward, 1980; *Publishers Weekly,* February 27, 1981.

MARKS, Burton 1930-

BRIEF ENTRY: Born August 11, 1930, in Akron, Ohio. A free-lance writer since 1976, Marks previously was employed for fifteen years as a writer and toy designer at the Saalfield Publishing Co. in Ohio. He and his wife, Rita J. Marks, have collaborated on five books that provide a wealth of information on activities of special interest to children, such as putting on a magic show, making kites, and planning a Halloween party.

Reviewers have praised the Marks' casual yet enthusiastic writing style and the easily understood instructions that accompany their texts. *Booklist* called *Give a Magic Show!* (Lothrop, 1977) "sure encouragement for those dabbling in magic." "There are instructions for related items children can make," added *New York Times Book Review*, "and suggestions for showmanship skills." *Kites for Kids* (Lothrop, 1980) was described by *Horn Book* as "a thoughtful, comprehensive handbook written by two experts," appealing to both "neophytes as well as more experienced kite fanciers." Likewise, *Booklist* noted that *The Spook Book* (Lothrop, 1981) contains "enough ideas . . . to fill several Halloweens with holiday fun." "Games, party invitations, activities," enumerated *School Library Journal*, "scary decorations, sound effects, and amazingly wholesome and yummy sounding . . . snack recipes are included." The Marks' other titles are *Magic Tricks* (Troubador Press, 1981) and *Puppet Plays and Puppet Making* (Plays, 1982). *Home:* 1512 Tiffany Circle, Akron, Ohio 44313.

FOR MORE INFORMATION SEE: Contemporary Authors, Volume 107, Gale, 1983.

MARRIN, Albert   1936-

BRIEF ENTRY: Born July 24, 1936, in New York, N.Y. Educator and author of books for adults and young people. After graduating from City College in 1958, Marrin was a high school social studies teacher in New York City for about ten years. In 1968 he joined the department of history at Yeshiva University, where he is currently employed. Among his writings are a number of historical accounts for young people, all published by Atheneum. Many of Marrin's titles focus on the topic of war, and he has earned critics' praise for his fast-paced and exciting narratives. *Horn Book* described *Overlord: D-Day and the Invasion of Europe* (1982) as "a straightforward and eminently readable account of the D-Day invasion . . . [which is] well described and enlivened by small but telling details." Similarly, *School Library Journal* noted that *The Airman's War: World War II in the Sky* (1982) is "filled with the sights and sounds of battle and the fears and feelings. . . ." Marrin also wrote *The Sea Rovers: Pirates, Privateers, and Buccaneers* (1984), which *Horn Book* found "vividly recounts the exploits of the colorful men and women who terrorized the seas." His other works for young people are: *Victory in the Pacific* (1983), *War Clouds in the West: Indians & Cavalrymen, 1860-1890* (1984), and *Eighteen Twelve: The War Nobody Won* (1985). *Office:* Department of History, Yeshiva University, 500 West 185th St., New York, N.Y. 10033.

FOR MORE INFORMATION SEE: Contemporary Authors, Volumes 49-52, Gale, 1975.

MARTIN, Patricia Miles   1899-
(Patricia A. Miles; Jerry Lane, Miska Miles, pseudonyms)

PERSONAL: Born November 14, 1899, in Cherokee, Kans.; daughter of Thomas J. and Nellie Ada (White) Miles; married: Edward R. Martin, October 24, 1942 (died, 1979). *Education:* Attended University of Wyoming. *Home:* 910 Bromfield Rd., San Mateo, Calif. 94402.

CAREER: Writer of children's books. *Member:* Authors Guild, Authors and Artists Workshop, Burlingame Writers Club.

Awards, honors: New York Herald Tribune Children's Spring Book Festival Honor Book Award, 1959, for *The Pointed Brush; Mississippi Possum* was on the *New York Times* list of seventy-five recommended titles, 1965; Commonwealth Club of California Medal, 1971, American Library Association Honor Book Award, Christopher Medal, Woodward Park School Award, and Newbery honor book, all 1972, and Brooklyn Museum-Brooklyn Public Library Art Books for Children Citation, 1973, all for *Annie and the Old One;* New York Academy of Sciences Citation, 1973, for *Wharf Rat.*

WRITINGS: Sylvester Jones and the Voice in the Forest, Lothrop, 1958; *The Pointed Brush* (illustrated by Roger Duvoisin), Lothrop, 1959; *Chandler Chipmunk's Flying Lesson,* Abingdon, 1960; *Little Brown Hen* (illustrated by Harper Johnson), Crowell, 1960; *Suzu and the Bride Doll* (illustrated by Kazue Mizumura), Rand McNally, 1960; *Happy Piper and the Goat* (illustrated by Kurt Werth; Junior Literary Guild selection), Lothrop, 1960; *Benjie Goes into Business,* Putnam, 1961; *The Raccoon and Mrs. McGinnis* (illustrated by L. Weisgard), Putnam, 1961; *Show and Tell* (illustrated by Tom Hamil), Putnam, 1962; *Rice Bowl Pet* (illustrated by Ezra J. Keats), Crowell, 1962; *The Lucky Little Porcupine* (illustrated by L. Smith),

PATRICIA MILES MARTIN

"It is here that I learned to dive," Kumi's mother said. ■ (From *Kumi and the Pearl* by Patricia Miles Martin. Illustrated by Tom Hamil.)

One slash of a paw could break the neck of a horse. The boy was afraid. ■ (From *Eddie's Bear* by Miska Miles. Illustrated by John Schoenherr.)

Putnam, 1963; *The Birthday Present* (illustrated by Margo Locke), Abingdon, 1963; *Little Two and the Peach Tree* (illustrated by Joan Berg; Junior Literary Guild selection), Atheneum, 1963; *Calvin and the Cub Scouts* (illustrated by T. Hamil), Putnam, 1964; *No, No, Rosina* (illustrated by Earl Thollander), Putnam, 1964; *The Greedy One* (illustrated by K. Mizumura; Junior Literary Guild selection), Rand McNally, 1964.

The Broomtail Bronc (illustrated by M. Locke), Abingdon, 1965; *Jump, Frog, Jump* (illustrated by E. Thollander; Junior

Literary Guild selection), Putnam, 1965; *The Bony Pony* (illustrated by G. Dines), Putnam, 1965; *Rolling the Cheese* (illustrated by Alton Raible), Atheneum, 1966; *The Pumpkin Patch* (illustrated by T. Hamil), Putnam, 1966; *Sing, Sailor, Sing* (illustrated by G. Booth), Golden Gate, 1966; *Mrs. Crumble and Fire Engine Number 7*, Putnam, 1966; *Woody's Big Trouble* (illustrated by Paul Galdone), Putnam, 1967; *Dolls from Cheyenne* (illustrated by Don Almquist), Putnam, 1967; *Friend of Miguel* (illustrated by Genia), Rand McNally, 1967; *Trina's Boxcar* (illustrated by Robert L. Jefferson), Abingdon, 1967; *Grandma's Gun* (illustrated by Robert Corey), Golden

Gate, 1968; *A Long Ago Christmas* (illustrated by Albert Orbaan), Putnam, 1968; *Kumi and the Pearl* (illustrated by T. Hamil), Putnam, 1968; *One Special Dog* (illustrated by Lucy Hawkinson and John Hawkinson; Junior Literary Guild selection), Rand McNally, 1968; *Stanley, the Dog Next Door*, Ginn, 1969; *The Dog and the Boat Boy* (illustrated by E. Thollander), Putnam, 1969.

Indians: The First Americans (nonfiction; illustrated by Robert Frankenberg), Parents Magazine Press, 1970; *The Eskimos: People of Alaska* (nonfiction; illustrated by R. Frankenberg), Parents Magazine Press, 1970; *That Cat 1-2-3*, Putnam, 1970; *Navajo Pet* (illustrated by John Hamberger), Putnam, 1971; *There Goes the Tiger!* (illustrated by T. Hamil), Putnam, 1971; *Chicanos: Mexicans in the United States* (nonfiction; illustrated by R. Frankenberg), Parents Magazine Press, 1971; *Be Brave, Charlie* (illustrated by Bonnie Johnson), Putnam, 1973; *Two Plays about Foolish People* (illustrated by Gabriel Lisowski), Putnam, 1973.

Biographies; all published by Putnam: *Abraham Lincoln* (illustrated by G. Schrotter), 1964; *Pocahontas* (illustrated by P. Takajian), 1964; *John Fitzgerald Kennedy* (illustrated by Paul Frame), 1965; *Daniel Boone* (illustrated by G. Dines), 1965; *Jefferson Davis* (illustrated by S. Tamen), 1966; *Andrew Jackson* (illustrated by S. Tamer), 1966; *Dolly Madison* (illustrated by Unada), 1967; *John Marshall* (illustrated by S. Tamer), 1967; *Jacqueline Kennedy Onassis* (illustrated by P. Frame), 1969; *James Madison*, 1970; *Zachary Taylor*, 1970; *Thomas Alva Edison* (illustrated by Fermin Rocker), 1971.

Under pseudonym Miska Miles; all published by Atlantic-Little, Brown, except as indicated: *Kickapoo* (illustrated by Wesley Dennis; Junior Literary Guild selection), 1961; *Dusty and the Fiddlers* (illustrated by Erik Blegvad), 1962; *See a White Horse* (illustrated by W. Dennis; Junior Literary Guild selection), 1963; *Pony in the Schoolhouse* (illustrated by E. Blegvad), 1964; *Mississippi Possum* (illustrated by John Schoenherr), 1965; *Teacher's Pet* (illustrated by Fen H. Lasell; Junior Literary Guild selection), 1966; *Fox and the Fire* (illustrated by J. Schoenherr; Horn Book honor list; ALA Notable Book), 1966; *Rabbit Garden* (illustrated by J. Schoenherr), 1967; *The*

Pieces of Home (illustrated by Victor Ambrus; Junior Literary Guild selection), 1967; *Uncle Fonzo's Ford* (illustrated by Wendy Watson; Junior Literary Guild selection), 1968; *Nobody's Cat* (illustrated by J. Schoenherr; ALA Notable Book), 1969; *Apricot ABC* (illustrated by Peter Parnall), 1969; *Hoagie's Rifle-Gun* (illustrated by J. Schoenherr; Junior Literary Guild selection), 1970; *Gertrude's Pocket* (illustrated by Emily McCully; Junior Literary Guild selection), 1970; *Eddie's Bear* (illustrated by J. Schoenherr), 1971; *Annie and the Old One* (illustrated by P. Parnall; Horn Book honor list; ALA Notable Book; Junior Literary Guild selection), 1971; *Wharf Rat* (illustrated by J. Schoenherr), 1972; *Somebody's Dog* (illustrated by J. Schoenherr), 1973; *Otter in the Cove* (illustrated by J. Schoenherr), 1974; *Tree House Town* (illustrated by E. McCully), 1975; *Swim, Little Duck* (illustrated by Jim Arnosky; Junior Literary Guild selection), 1976; *Aaron's Door* (illustrated by Alan E. Cober), 1976; *Chicken Forgets* (illustrated by J. Arnosky), 1976; *Small Rabbit* (illustrated by J. Arnosky), 1977; *Beaver Moon* (illustrated by J. Schoenherr), 1978; *Noisy Gander* (illustrated by Leslie Morrill), Dutton, 1978; *Mouse Six and the Happy Birthday* (illustrated by L. Morrill), Dutton, 1978; *Jenny's Cat* (illustrated by W. Watson), Dutton, 1979; *This Little Pig* (illustrated by L. Morrill), Dutton, 1980; (with Ted Clymer) *Horse and the Bad Morning* (illustrated by L. Morrill), Dutton, 1982.

Under pseudonym Jerry Lane; all published by Ginn: *In the Zoo*, 1974; *Run!*, 1974.

ADAPTATIONS: "Annie and the Old One" (film), Greenhouse Films, 1976; "Annie and the Old One (filmstrip with Cassette and teacher's guide), Newbery Award Records, 1980.

SIDELIGHTS:"I was born in Cherokee, Kansas [in 1899]. I remember a big tree that stood behind the house. Under the tree was a team of wooden rocking horses, with a seat between. I remember sitting there and pretending to read from a magazine, making up my stories as I went along, painstakingly pointing out the words. I am still painstakingly pointing out the words, but at least now I can give them the correct meanings."

That evening, when he was very hungry, he ventured out timidly and looked around for food. ■
(From *Rabbit Garden* by Miska Miles. Illustrated by John Schoenherr.)

Martin's youth was spent in the Midwest, attending schools in Monette, Missouri, and in Denver, Colorado, as well as in Kansas. "Many of my stories seem to come from the summers I spent on my grandfather's farm in Kansas. That was when I started writing. At Grandfather's, I used to go up into the barn loft—one step on a manger, another on a two-by-four nailed to the wall, the next on a crosspiece dividing the stall—and then there was the little opening, and I hauled myself up without benefit of a ladder.

"The barn was always partly full of hay, and the smell was dusty and sweet. I remember sitting in the big open doorway listening to the rain on the roof, smelling the sweet country fragrance, a lined tablet on my lap, describing the things I saw and smelled and heard.

"Much of my life was spent alone. I found serenity in this aloneness. I had cats and horses and chickens and ducks, and once, a frog. His deep and resonant voice had something to do with my writing about the annual jumping frog contest in Calaveras County here in California. There is something irresistible and almost dinosaurish about a frog. And it seemed to me that a frog and a fair naturally go together."

At a very young age Martin was interested in writing stories, although she never considered writing as a profession. "All my life I wrote poems. I started thinking about writing before I was old enough actually to put the words on paper. When I was about five years old I sat on the front steps of our little white house in Monette and made up my first rhyme: 'See the little butterfly/Flutter by.'"

Martin attended the University of Wyoming and then taught school for four years in Colorado and Wyoming before her marriage. In 1942, after marrying Edward R. Martin, she moved to a town near San Francisco, California, called San Mateo. Martin, who has written numerous books for children either under her full name or her penname, Miska Miles, became a writer quite by accident. "One day in 1957 we had a chair that needed upholstering, and I decided to attend a class in upholstery which was given at the College of San Mateo. When I went to enroll, the class was full. I walked by another classroom and looked in the door. There were a few empty desks there. It was a class in creative writing, and there was room for me. I found my desk and sat down to write."

Since her first book was published in 1958, Martin has written over seventy children's books, many of which were ALA Notable Books, Junior Literary Guild selections, or *Horn Book* honor books. "I try to pace my stories. First, I may write about that Midwest of mine, which takes me on a nice trip backward in time, and then I write about the Orient which takes me across a sea. *Little Two and the Peach Tree* was written because I wanted to say that a picture is worth ten thousand words.

"I write about the things that are most important to me—children, animals, birds. And the backgrounds that presently hover in my mind are my own—a wonderful Kansas farm, our neighborhood today, and a Navajo reservation.

"My days—generally—are uneventful. I pop out of bed very early in the morning, have coffee, feed the birds, put a stew in the Crock Pot for dinner, then to the typewriter as soon as possible. My life is serene in a not-so-serene world. I have my own private crusade—to pass on to children the values I live by.

"Before I start a story, I must have one line—one thought that I consider important enough to share with my readers. Then, having that thought, I know where I'd like to set the story, and whether a boy or girl or an animal will be best suited to tell what I want to tell.

"As an example, I wanted to share this thought with my young readers: in times of emergency, enemies forget enmity. In connection with this particular thought, I traveled to Sonoma, where a devastating fire had swept the forests around the Valley of the Moon, and this area became the setting for *The Fox and the Fire,* in which natural enemies, the fox and the rabbit, travel together to escape the fire.

"I am a meticulous researcher in connection with each story. (I write every day, sometimes starting as early as six o'clock in the morning, and work a minimum of six hours a day.) Even though the setting may not be definitely located in the text of the book, it is accurately and definitely located in my mind. The flower that I might mention will be correctly blooming there."

HOBBIES AND OTHER INTERESTS: Collecting old kerosene lamps.

FOR MORE INFORMATION SEE: Young Readers' Review, April, 1966, April 1967; *Christian Science Monitor,* May 4, 1967, November 2, 1967; *Book World,* November 9, 1969; *Detroit News,* November 28, 1971; *Top of the News,* April 19, 1972; *New York Times Book Review,* July 24, 1977, November 13, 1977; D. L. Kirkpatrick, *Twentieth-Century Children's Writers,* St. Martin's Press, 1978; Doris de Montreville and Elizabeth D. Crawford, editors, *Fourth Book of Junior Authors and Illustrators,* H. W. Wilson, 1978; *Writer's Digest,* March, 1981.

JOSEPH P. MATHIEU

All the while his friends were searching for him,
Big Bird was sound asleep on the roof.

(From *Christmas Eve on Sesame Street,* based on the television special created by Jon Stone. Illustrated by Joe Mathieu.)

MATHIEU, Joseph P. 1949-
(Joe Mathieu)

PERSONAL: Born January 23, 1949, in Springfield, Vt.; son of Joseph A. (a car dealer) and Patricia (a housewife; maiden name, Biner) Mathieu; married Melanie Gerardi, September 7, 1970; children: Kristen and Joey. *Education:* Rhode Island School of Design, B.F.A., 1971. *Residence:* 258 Pheasant Lane, Brooklyn, Conn. 06234.

CAREER: Author and illustrator of books for children. *Awards, honors: The Magic Word Book, Starring Marko the Magician!* was named one of the 50 Best Books by the American Institute of Graphic Arts, 1973; *Ernie's Big Mess* was selected as a Children's Choice by the International Reading Association, 1982.

WRITINGS—All picture books for children; all written under name Joe Mathieu; all self-illustrated; all published by Random House, except as indicated: *The Amazing Adventures of Silent "E" Man*, 1973; *The Magic Word Book, Starring Marko the Magician!*, 1973; *Big Joe's Trailer Truck*, 1974; *I Am a Monster* (a "Sesame Street" book), Golden Press, 1976; *The Grover Sticker Book*, Western Publishing, 1976; *The Count's Coloring Book*, Western Publishing, 1976; *The Sesame Street Mix or Match Storybook: Over Two Hundred Thousand Funny Combinations*, 1977; *Who's Who on Sesame Street*, Western Publishing, 1977; *Busy City* (nonfiction), 1978; *The Olden*

Days (nonfiction), 1981; *Bathtime on Sesame Street* (edited by Janet Schulman), 1983; *Big Bird Visits the Dodos*, 1985.

Illustrator: Ossie Davis, *Purlie Victorious*, Houghton, 1973; Scott Corbett, *Dr. Merlin's Magic Shop*, Little, Brown, 1973; Genevieve Gray, *Casey's Camper*, McGraw, 1973; Byron Preiss, *The Electric Company: The Silent "E's" from Outer Space*, Western Publishing, 1973; S. Corbett, *The Great Custard Pie Panic*, Little, Brown, 1974; Suzanne W. Bladow, *The Midnight Flight of Moose, Mops, and Marvin*, McGraw, 1975; Howard Liss, *The Giant Book of Strange but True Sports Stories*, Random House, 1976; Hedda Nussbaum, *Plants Do Amazing Things* (nonfiction), Random House, 1977; Katy Hall and Lisa Eisenberg, *A Gallery of Monsters*, Random House, 1981; Cindy West, *The Superkids and the Singing Dog*, Random House, 1982; Harold Woods and Geraldine Woods, *The Book of the Unknown* (nonfiction), Random House, 1982; H. Liss, *The Giant Book of More Strange but True Sports Stories*, Random House, 1983.

All part of the "Sesame Street" series; all published by Random House, except as indicated: Matt Robinson, *Matt Robinson's Gordon of Sesame Street Storybook*, 1972; Emily Perl Kingsley and others, *The Sesame Street 1,2,3 Storybook*, 1973; Norman Stiles and Daniel Wilcox, *Grover and the Everything in the Whole Wide World Museum: Featuring Lovable, Furry Old Grover*, 1974; Jeffrey Moss, N. Stiles, and D. Wilcox, *The Sesame Street ABC Storybook*, 1974; Anna Jane Hays,

See No Evil, Hear No Evil, Smell No Evil, Western Publishing, 1975; E. P. Kingsley, David Korr, and J. Moss, *The Sesame Street Book of Fairy Tales*, 1975; N. Stiles, *Grover's Little Red Riding Hood*, Western Publishing, 1976; N. Stiles, *The Ernie and Bert Book*, Western Publishing, 1977; Patricia Thackray, *What Ernie and Bert Did on Their Summer Vacation*, Western Publishing, 1977; E. P. Kingsley, *The Exciting Adventures of Super-Grover*, Golden Press, 1978; Sharon Lerner, *Big Bird's Look and Listen Book*, 1978; P. Thackray, *Grover Visits His Granny*, 1978; D. Korr, *Cookie Monster and the Cookie Tree*, Western Publishing, 1979; Valjean McLenigham, *Ernie's Work of Art*, Western Publishing, 1979.

Linda Hayward, *The Sesame Street Dictionary*, 1980; Sarah Roberts, *Ernie's Big Mess*, 1981; Jon Stone and Joe Bailey, *Christmas Eve on Sesame Street* (based on the television special "Christmas Eve on Sesame Street"), 1981; S. Roberts, *Nobody Cares about Me!*, 1982; Dan Elliott, *Ernie's Little Lie*, 1983; D. Elliott, *A Visit to the Sesame Street Firehouse*, 1983; S. Roberts, *Bert and the Missing Mop Mix-Up*, 1983; N. Stiles, *I'll Miss You, Mr. Hooper*, 1984; D. Elliott, *Two Wheels for Grover*, 1984; S. Lerner, *Big Bird's Copycat Day*, 1984; D. Elliott, *My Doll Is Lost*, 1984; S. Roberts, *The Adventures of Big Bird in Dinosaur Days*, 1984; S. Roberts, *I Want to Go Home*, 1985; Deborah Hautzig, *A Visit to the Sesame Street Hospital*, 1985; S. Lerner, *Big Bird Says*, 1985; D. Hautzig, *A Visit to the Sesame Street Library*, 1986.

SIDELIGHTS: "I became addicted to drawing pictures at about three years old. I was never interested in drawing completely straight. It's almost impossible for me to avoid humor, caricature and lots of action.

"I don't feel that an artist has to be particularly encouraged to draw. I think he'll draw no matter what. The same with a writer or a musician for that matter.

"As a youngster, I became enamoured of Jim Henson and the Muppets long before they were really famous. I would beg permission to miss the bus if they were going to appear on the 'Dave Garroway Show' or I'd get special permission to stay up late if they were scheduled for Jack Parr.

"When Random House and CTW ('Children's Television Workshop') started looking for illustrators to interpret the Muppet characters from 'Sesame Street,' I just fell into it and I love drawing them. The 'Sesame Street' characters are my favorites of all the many Muppet characters.

"I have also spent a sizable amount of time in the past few years developing my drawing through album cover design. I love the format and the challenges. I've illustrated about two dozen covers for a wonderful label called 'Stomp Off' which specializes in jazz of the 1920s and ragtime.

"I feel that drawing a subject matter that the artist loves is probably the single most important factor in making illustration a satisfying career.

"My favorite way to spend time away from my studio is cycling. I love touring the New England states during the summer and I ride almost every day. It helps me keep a fresh mind and a positive attitude and a sense of humor for my drawing and life in general.

"I'm also a rabid jazz fan. All my trips to see my publisher in New York are timed around visits to hear jazz piano. I'll travel anywhere to hear a good jazz band—from Boston to Breda, Holland.

"An extensive record collection sets the mood in my studio and I play ragtime piano between drawings."

MATULAY, Laszlo 1912-

PERSONAL: Born in 1912, in Vienna, Austria; came to United States in 1935. *Education:* Attended Academy of Applied Arts, Vienna, Austria, 1930-35, and New School for Social Research.

CAREER: Free-lance illustrator, 1950—. Has also been employed as a commercial artist and an art director. *Military service:* U.S. Army Infantry, 1943-46.

WRITINGS: Then and Now (drawings), Alpine Fine Arts Collection, 1981.

Illustrator; all for children, unless otherwise indicated: Lev Nikolaevich Tolstoy, *Anna Karenina* (adult), translated from the Russian by Constance Garnett, World Publishing, 1946; Dorothy G. Hosford, *By His Own Might: The Battles of Beowulf*, Holt, 1947; Gustave Flaubert, *Madame Bovary* (adult), translated by Eleanor Marx Aveling, World Publishing, 1948;

(From *By His Own Might: The Battles of Beowulf* by Dorothy Hosford. Illustrated by Laszlo Matulay.)

Aristophanes, *Five Comedies* (adult), World Publishing, 1948; Libby M. Klaperman, *Dreidel Who Wouldn't Spin*, Behrman, 1950; Lewis Carroll (pseudonym of Charles Lutwidge Dodgson), *Adventures from the Original Alice in Wonderland*, adapted by Marcia Martin, Wonder-Treasure Books, 1951; Bernice W. Carlson, *Do It Yourself: Tricks, Stunts, and Skits*, Abingdon, 1952; Robert Louis Stevenson, *Treasure of Franchard*, Rodale, 1954; B. W. Carlson, *Act It Out*, Abingdon, 1956; Iris Vinton, *Longbow Island*, Dodd, 1957; Felix Sutton, *We Were There at the First Airplane Flight*, Grosset, 1959; Azriel L. Eisenberg, *Voices from the Past: Stories of Great Biblical Discoveries*, Abelard, 1959.

Freya Littledale, editor, *Treasure Chest of Poetry*, Parents Magazine Press, 1964; A. L. Eisenberg, *Feeding the World: A Biography of David Lubin*, Abelard, 1965; Barbara Taylor Bradford, *Children's Stories of Jesus from the New Testament*, Lion Press, 1966; B. T. Bradford, *Children's Stories of the Bible from the Old Testament*, Lion Press, 1966; Robin Fox, adapter, *Le Poulet: A Rooster Who Laid Eggs*, Lion Press, 1967; Mary Batten, *Discovery by Chance: Science and the Unexpected*, Funk, 1968; Ruth Samuels, *Bible Stories for Jewish Children, from Joshua to Queen Esther*, Ktav, 1973; Robert Garvey, *What Feast?, and Other Tales*, Ktav, 1974; Dorothy K. Kripke and Myer S. Kripke, *Let's Talk about Loving: About Love, Sex, Marriage, and Family*, Ktav, 1980.

SIDELIGHTS: "I was born of Hungarian parents. My father was a fine artist and my mother a dressmaker. Thus my first impressions and inspirations came from a workshop, which was my home. My training started early, copying from picture books and later art books and museums. My first artistic triumph was in the first grade. It was a large colored chalk drawing of a wreath to commemorate All Souls Day. It was left on the blackboard for many months. I decided early to become an artist and after the Gymnasium I studied at the Academy of Fine and Applied Arts from 1930 to 1935. My summer vacations were spent in Austria, Hungary, the Balkans and Italy on walking and hitch-hiking expeditions, always with sketchbook under my arm. My most important artistic ideals are the following: my father, the Greek Classics, the Vase Drawings, Rembrandt, Michelangelo, Oscar Kokosehka, Egon Schiele, the French Impressionists—Lautrec, van Gogh, and Picasso—a most impressive list. Since 1935 I have lived in the United States working in many fields of commercial art both promotional and editorial, but always returning to the easel. My most important teachers were: my father, Eugene Steinhof, Dr. Oskar Strand, Paul Rand and Alexy Brodovitch." [Bertha E. Miller and others, compilers, *Illustrators of Children's Books: 1946-1956*, Horn Book, 1958.]

MAYNARD, Christopher 1949-
(Chris Maynard)

BRIEF ENTRY: Born in 1949, in Canada. Author of books for adults and young people. Maynard began his career in 1972 as an editor for Macdonald Educational Ltd. in London, England. He has also been employed as an editor for Intercontinental Book Productions Ltd. in Berkshire, England and is currently the director of both Oasis Press and Maynard & How Publishing. The majority of Maynard's writings are nonfiction books for young people. Among them is *Great Men of Science* (Warwick Press, 1979), which looks at the developments in science and technology from ancient Egypt to modern times. *Science Books and Films* described it as "an excellent volume for anyone wishing a capsule view of the evolution of sci-

ence." In addition, he wrote *All about Ghosts* (EMC Corp., 1978) and *The Young Scientist Book of Stars and Planets* (EMC Corp., 1978), part of the "Young Scientist Books" series. Maynard's other books for young people include *Planet Earth* (Warwick Press, 1976), *The Amazing World of Dinosaurs* (Angus & Robertson, 1976), *Meet the Razzmataz Gang* (Sackett & Marshall, 1978), *War Vehicles* (Lerner Publications, 1980), and *Aircraft* (Rand McNally, 1982). *Home:* 28-32 Shelton St., London, WC2, England.

FOR MORE INFORMATION SEE: The Writers Directory: 1984-86, St. James Press, 1983.

MELCHER, Daniel 1912-1985

OBITUARY NOTICE: Born July 10, 1912, in Newton Center, Mass.; drowned following an epileptic seizure, July 22, 1985, in Charlottesville, Va. Publisher and author. Former president of R. R. Bowker and founder of the *Books in Print* index, Melcher began his publishing career in 1934 as an assistant at Allen & Unwin, later holding positions at Holt, Oxford University Press, Alliance Book, and Viking. In 1947 he joined Bowker as promotion manager and publisher of *Library Journal*. The following year marked the first appearance of *Books in Print*, an annual reference work containing authors and titles of books published in America. Melcher was credited with developing a mechanical and photographic system that made publication of such a book possible. Similar titles followed, including *Paperbound Books in Print*, *Subject Guide to Books in Print*, *American Book Publishing Record*, and *Forthcoming Books*. He also founded *Junior Libraries*, known as *School Library Journal* since 1961.

Melcher became president of Bowker in 1963 and was named board chairman in 1968, the same year the company was sold to Xerox. He resigned early in 1969. Melcher remained professionally active throughout the 1970s, serving as board member of the Institute for the Achievement of Human Potential, board chairman of Gale Research, 1971-73, and member of the Council of the American Library Association, 1972-74. He also succeeded his father, publisher Frederic G. Melcher, as bestower of the annual Newbery and Caldecott Medals. Among Melcher's writings are the juvenile career book *Young Mr. Stone, Book Publisher*, *The Printing and Promotion Handbook*, written with Nancy Larrick, and *Melcher on Acquisition*, written with his wife, Margaret Saul Melcher.

FOR MORE INFORMATION SEE: Contemporary Authors, Volumes 33-36, revised, Gale, 1978; *Who's Who in Library and Information Services*, American Library Association, 1982. Obituaries: *New York Times*, July 31, 1985; *Publishers Weekly*, August 9, 1985; *School Library Journal*, September, 1985.

MITCHELL, Joyce Slayton 1933-

BRIEF ENTRY: Born August 13, 1933, in Hardwick, Vt. Author of books for adults and young people. A graduate of Denison University, Mitchell received her M.S. from the University of Bridgeport and did further graduate study at Columbia University. She began her career as a physical education teacher in junior high schools and later served as a high school counselor. In 1962 she began consultant work and, in 1975, was a visiting lecturer at Johnson State College. She is also a member of several organizations, including the American Personnel and Guidance Association and the National Association of College Admissions Counselors.

Among Mitchell's writings are several career guidebooks geared to young adults. One of these, *Choices and Changes: A Career Book for Men* (College Entrance Examination Board, 1982) was described by *Kliatt* as "a good starting place for a future job seeker," while *Booklist* found it "contributes enthusiastic yet thoroughly realistic counsel." She also wrote *See Me More Clearly: Career and Life Planning for Teens with Physical Disabilities* (Harcourt, 1980), which *Voice of Youth Advocates* called "a much needed tool to help disabled youth make plans for their futures." In addition, *School Library Journal* deemed it a "well-done book" and "a first and major contribution" to its category. Mitchell's other young adult books include *Be a Mother and More: Career and Life Planning for Young Women* (Bantam, 1980) and *Your Job in the Computer Age: The Complete Guide to the Computer Skills You Need to Get the Job You Want* (Scribner, 1984). She also wrote the children's book *My Mommy Makes Money* (Little, Brown, 1984).

FOR MORE INFORMATION SEE: Contemporary Authors, New Revision Series, Volume 15, Gale, 1985.

MOZLEY, Charles　1915-

PERSONAL: Born May 29, 1915, in Sheffield, England; married; children: five. *Education:* Attended Sheffield School of Art; graduated from Royal College of Art, 1937.

CAREER: Free-lance artist and illustrator. Camberwell School of Art, Camberwell, England, teacher of lithography, life drawing, and anatomy, 1938-39. Commissioned work includes auto-lithographic posters for Lyric Theatre, Hammersmith, England, film posters for Alexander Korda at Pathé and Ealing Studios, and a mural for Festival of Britain Exhibition, 1951. Work has appeared in various exhibitions, including AIA Gallery, London, 1957, and one-man exhibition at Savage Gallery, 1960. Work is represented in permanent collections of Klingspor-Museum, Offenbach, West Germany; Victoria and Albert Museum, London; and Imperial War Museum. *Military service:* British Army, World War II; served as staff officer.

WRITINGS: The First Book of Tales of Ancient Araby (juvenile; self-illustrated), F. Watts, 1960; *The First Book of Tales of Ancient Egypt* (juvenile; self-illustrated), F. Watts, 1960; *Wolperiana: An Illustrated Guide to Berthold L. Wolpe* (adult), Merrion Press, 1960.

Illustrator; for children, unless otherwise indicated: Carlo Collodi (pseudonym of Carlo Lorenzini), *The Adventures of Pinocchio,* translated by Jane McIntyre, F. Watts, 1959; Charles Perrault, *Famous Fairy Tales,* translated by Sarah Chokla Gross, large-type edition, F. Watts, 1959; Johanna Spyri, *Heidi,* translated by Joy Law, F. Watts, 1959; Jean Neville Ure, compiler and translator, *Pacala and Tandala, and Other Rumanian Folk-Tales,* Methuen, 1960, published as *Rumanian Folk Tales,* Watts, 1961; Oscar Wilde, *Fairy Tales,* Bodley Head, 1960, published as *The Complete Fairy Tales,* F. Watts, 1961; René Guillot, *Nicolette and the Mill,* translated by Gwen Marsh, Abelard, 1961; Elisabeth Kyle (pseudonym of Agnes M. R. Dunlop), *Girl with a Pen,* Evans, 1963, published as *Girl with A Pen: Charlotte Bronte,* Holt, 1964; Noel Streatfeild, *A Vicarage Family,* Collins, 1963, F. Watts, 1964; George MacDonald, *At the Back of the North Wind,* Nonesuch Press,

(From *A Vicarage Family* by Noel Streatfeild. Illustrated by Charles Mozley.)

1963, F. Watts, 1964; E. Kyle, *Girl with a Destiny,* F. Watts, 1964; Anna Sewell, *Black Beauty,* large-type edition, F. Watts, 1967; H. G. Wells, *The Invisible Man,* Heritage Press, 1967; Andrew Lang, compiler, *King Arthur: Tales of the Round Table,* large-type edition, F. Watts, 1968; Elvajean Hall, compiler, *Psalms: A Selection,* F. Watts, 1968; Alfred E. Housman, *A Shropshire Lad* (young adult), F. Watts, 1968; Charles Dickens, *A Christmas Carol,* F. Watts, 1969; Margaret Mahy, *The Procession,* F. Watts, 1969; Samuel Taylor Coleridge, *The Rime of the Ancient Mariner,* F. Watts, 1969; William Shakespeare, *Shakespeare's Sonnets* (young adult), F. Watts, 1969.

Aladdin and His Wonderful Lamp, F. Watts, 1970; M. Mahy, *The Little Witch,* F. Watts, 1970; E. Hall, compiler, *The Proverbs: A Selection,* F. Watts, 1970; Robert Erskine Childers, *The Riddle of the Sands,* Dutton, 1970; John Keats, *Selected Poems of John Keats* (young adult), F. Watts, 1970; Robert Browning, *Selected Poems of Robert Browning* (young adult), F. Watts, 1970; *The Sleeping Beauty,* F. Watts, 1970; Martha Shapp and Charles Shapp, *Words about Air Travel,* F. Watts, 1970; Stephen Crane, *The Red Badge of Courage* (young adult), Dutton, 1971; *Sinbad the Sailor,* F. Watts, 1971; James Otis, *Toby Tyler,* abridged by Grace Hogarth, Collins, 1971; Frank Waters, *The First A.B.C.,* F. Watts, 1972; M. Mahy, *Seventeen Kings and Forty-Two Elephants,* Dent, 1972; Norris McWhirter and Ross McWhirter, *Surprising Facts about Kings and Rulers,* F. Watts (London), 1973; Edith Nesbit, *The Railway Children,* Dent, 1975; Bill Naughton, *A Dog Called Nel-*

(From *The Invisible Man* by H. G. Wells. Illustrated by Charles Mozley.)

son, Dent, 1976; N. Streatfeild, *Far to Go,* Collins, 1976; N. Streatfeild, *Gran-Nannie,* M. Joseph, 1976; Cyril Ray, *Lickerish Limericks,* Dent, 1979; Oscar Wilde, *Oscar Wilde Fairy Tales,* Merrimack, 1980.

Illustrator; for adults: Benita Pérez Galdós, *The Spendthrifts,* translated by Gamel Woolsey, Farrar, Straus, & Young, 1952; B. Pérez Galdós, *Torment,* translated by J. M. Cohen, Weidenfield & Nicolson, 1952; Daniel Defoe, *The Fortunes and Misfortunes of the Famous Moll Flanders,* Zodiac Press, 1962; Edmund Spenser, *An Hymne of Heavenly Beautie,* Stellar Press, 1963; John Galsworthy, *The Man of Property* (introduction by Evelyn Waugh), Limited Editions Club, 1964; Henri Maupassant, *The Tellier House,* translated by Desmond Flower, Cassell, 1964; Bergen Evans, *Dictionary of Mythology,* Centennial Press, 1970; Denis Diderot, *The Nun,* translated by Leonard Tancock, Folio, 1972; Anthony Trollope, *The Duke's Children,* Oxford University Press, 1973.

SIDELIGHTS: "Soon after completing my training at the Royal College of Art, I was called up into the Army in World War II for six years. After the war I did posters for different theatre and film companies and soon after that began doing book jackets and illustrations." [Lee Kingman and others, compilers, *Illustrators of Children's Books: 1957-1966,* Horn Book, 1968.[1]]

Noel Streatfeild's *The Vicarage Family* [Collins, 1963] was illustrated by Mozley. Streatfeild paid tribute to Mozley: "What a man is Charles Mozley to work with! He is a great believer in getting impressions down on paper immediately. Does this

North Wind met him, took him by the hand, and hurried down and out of the house. ■ (From *At the Back of the North Wind* by George MacDonald. Illustrated by Charles Mozley.)

mean he turns up with a drawing block and pencils? It does not. We discussed the illustrations in Helen Hoke Watts' room at the Savoy Hotel, London.

"'I know what you mean,' Charles would say, looking wildly around the room. 'Paper, paper—and a good pencil.' And we rushed to find them. Sometimes foolscap would do; but often he needed something larger, and the lining paper would be snatched from the drawers of the wardrobe. Sometimes he needed color to express what was in his mind. Naturally there were no paints in Helen's room, but her dressing table was nearby; so, undeterred, Charles got his effects with lipstick, eyebrow pencils—*anything* at hand.

"One day the lushness of this hotel bedroom in which we were working got on his nerves. 'It's all so grand,' he muttered. He strode over to the long glass of the wardrobe and brilliantly, with a black grease pencil, in a few strokes made it look as if it had been cracked by a bullet. 'That's better,' he said when he had finished. (The floor housekeeper almost had a heart attack when she saw it the next morning.)

"Such arguments we had: 'I never wore boots,' I complained. 'We wore black, laced shoes.'

"Nevertheless, Charles drew boots, merely murmuring, 'I like drawing boots.'

"Sometimes *I* won. 'A cook,' I said, 'never wore black. Her dresses were of sprigged print.'

"'Bother,' said Charles, 'I must alter that.' And, eventually, he did.

"There was no guessing between one meeting and another what Charles would turn up with. As a parson's daughter I could not accept that a picture showing a quiet day for clergy held in the vicarage included a bishop. But Charles was crazy on drawing gaiters. 'I like them!' he said ecstatically. 'See how well they look.'

"'But they weren't *there,*' I protested.

"'Who cares?' murmured Charles, sketching yet more gaiters on a clean sheet of lining paper from one of Helen's wardrobe drawers.

"One of the most fascinating things about working with Charles was that he was unpredictable. He would telephone to say, 'Can I bring around a sketch I have made of the parish concert?' If he turned up at the agreed time—and this was always a hazard—I could be certain that the parish concert was forgotten and, by now, his entire attention given to a totally different scene. It was on such an occasion that he brought along my favorite of his illustrations: a picture of us all, including my father, paddling. He has caught the period superbly. Nothing has changed more than the seaside, and somehow Charles knew it. There are no 'bathing machines' visible, but you know they are just out of sight. There are no shorts—skirts are turned up over petticoats. Above all, there are hats. Those straw hats trimmed with flowers on Sundays and a plain ribbon on weekdays which, for some reason, no little girl's head was ever without.

"How wonderfully Charles Mozley has caught the essence of us as a family—better probably than I have caught us in the writing. Maybe it's easier when you do not rely on 'I remember. . . .'" [Noel Streatfeild, "The Album and the Artist," *Horn Book,* April, 1964.[2]]

The wolf tried to sound less gruff as he replied, "Pull the catch to lift the latch and the door will open, dear." ▪ (From "Little Red Riding Hood," in *Famous Fairy Tales* by Charles Perrault. Illustrated by Charles Mozley.)

(From *The Red Badge of Courage* by Stephen Crane. Illustrated by Charles Mozley.)

Mozley's works are included in the Kerlan Collection at the University of Minnesota.

FOR MORE INFORMATION SEE: John Ryder, *Artists of a Certain Line,* Bodley Head, 1960; *Horn Book,* April, 1964; Lee Kingman and others, compilers, *Illustrators of Children's Books: 1957-1966,* Horn Book, 1968; Lee Kingman and others, compilers, *Illustrators of Children's Books: 1967-1976,* Horn Book, 1978.

Matilda told such dreadful lies,
It made one gasp and stretch one's eyes;
Her aunt, who, from her earliest youth,
Had kept a strict regard for truth,
Attempted to believe Matilda;
The effort very nearly killed her.

—Hilaire Belloc

MULFORD, Philippa Greene 1948-

PERSONAL: Born May 29, 1948, in New York, N.Y.; daughter of Philip Murray (a radio station owner) and Constance (an author of books for young people; maiden name, Clarke) Greene; married Andrew S. Kennedy, January 9, 1971 (divorced); married R. Edward Mulford (a businessman), September 29, 1978; stepchildren: Nicholas, Leslie. *Education:* Skidmore College, B.A., 1971. *Home and office:* Rural Delivery 1, Box 14, Norton Ave., Clinton, N.Y. 13323. *Agent:* Marilyn Marlow, Curtis Brown, Ltd., 575 Madison Ave., New York, N.Y. 10022.

CAREER: Steuben Glass, New York, N.Y., sales clerk, and later in customer relations department; *Clinton Courier* (weekly newspaper), Clinton, N.Y., feature writer, 1971-73; Central New York Community Arts Council, Inc., Utica, N.Y., executive director, 1971-78; full-time writer, 1978—. Consultant to the New York State Council on the Arts, 1973-79. Member, Arts Service Organization Panel, New York State Council on the Arts, 1976-78.

WRITINGS: If It's Not Funny, Why Am I Laughing? (young adult novel), Delacorte, 1982; *The World Is My Eggshell*, Delacorte, 1986.

SIDELIGHTS: "Having a mother who wrote for as long as I can remember is probably the main reason I became a writer. My brother, Shep Greene, has also published a young adult novel, *The Boy Who Drank too Much*, and that really spurred me on. Talk about sibling rivalry—I know quite a lot about it coming from a family of five children. You'll probably be seeing more books over the years from Greenes, as my two sisters and younger brother have to keep up with me *and* Shep now. I like to laugh and make other people laugh, and the teenage years are chock-full of reasons to laugh (rather than cry)."

PHILIPPA GREENE MULFORD

HOBBIES AND OTHER INTERESTS: "My interests include tennis, water and snow skiing, and my two stepchildren who keep me on my toes. I am also an avid bluefisherwoman (meaning I fish blues off of Chappaquiddick Island where we have a house)."

MURRAY, Ossie 1938-

PERSONAL: Born May 28, 1938, in Kingston, Jamaica, British West Indies; emigrated to England, 1959; son of William Nataniel (a shoemaker) and Mary (a homemaker; maiden name, Marsh) Murray. *Education:* Attended Kingston Senior Tutorial College, Jamaica; East Ham College, London, England; and Walthamstow Technical College, London, England. *Home:* 16 Barley Lane, Goodmays, Ilford, Essex, England.

CAREER: Artist and illustrator of books for children. *Exhibitions:* (One-man show) Jamaican High Commission, London, England, 1976; Second World Festival of Black Arts and African Culture in Lagos, Festival, 1977; (one-man show) International Press Centre, 1977; (one-man show) Keskidee Centre, 1979; Air Jamaica, 1980. Work has been exhibited at the Commonwealth Institute, and at the Empire Ballroom.

ILLUSTRATOR—All for children; all written by Petronella Breinburg, except as indicated; all published by Bodley Head, except as indicated: *Sally-Ann's Umbrella*, 1975, Merrimack,

OSSIE MURRAY

All morning Sally-Ann went up and down the slope in Sandra's box.

(From *Sally-Ann in the Snow* by Petronella Breinburg. Illustrated by Ossie Murray.)

1979; *Sally-Ann in the Snow*, 1977, Merrimack, 1979; *Sally-Ann's Skateboard*, 1979; Jamila Gavin, *The Orange Tree and Other Stories*, Methuen, 1979; Hugh Sinclair, *Explore a Story*, Collins, 1979. Also illustrator of *The Black Rose* by Mall Bell, published by Affor Publication. Also illustrator of books for the London Inner Education Authority.

SIDELIGHTS: Born in Jonestown, Jamaica, the poor district of Kingston, Murray was the youngest of twelve children, son of a modest shoemaker. Very early in his childhood Murray discovered that drawing came naturally to him. This artistic ambition sustained him throughout his early poverty-stricken years in Jamaica.

Quitting school before he was sixteen, Murray tried to earn his living at several craftskills such as leather-tanning and cabinet-making. He continued to sketch his environment and the people who lived and worked around him.

By 1959, Murray had moved from his Jamaican home to England in search of greater opportunities in earning a living as an artist. His first job in England, however, was making sweets in a candy factory. He continued to draw the world around him. Realizing that there was no commercial outlet for his work, he took up a trade skill—screen process-printing in Croydon.

Some of his landscapes and portraits were exhibited at the Commonwealth Institute. Judy Taylor of The Bodley Head publishing company in London was so impressed with his exhibited work that she introduced him to her company. "They thought my style of work would go down very well with chil-

dren, and although this was something I had always considered, I just never got round to getting really involved. Now that I have . . . published . . . and . . . illustrated for the London Inner Education Authority, I feel quite at home." [Lee Kingman and others, compilers, *Illustrators of Children's Books: 1967-1976*, Horn Book, 1978.[1]]

HOBBIES AND OTHER INTERESTS: Cricket and music.

NATHAN, Robert (Gruntal) 1894-1985

OBITUARY NOTICE—See sketch in *SATA* Volume 6: Born January 2, 1894, in New York, N.Y.; died of kidney failure, May 25, 1985, in Los Angeles, Calif. Novelist, poet, playwright, and screenwriter. A prolific author, Nathan wrote over fifty books during his more than seventy years as a writer. After leaving Harvard University in 1915, Nathan was a solicitor for a New York City advertising firm. He later became a lecturer at New York University School of Journalism and, during the 1940s, was a screenwriter for Metro-Goldwyn-Mayer. Probably one of his best known works of interest to young people is *Portrait of Jennie*, a fantasy novel about a penniless artist who meets a mysterious young girl. The book was made into a movie in 1949, starring Jennifer Jones and Joseph Cotten. Nathan's other well-known novel is *One More Spring*, the story of three strangers, hit hard by the Depression, who meet in Central Park and decide to pool their resources. It was also successfully adapted to film in 1935, with Janet Gaynor and Warner Baxter. Nathan's numerous books include novels for young people like *The Snowflake and the Starfish* and *Tappy*. His autobiography, *Portrait of Nathan: Robert Nathan at Ninety-One,* written with Jeffrey M. Elliot, was published in 1985.

FOR MORE INFORMATION SEE: The Dictionary of Literary Biography, Volume IX, Gale, 1981; *Contemporary Authors, New Revision Series,* Volume 6, Gale, 1982. Obituaries: *Los Angeles Times,* May 26, 1985; *Milwaukee Journal,* May 27, 1985; *Washington Post,* May 27, 1985; *New York Times,* May 28, 1985; *Times* (London), May 30, 1985; *Facts on File,* May 31, 1985; *Newsweek,* June 10, 1985; *Time,* June 10, 1985.

NEY, John 1923-

PERSONAL: Surname rhymes with ''hay''; born May 3, 1923, in St. Paul, Minn.; married Marian Wallace (a teacher), August 17, 1954; children: Sarah, Janet, Peter. *Office:* Warfield Co., P.O. Box 537, Indiantown, Fla. 33456.

CAREER: President of Warfield Co. (investment organization), Indiantown, Fla. *Awards, honors: Ox Goes North: More Trouble for the Kid at the Top* was chosen one of *New York Times* Outstanding Books of the Year, 1973; National Book

JOHN NEY

Award, Children's Book Category, finalist, 1977, for *Ox Under Pressure*.

WRITINGS: Whitey McAlpine: A Tale of Ambition (adult novel), C. N. Potter, 1962; *Palm Beach: The Place, the People, Its Pleasures and Palaces* (adult nonfiction), Little, Brown, 1966; *The European Surrender: A Descriptive Study of the American Social and Economic Conquest* (adult nonfiction), Little, Brown, 1970; *Ox: The Story of a Kid at the Top* (young adult novel), Little, Brown, 1970; *Ox Goes North: More Trouble for the Kid at the Top* (young adult novel), Harper, 1973; *Ox Under Pressure* (young adult novel), Lippincott, 1976; *Ox and the Prime-Time Kid* (young adult novel), Pineapple Press, 1985. Also author of movie scripts.

WORK IN PROGRESS: For adults, *An Intelligent Woman's Guide to American Failure*.

FOR MORE INFORMATION SEE: Martha E. Ward and Dorothy A. Marquardt, *Authors of Books for Young People,* supplement to the second edition, Scarecrow, 1979.

NORTON, Alice Mary   1912-
(Andrew North, André Norton; Allen Weston, a joint pseudonym)

PERSONAL: Born February 17, 1912, in Cleveland, Ohio; legally adopted name André Norton, 1934; daughter of Adalbert Freely (a salesman) and Bertha (Stemm) Norton. *Education:* Attended Western Reserve University (now Case Western Reserve University), 1930-31. *Politics:* Republican. *Religion:* Presbyterian. *Home and office:* 682 South Lake-

(Jacket illustration by Bruce Waldman from *Iron Cage* by André Norton.)

mont, Winter Park, Fla. 32789. *Agent:* Larry Sternig, 742 Robertson St., Milwaukee, Wis. 53212.

CAREER: Cleveland Public Library, Cleveland, Ohio, children's librarian, 1932-41, 1942-51; Mystery House (book store and lending library), Mount Ranier, Md., owner and manager, 1941; free-lance writer of juvenile fiction and science fiction, 1950—. Worked as a special librarian for a citizenship project in Washington, D.C. and at the Library of Congress, 1941. Reader, Gnome Press, 1950-58. *Member:* American Penwomen, Women in Communications, Science Fiction Writers of America, American League of Writers, Swordsmen and Sorcerers Association. *Awards, honors:* Award from Dutch government, 1946, for *The Sword Is Drawn;* Ohioana Library Juvenile Award honor book, 1950, for *Sword in Sheath;* Boys' Club of America Medal, 1951, for *Bullard of the Space Patrol,* and Certificate of Merit, 1965, for *Night of Masks;* Hugo Award nomination, 1962, for *Star Hunter,* 1964, for *Witch World,* and 1968, for "Wizard's World"; Headliner Award, Theta Sigma Phi, 1963; Invisible Little Man Award for sustained excellence in science fiction, 1963; Phoenix award, 1975; Gandalf Master of Fantasy award, 1977, for lifetime achievement in fantasy; André Norton Award, Women Writers of Science Fiction, 1978; Balrog Fantasy Award, 1979; Ohioana Award, 1980, for body of work; Ohio Women's Hall of Fame, 1981; Fritz Leiber Award, for her work in the field of fantasy, 1983; Nebula Grand Master Award, for life achievement, 1984; Jules Verne Award, for her work in the field of Science Fiction, 1984.

ALICE MARY NORTON

WRITINGS—Under name André Norton, except as indicated: *The Prince Commands* (illustrated by Kate Seredy), Appleton, 1934; *Ralestone Luck* (illustrated by James Reid), Appleton, 1938; *Follow the Drum*, Penn, 1942; *The Sword Is Drawn* (illustrated by Duncan Coburn; Junior Literary Guild selection), Houghton, 1944; *Rogue Reynard* (illustrated by Laura Bannon), Houghton, 1947; *Scarface* (illustrated by Lorence Bjorklund), Harcourt, 1948; *Sword in Sheath* (illustrated by L. Bjorklund), Harcourt, 1949 (published in England as *Island of the Lost*, Staples Press, 1953); *Huon of the Horn* (illustrated by Joe Krush; ALA Notable Book), Harcourt, 1951; *Star Man's Son 2250 A.D.* (illustrated by Nicolas Mordvinoff), Harcourt, 1952, published as *Daybreak—2250 A.D.*, Ace Books, 1954; *At Swords' Points*, Harcourt, 1954; (with Grace Allen Hogarth; under joint pseudonym Allen Weston) *Murder for Sale*, Hammond-Hammond, 1954; *Yankee Privateer* (illustrated by Leonard Vosburgh), World Publishing, 1955; *Stand to Horse*, Harcourt, 1956; *Sea Seige*, Harcourt, 1957; *Star Gate*, Harcourt, 1958, revised edition, Ace Books, 1963; *Secret of the Lost Race*, Ace Books, 1959 (published in England as *Wolfshead*, R. Hale, 1977).

The Sioux Spaceman, Ace Books, 1960; *Shadow Hawk*, Harcourt, 1960; *Star Hunter*, Ace Books, 1961; *Ride Proud, Rebel!*, World Publishing, 1961; *Catseye*, Harcourt, 1961; *Eye of the Monster*, Ace Books, 1962; *Rebel Spurs*, World Publishing, 1962; *Night of Masks*, Harcourt, 1964; *The X Factor*, Harcourt, 1965; *Steel Magic* (illustrated by Robin Jacques), World Publishing, 1965, revised edition published as *Grey Magic*, Scholastic Book Services, 1967; *Octagon Magic* (illustrated by Mac Conner), World Publishing, 1967; *Operation Time Search*, Harcourt, 1967; *Dark Piper*, Harcourt, 1968; *Fur Magic* (illustrated by John Kaufmann), World Publishing, 1968; (with mother, Bertha Stemm Norton) *Bertie and May* (illustrated by Fermin Rocker), World Publishing, 1969.

High Sorcery (story collection), Ace Books, 1970; *Ice Crown*, Viking, 1970; *Dread Companion*, Harcourt, 1970; *Android at Arms*, Harcourt, 1971; *Dragon Magic* (illustrated by R. Jacques), Crowell, 1972; *Breed to Come*, Viking, 1972; *Garan the Eternal* (story collection), Fantasy Publishing, 1972; *Forerunner Foray* (Science-Fiction Book Club selection), Viking, 1973; *Here Abide Monsters*, Atheneum, 1973; *Lavender-Green Magic* (illustrated by Judith G. Brown), Crowell, 1974; *The Many Worlds of André Norton* (story collection), edited by Roger Elwood, Chilton, 1974, published as *The Book of André Norton*, DAW Books, 1975; *The Jargoon Pard*, Atheneum, 1974; *Iron Cage*, Viking, 1974; *Outside* (illustrated by Bernard P. Colonna), Walker, 1974; (with Michael Gilbert) *The Day of the Ness* (illustrated by M. Gilbert), Walker, 1975; *The White Jade Fox*, Dutton, 1975; *Merlin's Mirror*, DAW Books, 1975; *No Night without Stars*, Atheneum, 1975; *Knave of Dreams*, Viking, 1975; *Perilous Dreams* (story collection), DAW Books, 1976; *Wraiths of Time*, Atheneum, 1976; *Red Hart Magic* (illustrated by Donna Diamond), Crowell, 1976; *Velvet Shadows*, Fawcett, 1977; *The Opal-Eyed Fan*, Dutton, 1977; *Quag Keep*, Atheneum, 1978; *Yurth Burden*, DAW Books, 1978; (with Phyllis Miller) *Seven Spells to Sunday*, McElderry, 1979; *Snow Shadow*, Fawcett, 1979.

Iron Butterflies, Fawcett, 1980; *Voor Loper*, Ace Books, 1980; *Forerunner*, Tor Books, 1981; *Horn Crown*, DAW Books, 1981; *Ten Mile Treasure*, Archway, 1981; *Moon Called*, Pinnacle Books, 1983; *Stand and Deliver*, Dell, 1984; *Were-Wrath*, Cheap Street, 1984; *Wheel of Stars*, Tor Books, 1984; (with

(Jacket illustration by Charles Mikolaycak from *Forerunner Foray* by André Norton.)

It was all right, everything would be everlastingly all right from now on. ▪ (From *Star Ka'at* by André Norton and Dorothy Madlee. Illustrated by Bernard Colonna.)

P. Miller) *House of Shadows,* Atheneum, 1984; *Forerunner: The Second Venture,* Tor Books, 1985.

"Central Control" series: *Star Rangers,* Harcourt, 1953, published as *The Last Planet,* Ace Books, 1955; *Star Guard,* Harcourt, 1955.

"Pax" series; published by World Publishing: *The Stars Are Ours!,* 1954; *Star Born,* 1957.

"Solar Queen" series: *Sargasso of Space,* Gnome Press, 1955, Ace Books, 1971 (originally published under pseudonym Andrew North); *Plague Ship,* Gnome Press, 1956, Ace Books, 1972 (originally published under pseudonym Andrew North); *Voodoo Planet,* Ace Books, 1959, reprinted, 1968 (originally published under pseudonym Andrew North); *Postmarked the Stars,* Harcourt, 1969.

"Blake Walker" series: *The Crossroads of Time,* Ace Books, 1956; *Quest Crosstime,* Viking, 1965 (published in England as *Crosstime Agent,* Gollancz, 1975).

"Time Travel" series; published by World Publishing: *The Time Traders,* 1958; *Galactic Derelict,* 1959; *The Defiant Agents,* 1962; *Key Out of Time,* 1963.

"Hosteen Storm" series; published by Harcourt: *The Beast Master,* 1959; *Lord of Thunder,* 1962.

"Planet Warlock" series: *Storm over Warlock,* World Publishing, 1960; *Ordeal in Otherwhere,* World Publishing, 1964.

"Janus" series; published by Harcourt: *Judgement on Janus,* 1963; *Victory on Janus,* 1966.

"Witch World" series; published by Ace Books, except as indicated; novels, except as indicated: *Witch World,* 1963; *Web of the Witch World,* 1964; *Three against the Witch World,* 1965; *Year of the Unicorn,* 1965; *Warlock of the Witch World,* 1967; *Sorceress of the Witch World,* 1968; *Spell of the Witch World* (story collection), DAW Books, 1972; *The Crystal Gryphon,* Atheneum, 1972; *Trey of Swords* (story collection), 1977; *Zarsthor's Bane,* 1978; *Lore of Witchworld,* DAW Books, 1980; *Gryphon in Glory,* Atheneum, 1981; *'Ware Hawk,* Atheneum, 1983; *Gryphon's Eyrie,* Tor, 1984.

"Free Traders" series; published by Viking: *Moon of Three Rings* (Junior Literary Guild selection), 1966; *Exiles of the Stars,* 1971.

"Jern Murdock" series; published by Viking: *The Zero Stone,* 1968; *Uncharted Stars,* 1969.

"Star Ka'at" series, with Dorothy Madlee; published by Walker: *Star Ka'at* (illustrated by B. P. Colonna), 1976; *Star Ka'at World* (illustrated by Jean Jenkins), 1978; *Star Ka'ats and Plant People* (illustrated by J. Jenkins), 1979; *Star Ka'ats and the Winged Warriors* (illustrated by J. Jenkins), 1981.

Editor: Malcolm Jameson, *Bullard of the Space Patrol,* World Publishing, 1951; *Space Service,* World Publishing, 1953; *Space Pioneers,* World Publishing, 1954; *Space Police,* World Publishing, 1956; (with Ernestine Donaldy) *Gates to Tomorrow: An Introduction to Science Fiction,* Atheneum, 1973; (compiler) *Small Shadows Creep: Ghost Children,* Dutton, 1974; (with Robert Adams) *Magic in Ithkar,* Tor, 1985.

Contributor to anthologies: T. E. Dikty, editor, *Best Science Fiction Stories and Novels, 1955,* Frederick Fell, 1955; Donald A. Wollheim, editor, *Swordsmen in the Sky,* Ace Books, 1964; Roger Elwood and Sam Moskowitz, editors, *The Time Curve,* Tower, 1968; R. Elwood and S. Moskowitz, editors, *Alien Earth and Other Stories,* Macfadden-Bartell, 1969; Ben Bova, editor, *Many Worlds of Science-Fiction,* Dutton, 1971; Jane Yolen, editor, *Zoo 2000: Twelve Stories of Science-Fiction and Fantasy Beasts,* Seabury, 1973; R. Elwood and Virginia Kidd, editors, *In Saving Worlds: A Collection of Original Science-Fiction Stories,* Doubleday, 1973; R. Elwood, editor, *Science-Fiction Adventures from Way Out,* Western Publishing, 1973; Lin Carter, editor, *Flashing Swords! #2,* Nelson Doubleday, 1973; R. Elwood, editor, *The Long Night of Waiting by André Norton and Other Stories,* Aurora, 1974; R. Elwood, *The Gifts of Asti and Other Stories,* Follett, 1975; D. A. Wollheim, editor, *The DAW Science-Fiction Reader,* DAW Books, 1976; Seon Manley and Gogo Lewis, editors, *Sisters of Sorcery: Two Centuries of Witchcraft Stories by the Gentle Sex,* Lothrop, 1976; L. Carter, *Flashing Swords! #3: Warriors and Wizards,* Dell, 1976; (author of introduction) *Baleful Beasts and Eerie Creatures* (illustrated by Ruth Rod), Rand McNally, 1976; Andrew J. Offrett, editor, *Swords Against Darkness II,* Zebra Books, 1977; Jane Mobley, editor, *Phantasmagoria: Tales of Fantasy and the Supernatural,* Anchor Books, 1977.

Contributor of stories to *Fantasy Book* (under pseudonym Andrew North), *Fantastic Universe* (under pseudonym A. North), *Magazine of Fantasy and Science-Fiction, Phantom Magazine, Golden Magazine for Boys and Girls, Worlds of If, Spaceway Science-Fiction,* and *Worlds of Fantasy.* Also contributor of reviews to *Cleveland Plain Dealer* and *Cleveland Press.*

SIDELIGHTS: **February 17, 1912.** Born in Cleveland, Ohio. "I am of pioneer American stock (including an Indian strain introduced in the late 1700s). My father's mother was an Abbey whose family established the town of Enfield, Connecticut; her ancestors there fought in King Phillip's War in the late 1600s. Her branch of that line is directly descended from a man and his wife who were witnesses at the Salem Witchcraft trials. My mother's line were Scotch-Irish-English-Penn Dutch and part of the clan were established in Ohio on those land grants paid to Revolutionary War soldiers for arrears in army pay." [Paul Walker, "An Interview with André Norton," *Luna Monthly,* number 40, September, 1972.[1]]

"Both my parents were readers. My father had spent some time out west in Ellsworth, Kansas in the days after Wyatt Earp. He loved to read westerns and would watch all the western shows on our first television set criticizing their lack of authenticity. My mother read to me from the time I was one year old." "[She] knew a great deal of poetry and could tell wonderful stories—I was reading aloud long before I went to school. The Oz books were my pride and joy, and for every

report card which matched my mother's standard of approval, volumes were added to my collection."[1]

"With my first library card, I headed immediately for the fourth and fifth grade levels. I'm well read. I used to buy pulp magazines which contained some darned good writing. I read less-known authors Dornford Yates, Ann Pat McCaffrey, Edgar Wallace, and the more familiar Jules Verne and H. G. Wells.

"I wrote fiction and book reviews for *The Collingwood Spotlight,* my high school paper. I joined 'The Quill and Scroll,' a special club under the tutelage of Sylvia Cochran. We would stay after school to do our writing. My mother encouraged me. In fact, she aspired to become a writer herself. After she died, I found amongst her papers a book that she had begun about her childhood. I completed it for her, and had it published as *Bertie and May.*

"Collingwood High had its own print shop as well, and upon graduation, we were allowed to publish our own book. There were twelve of us in the club, five members of whom became professional writers—one as head of a news bureau in Washington, one in advertising, one editor, and I, a fiction writer. We shared a great sense of responsibility and self-motivation in those days.

"Ware boarders!" Fritz cried out. ■ (From *Yankee Privateer* by André Norton. Illustrated by Leonard Vosburgh.)

"I won the English trophy during my senior year and placed first in the History department's final exam. I intended to become a history teacher."

1930-1931. Attended Flora Stone Mather College of Western Reserve University (now Case Western Reserve) as a history major. "These were the depression years. I attended Western Reserve College for a year, and then had to leave to find a job. I was lucky to find a job at the Cleveland Public Library. I continued my education in the adult division of Western Reserve University at night, taking every writing course they offered, including journalism and creative writing. One of these classes was taught by a literary editor. He wrote book reviews and later invited me to review mystery stories for his publication. I soon learned that no one can teach writing. What you can get out of a writing course, however, is the ability to look critically at your weaknesses.

"There were fifty-two branches of the Cleveland Public Library, and I covered forty-eight of them. I started at the desk checking out books and moved up to become the children's librarian. Working from noon until nine o'clock, I was able to save my mornings for writing. I still write in the mornings.

"My first novel *Ralestone Luck* was written in high school. I later rewrote it using all I had learned along the way and had it published in 1938 as my second novel. By this time I had learned how to make conversation work. I had developed as a writer. I could feel when something was working."

1934. Published first novel, *The Prince Commands,* a historical fantasy, and legally adopted the name André Norton. "I chose the name André Norton because it was neither male or female. I was writing men's books at the time, and publishers would not accept such books by a woman. *The Prince Commands* was my first published novel, though it was the third I'd written. I sent the manuscript to the first name on my alphabetized list of publishers. It was accepted.

"Editor-writer relationships have changed over the years. It is necessary that an author know that the editor will be with a publishing house for at least two or three years to establish a stable relationship. It seems, however, that companies are bought and sold in such rapid succession that that kind of relationship is not possible any more. There are no guarantees that an editor will *be* there from one week to the next. I've written letters to one editor, and by the time it reaches him, he's gone."

1941. "Just before the war, I went to Mount Ranier, Maryland and opened a bookshop/lending library for about eight months. I sold the business and took a job as a librarian in Washington D.C. for a special government agency, which rewrote material in basic English for immigrants. The project was axed with the start of the war and I went to work for the Library of Congress."

1941-1944. Returned home to Cleveland to care for her elderly parents, taking a position with the Cleveland Public Library. *The Sword Is Drawn,* an espionage novel which chronicles the

Fox eyes—gems—moonlight—a dancer with the form of a woman, but a sharp pointed, red-furred muzzle for a face—Fox face—fox eyes—. ■ (Jacket illustration by David K. Stone from *The White Jade Fox* by André Norton.)

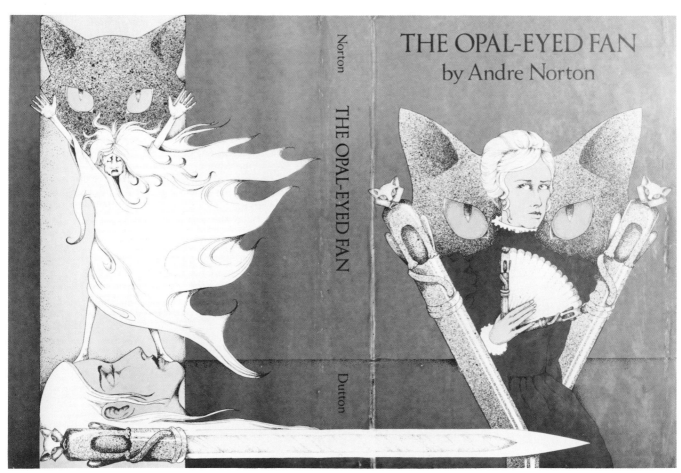

It stirred in her again that other fear, the one which had gripped her last night when she had stood in the hall sure that a "presence" had passed her by. ■ (Jacket illustration by Jack Crane from *The Opal-Eyed Fan* by André Norton.)

activities of the Dutch underground during World War II, was published in 1944. Norton was awarded an enamel plaque by the Dutch government for the book's authenticity and for its portrayal of the heroic efforts of the underground. "*Sword Is Drawn* was written at the request of the World Friend's Club in Cleveland. The second novel of that series, *Sword in Sheath* was written after the war, at which time I contacted a man who had been one of the leaders of the Dutch resistance. He sent me a great deal of information, letters and photographs which were very helpful."

1947-1948. Wrote *Scarface, Being the Story of One Justin Blade, Late of the Pirate Isle of Tortuga, and How Fate Did Justly Deal with Him, to His Great Profit*. The idea for the novel came to Norton when at twenty-three, she was a passenger on a Dutch freighter. "I was on a vacation trip through the West Indies. I didn't decide to write the book then, but later, I went back to write it, based on what I had seen during my travels. I wrote the book after I had read a great deal about the history of the pirates and the pirateers in the Caribbean."

1950-1958. Left the Cleveland Public Library System to work as a reader for Martin Greenberg at Gnome Press. Wrote first science-fiction novel, *Star Man's Son 2250 A.D.*, which has sold over one million copies. The increased income allowed her to devote full time to writing. "By the time I was able to support myself with my own writing, the science-fiction field had opened up.

"I had tried to write science fiction before, but was rejected because there was no market for it. Most science-fiction writing was in short story form, a form I find difficult to write in. No one would take a chance on book-length science fiction. A market was created, however, with the rise in paperback publication and the advent of the space program, which popularized science fiction.

"I'm not a 'hard' science-fiction writer. I write science-fiction adventure. There are a great many science-fiction writers whose work I admire—Alison Peters, Ardath Mayhar, Ann McCarthy, Dell Shannon, and Jane Yolen, to name a few."

1958-1978. Norton wrote sixty-seven novels, three short story collections, edited five anthologies and published twenty-three short stories. "I'm drawn to the science-fiction genre because it imposes no limits on my imagination. I've written some books from pictures. One novel grew out of a footnote in a book. I read archeology, anthropology, natural history, history, folklore, travel, and psycho-esper research. I come across things that give me ideas, then I start building. I get my alien animals by going through naturalist books, finding very rare animals, and making slight changes. I do the same with foliage and landscape. I consult experts. For example, if I am interested in a certain occult practice, such as tarot card readings, I have someone demonstrate it for me. Science fiction flows naturally into areas like telepathy, and of course, reading folklore and fantasy as I do for background, leads me to the occult.

Grandma took the page in turn, rammed up her glasses high and hard on her nose. ■ (From *Lavender-Green Magic* by André Norton. Illustrated by Judith Gwyn Brown.)

"... I am not one of the 'new wave' writers, but rather a very staid teller of old-fashioned stories with firm plots and morals. . . . I prefer reading the type of story I write—that is, a tightly plotted action story. The 'new wave' fiction, with sprawling action and the anti-hero, is certainly NOT to my taste. And I see no reason for piling in sex scenes—much more can be accomplished by putting the reader's imagination to work—under-stating rather than over-stating. That, to me, is the better course in writing.

"The primary concern of fiction is to tell an entertaining story; not to display the whining weaknesses of main characters, but to give [attention to] a hero or a heroine who stands up to difficulties as best he or she can and does not 'cop out' when the going gets rough. But then I am of the generation trained in the Depression and this was hammered into us in that day and age.

"A firm plot is one in which the action flows steadily in a pattern and is not entangled in whirls which add nothing to the story line and leave the reader baffled. (There are a number of writers now in the field whom I frankly confess leave me feeling that I am faced with merely grandiose masses of un-intelligible sentences.)

"I do all my own research. I have at my disposal a huge personal library, which is used by other writers as well. Most of my collection comes from bookshops and remainder houses. I read catalogues from places like Hamilton and Publisher's Bureau and that is how I collect most of my nonfiction.

"My practise is to write directly on the typewriter. I don't work by increments of time, I work by number of pages. My writing is very visual. I see a mental picture of the story and then describe it on paper. Even as a child I used to tell myself stories and act them out with small dolls and animals.

"My first draft is always a terrible mess because I pay no attention to spelling or grammar. The important thing is to get the story on paper. I make my corrections and give it to a typist who types it into a second draft on yellow paper. I revise the second draft, making changes by hand. The typist makes a third draft for the editor. The most intensive writing happens in the first draft, but the book does not become clear until I start working on the second draft.

"My themes haven't really changed over the years. I've always written stories about the loner, the person who doesn't give up. I use female protagonists because it makes for a better story. When I started writing, you couldn't put a female character in an adventure story, it was taboo. The first story I wrote had a female protagonist, and nobody would publish it at first because editors believed that girls didn't read science fiction, and boys wouldn't read about girls. Now more than half of the readers of science fiction are women, and the writers of fantasy, LeGuin, L'Engle, Marion Zimmer Bradley, and myself are all women. I think the fantasy form comes more easily to women than hard science. Perhaps because it is a form which has its roots in the old fairy tales, and women have always read and told stories to children."

One of Modred's men had drawn sword, was stabbing down at the ground. ■ (From *Dragon Magic* by André Norton. Illustrated by Robin Jacques.)

The priestess pointed from her knife to the rod, and then to the knife again. Was she trying to say that the rod was as much of a weapon as the blade she had drawn. . . ? ■ (Jacket illustration by Jack Gaughan from *Wraiths of Time* by André Norton.)

"Usually I do not intend to write series books at all—in fact, the only series which was actually planned to be one from the first was that dealing with the Solar Queen. The others developed from a first book because I received so many letters from readers asking for more about the same characters. The 'Witch World' tales, for example, were only supposed to be the first book, but I found that setting so interesting, and had so many inquiries, I kept returning to it. . . . The 'Witch World' books lean heavily on my research into Celtic and British mythology and three of them are retellings of very ancient themes. *Warlock of the Witch World* is based on the early Anglo-Saxon 'Childe Roland'; *Sorceress of the Witch World* on 'Sleeping Beauty'; and *Year of the Unicorn* on 'Beauty and the Beast.'

"In my science fiction, *Dread Companion* is based heavily, once again, on English folklore, and *Dark Piper* is a retelling of the 'Pied Piper.' *Ice Crown,* on the other hand, was an experiment to see if the old time mythical kingdom romance could be successfully combined with science fiction.

"The characters grow with the book. I do have an idea as to my main characters in type and background, but once the story begins, the characters take over, and often times the ending of the book is far different from that which I had first blocked out. Luckily my publishers know this and make allowances for such changes from the outlines I submit before I begin work.

"I think everyone realizes now . . . that 'mythology' does have a very ancient core of fact. More and more research has been instigated into this very subject. My own full interest has always been in ancient history and archeology—therefore 'mythology' is kindred to this.

"Writing for young people came to me because I wanted to write adventure stories and . . . to develop the action story for young readers. I do not find the piling on of sex of any benefit and never did, and to my mind the straight action story does not need this. Thus—writing without this element when I began made it fall directly into the 'young people's' field. But, of course, this has also changed drastically in the past few years. Many of the taboos of earlier days have disappeared. Also, the stories are growing grimmer and darker all the time. I agree with some of the removal of taboos, but I do not agree with fiction that is preoccupied with the seedier sides of life. One reads fiction for escape, not to be plunged into degrading and sordid scenes."[1]

"I advise young writers to read about as many subjects as possible. Write something every day, even if it's just a sentence or two for the discipline of producing when you are not, as they say, inspired. A writer is inspired very little. Writing is just hard work.

"Over the past couple of years, however, it has taken me longer to write each book because of my arthritis. In my peak years, I was able to write three books a year, though I can't work on many books simultaneously as some authors do. I write one book at a time, and when I get ideas for new books while I'm working, I take notes and set them aside for the time being. I keep extensive notebooks.''

Since 1966 Norton has lived in Florida with her seven cats, large library, and figurines. ''I don't travel much now. Since 1950 I have been more or less an invalid, which is also why I had to quit my work in the library. I'm agoraphobic. When it first struck me it was a rather mysterious illness, which no one knew how to treat. I didn't know what I had or what was the matter with me. I had been working under particularly hard conditions, and that brought it on. The condition was so bad at first that I couldn't get out of bed without terrible dizziness. Still, I kept writing, even while I was in bed, using a lapboard as a desk. For the past three years, I have found a medication that controls it, so I can get around, though I don't travel.''

HOBBIES AND OTHER INTERESTS: Collecting antiques and old dolls, needlework.

FOR MORE INFORMATION SEE: Library Journal, September 15, 1952; *Current Biography,* January, 1957; Muriel Fuller, editor, *More Junior Authors,* H. W. Wilson, 1963; *Horn Book,* December, 1965; *Book World,* December 29, 1968; *Times Literary Supplement,* June 6, 1968, June 26, 1969, October 16, 1969, July 2, 1971, September 28, 1973; *Books and Bookmen,* December, 1969; *Observer Review,* December 7, 1969, April 4, 1971; *Riverside Quarterly,* January, 1970; John Rowe Townsend, *A Sense of Story: Essays on Contemporary Writers for Children,* Lippincott, 1971; *New Statesman,* June 4, 1971; *New York Times,* September 20, 1971; Marcus Crouch, *The Nesbit Tradition: The Children's Novel in England, 1945-1970,* Benn, 1972; Paul Walker, ''An Interview with André Norton,'' *Luna Monthly,* September, 1972; John Wakeman, editor, *World Authors 1950-1970,* H. W. Wilson, 1975; D. L. Kirkpatrick, *Twentieth-Century Children's Writers,* St. Martin's Press, 1978; Roger Schlobin, *André Norton: A Primary and Secondary Bibliography,* Gregg, 1979; (under name André Norton) *Contemporary Literary Criticism,* Volume XII, Gale, 1980; *Contemporary Authors, New Revision Series,* Volume 2, Gale, 1981; *Dictionary of Literary Biography,* Volume 8, Gale, 1981.

PALMER, Robin 1911-

PERSONAL: Born in 1911, in New York, N.Y.; married Douglas S. Riggs (a medical doctor and professor). *Education:* Attended Vassar College.

CAREER: Author of books and articles for young people.

WRITINGS—All for young people except as noted: *Furry Ones: An Animal Picture Book* (illustrated by Bray Educational Pictures), Whitman Publishing, 1938; *Mickey Never Fails* (illustrated by Walt Disney Studio), Heath, 1939; *Ship's Dog* (illustrated by Rafaello Busoni), Grosset, 1945; *The Barkingtons* (illustrated by Flavia Gàg), Harper, 1948; *Wise House* (illustrated by Decie Merwin), Harper, 1951; (with Pelagie Doane) *Fairy Elves: A Dictionary of the Little People with Some Old Tales and Verses about Them* (illustrated by Don Bolognese), Walck, 1964; *Dragons, Unicorns, and Other Magical Beasts: A Dictionary of Fabulous Creatures with Old Tales and Verses about Them* (illustrated by D. Bolognese), Walck, 1966; (editor) *Wings of the Morning: Verses from the Bible* (adult; il-

lustrated by Tony Palazzo), Walck, 1968; *Centaurs, Sirens, and Other Classical Creatures: A Dictionary, Tales, and Verse from Greek and Roman Mythology* (illustrated by D. Bolognese), Walck, 1969; *A Dictionary of Mythical Places* (illustrated by Richard Cuffari), Walck, 1975; *Demons, Monsters, and Abodes of the Dead,* Scholastic Book Services, 1978.

Contributor of stories to numerous periodicals, including *Jack and Jill, Child Life,* and *Story Parade.*

FOR MORE INFORMATION SEE: New York Herald Tribune Weekly Book Review, May 9, 1948; *New York Times,* June 20, 1948, November 18, 1951; *Saturday Review of Literature,* November 10, 1951; Martha E. Ward and Dorothy A. Marquardt, *Authors of Books for Young People,* Scarecrow, 1964; *Times Literary Supplement,* November 30, 1967; *Commonweal,* November 19, 1976.

PETERSEN, P(eter) J(ames) 1941-

BRIEF ENTRY: Born October 23, 1941, in Santa Rosa, Calif. As an author of novels for young adults, Petersen concerns himself with what he terms ''the difficult ethical problems that young adults face.'' In *Would You Settle for Improbable?* (Delacorte, 1981), ninth-grader Michael Parker and friends attempt to change the antisocial, self-destructive behavior of newcomer Arnold Norberg, a former resident of Juvenile Hall. *Horn Book* called it ''a finely crafted novel, at once funny and touching . . . [with] a memorable cast of characters.'' *School Library Journal* agreed, noting Petersen's use of ''exaggerated caricatures and broad humor to make an improbable plot fun to read.'' His second novel, *Nobody Else Can Walk It for You* (Delacorte, 1982), is the story of eighteen-year-old Laura and seven younger adolescents who confront three menacing motorcyclists while on a backpacking trip. ''A cliff-hanger from page one'' and ''tense adventure'' were phrases used by *Booklist* to describe the action. ''The characterization is superb,'' added *Bulletin of the Center for Children's Books,* ''from the vicious leader of the motorcycle group to the fearful but courageous youngsters, all well-differentiated.''

Petersen focuses on the dilemma of runaway teens in *The Boll Weevil Express* (Delacorte, 1983) as he unveils the plight of three youths who become, according to *School Library Journal,* ''trapped in a sordid struggle for survival. . . . Petersen's simplistic style has considerable flexability: from the convincing funny dialogue . . . to . . . the sad undercurrent of their yearning for a home.'' The cast of *Would You Settle for Improbable?* reappears in Petersen's companion novel, *Here's to the Sophomores* (Delacorte, 1984). The problem of dealing with peer pressure comes to the fore, as *Horn Book* observed: ''The fast action, snappy dialogue, and authentic atmosphere add to . . . [this] thoughtful novel on accepting differences and standing up for one's beliefs.'' Petersen's latest work is *Corky and the Brothers Cool* (Delacorte, 1985), in which a streetwise con artist tries to lead two friends astray. ''A well-told story,'' remarked *School Library Journal,* ''whose worthwhile message is delivered softly with grace and care.'' In addition to writing, Petersen has been employed as an English instructor at Shasta College since 1964. He is currently working on a book for younger children and an outdoor novel entitled *Going for the Big One. Home:* 1243 Pueblo Court, Redding, Calif. 96001.

FOR MORE INFORMATION SEE: Contemporary Authors, Volume 112, Gale, 1985.

PLOWHEAD, Ruth Gipson   1877-1967

PERSONAL: Born December 11, 1877, in Greeley, Colo.; died in 1967, in Caldwell, Ida.; daughter of Albert E. and Lina (West) Gipson; married Edward Hayes Plowhead, June 20, 1906 (deceased); children: Ruth (Mrs. Kenneth Wiltsie), Eleanor (Mrs. George Harris). *Education:* Graduated from College of Idaho Academy, 1896; attended University of Idaho, 1900-01. *Politics:* Republican. *Religion:* Presbyterian. *Residence:* Caldwell, Idaho.

CAREER: Editor of several newspapers in Idaho and Washington, 1896-1916; author of books for children. *Member:* American Rose Society, Daughters of the American Revolution (historian of Pocahontas chapter), Idaho Writers League, Beta Sigma (now Delta Gamma), Plain Dirt Gardeners. *Awards, honors:* Honorary M.A. from College of Idaho, 1941.

WRITINGS—All for children; all illustrated by Agnes Randall Moore, except as noted; all published by Caxton: *Lucretia Ann on the Oregon Trail,* 1931, reprinted, 1969: *Lucretia Ann in the Golden West,* 1935; *Lucretia Ann on the Sagebrush Plains,* 1936; *Josie and Joe* (Junior Literary Guild selection; illustrated by Marguerite de Angeli), 1938; *Holidays with Betty Sue and Sally Lou,* 1939; *Josie and Joe Carry On* (illustrated by Johanna E. Lund), 1942; *Mile High Cabin* (illustrated by J. E. Lund), 1945; *The Silver Nightingale, and Other Stories,* 1955.

Also author of plays "Benjamin and the Indians," 1959, and "The Cat on the Oregon Trail," 1961, both adaptations of "Lucretia Ann" books. Contributor of stories to children's magazines such as *Child Life, Junior,* and *Story Parade,* and of feature articles to periodicals, including *Woman's Home Companion, Country Life,* and *American.*

Lucretia Ann stretched her neck the better to see. ■ (From *Lucretia Ann on the Oregon Trail* by Ruth Gipson Plowhead. Illustrated by Agnes Kay Randall Moore.)

RUTH GIPSON PLOWHEAD

SIDELIGHTS: "I was born in Colorado, and lived in Greeley and Denver. When I was twelve years old my mother, father, four brothers and three sisters, and I moved to Idaho. It's a wonderful state in which to live.

"I always made up stories in my head, and always planned to write. I won a dollar in a prize story contest for children when I was twelve years old, and my first story was published in *Leisure Hours* magazine.

"After we moved to Idaho I decided to write a book. I was thirteen years old. It was a great adventure story, and to make it more vivid, I decided to make my own drawings to illustrate it. I wanted to be an artist as well as an author. I finally laid this book aside, and when I was about sixteen, I started another book; the 'Josie and Joe' stories. When I was attending the University of Idaho in Moscow, our house burned to the ground and both my books with it. I wish I might see that funny first book I tried to write. Many, many years later I rewrote the 'Josie and Joe' story.

"When my two daughters, Ruth and Eleanor, were young I told them many stories which they liked so well I started writing them. That is the way some of my books happened to be written.

"You learn to write by writing. . . . I wrote for our school paper and our university paper. I wrote news and society for local papers. I edited a garden column in a farm paper for many years. I wrote feature stories about my garden, and illustrated them with my camera. I wrote dozens and dozens of stories for *Child Life, Children's Activities, Story Parade,* and other magazines.'' Plowhead's advice is to ''read all you can, study your grammar, your English, your literature; practice writing in every way you can.''

HOBBIES AND OTHER INTERESTS: Flower growing.

FOR MORE INFORMATION SEE: Idaho Writer's Leagazette, December, 1955; *Idaho Daily Statesman,* January 30, 1959; *News-Tribune* (Caldwell, Idaho), January 28, 1959, August 17, 1959, August 17, 1961.

PLUME, Ilse

BRIEF ENTRY: Born in Dresden, Germany. Reteller and illustrator of books for children. Plume and her family emigrated to the United States when she was about five years old. Her love for drawing developed early in her childhood and continued throughout her adolescent years. In 1968 she graduated with a degree in art from Duke University; two years later, she earned her M.F.A. from the same university. During the 1970s, she held positions as art instructor at Iowa State University, the Minneapolis College of Art and Design, and the University of Wisconsin-Eau Claire.

Plume's first book is a retelling of a familiar Grimm Brothers' tale, *The Bremen Town Musicians* (Doubleday, 1980). In 1980 it received the Parents' Choice Award for illustration and, the following year, was chosen a Caldecott Honor Book. *School Library Journal* praised the ''realistic illustrations'' accompanying the text. ''The style of the crayon-like paintings is pleasantly naive, the atmosphere is warm with yellow and orange.'' *New York Times Book Review* agreed, noting in particular the ''lovely, soft, glowing pictures of gentle barnyard animals wandering through a sunlit forest.'' In her second picture book, *The Story of Befana: An Italian Christmas Tale* (Godine, 1981), Plume provides a retelling of the Italian folktale that has endured for centuries. ''The full page illustrations are executed with a sure hand,'' observed *Booklist.* ''They glow with a jewellike intensity. . . .'' Plume is also the illustrator of a 1983 Godine edition of Margery Williams's classic children's story, *The Velveteen Rabbit; or, How Toys Become Real. Residence:* Massachusetts.

FOR MORE INFORMATION SEE: Fifth Book of Junior Authors and Illustrators, H. W. Wilson, 1983.

REANEY, James 1926-

PERSONAL: Born September 1, 1926, in South Easthope, Ontario, Canada; son of James Nesbitt (a farmer) and Elizabeth (a teacher; maiden name, Crerar) Reaney; married Colleen Thibaudeau, December 29, 1951; children: James Stewart, Susan Alice. *Education:* University of Toronto, B.A., 1948, M.A., 1949, Ph.D., 1958. *Agent:* Sybil Hutchinson, Apt. 409, Ramsden Pl., 50 Hillsboro Ave., Toronto, Ontario, Canada M5R 1S8. *Office:* Department of English, University of Western Ontario, London, Ontario, Canada N6A 3K7.

CAREER: University of Manitoba, Winnipeg, faculty member, 1949-57, assistant professor of English, 1957-60; University of Western Ontario, London, associate professor, 1960-63, professor of English, 1964—. *Member:* Association

JAMES REANEY

of Canadian University Teachers of English, Canadian Association of University Teachers, Canadian Theatre Co-op, League of Canadian Poets, Royal Society of Canada, Guild of Canadian Playwrights, Canadian Child and Youth Drama Associations. *Awards, honors: The Boy with an ''R'' in His Hand* was selected as a Notable Canadian Children's Book, 1983.

*WRITINGS—*Poetry: *The Red Heart,* McClellan & Stewart, 1949; *A Suit of Nettles,* Macmillan, 1958, 2nd edition, 1975; *Twelve Letters to a Small Town,* Ryerson, 1962; *The Dance of Death at London, Ontario,* Alphabet Press, 1963; *Selected Poems,* edited by Germaine Warkentin, New Press, 1972; *Selected Shorter Poems,* edited by G. Warkentin, Porcépic, 1976; *Selected Longer Poems,* edited by G. Warkentin, Porcépic, 1976.

Plays: *The Killdeer and Other Plays* (contains ''Night-Blooming Cereus,'' broadcast as radio play, 1959, first produced in Toronto, 1960; ''The Killdeer,'' [also see below], first produced in Toronto, 1960; ''One-Man Masque,'' produced in Toronto, 1960; ''Sun and Moon,'' first produced in Winnipeg, 1972), Macmillan, 1962; (with Alfred Kunz) *Let's Make a Carol: A Play with Music for Children,* Waterloo Music Co., 1965; *Colours in the Dark* (first produced in Stratford, Ontario, 1967), Talonbooks-Macmillan, 1969; *Masks of Childhood* (contains ''The Killdeer,'' revised version, first produced in Vancouver, 1970; ''The Easter Egg,'' first produced in Hamilton, Ontario, 1962; ''Three Desks,'' first produced in Calgary, Alberta, 1967), edited by Brian Parker, New Press, 1972; *Listen to the Wind* (three-act; first produced in London, Ontario, 1965), Talonbooks, 1972; *Apple Butter and Other Plays for Children* (contains ''Names and Nicknames,'' first produced in Winnipeg, 1963; "Apple Butter," first produced in London, Ontario, 1965; "Ignoramus," first produced at York Mills Collegiate School, Toronto, 1967; "Geography Match"), Talonbooks, 1973 (all published separately, 1978); *The Donnellys: A Trilogy*, Part I: *Sticks and Stones* (first produced in Toronto, 1973), Porcépic, 1975, Part II: *The Saint Nicholas Hotel* (first produced in Toronto, 1974), Porcépic, 1976, Part III: *Handcuffs* (first produced in Toronto, 1975), Porcépic, 1976, published as *The Donnelly Trilogy*, Porcépic, 1983; (with John Beckwith) *All the Bees and All the Keys* (illustrated by Rudy McToots; music by J. Beckwith), Porcépic, 1976; (with C. H. Gervais) *Baldoon* (two-act), Porcupine's Quill, 1976; *The Dismissal*, Porcépic, 1978: *King Whistle*, Brick, 1979; *Wacousta*, Porcépic, 1980.

Other: *The Boy with the "R" in His Hand* (juvenile novel; illustrated by Leo Rampen), Macmillan of Canada, 1965; *Fourteen Barrels from Sea to Sea* (travel diary), Porcépic, 1977; *Take the Big Picture* (juvenile), Porcupine's Quill (Ontario), 1985. Contributor to Jay Macpherson's, *Spirit of Solitude*, Yale, 1983. Editor and founder of *Alphabet*, 1960-71.

ADAPTATIONS: Ron Cameron, adapter, *Masque* (one-act play; adapted from play, "One-Man Masque"), Simon & Pierre, 1975.

WORK IN PROGRESS: Zamorna, a two-part opera based on the Brontë juvenilia; "Serinette," an opera about life at Sharon Temple with composer Harry Somers.

SIDELIGHTS: Reaney was born on a farm near Stratford, Ontario, one of three children. "My father won a mime contest at school when he was ten; he did such a brilliant imitation of milking a cow that it was repeated for the benefit of the entire neighbourhood. Afterwards he was given a box of chocolates. That would be in 1899. That's where I get my interest in acting, and from my mother I get my urge to write plays and direct them. With the local young people, the farmers and their wives, she produced and directed such epics as 'Dot the Miner's Daughter.' A teacher, her board of trustees fired her for putting on too many plays with the young people; so she married my father instead. My passion for theatre was further whetted by a visit in 1934 to Ringling Brothers Circus playing a vacant Stratford lot. Back home, I took over a deserted room in my father's farmhouse and produced my own circus with the help of three visiting cousins. At school I produced my first play—a ghost story with two tar paper towers, red paper windows, and flashlight for supernatural effects. Christmas concerts were my delight, and my career ambition was to become a primary school teacher with great emphasis on producing a proper Christmas concert. No doubt I would have been fired by the trustees, but by accident I eventually ended up at the University of Toronto and fell under the spell of Northrop Frye whose criticism has particularly influenced me with regard to my work in marionettes and in plays specially written for children.

"Getting married and having children of my own started me writing for children; I also had a little magazine, *Alphabet*, that needed money to keep it coming out, so I used to enter contests for children's plays and novels. I never won, but the results were performed—John Hirsch directing the Winnipeg premiere of 'Names and Nicknames' in 1963. Using bare stage and a few props, but lots of kids and six grown-ups, this play was inspired by an old speller of my father's in which the spelling lessons took the form of suites—all the words, for example, connected with the landscape around a farm, the yard, the road and so forth. So instead of having sets in 'Names and Nicknames' we simply had the children chant and mime such lists of words as 'Vale, hill, dell, dale,' with huge savings in sets and also a cinematic ability to dart from one scene to another.

"After 'Names,' I decided to write a series of graded plays for children—a marionette play, 'Apple Butter' for tots; 'Geography Match' for twelvers, and 'Ignoramus' for high schools. In the case of 'Apple Butter' I carved him myself and produced the whole show at the local fall fair in 1965; children relate to him as if he were a doll or Teddy Bear, and when he leaves town on tour quite a few kids have come to the station to see him off.

"Very few of my adult plays cannot be enjoyed by children unless they come with at least one parent, and in these plays I find that unconsciously I have based them on either children's games or children's toys; in the 'Donnelly Trilogy,' a tragedy about a mob who executed a whole family not twenty-five miles from where I was born, the imagery in the opening play is nevertheless based on a game the kids played in my first schoolyard—Prisoner's Base, while the middle play about the Donnellys' stage coach feud uses spinning tops to carry across the theme of hate-whips that spin you on to your doom.

"Some people have the attitude about me and my work that I am too interested in children, and even childishly so. But I reject this; Christianity is child-centred, it is mature to have children and to care deeply about their spiritual development, a matter in which plays, poems, stories, toys, and games are of supreme importance. For two years in the sixties I ran a weekly workshop for young people, called Listeners' Workshop, a spin-off from a play of mine called 'Listen to the Wind.' In our investigation of local history, the Bible, classical legends, and poetry during that very happy time, I saw what can redeem the world if only every child gets it early enough, and that is the power of images that both body and mind respond to in mime, dance, language, and improvised response. Perhaps what I am saying is that when at school I learned my most important lessons in the games played and the stories told by the children themselves, not always in the school, but out in the schoolyard. Yes, I also draw for children, usually to help them with my poems, a great many of which children, helped by adults, can arrive at the joy I feel all around me, free, in a world which, with very little effort really, we could make such a better place."

Reaney has the following advice to aspiring writers: "It's the reading, I think. I started writing far too soon. I should have waited until I was about thirty. Just keep reading away, and read what you want to read. If you are at college, of course, do what you have to do there. But quite often following through an enthusiasm is important. And I can see that there are going to be people who don't read. Okay, look at TV—really go for it. Follow that through and eventually it will educate you, I'm pretty sure. But I'm more doubtful about the TV than I am about reading. I think reading is the best way of transferring culture. But I can see that when computers come in we're going to have to fight for people to read at all. The electronic stuff will have to sort itself out. I've just recently done a videotape on cat's cradles with little kids. I think that shows I'm moving towards film before it's too late!" [Catherine Ross, "An Interview with James Reaney," *Canadian Children's Literature,* number 29, 1983.]

FOR MORE INFORMATION SEE: Alvin Lee, *James Reaney*, Twayne, 1969; Ross Woodman, *James Reaney*, McClelland & Stewart (Toronto), 1972; James Stewart Reaney, *James Reaney,* Gage, 1977; Catherine Ross, "An Interview with James Reaney," *Canadian Children's Literature*, number 29, 1983.

RICHARDS, R(onald) C(harles) W(illiam) 1923-
(Allen Saddler, K. Allen Saddler)

BRIEF ENTRY: Born April 15, 1923, in London, England. British writer and theater critic. Richards has been employed as a theater critic for the *Guardian* newspaper in London since 1972. Under the pseudonym K. Allen Saddler, he is the author of four adult novels, including *The Great Brain Robbery* and *Betty.* As Allen Saddler, he has produced several books for children. Among these are *The Clockwork Monster* (Hodder & Stoughton, 1981), *Mr. Whizz* (Blackie & Son, 1982), and six books in "The King and Queen" series published by Oxford University Press. Aimed at preschool and early primary-grade readers, the series features cartoon-like drawings by illustrator Joe Wright in titles like *The Archery Contest* (1982), *The King Gets Fit* (1982), *The King at Christmas* (1983), and *The Queen's Painting* (1983). Richards' other works include a number of radio plays for the British Broadcasting Corp., a television documentary script, and several stage plays. *Home:* 6 South St., Totnes, Devon TQ9 5DZ, England.

FOR MORE INFORMATION SEE: The International Authors and Writers Who's Who [and] International Who's Who in Poetry, 9th edition, International Biographical Centre, 1982; *Contemporary Authors, New Revision Series,* Volume 10, Gale, 1983; *The Writers Directory: 1984-1986,* St. James Press, 1983.

RICO, Don(ato)   1917-1985

OBITUARY NOTICE: Born September 26, 1917, in Rochester, N.Y.; died of cancer, March 27, 1985. Illustrator, artist, editor, and author. Rico was best known as the author and illustrator of Marvel Comics publications such as *Captain America* and *Daredevil.* He was also the originator of the "Blackout," "Gary Stark," and "Stevie Starlight" comic strips. In addition to his work on comic books and strips, Rico wrote western novels and mysteries for adults, including *Last of the Breed, Daisy Dilemma,* and *Bed of Lesbos,* and contributed scripts to the television series "Adam-12." He also produced wood engravings, many of which are on exhibit at the Metropolitan Museum of Art, and co-founded the Comic Arts Professional Society.

FOR MORE INFORMATION SEE: Contemporary Authors, Volumes 81-84, Gale, 1979. Obituaries: *Chicago Tribune,* April 20, 1985.

RIDGE, Martin   1923-

PERSONAL: Born May 7, 1923, in Chicago, Ill.; son of John and Ann (Lew) Ridge; married Marcella Jane VerHoef, March 17, 1948; children: John Andrew, Curtis Cordell, Wallace Karsten, Judith Lee. *Education:* Chicago Teacher's College, A.B., 1943; Northwestern University, A.M., 1949, Ph.D., 1951. *Politics:* Democrat. *Religion:* Protestant. *Office:* Huntington Library, San Marino, Calif. 91109; and Department of History, California Institute of Technology, 1201 East California Blvd., Pasadena, Calif. 91125.

CAREER: Historian and educator. Westminster College, New Wilmington, Pa., 1951-55, began as instructor, became assistant professor of American history; San Diego State College,

San Diego, Calif., assistant professor of history, 1955-66; Indiana University, Bloomington, professor of history, 1966-77; Henry E. Huntington Library, San Marino, Calif., senior research associate, 1977—; fellow, California Institute of Technology, 1980—. Member of board of directors, California Historical Landmarks Commission, 1954-64; visiting professor at Northwestern University, summer, 1959, and University of California, Los Angeles, summer, 1963. *Military service:* U.S. Maritime Service, 1943-54. *Member:* American Historical Association, Organization of American Historians, Agricultural History Society, Southern Historical Association, Western History Association. *Awards, honors:* Fellow, William Randolph Hearst Foundation, 1950, Social Science Research Council, 1952, American Council of Learned Societies, 1960, Newberry Library, 1962, Guggenheim Foundation, 1965-66, Henry E. Huntington Library, 1973-74; Best Book award, American Historical Association, 1963, and Best Book award, Phi Alpha Theta, 1963, both for *Ignatius Donnelly: The Portrait of a Politician;* Annenberg scholar at University of Southern California, Los Angeles, 1979-80.

WRITINGS—Adult, except as noted: *Ignatius Donnelly: The Portrait of a Politician,* University of Chicago Press, 1962; (with Vanza Devereau) *Work and Workers in California,* Wagnar, Harr, 1963; (with Walker D. Wyman) *The American Ad-*

MARTIN RIDGE

venture: A History, Lyons & Carnahan, 1964; (editor with Ray Allen Billington) *America's Frontier Story: A Documentary History of Western Expansion,* Holt, 1969; (with Raymond J. Wilson and George Spiero) *Liberty and Union: A History of the United States* (juvenile textbook), two volumes, Houghton, 1973; (with R. A. Billington) *American History after 1865,* 9th edition, Littlefield, Adams, 1981 (Ridge was not associated with earlier editions); (editor) *The New Bilingualism: An American Dilemma,* University of Southern California Press, 1981; (with R. A. Billington) *Westward Expansion: A History of the American Frontier,* 5th edition, Macmillan, 1982 (Ridge was not associated with earlier editions). Editor of *Journal of American History.*

WORK IN PROGRESS: A social history of silver.

ROTH, Arthur J(oseph)   1925-
(Nina Hoy, Barney Mara, Slater McGurk, Pete Pomeroy)

PERSONAL: Born August 3, 1925, in New York, N.Y.; son of Joseph (a printer) and Bella (a maid; maiden name, McGurk) Roth; married Ruth E. Buchalter, June 29, 1958; children: Mark. *Education:* Arizona State University, B.A., 1954; Columbia University, M.A., 1961. *Home:* 34-A Buell Lane Ext., East Hampton, N.Y. 11937. *Agent:* Curtis Brown, 10 Astor Place, New York, N.Y. 10003.

CAREER: Has worked as a bartender, carpenter, coalminer, factory worker, logger, farmer, high school teacher of Spanish, college instructor in writing, clerk-typist, and truck driver; currently full-time writer. *Military service:* Irish Army, 1944-46; U.S. Air Force, 1950-51. *Awards, honors: Two for Survival* was selected as one of the children's books of the year, 1976, by the Children's Book Committee of the Child Study Association.

WRITINGS—Young adult novels, except as indicated: *A Terrible Beauty* (adult novel), Farrar, Straus, 1958; *What Is the Stars?* (adult novel), Farrar, Straus, 1959; *The Shame of Our Wounds* (adult novel), Crowell, 1961; (under pseudonym Pete Pomeroy) *Wipeout!,* Four Winds, 1968; (under pseudonym Pete Pomeroy) *The Mallory Burn* (Junior Literary Guild selection), Grosset, 1971; (under pseudonym Pete Pomeroy) *Crash at Salty Bay,* Action Books, 1972; *The Iceberg Hermit* (Junior Literary Guild selection), Four Winds, 1974.

Snowbound, Sprint Books, 1975; (under pseudonym Barney Mara) *Forest Fire,* Action Books, 1975; *The Strikeout Gang Strikes Again,* Action Books, 1976; *Two for Survival,* Scribner, 1976; *The Secret Lover of Elmtree,* Four Winds, 1976; *Demolition Man,* Action Books, 1978; *Black and White Jones,* Sprint Books, 1978; (under pseudonym Nina Hoy) *The Runaways,* Action Books, 1979; *Avalanche,* Scholastic Book Services, 1979; *You and Your Bicycle* (illustrated by Stephanie Baloghy), Dandelion Press, 1979; *The Yucky Monster* (illustrated by Tom O'Sullivan), Dandelion Press, 1979; *The Caretaker,* Four Winds, 1980; *Great Spy Stories,* Scholastic, 1981; *Eiger: Wall of Death* (adult nonfiction), Norton, 1982; *Against Incredible Odds,* Scholastic, 1983; *The Castaway,* Scholastic, 1983; *Crash Landing!* (illustrated by David Febland), Scholastic, 1983.

Mystery novels; under pseudonym Slater McGurk: *The Grand Central Murders,* Macmillan, 1964; *The Denmark Bus,* Walker & Co., 1966; *The Big Dig,* Macmillan, 1968.

ARTHUR J. ROTH

Author of column "From the Scuttlehole," *East Hampton Star,* 1966—. Contributor of short stories and articles to magazines.

WORK IN PROGRESS: Novels for adults and young people.

SIDELIGHTS: Roth comments on his beginning career as a writer. "I began writing as the result of a fluke. While in the Air Force I wrote a humorous letter to the editor of the base newspaper complaining about flies in the mess hall. The editor asked me if I would like to write full time for the paper. They needed someone with a light touch.

"I transferred to the newspaper and found an office full of bright journalism graduates who taught me much about writing, but in particular taught me a certain measure of self-confidence in my own abilities. At this time, I had only a grade-school education, though a wide education in life, having been a bartender, a miner, a factory worker, and a truck driver. That transfer and those college lads sparked something in me and, thanks to the G. I. Bill, my life took a complete turn."

Roth climbed the 1,300-foot "Devil's Tower" mountain in Wyoming in mid-August, 1985 with son, Mark, as the lead. Two weeks prior, Roth led his son on a climb of "Bastille Crack" in Eldorado Canyon, Colo.

HOBBIES AND OTHER INTERESTS: Repairing antique clocks, running marathons, mountain climbing.

FOR MORE INFORMATION SEE: New York Times Book Review, January 26, 1975, November 28, 1976; *Kliatt,* fall, 1979; Dorothy A. Marquardt and Martha E. Ward, *Authors of Books for Young People,* 2nd edition supplement, Scarecrow, 1979.

SCOTT, Sally Fisher   1909-1978

PERSONAL: Born July 30, 1909, in Arlington, Vt.; died September 6, 1978, at her home in Bowling Green, O.; daughter of John Redwood and Dorothy (a children's author; maiden name, Canfield) Fisher; married John Paul Scott, June 18, 1933; children: Jean (Fru Eugen Franck), Vivian, John Paul, David. *Education:* Swarthmore College, A.B., 1930; Oxford University, A.B., 1932, M.A., 1934.

CAREER: Author of children's books. *Awards, honors:* Boys' Club Junior Book Award, 1953, for *Benjie and His Family.*

WRITINGS—All for children; all published by Harcourt, except as indicated; all illustrated by Beth Krush, except as indicated: *Molly and the Tool Shed* (illustrated by Ellen Segner), 1943; *Silly Billy* (illustrated by Priscilla Pointer and Marjorie Hartwell), 1945; *Mr. Doodle,* 1947; *Sue Ann's Busy Day* (illustrated by Madye Lee Chastain), 1948; *Judy's Baby* (illustrated by Jane Toan), 1949; *Tippy,* 1950; *Rip and Royal,* 1950; *Little Wiener,* 1951; *Benjie and His Family,* 1952; *Binky's Fire,* 1952; *Jonathan,* 1953; *Bobby and His Band,* 1954; *Chica* (illustrated by Joe Krush), 1954; *Jason and Timmy,* 1955; *The Brand New Kitten,* 1956; *What Susan Wanted,* 1956; *Bitsy,* 1957; *Judy's Surprising Day,* 1957; *Tinker Takes a Walk,* 1958; *There Was Timmy!,* 1959; *Judy's Summer Adventure,* 1960; *Sunny Jim: The Uppity Kitten,* 1962; *Jenny and the Wonderful Jeep,* 1963.

SHEARER, John   1947-

PERSONAL: Born in New York City in 1947; son of Ted (a cartoonist and illustrator) and Phyllis (a deputy commissioner of social services; maiden name, Wildman) Shearer. *Education:* Attended Rochester Institute of Technology and School of Visual Arts. *Home:* Tatomuck Rd., Pound Ridge, N.Y. 10576. *Office:* School of Journalism, Columbia University, Broadway and West 116th St., New York, N.Y. 10027.

CAREER: Photographer, and author of books for children. Staff photographer, *Look,* 1970—, *Life,* 1971-73; Columbia University School of Journalism, New York, N.Y., teacher, 1975—. Shearer Visuals, White Plains, N.Y., president, 1980-84. Producer of films for "Sesame Street" featuring "Billy Jo Jive" and "Susie Sunset." Work has been included in the "Harlem on My Mind" exhibit at the Metropolitan Museum of Art, New York, N.Y., and in shows at Grand Central Station in New York City, IBM Galleries in New York City, and Eastman Kodak Co. *Awards, honors:* Recipient of over twenty national awards. Ceba award, 1978, for animated film "Billy Jo Jive Super Private Eye: The Case of the Missing Ten Speed Bike," and 1978, for communications.

WRITINGS—All for children; all fiction, except as indicated: *I Wish I Had an Afro* (nonfiction; self-illustrated with photographs), Cowles Book, 1970; *Little Man in the Family* (nonfiction; self-illustrated with photographs; foreword by Gordon Parks), Delacorte, 1972; *Billy Jo Jive Super Private Eye: The Case of the Missing Ten Speed Bike* (illustrated by father, Ted Shearer), Delacorte, 1976; *Billy Jo Jive: The Case of the Sneaker Snatcher* (illustrated by T. Shearer), Delacorte, 1977; *Billy Jo Jive and the Case of the Missing Pigeons* (illustrated by T. Shearer), Delacorte, 1978; *Billy Jo Jive and the Walkie Talkie Caper* (illustrated by T. Shearer), Delacorte, 1981; *Billy Jo Jive and the Case of the Midnight Voices* (illustrated by T. Shearer), Delacorte, 1982. Also contributor of photographs to magazines such as *Popular Photography, Infinity,* and *Look.*

ADAPTATIONS: "Billy Jo Jive Super Private Eye: The Case of the Missing Ten Speed Bike" (animated film), Shearer Visuals, 1978.

WORK IN PROGRESS: Semi-autobiographical novel.

SIDELIGHTS: Shearer's first two books for children included his own photographs, although his subsequent books were illustrated by his father, Ted Shearer. The series, published by Delacorte Press, is a mystery series about two characters, Billy Jo Jive and Susie Sunset. ". . . Jive came largely out of a lot of experiences that I've had in my lifetime. I think that everything you do is kind of autobiographical. There are a lot of things about Jive that are about my childhood and I also think Jive started because I wanted to really write.

"I started to get ideas and to talk with my dad to interest him in working on the project with me. It was the first time we worked together and we've had a lot of fun.

JOHN SHEARER

(From *Billy Jo Jive and the Walkie-Talkie Caper* by John Shearer. Illustrated by Ted Shearer.)

"... Dad has a really tremendous feeling for book structure and pacing that is so important in doing picture books—making the story work and making it happen. Dad's been very good about helping me learn all about that.

"The foremost idea we were concerned with at the beginning was designing a character that had a hook, one that would get the little guys who didn't like to read much, who like to play basketball. The books are written in street language the way they really speak and the characters talk about things they're familiar with. One thing I don't want to lose is that feeling. I want to make the stories real to those kids, make it possible for them to relate to the characters.

"When we first started, we had two boys in the story but it just didn't seem to be working. We wanted to talk to a larger audience and so we developed the Susie Sunset character, who really comes from my niece, Schatzi ... I get an awful lot of ideas for Sunset from her. In the first book, Jive overpowered the Susie Sunset character. But in the second and even more in the third, she plays a bigger part.

Besides writing and photography, Shearer combines his two careers into a third career—teaching photojournalism at Columbia University. "I take pictures, teach class at Columbia, go home and start to write about eleven o'clock until three in the morning, then get up at six and start all over again. I do it because I love what I'm doing, writing and photography. I just wish there were about ten more hours in every day."

FOR MORE INFORMATION SEE: Dorothy A. Marquardt and Martha E. Ward, *Authors of Books for Young People,* 2nd edition supplement, Scarecrow, 1979.

SHEARER, Ted 1919-

PERSONAL: Born November 1, 1919, in Maypen, Jamaica, West Indies; son of Samuel and Sophie (Parnell) Shearer; married Phyllis Wildman (a deputy commissioner of social services), December 23, 1945; children: John, Kathleen. *Education:* Attended Art Students' League, 1938-40, and Pratt Institute, 1946-47. *Home and office:* Route 1, Box 56, Tatomuck Rd., Pound Ridge, N.Y. 10576.

CAREER: Television art director for Batten, Barton, Durstine, & Osborn advertising agency, 1956-70; creator, writer and illustrator of comic strip "Quincy," 1970—. Producer of films for "Sesame Street" featuring "Billy Jo Jive" and "Susie Sunset." *Military service:* U.S. Army, 1941-45. *Member:* Cartoonist Society, Comic Council. *Awards, honors:* Received five art director awards for television commercials from Batten, Barton, Durstine & Osborn; Ceba award of merit in advertising and communication, 1978.

WRITINGS: Quincy's World (cartoons), Tempo Books, 1973.

Illustrator; "Billy Jo Jive" series; all written by son, John Shearer; all fiction for children; all published by Delacorte: *Billy Jo Jive Super Private Eye: The Case of the Missing Ten Speed Bike,* 1976; *Billy Jo Jive: The Case of the Sneaker Snatcher,* 1977; *Billy Jo Jive and the Case of the Missing Pigeons,* 1978; *Billy Jo Jive and the Walkie-Talkie Caper,* 1981; *Billy Jo Jive and the Case of the Midnight Voices,* 1982.

Contributor of cartoons to *Saturday Evening Post, Colliers, This Week of the Herald Tribune, Ladies' Home Journal,* and *Amsterdam News.*

ADAPTATIONS: "Billy Jo Jive Super Private Eye: The Case of the Missing Ten Speed Bike" (animated film), Shearer Visuals, 1978.

SIDELIGHTS: "As long as I can remember, I've wanted to have my own comic strip, but first I had to be a newspaper deliverer, busboy, waiter, package wrapper, gallery boy, freelance cartoonist, Army sergeant, sketchman and art director.

"I must have been about thirteen when I started to mail my drawings to the *Amsterdam News,* but as fast as I sent them, they mailed them right back to me.

"Somehow, I found out that Dr. C. B. Powell, the editor and publisher, arrived at his office on Saturday mornings about eleven o'clock. I discovered the lot where he parked his car; so every Saturday morning as he drove in, guess who was waiting? ... me, with a brand new set of cartoons. As he walked to his office, I would be explaining my drawings, reading the captions and telling him why he should buy them. He never said a word until he got to his door, then he'd shake his head, 'No, Ted, they're not quite right yet!'

"This went on for about six months, until one Saturday, as he was getting out of his car, he greeted me with, 'You know, Ted, I was thinking about a cartoon you showed me last Saturday....'

"I ran all the way from 134th Street on Seventh Avenue to my house on 113th Street to tell my Mom that I'd sold my first cartoon. I was fifteen years old and in heaven!!

"Shortly after that, I started to do a regular feature for the *Amsterdam News* called 'Around Harlem' and over the years I've continued to do cartoons for them.

TED SHEARER

(From the comic strip "Quincy," which made its debut June 17, 1970. Created, written, and illustrated by Ted Shearer. Copyright by King Features Syndicate, Inc.)

"Another high spot for me when I was in my teens came when I worked as a busboy at S. H. Kress on Fifth Avenue. The manager of the cafeteria, who saw that I was always drawing, suggested that the store give me a little exhibit. I brought in my sketches and they put them on display in the area which was available for that sort of thing. As I picked up dishes, I could see people stopping to look at my work. Boy, what a charge I got out of that!

"I had graduated from high school and was attending the Art Students' League at night on a scholarship. In the daytime, I worked as a gallery boy—a job which my high school art teacher, Joe Hauser, got for me. My function at the gallery was to hang pictures, deliver paintings, clean the place and make myself generally useful. It was a job I loved because I was around art all day. I got to know a number of the top painters: Charles Sheeler, Kuniyoshi, Julian Levi, Jack Levine, Raphael Soyer, to name a few.

"Edith Halpert, who was the curator of the gallery, took a great interest in me. There was a small room in the back where the mop, bucket, broom and wrapping paper were kept. There were also a table and chair there, just big enough for a guy to sit down and draw. With Mrs. Halpert's blessing, this became my studio. I would get to work in the morning—give the place a 'lick and a promise'—rush into the back room and start working on a painting, cartoon, piece of sculpture or mobile. This went on for about two years—then one day, Mrs. Halpert appeared in my little room. Looking at some of my work, she said, 'Teddy, you've come a long way with your art. I think it is time you go out and give it a try. I'm going to give you a month's severance pay . . . !'

We just had to get to the bottom of this. Two dudes were missing and everyone in the cabin was real uptight. ■ (From *Billy Jo Jive and the Case of the Midnight Voices* by John Shearer. Illustrated by Ted Shearer.)

I needed a new lead. ■ (From *Billy Jo Jive and the Walkie-Talkie Caper* by John Shearer. Illustrated by Ted Shearer.)

"I've never been fired so nicely. When Edith Halpert died, . . . she was one of America's leading art spokesmen. Through the years she was always a great source of encouragement. I will always remember her with affection.

"What I recall of my free-lance cartooning days was being on a roller coaster. There were high points like the OK's from *Colliers, Saturday Evening Post* and *Ladies' Home Journal.* Then there were those dog days when I couldn't *buy* an OK. I could never make plans. Everything was 'cash and carry.' My wife at that time was both a mother and a struggling lawyer, with diaper pins in her mouth and law books under her arm. We often found ourselves short on cash but long on dreams. With the demands of a growing family, one son and one daughter, I felt the urge to find something steady.

"For the next fifteen years I hung my hat at the advertising agency of Batten, Barton, Durstine and Osborn, where I learned discipline and was truly challenged creatively. I became a TV art director on accounts which included Schaefer Beer, Betty Crocker, Armstrong Cork Company and DuPont. Looking back, it seems as if there were unending deadlines, working late at night and many anxious moments but, strangely enough, I learned not only to live with pressure, but to love it.

"After fifteen years in the business, complete with headaches, loss of hair and art director's awards, it happened! I found myself with the job I've always wanted—my own comic strip, 'Quincy,' which is syndicated by King Features. For this pleasure, I only work eight days a week.

"For a Black artist, bringing a Black youngster to the comic pages is a challenge and a responsibility. There is the responsibility of the humor which is expected by the general public and the challenge of truly portraying what it's like to be poor, Black and young. The good times and hard times of being a kid—a Black kid—that's what 'Quincy's' all about!"

SMITH, Betsy Covington   1937-

BRIEF ENTRY: Born July 29, 1937, in Omaha, Neb. Author. Smith graduated from Vassar College in 1959 and has been a member of women's boards of the Chicago Symphony Orchestra, St. Luke's Hospital, and the Chicago Urban League. She began writing in the late 1960s and is now the author of several books for young people. Most of her books are career guidebooks with biographies of contemporary women and explanations of their professions. In Smith's view, ''To convey . . . [a] person's life story onto a piece of paper, to make that person as alive and unique to the reader as he/she was to me seems such an awesome responsibility.'' *School Library Journal* said of *Breakthrough: Women in Law* (Walker & Co., 1984), ''Smith's . . . style brings each of the women to life.'' *Booklist* also found the text provided ''a real sense of each woman.'' Similarly, *School Library Journal* noted the ''lively interviews'' in *Breakthrough: Women in Television* (Walker & Co., 1981) and called the book ''an upbeat, useful collection.'' Smith also wrote *Breakthrough: Women in Religion* (Walker & Co., 1978), which *Horn Book* described as ''a lucid, enthusiastic account of five women and their individual struggles to attain positions in the ministry and the life of the church.'' Smith's other books for young people are *A Day in the Life of a Firefighter* (Troll Associates, 1981), *A Day in the Life of an Actress* (Troll Associates, 1984), and *The Lewis and Clark Expedition* (Silver Burdett, 1985). *Home and office:* 755 Park Ave., New York, N.Y. 10021.

FOR MORE INFORMATION SEE: Contemporary Authors, Volume 111, Gale, 1984.

SMITH, Susan Mathias 1950-

PERSONAL: Born January 23, 1950, in Rockingham County, Va.; daughter of Charles E. (a farmer) and Laura (a nurse; maiden name, Raynes) Mathias; married John P. Smith III (a photographer), December 26, 1972. *Education:* Madison College (now James Madison University), B.A., 1972, graduate student, 1985—. *Religion:* United Methodist. *Address:* P.O. Box 624, New Market, Va. 22844.

CAREER: Variously employed as a gift shop manager, waitress, and supply clerk, 1973-76; Stonewall Jackson High School, Mt. Jackson, Va., teacher of accelerated English, 1976—. *Member:* National Education Association.

WRITINGS—All for children: *The Night Light* (illustrated by Terry L. Wickart), Follett, 1981; *No One Should Have Six Cats!* (illustrated by Judith Friedman), Follett, 1982.

WORK IN PROGRESS: The Booford Summer, Bob Cat, and *Spring Grows up the Mountain,* all for children.

Every morning she licks my face and wakes me up. ■ (From *No One Should Have Six Cats!* by Susan Mathias Smith. Illustrated by Judith Friedman.)

SIDELIGHTS: "I wrote *The Night Light* in 1972 to finance a trip to Texas. The book wasn't sold until eight years later. I did visit Texas—on tips from a waitressing job! All of my other early books, most of which were never sold, were written for my horses. One of the horses had severe medical problems resulting in high vet bills. Both horses are in heaven now.

"Almost all of my books, published and in progress, are about animals. I think that I still retain a child's delight in animals. Too, I want to encourage that delight so that a child will not only play with his pet, but will give that pet proper care and love.

"*No One Should Have Six Cats!* is basically a true story. Herkie, cat number one, did lose her front leg; it did not get well as the story explained. Everything else, except for the cats' names, is true.

"My works in progress, *The Booford Summer, Bob Cat* and *Spring Grows up the Mountain*, are also about animals. *The Booford Summer* is the story of a little girl's efforts to get her neighbor, of whom she is afraid, to walk his dog Booford. *Bob Cat* is the story of a missing Siamese cat and the three children who search for him. *Spring Grows up the Mountain* is about twelve-year old Carolina's acceptance of the death of her horse.

"My animal stories do become, in many cases, stories about the 'big things' of life—love and death and fear and hope.

"Besides animals, another motivation for me has been my sisters. They all three teach kindergarten and tell me almost every Sunday at dinner, 'I need a book about. . . .' In fact, it was a sister who suggested a book about a child's fear. *The Night Light*, my first published book, resulted.

"Sometimes when I cannot think of ideas or when I am discouraged, I go to the library and read children's books. I read until I laugh or smile or feel touched in some way. Then I drive home and I think and I write. Hopefully, what I write will cause a child to smile, to cry, to laugh, to feel."

FANNIE STEINBERG

STEINBERG, Fannie 1899-

PERSONAL: Born April 6, 1899, in Russia; came to the United States about 1903; daughter of Maierchaim (a scholar) and Mindel (Rubinstein) Karshmev; married David Steinberg (a realtor; deceased); children: Marvin E. *Education:* Rutgers University, B.A., 1931, M.A., 1947, graduate study, 1976. *Religion:* Jewish. *Home:* 212 South First Ave., Highland Park, N.J. 08904.

CAREER: Elementary schoolteacher at public schools in New Brunswick, N.J.; writer, beginning about 1976. President, Middlesex County Women's Democratic Organization. *Member:* B'nai B'rith Women.

WRITINGS: Birthday in Kishinev (juvenile fiction; illustrated by Luba Hanuschak), Jewish Publication Society, 1979. Author of article "Tribute to a Mother," published in U.S. Congressional Records; contributor to political journals.

WORK IN PROGRESS: To the Golden Door, a sequel to *Birthday in Kishinev*.

SIDELIGHTS: Steinberg describes herself as "a potential Grandma Moses." Most of her life was spent teaching ele-

mentary school; upon her retirement, she managed her husband's real estate and insurance business. In 1976, at the age of seventy-seven, she returned to her alma mater to take a course in creative writing. Her study resulted in *Birthday in Kishinev*, a fictionalized account of Steinberg's survival of the anti-Jewish pogrom which took place in Kishinev in 1903. She is currently working on a sequel, *To the Golden Door*, which chronicles her family's escape from Russia to the United States.

FOR MORE INFORMATION SEE: Margaret Teringer, "Tale of Dreaded Pogrom Told by Eighty-Year-Old Author," *Home News* (New Brunswick, N.J.), February 12, 1979.

STRETTON, Barbara (Humphrey) 1936-

PERSONAL: Born June 23, 1936, in Salt Lake City, Utah; daughter of Eugene O. (an engineer) and Lucille (a homemaker; maiden name, Howe) Humphrey; married Guy R. Stretton (an accountant), February 23, 1978. *Education:* University of Utah, B.S., 1959; Southern Connecticut State College, M.L.S., 1974. *Home:* 62 North Ridge Rd., Old Greenwich, Conn. 06870. *Agent:* James Seligmann Agency, 175 5th Ave., New York, N.Y. 10010.

CAREER: Teacher of English at schools in Salt Lake City, Utah, 1959-68; librarian at schools in Darien, Conn., and Greenwich, Conn., 1968-81; full-time author of books for young adults, free-lance educational and business writer, and instructor in adult education, 1981—.

WRITINGS—Novels for young adults: *A Deeper Season,* Fawcett, 1980; *You Never Lose,* Knopf, 1982; *The Truth of the Matter,* Knopf, 1983. Also author of filmstrip series for Educational Dimensions Corp. and Sunburst Communications, teachers' guides for CBS-TV Reading Program, audio programs for 3-M Co., and study guides for Listening Library, Inc.

WORK IN PROGRESS: Another novel for young adults, *Command Performance.*

SIDELIGHTS: "I began writing before I could spell my name, little illustrated books about animals. Somewhere along the way my writing out-distanced my art. Though writing was my great love—I was editor of the high school paper, frequently appeared in the literary magazine, and wrote the lyrics to the school song—I became a teacher. This brought me into close contact with teenagers and eventually led to my becoming a young adult writer.

"I dabbled at writing for a number of years and attended writers conferences every summer at the University of Utah. At one of these conferences, a visiting novelist, Alec Waugh, suggested I try a novel. By the next summer I had written *A Deeper Season.* Then I moved to Connecticut and had to adjust to some changes in my life, so the novel lay in the bottom drawer for many years. In 1974 I took it out again and rewrote it. It was published in 1980.

"I'd changed my career from teaching to school library work, which gave me exposure to the young adult field and the fine writers in this area. I met such people as Robert Cormier and

Richard Peck and decided this was an excellent field to work in. I was already in it anyway, with my first novel, so whenever I come upon an idea, I translate it into 'teenage' terms.

"My second novel, *You Never Lose,* came out of an incident at the junior high where I was working. A fine teacher was dying of cancer. He'd come to school whenever he could until he died that spring. What impressed me was his son, a ninth grader, who'd come into the library and sit by himself, looking sad. I'd been working on a story about a father who'd been a football star and was forcing a reluctant son to follow in his footsteps. I combined the two ideas in *You Never Lose.*

"In 1981 I left library work to become a full-time writer and teacher of adults. After two years of writing educational filmstrips and teachers' guides, I worked full time writing training scripts for a corporation. I now have my own business writing for industry and education.

"I love writing about teenagers, though I'm not fond of the young adult marketing category. It seems to fall into a never-never land somewhere between children's and adult books. Even the term 'young adult' is distasteful. But the main problem is that adults miss out on such wonderful books, books that tell a good story, create interesting characters, use an economy of language, and above all, touch on genuine themes. Too bad."

SUTTON, Jane 1950-

BRIEF ENTRY: Born May 11, 1950, in New York, N.Y. Author of children's books. Sutton graduated magna cum laude from Brandeis University in 1972. That same year, she became a mental health worker with retarded adults at Harlem Valley State Hospital in Wingdale, N.Y. She later worked as a staff writer for *Mid-Hudson Leisure* in Poughkeepsie, N.Y. Since 1975 she has been employed in public relations at Instrumentation Laboratory, Inc. Also the author of four works of fiction for children, Sutton commented, "I enjoy writing for children . . . in children's works I can express a strong moral message. . . ." In *Not Even Mrs. Mazursky* (Dutton, 1984), fourth-grader Stella adores her third-grade teacher, Mrs. Mazursky. But when the teacher verbally harasses Stella and her teammates during a softball game between the third and fourth grades, Stella is disillusioned. The girl eventually realizes that nobody is perfect after she examines some of her own bad behavior. *Booklist* called the book a "frank and funny slice-of-life novel."

Confessions of an Orange Octopus (Dutton, 1983) recounts the adventures of nine-year-old Clarence Slagovsky, who likes to juggle oranges. When he seeks to become a performer, he encounters opposition from different adults, even his parents. "There's a clean, healthy quality to the whole [story]," observed *School Library Journal,* "that gives it a refreshing appeal." Sutton also wrote the humorous stories *What Should a Hippo Wear?* (Houghton, 1979) and *Me and the Weirdos* (Houghton, 1981). *Office:* Instrumentation Laboratory, Inc., 113 Hatwell Ave., Lexington, Mass. 02173.

FOR MORE INFORMATION SEE: Lexington Minute-Man, May 17, 1979; *Contemporary Authors,* Volumes 89-92, Gale, 1980.

BARBARA STRETTON

Give a little love to a child, and you get a great deal back.

—John Ruskin

TALLON, Robert 1939-

PERSONAL: Born September 21, 1939, in New York, N.Y.; son of Charles A. and Anne E. Tallon. *Education:* Attended Metropolitan Opera Studios, 1953-55; New York University, 1957-61, and New York School of Visual Arts, 1963-65. *Home:* 196 E. 75th St., New York, N.Y. 10021.

CAREER: Artist, author and illustrator of children's books. Batton, Barton, Durstine & Osborn (advertising agency), artist, 1965-66; *New Yorker,* cover artist, 1974—. *Exhibitions:* Marble Arch Gallery, New York, N.Y.; Walker Gallery, Weston, Conn.; Pastiche Gallery, New York, N.Y.; J. Walter Thompson Gallery, New York, N.Y.; Pan Am Gallery, New York, N.Y.; Myra James Gallery, East Hampton, N.Y.; Peter Flanagan Gallery, New York, N.Y.; Daniel Douglas Gallery, New York, N.Y.; Elizabeth Ives Bartholet Gallery, New York, N.Y.; The Museum of Fine Arts, Houston, Tex. Works are included in the permanent collection at Smithsonian Institution National Portrait Gallery, Washington, D.C. *Military service:* U.S. Army. *Awards, honors: The Thing in Dolores' Piano* was included in the American Institute of Graphic Arts Children's Book Show, 1971-72; Brooklyn Art Books for Children citation, 1975, for *Rhoda's Restaurant.*

WRITINGS—For children, except as noted: *Conversations, Cries, Croaks, and Calls* (adult; self-illustrated), Holt, 1963; *A.B.C. . . . in English and Spanish* (self-illustrated), Lion Press, 1970; *The Thing in Dolores' Piano* (self-illustrated), Bobbs-Merrill, 1970; *Zoophabets* (self-illustrated), Bobbs-Merrill, 1971; *Handella* (self-illustrated), Bobbs-Merrill, 1972; *Rhoda's Restaurant,* Bobbs-Merrill, 1973; *Rotten Kidphabets* (self-illustrated), Holt, 1975; *ZAG: A Search through the Alphabet* (self-illustrated), Holt, 1976; *Fish Story* (self-illustrated), Holt, 1977; *Flea Story* (self-illustrated), Holt, 1977; *Worm Story* (self-illustrated), Holt, 1978; *Little Cloud* (self-illustrated),

"Here it is! Fried fish with pickles, mayonnaise, banana tips, ketchup and mustard. I'm starved!" ■ (From *Fish Story* by Robert Tallon. Illustrated by the author.)

Parents Magazine Press, 1979; *The Alligator's Song* (self-illustrated), Parents Magazine Press, 1981; *Latouse My Moose* (self-illustrated), Knopf, 1983; *Mooseberry and the Fuzzo Makers* (self-illustrated), Knopf, 1984.

Illustrator; for children: *Fables for the Fair,* Holt, 1964; Ruth Leslie Smith, *Hurry! Dinner Is at Six,* Bobbs-Merrill, 1969; Robyn Supraner, *Sam Sunday and the Strange Disappearance of Chester Cats,* Parents Magazine Press, 1979. Also designer of films for television shows including "Sesame Street" and "Electric Company."

ADAPTATIONS: "Little Cloud" (recording), read by Debbie Allen, Triton, 1978; "Latouse My Moose" (animated television special), ABC-TV, 1985.

WORK IN PROGRESS: A movie script; an art show.

SIDELIGHTS: **September 21, 1939.** Born in New York City. "I grew up in Forest Hills, Long Island, and wasn't exposed to museums. When I was older, I spent a lot of time in museums—they were more or less my art school. You can learn a great deal from looking at art.

"I think most children have an artistic ability, but it's suppressed at a certain level. My parents never said, 'You can't

ROBERT TALLON

Selfish Sam

(From *Rotten Kidphabets* by Robert Tallon. Illustrated by the author.)

(From *A. B. C. . . . in English and Spanish* by Robert Tallon. Illustrated by the author.)

do this or you can't do that.' They always told us we could do whatever we wanted to do. Had I told them that I wanted to become a Mexican Jumping Bean, they'd have said, 'Well . . . okay. But where do you think you'll want to go with that?' They never pressured me, and always praised. When kids draw or express themselves in other ways and are criticized for it with, 'That doesn't look right' or, 'That doesn't look anything like an apple,' they'll soon become discouraged and their creativity becomes stifled. We were never criticized for our efforts. If a kid thinks he's great, he'll stay with his drawing or writing. Most of the arts are about *doing,* and, as they say, 'practice makes perfect.' Even as a young lad, I spent countless hours drawing, painting and writing. That's what it's all about.

"My mother was a singer/dancer as a young girl and performed in off-Broadway shows and with road companies. She gave up her career once she married, but reared us with a love for the theatre. My whole family was interested in singing, dancing and acting.

"My two brothers, sister, and I had an almost Fellini-type childhood—some of the things that happened to us were unbelievable! Many writers I know had a great interest in chil-

dren's books when they were young, but we never had children's books, so we made our own. We were quite poor and had to learn to entertain ourselves.

"After suffering a heart attack, my father was forced to work at jobs below his educational level. When his doctor suggested we move to the country, we settled in Long Island, where my father ran a chicken farm, knowing absolutely *nothing* about chickens or farming. He ran the farm for two dentists who didn't want anything to do with the business, but needed the tax write-offs. They told him how refreshing it would be to live a country life. *Refreshing?* Have you ever smelled three thousand chickens?

"Imagine, we arrived at the farm in the middle of the night, opened the doors to the little farmhouse, put on the lights, and discovered that the walls had been painted with tremendous bouquets of flowers. It was startlingly beautiful. Whoever had lived there before us must have been a mad, but wonderful, artist who had spent long winters with the chickens. That began our country life. The first week, my father managed to let three thousand chickens loose. My brother and I, who were horrified by the birds, ran all over the yard with shopping bags trying to catch them.

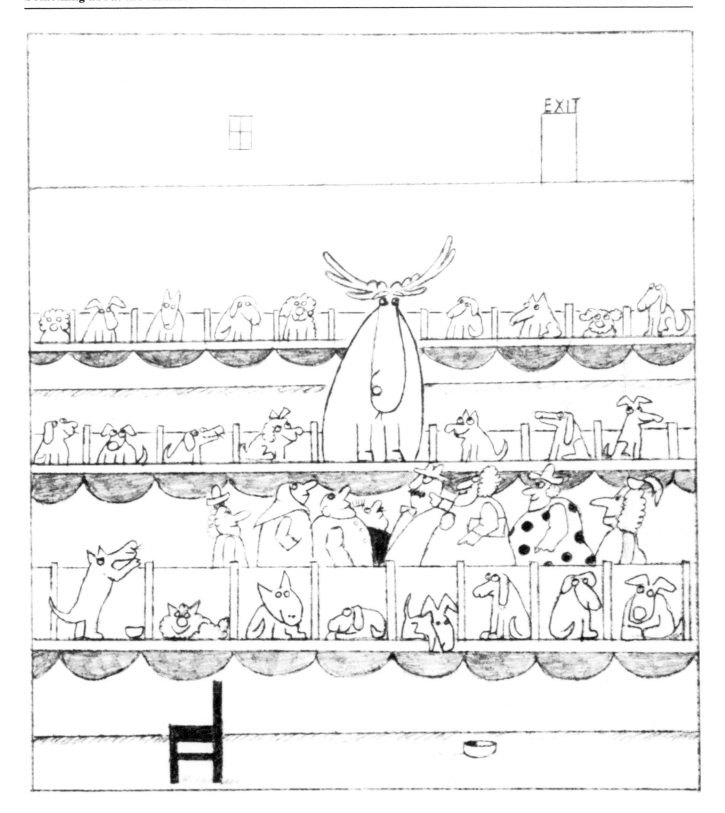

Latouse really stood out, as he was the only rare West Tibetan Mountain Dog entered. ■ (From *Latouse, My Moose* by Robert Tallon. Illustrated by the author.)

''My father was a great storyteller—in the Irish tradition—with a terrific sense of humor. He would often mimic all the characters in his tales to make us laugh. There was a piano in the house and my mother with her great voice, encouraged us to sing. We enjoyed entertaining as children and were often given the floor as stage. When company came, my parents would insist that we 'Get up and sing a song!'

''We had many ups and downs, but I think that's what made me a writer. I know that my humor comes from my family. My relatives were all very funny. You'd be in a room full of Fitzpatricks and they would have something to say about everybody.

''We have stayed close over the years. We also have felt very strong psychic connections and have had many interesting experiences with extrasensory perception. I believe that ESP has to do with being sensitive to what's going on around and beyond you. We were very sensitive children, and perhaps this particular trait runs in families, because my mother was also very psychic. We even had a 'ghost' dog. Every night at eleven, we'd be watching television and this little white thing would move across the floor, up the stairs and stop. I thought I was really cracking up when I first saw it. (I knew we were crazy, but this was too much!) Then one night I asked my sister if she had seen what I thought I had seen. She had also seen a little white 'ghost' dog.

''We lived in the house for seven years without trouble. The night before we moved something unusual occurred. We heard an ungodly noise coming from the living room. When we turned on the light, the noise would stop; when we flipped it off, it continued. In the morning, believe it or not, all the packing boxes had been placed against the walls of the room. We had no idea who had done that. Something in the house didn't want us to go, or it wanted to come with us. I like to think that it was a happy ghost. Years later I read that if you live in a house with a happy ghost, he wants to move with you and will attempt to climb into the boxes the night before you leave.''

K   KINKA
Lives in   Keyholes
Eats   Knotholes with ketchup

■ (From *Zoophabets* by Robert Tallon. Illustrated by the author.)

One of the numerous covers Tallon created for *The New Yorker* magazine.

Yes, Glory Oliver, you are my prize pupil. ■ (From *Conversations: Cries, Croaks, and Calls* by Robert Tallon. Illustrated by the author.)

Nobody ate at Rhoda's Restaurant, because Rhoda was a rotten cook. ■ (From *Rhoda's Restaurant* by Robert Tallon. Illustrated by the author.)

1953. Won a two-year music scholarship to the Metropolitan Opera Studios during his high school years. "I didn't know too much about opera, but I did have a great little voice to be developed. I really wanted to become a singer. I studied and sang very seriously two or three nights a week at the old Metropolitan on 42nd Street with a semi-retired opera singer who had a studio in the Metropolitan, where he also lived."

A bout with bulbar polio ended Tallon's plans for a musical career. He found, however, as he convalesced, that he had talent for art. "I just woke up one morning and couldn't swallow or talk. I felt as if I were choking to death—I couldn't breathe. I was diagnosed as having bulbar polio of the throat and spine, the most dangerous polio at the time, and was placed in an iron lung. Only a child, I knew nonetheless that I was dying. I was in that half-way world between life and death, and for days on end, slipped in and out of it, watching my mother and father standing at the end of my bed. One night, I was sure I was dying. I fought hard for three or four weeks, and finally pulled through.

"I had to convalesce for several years. I couldn't talk, swallow, or eat food, except for liquid jello—not a wonderful thing to eat! Of course I couldn't go back to singing. It wasn't until my illness that I began to seriously paint and draw. I was also very interested in puppetry and theatre, and in writing. I wrote stories and acted out all the parts I'd written with different puppets in the puppet theatre I built myself."

Art became Tallon's major ambition after his illness. From 1957 to 1961, he attended New York University and from 1963 to 1965, the New York School of Visual Arts. His first book, entitled *Conversations, Cries, Croaks, and Calls,* was published in 1963. "I had written and illustrated an adult humor book, which was a series of monologues. At the time I was working at an advertising agency in the same building as publishers Holt, Rinehart & Winston. I worked on the book for a good year without showing it to anyone. When I finished it, I trotted downstairs with my book under my arm to talk with the secretary at Holt. 'I'd like to show my book to an editor,' I said. She laughed because I'm sure she'd heard that line a million times, but to my surprise, she asked me which editor I'd like to have see it. I had no idea. I was asked to wait. Later Sam Stewart, one of the head editors came in and told me to leave the book with him.

"'When can I call you? Tomorrow morning?' I asked. He chuckled and told me to wait a few days. The next morning, just as I arrived at work, Stewart called to tell me that he liked the book enough to publish it. 'How easy!' I thought. They paid me next to nothing, but did beautiful reproductions, which pleased me.

"I had a nice group of people behind me from the beginning, and nothing compared with the moment when they brought me the first copy of the book wrapped in a blanket like a baby. I walked home twenty-five feet off the ground that night. Since then, everything else has been hard labor."

In 1970, Tallon had two self-illustrated books published. "Miriam Chaikin, an editor with Bobbs-Merrill Company, gave me my first break with children's books. My sister held a temporary position as receptionist with Bobbs-Merrill at the time. She asked Miriam to look over my portfolio. Miriam agreed, looked it over, and exclaimed, 'Robert *Tallon!* . . . Is he the fellow who did the Haines stocking campaign? I've had his artwork in my files for six years, and have been looking for him.' I was in her office the next day. Miriam and I were

on the same wavelength, and since then, have done many books together."

1971. Tallon's first children's book, *The Thing in Dolores' Piano* was selected for the American Institute of Graphic Arts Children's Book Show. That same year *Zoophabets* was published. "*Zoophabets* has an interesting history. I had drawn one or two of the animals and always felt that they would make a great book some day. I met the head of Simon & Schuster who recommended that I work on a book with Ogden Nash. Nash wanted to put poetry with my creatures and agreed to work with me. He offered to take the drawings back to his home in Baltimore. Shortly afterward, Nash sent back some little bits of poetry, which were wonderful. This was the direction we were moving with the book until he died.

"The project was abandoned until I suggested to Miriam that we turn it into an alphabet book. It worked, and *Zoophabets* has been a great success. Miriam tells me that children love the book. I receive beautiful letters from kids with their own 'Zoophabets,' which are usually better than mine!"

Tallon's picture books are imbued with a strong sense of the ridiculous. The artwork and texts attract younger readers, who enjoy his sense of humor. "Humor is a way of coping. We all have to have an edge, and that edge has to become bigger and bigger because it's becoming harder and harder to live in the world today. Children, too, need this edge to live in our world.

"I thought of *Fish Story, Flea Story,* and *Worm Story* as a series of parables. I was pleased when a Japanese company published the books as a series a few years ago. They are so beautifully designed, with interesting Japanese characters. I searched the covers to find what my name looked like in Japanese!"

Aside from children's books, Tallon has been working as a cover artist for the *New Yorker* magazine for over eleven years. "I enjoy doing the *New Yorker* covers, though often it seems I will never come up with another idea. The people at the *New Yorker* are very nice."

He works out of his New York city studio. "I have a small studio in my home. I work in acrylic or Dr. Martin's water colors, whatever I think is best. For the books I do four-color paintings. I dislike working with separations and usually stay away from them. I use whatever method is appropriate for a particular book.

"I find that lately when I want to concentrate on an idea I have for a book, I sit down and work for two hours writing the story and then from time to time work on the visuals while I'm writing. Artwork often helps me go on with the story." Unlike many illustrators who use models, Tallon paints from his imagination. "At one time I painted in a more realistic style, but now I've moved beyond that and learned the techniques that help me do what I want."

Commercial art requires enthusiasm, dedication, and hard work, as well as talent. These essential requirements are all found in Tallon. "I've always been a worker. My whole life has really been about turning out work. I see people reaching an age where their responsibilities become less, and they often wonder what they'll do with their free time. I *know* what I'm going to do! I'm going to work even harder. I am very disciplined, and if I have a book to do, I usually come in way before the deadline. I try to do something every day, even if it's only

(From *The Thing in Dolores' Piano* by Robert Tallon. Illustrated by the author.)

scribbles. With children's books I try to blend everything together. Books are the last place, the *only* place where people are still producing quality. I would like to become more poetic with my children's books, although that is difficult, given the market at present.

"When I have a difficult time coming up with new ideas for books, I form a list. I go through the dictionary picking words I like, then I scrutinize my list. It really helps. One word can generate a multitude of images."

When Tallon takes a break from his busy work schedule, he enjoys photography. "I love photography. Art to me is work, writing is work, but I actually relax with photography. I would like to someday do a book for children using photography for the illustrations. I also hope to be able to work with kids, to get them interested in art and writing.

"We look at somebody's work, and we don't realize the pain and anguish that's gone into it. We make a judgement, and often do a lot of harm. My family, and my experiences, like having polio as a young boy, are what make me an artist. Experience is wonderful, because you learn from it; even if it's difficult while it's happening, in the long run, you profit."

FOR MORE INFORMATION SEE: Library Journal, September, 1970; Dorothy A. Marquardt and Martha E. Ward, *Authors of Books for Young People,* supplement to the 2nd edition, Scarecrow, 1979.

schizo; most writers are that way anyway, because they have to get inside another person's skin. It's hard when a manuscript wins a semi-finalist award for fiction but is reviewed as having 'nasty characters.' Why? Because all Chinese women are supposed to be passive and nice—they don't fit the stereotype. Then that is followed by a lawsuit for a million dollars for 'libel.'

"Why do I write? It is a source of creativity. I can get angry and have my characters shoot someone; I can fall in love and have my heroine get the man of her dreams. I can get angry at the apathy and cruelty of the world, but I am not a person who writes tirades or tracts. I hope to create characters who feel pain and can shout their fury to the gods. Some persons who knew me as a child in Minnesota and who read *It's Crazy to Stay Chinese in Minnesota* claimed I was 'bitter.' I guess the book missed its mark with them. *It's Crazy* is not an autobiography—it is the story of discovery by a teenager, the discovery of sex, the discovery that sex knows no race, and the discovery that growing up is painful for everyone, especially Chinese girls who are not passive and who hate being Chinese.

"What are important subjects? The relationships of human beings. Being mostly Chinese, I am fascinated by family—at one end of the spectrum the Asian concept of family and loyalty and subjugation of rights to the good of the members—at the other end, the Western ideology of individualism which becomes material. I learned from Edward McClure (E. Daniel

TELEMAQUE, Eleanor Wong 1934-

PERSONAL: Born January 1, 1934, in Albert Lea, Minn.; daughter of Sang and Mei-Lee (See) Wong; married Jean-Raoul Middleton, 1953 (divorced); married Maurice Telemaque (in business), April 11, 1960; children: (second marriage) Adrienne Love. *Education:* Attended University of Chicago, 1947-49; University of Minnesota, B.A., 1952. *Home:* 230 East 88th St., New York, N.Y. 10028. *Agent:* Frances Schwartz Literary Agency, 60 East 42nd St., Suite 413, New York, N.Y. 10017. *Office:* U.S. Commission on Civil Rights, 26 Federal Plaza, Suite 1639, New York, N.Y. 10278.

CAREER: Member of UNESCO relations staff in Washington, D.C., 1952-54; CARE, Inc., New York City, researcher, 1956-59; New York City Commission on Human Rights, New York City, in public relations, 1963-70; U.S. Department of Justice, Community Relations Service, Northeast Regional Office, New York City, communications specialist, 1970-73; Equal Employment Opportunity Commission, Newark, N.J., conciliator, 1973-74; U.S. Commission on Civil Rights, New York City, field representative in Massachusetts, 1974-79, New Hampshire, 1974-79, and New York City, 1974—. Once active in civil rights and anti-war movements; gives readings.

WRITINGS: It's Crazy to Stay Chinese in Minnesota (novel), Thomas Nelson, 1978; *Haiti through Its Holidays* (juvenile), Edward Blyden, 1981. Also author of *Ru-Wen Goes to the Golden Mountain* (juvenile), Council on Urban Education (New York City).

Co-author of "Picture Bride for Peter," a film released by Revue Studios. Contributor to *New York* and *Village Voice.*

SIDELIGHTS: "It has been difficult being a minority writer reviewed by Caucasians from their point of view. You become

(Jacket photograph by Peter K. Fine from *It's Crazy to Stay Chinese in Minnesota* by Eleanor Wong Telemaque.)

McClure), who wrote a marvelous book called *Freckles* about how we are all interrelated—one family—black, white, yellow—we all are 'others.'''

TRNKA, Jiri   1912-1969

PERSONAL: Name is pronounced "*Jeer* ee *trink* a"; born February 24, 1912, in Pilsen, Czechoslovakia; died of a heart ailment, December 30, 1969, in Prague, Czechoslovakia; son of Rudolph Trnka (a plumber) and a seamstress; married Helena Chvojkova (a writer); children: five. *Education:* Graduated, Prague Academy of Art, 1935; studied puppetry under Josef Skupa. *Residence:* Prague, Czechoslovakia.

CAREER: Puppet film producer, animator, stage designer, artist and illustrator of books for children. Began his career at an early age as an apprentice to puppeteer Josef Skupa; became stage designer and illustrator of books for children, 1935; briefly established own puppet theater, Prague, Czech., 1936; collaborated with "Trick Brothers," an animated film group; animated film producer, 1945-53; established own puppet film studio, Prague, 1946-69.

AWARDS, HONORS: Recipient of numerous awards for films, including Prize of Bohemia, 1946, and prize, Cannes International Film Festival, 1946, both for "The Animals and the Brigands"; Czechoslovak Film Critics prize, 1947, Venice Biennale Gold Medal, 1948, Prix Melies, 1948, and first prize, International Film Festival of Cartoons and Puppets, 1949, all for "The Czech Year"; Czechoslovak National Film Prize, 1950, for "Bayaya"; Prix Melies, 1950, Prix de la critique, 1951, and Golden Reel, American Film Academy, 1955, all for "The Emperor's Nightingale"; Prix Melies, 1952, and British Film Academy prize, 1955, both for "The Song of the Prairie"; special honorable mention, London Film Festival, 1958, for "The Lutchan War"; prize for best national selection, Cannes International Film Festival, 1959; second prize, Montevideo Film Festival, 1960, for "A Midsummer Night's Dream," and many more. Also recipient of Czechoslovak Honour of Merited Artist, 1955; Czechoslovak Peace Prize, 1958; awarded title of National Artist of Czechoslovakia, 1963; Hans Christian Andersen Medal, 1968, for entire body of illustrated work.

WRITINGS—Selected works; all for children; all self-illustrated: (With Frantisek Hrubin) *The Enchanted Forest,* translated by Daphne Rusbridge, Artia, 1954; (with F. Hrubin) *Let's Tell a Tale Together,* translated by D. Rusbridge, Artia, 1954; *Zahrada,* SNDK, 1962, translation published as *Through the Magic Gate,* Golden Pleasure Books, 1963.

Illustrator; selected works; all for children: Josef Menzel, *Misa Kulicka v rodnem lese,* Melantrich, 1939, translation published as *Bruin Furryball in His Forest Home,* Dakers, 1957; J. Menzel, *Misa Kulicka v cirkuse,* Melantrich, 1940, translation published as *Bruin Furryball in the Circus,* Dakers, 1957; Jan Karafiat, *Broucci,* J. Otto, 1940, translation published as *The Fireflies,* adapted by Max Bollinger, translated by Roseanna Hoover, Atheneum, 1970; J. Menzel, *Misa Kulicka v zoo,* Melantrich, 1941, translation published as *Bruin Furryball in the Zoo,* Dakers, 1957; Wilhelm Hauff, *Karavana,* Melantrich, 1941, translation published as *Caravan,* Hamlyn, 1961; Jakob Ludwig Grimm and Wilhelm Karl Grimm, *Pohadky a legendy,* J. R. Vilimek, 1942, translation published as *Fairy Tales,* Hamlyn, 1961, new edition, 1969; Frantisek Hrubin, *Pohadka o Kvetusce a jeji zahradce,* SNDK, 1955,

JIRI TRNKA

translation published as *Primrose and the Winter Witch,* retold by James Reeves, Hamlyn, 1964; Hans Christian Andersen, *Pohadky,* SNDK, 1955, translation published as *Fairy Tales,* Hamlyn, 1959; J. Menzel, *Mischa Kugelrund im Puppentheater,* Artia, 1956, translation published as *Bruin Furryball in the Puppet Theatre,* Dakers, 1957; J. Menzel, *Mischa Kugelrund im Spielzeugsparadies,* Artia, 1956, translation published as *Bruin Furryball in the Toyhouse,* Dakers, 1958; F. Hrubin, *Pohadky tisice a jedne noci,* Cesoslovensky spisovatel, 1957, translation published as *Tales from the Arabian Nights,* Hamlyn, 1960; Brothers Grimm and Hans Christian Andersen, *Favorite Tales from Grimm and Andersen,* Artia, 1959, reprinted, Exeter Books, 1983; William Shakespeare, *Sen noci svatojanske,* translation by Jean Layton published as *A Midsummer Night's Dream,* adapted by Eduard Petiska, Artia, 1960; Alois Jirasek, *Stare povesti ceske,* SNDK, 1960, translation published as *Legends of Old Bohemia,* Hamlyn, 1963; Jean de la Fontaine, *Bajky detem,* SNDK, 1961, translation by I. T. Havlu published as *Fables,* adapted by Oldrich Syrovatka, Golden Pleasure Books, 1963; Sergei Prokofiev, *Peter and the Wolf,* Hamlyn, 1965.

Also illustrator of over forty additional works published in Czechoslovakian.

Films; all puppet, except as noted: "Grandpa Planted a Beet" (animated cartoon), 1945; "The Gift" (animated cartoon), 1946; "The Chimney Sweep" (animated cartoon), 1946; "The Animals and the Brigands" (animated cartoon), 1946; "The Fox and the Jug" (animated cartoon), 1947; "The Czech Year," 1947; "The Emperor's Nightingale," 1948; "The Song of the Prairie," 1949; "The Story of the Double-Bass," 1949; "Bayaya," 1950; "The Devil's Mill," 1951; "The Golden Fish" (animated cartoon), 1951; "The Gingerbread Cottage," 1951; "The Happy Circus" (paper cut-outs), 1951; "How

(From "The Swineherd" by Hans Christian Andersen,
in *Favorite Tales from Grimm and Andersen.* Illustrated by Jiri Trnka.)

Grandpa Changed Till Nothing Was Left" (animated cartoon), 1952; "Kutasek and Kutilka," 1952; "Old Czech Legends," 1953; "The Two Frosts" (animated cartoon), 1954; "A Drop Too Much," 1954; "The Good Soldier Schweik," 1954; "There Was Once a King" (motion picture), 1955; "Circus Hurvinek," 1955; "The Hussite Warrior" (motion picture), 1955; "Spejbl on the Track," 1955; "Jan Zizka" (motion picture), 1956; "Against All" (motion picture), 1956; "The Little Umbrella," 1957; "A Midsummer Night's Dream," 1959; "Pas-

sion," 1961; "The Cybernetic Grandma," 1963; "Tillie, the Unhappy Hippopotomus" (animated cartoon), 1979. Also author of animated short film "The Hand."

SIDELIGHTS: Trnka was born in the city of Pilsen, western Czechoslovakia. The son of a plumber and a seamstress, Trnka became acquainted with the art of dollmaking at an early age since his parents and grandmother all made toys in their spare

(From "The Ugly Duckling" by Hans Christian Andersen, in *Favorite Tales from Grimm and Andersen.* Illustrated by Jiri Trnka.)

(From "The Snow Queen" by Hans Christian Andersen, in *Favorite Tales from Grimm and Andersen.* Illustrated by Jiri Trnka.)

time. "Andersen's fairy tales always bring me back to the depth of my childhood. I was reading them when I was six or seven. My very first drawing from Andersen originated when I was ten years old and illustrated *The Emperor's New Clothes*. I have been dealing with Andersen ever since. In 1939, five of my illustrations of his fairy tales were displayed at the museum. Andersen still fascinates me and always will."

Young Trnka won his first puppet competition at the age of nine. At school, he was introduced to the Pilsen puppet theater by art teacher and famous puppeteer, Josef Skupa. Later, Skupa gave Trnka a job in an art supplies store and extra work in Skupa's theater. He was also influential in persuading Trnka's family to allow the young artist to attend the Prague Academy of Art.

While in art school, Trnka designed costumes for Skupa's puppets and worked as an illustrator for a children's magazine. A year after graduation, Trnka opened his own "Wooden Theater," so named because of the wooden puppets that he used. Unfortunately, the theater failed to attract audiences and was closed in less than a year.

From 1936 until 1946, Trnka did book illustrations, designed tapestries, worked at the Prague National Theater as costume and stage designer, and painted still lifes, portraits and landscapes. After World War II, Trnka produced cartoon and trick films. He was one of the founders of the Trick Brothers Studio which produced noteworthy cartoons. "At first, we all sat together and discussed what should be done. We then considered what it should be, and since no theme was at hand, I suggested this old idea of mine—to shoot 'Grandpa Planted a Beet.'"

The production of these films stirred an old ambition of his to create puppet films, and at the end of 1946 he opened his own studio in Prague. "I must admit that from the first I took a far greater interest in puppet films than in cartoons. Perhaps this can be explained by the fact that I had been engaged in work with puppets before, back in the days when I was director of the Prague Puppet Theatre for Children. I kept away from film-making for a long time, however. It was not until 1945 that I first took an active part in film creation, when I was offered a job in the Cartoon Film Studio within the framework of the then newly established unified organization of the Czechoslovak nationalized film industry.

"My first experience with the practical side of film, when I suddenly realized the unsuspected possibilities in the utilizing of the trick technique of cartoon films, reminded me of my old love of puppets, and with it, an ambition to animate on the screen, where everything is possible, the three-dimensional figures of puppets, moving in contradistinction to the heroes of cartoons, not within their own plane but in space. It never occurred to me at that time to adopt the puppet film technique of any of my predecessors. As a matter of fact, I was not even acquainted with their work, with the exception of Ptushko's *New Gulliver*. From the beginning, I had my own conception of how puppets could be handled—each of them to have an individual but static facial expression, as compared with the puppets that by means of various technical devices, can change their mien in an attempt to achieve a more life-like aspect. In practice, of course, this has tended not to enhance the realism, but rather conduce to naturalism.

"There are many reasons why I have remained faithful to puppet films ever since I started systematic work puppeteering before the camera. First of all, I am firmly convinced that puppet films keep much closer to the author's original manuscript in the portrayal of the figures, and that they make possible a much richer use of the imagination in the facial expression. This corresponds fully to the kind of lyrical film for which I have been striving since the outset of my film career. I should like to add, moreover, that in cartoons the different techniques of the many draftsmen participating in the actual piecing together of the film obscures the character of the original drawing. Apart from this, the very nature of cartoon figures calls for continual motion; it is not possible to stop them, and neither is it possible to bring them into a state of contemplation. All this, of course, limits the creative possibilities of cartoons. After my experience with puppet films, I would definitely not like to return to cartoons, as I would feel considerably tied down in the originality of my designs." [J. Broz, "The Puppet Film as an Art," *Film Culture*, Volume 1, number 5-6, winter, 1955.[1]]

(From "The Bremen Town-Musicians" by Jacob and Wilhelm Grimm, in *Favorite Tales from Grimm and Andersen.* Illustrated by Jiri Trnka.)

(From the puppet film "Passion." Produced by Short Prague—Cartoon and Puppet Film Studio, 1961.)

For over a quarter of a century, Trnka produced numerous films and received many international awards for his puppet films. ". . . Let me set right the frequently voiced fallacy, namely, that puppet films can present any and every kind of theme and topic, the effectiveness of the presentation depending solely on the author's powers of creative fantasy and his skill in all the contrivances of the technique of puppet films. After all that I have seen during my . . . years' experience in the field of puppet films, I can say that the potentialities there are boundless. But, as a matter of fact, in my opinion, this is not a matter for rejoicing, for these unlimited potentialities—as I know from past experience—can be easily over-exploited.

"On the whole, one may say that puppets are utilized to the best effect where a realistic presentation on the screen often places insurmountable obstacles in the way of convincing performances by humans. It is no mere chance that puppet films are most successful not only in the field of biting caricature and satire, but also in extremely lyrical tales and in those whose subject demands the portrayal of emotional fervour. I can confirm from my own experience that the most successful films produced by my production unit include those of the type of *The Song of the Prairie,* a satire on the Wild-West adventure films, and also such lyrical fairy tales as *The Emperor's Nightingale* and *Prince Bayaya.* And as far as I, myself, am concerned, I cannot imagine how the grand passion

of the scenes from the Czech mythology, which I endeavoured to bring to the screen under the guise of puppet figures in *Old Czech Legends,* could be conveyed as stirringly in a live action film. As I have already said, puppet films have unlimited possibilities; they could be adapted to any subject current in full-length live action features. There would however be no sense in that, for they would be mere imitations of repetitions. Puppet films stand on their own feet only when they are outside the scope of live action films—when the stylization of the scenery, the hyperlook of the human actors, and the lyrical content of the theme might easily produce an effect both unconvincing and ludicrous or even painful."[1]

Czechoslovak animated films have been long recognized as among the world's outstanding examples of this art form. The Czechoslovak puppet film derives from a long tradition of puppet theater of which Trnka was one of the most famous puppet filmmakers. Trnka explained the Czech interest in puppets: "The Czech artists have always looked for the world's reality not in size but rather in depth, not on the high mountains, but in the woods, the rivers, in the songs of birds and of young girls, in the sorrows and joys of children—it is in these places also that we find reality. Perhaps it is for this reason that we love puppets, because in this smallest of worlds we attempt to express everything about life, about beauty and about love. . . ." [Harriet R. Polt, "The Czechoslovak Animated Film," *Film Quarterly,* spring, 1964.[2]]

In the early 1960s, Trnka was among a group of Czech artists and writers who voiced their opposition to the Soviet domination of their country. His last film, "The Hand," which shows a happy sculptor losing his liberty and then his life when a giant hand forces him to make a statue of it, represented in allegory the Czech political situation. In 1963, he was awarded the title of National Artist of Czechoslovakia. "Nobody should rely on inspiration alone. Besides, it is a romantic concept. All of us have to work to be inspired. The most difficult thing is to start—this fear that seizes and paralyzes us in front of a blank sheet of paper until an impulsive force hurls us into the chasm. . . ."

Fifty-seven-year-old Trnka died on December 30, 1969 in Prague, Czechoslovakia of a chronic cardiac disease.

FOR MORE INFORMATION SEE: J. Broz, "The Puppet Film as an Art," *Film Culture,* Volume 1, number 5-6, winter, 1955; Harriet R. Polt, "The Czechoslovak Animated Film," *Film Quarterly,* spring, 1964; Jaroslov Bocek, *Jiri Trnka: Artist and Puppet Master,* translated by Till Gottheiner, Artia, 1965; Bettina Hürlimann, *Picture Book World,* translated and edited by Brian W. Anderson, Oxford University Press, 1968; Doris de Montreville and Donna Hill, editors, *Third Book of Junior Authors,* H. W. Wilson, 1972. Obituaries: *New York Times,* December 31, 1969.

VAN HORN, William 1939-

PERSONAL: Born February 15, 1939, in Oakland, Calif.; son of William Jennings (a machinist) and Virginia Ruth (a housewife; maiden name, Hygelund) Van Horn; married Frances Elaine Dixon (an operating room nurse), July 29, 1966; children: Noel Charles, Tish Johanna. *Education:* California College of Arts and Crafts, B.F.A., 1961. *Home and office:* 4562 Ranger Ave., North Vancouver, British Columbia, Canada V7R 3L7.

CAREER: Animator, director, and author of books for children. Imagination, Inc., San Francisco, Calif., background artist, 1961; Mills Animation, San Francisco, background animator, 1964-66; Walter Landor Associates, San Francisco, background animator, 1966-67; Davidson Films, San Francisco, art director, producer, head of animation department, 1967-75; Aesop Films, San Francisco, co-owner and art director, producer, head of animation department, 1975-77; freelance artist and illustrator, 1978—. Illustrator, designer, and author of metric system posters, California State Department of Education, 1975, and of metric system study prints, Encyclopaedia Britannica Corporation, 1976. *Military service:* U.S. Army, 1962-64, staff artist at Fort Lewis Washington.

AWARDS, HONORS: CINE Golden Eagle certificates from the Council on International Nontheatrical Events, 1970, for "Between Rational Numbers," 1970, for "The Wanderers," 1972, for "The Weird Number," 1973, for "Whatever Is Fun," 1975, for "Where Did Leonard Harry Go?"; two silver medals at Venice Children's Film Festival, 1970; first prize at both Columbus and Atlanta Film Festivals, 1971; best of festival citation at National Educational Film Festival, and certificate of merit at Chicago International Film Festival, both 1971; Calvin Workshop Notable Film Award, 1972; CINE Eagle Certificate, 1972 (Brussels), 1972 (Tehran), 1973 (Moscow), 1976 (Tehran), all for "The Weird Number"; Blue Ribbon, New York Educational Film Festival, 1973; "Where Did Leonard Harry Go?" was selected by the American Film Fes-

tival Board as one of the top eight comedy/satire film shorts of 1976.

WRITINGS—All for children; all self-illustrated: *Harry Hoyle's Giant Jumping Bean* (Junior Literary Guild selection), Atheneum, 1978; *Twitchtoe, the Beastfinder,* Atheneum, 1978; *Harry Hoyle's Slippery Shadow,* Scholastic Book Services, 1980; *The Very Special Birthday Present,* Atheneum, 1982; *The Wiggly Wobbly Boat Ride,* Scholastic Book Services, 1982; *A Picnic with Bert,* Scholastic Book Services, 1983; *The Big Sneeze,* Scholastic Book Services, 1985.

Films; all for children; all written and produced by the author; all animated: "Between Rational Numbers," Davidson Films, 1969; "The Wanderers," Davidson Films, 1969; "The Weird Number," Davidson Films, 1970; "Whatever Is Fun," Audio Brandon Films, 1973; "The Truth about Horsefeathers" (also filmstrip), Xerox Films, 1974; "Idiom's Delight" (also filmstrip), Xerox Films, 1974; "If You're a Horse" (also filmstrip), Xerox Films, 1974; "Where Did Leonard Harry Go?" (also filmstrip), Xerox Films, 1974; "The Telescope," Encyclopaedia Britannica Educational Corporation, 1976; "Zenith," Encyclopaedia Britannica Educational Corporation, 1977; (with Mitchell Rose) "The Reluctant Robot" (a television special), Free Sparlin, 1980.

Also producer of fifty-three sound cartoons and forty-five animated film shorts for organizations, including Silver Burdett, Xerox Corp., Encyclopaedia Britannica Corp., Macmillan, Baily Film Associates, Audio Brandon Films, "Sesame Street," Kaiser Broadcasting Company ("Snipets"), and Houghton Mifflin.

WORK IN PROGRESS: A book entitled *Uncle Rumpus Arrives;* a bimonthly comic book entitled *Nervous Rex.*

WILLIAM VAN HORN

Max smiled in the way that cats smile, and looked at Harry as if to say, "How should I know?" ■
(From *Harry Hoyle's Giant Jumping Bean* by William Van Horn. Illustrated by the author.)

SIDELIGHTS: "I began to draw when very young. Five or six. I drew mostly war scenes and pictures of Mickey Mouse. Later I tried my hand at Dick Tracy and the Lone Ranger. I really wasn't very good at any of them, but was mercifully too young to realize it. I was very interested in astronomy at one point, and spent quite a bit of time trying to draw a decent picture of the planet Saturn. When that didn't work out, I switched to dinosaurs. Drawing dinosaurs was much more satisfying somehow, and to this day I've had a love affair with the things. The characters in my latest books are two little dinosaurs named Charlie and Fred.

"From around 1954 on, I was determined that I would work someday in the animation business. In college I did my own films (or tried to) and gained just enough practical experience to land a job with an animation studio upon graduation. It was during my years in the animation business that I began to write. It was out of sheer necessity. We often received scripts for animated films (all for children, by the way) that were so lifeless and pedantic that something had to be done. With my partner, Mitchell Rose, I learned to put one word after another in a reasonably entertaining way. We must have done something right, because many of our films went on to win awards.

"Later I began to write my own scripts, seven of which were sold to distributors. I then produced the films, and a couple of them won awards.

"The first children's book I wrote was *Harry Hoyle's Giant Jumping Bean*. It sold on its first submission, and believe me, that was absolutely the last time it was ever so easy. Every book since then has been an uphill fight. I really think that a children's book is the most difficult thing to write, although many friends are under the impression that if the book can be read in ten minutes, it can't therefore have taken more than twenty to write.

"I was born and raised in Oakland, California, and lived for many years in San Francisco. I moved (in 1980) with my family to Vancouver, British Columbia. My wife Elaine is a Canadian citizen, so she was able to get the rest of us in. The children and myself are landed immigrants."

HOBBIES AND OTHER INTERESTS: "Collecting comic art, including originals of daily and Sunday strips and comic books from the forties and fifties."

FOR MORE INFORMATION SEE: Junior Literary Guild, March, 1978.

VENTURA, Piero (Luigi) 1937-

BRIEF ENTRY: Born December 3, 1937, in Milan, Italy. Italian author and illustrator of children's books. Ventura attended the Art School of Castello Sforzesco and the Architecture University before becoming associated with the Lambert advertising agency in 1959. He later worked as art director of P & T of Milan in Italy. A free-lance illustrator since 1978, Ventura has won reviewers' praise as an author/illustrator of books for children. As *Publishers Weekly* noted: "Precision plus imagination (to say nothing of an acute sense of color) are the hallmarks of . . . [his] works." In his first book, *Piero Ventura's Book of Cities* (Random House, 1975), the artist takes his young readers on a trip around the world as he explores the uniqueness of places like London, Moscow, New York, Paris, Tokyo, Rome, and more. "The overall effect of so many city sights and people, even if rose-colored, is exhilarating," observed *New York Times Book Review*. "Precise, intricate drawings," added *Booklist,* "feature an array of bright colors and an amazing variety of life-goes-on details." Ventura displayed the same adeptness for detail in his next book,

The Magic Well (Random House, 1976), described by *Horn Book* as "a marvelously comic fantasy in picture-book form . . . imbued with typically European satire. . . ."

For young adults and up, Ventura wrote and illustrated *Man and the Horse* (Putnam, 1982), a history of the relationship that has existed from cave days to modern times. *Publishers Weekly* commended the "smooth, readily comprehended writing" and the paintings that "are hard to surpass in grandeur, beauty and animation." Among his other works for children is *Great Painters* (Putnam, 1984) in which he creates what *School Library Journal* called "an unusual dimension" as he combines his own paintings with reproductions of master artists. "A wealth of accurate material is presented," added the same reviewer, "in a readable and spirited style." Ventura also collaborated with his artist wife, Marisa, on a children's story entitled *The Painter's Trick* (Random House, 1977). His illustrated work for others includes Guido Sperandio's *Vanuk, Vanuk* and Gian Paolo Ceserani's *Marco Polo*.

Ventura has received numerous awards, including an award of excellence from the Society of Illustrators in 1976 for *Piero Ventura's Book of Cities* which was also named book of the year in 1977 by both the American Institute of Graphic Arts and the Brooklyn Museum. *Home and office:* Via Domenichino 27, Milan 20149, Italy.

FOR MORE INFORMATION SEE: Contemporary Authors, Volume 103, Gale, 1982.

WADDELL, Martin   1941-
(Catherine Sefton)

PERSONAL: Born April 10, 1941, in Belfast, Northern Ireland; son of Mayne (a linen manufacturer) and Alice (Duffell) Waddell; married Rosaleen Carragher (a teacher), December 27, 1969; children: Thomas Mayne, David Martin, Peter Matthew. *Education:* "Almost nil." *Religion:* "Troubled agnostic." *Home and office:* 139 Central Promenade, Newcastle, County Down, Northern Ireland. *Agent:* Murray Pollinger, 4 Garrick St., London WC2E 9BH, England.

CAREER: Writer, 1966—. Has held various jobs, including bookselling and junk-stalling. Lectures to schools on children's literature and on promoting children's writing, for the Northern Ireland Arts Council. *Member:* Society of Authors. *Awards, honors: The Ghost and Bertie Boggin* (written under pseudonym Catherine Sefton), was a runner-up for the Federation of Children's Book Club Award, 1982; *Island of the Strangers* (under Sefton pseudonym), was nominated for a Carnegie Award in 1984.

WRITINGS—For children: *Ernie's Chemistry Set* (illustrated by Ronnie Baird), Blackstaff, 1978; *Ernie's Flying Trousers* (illustrated by R. Baird), Blackstaff, 1978; *Napper Goes for Goal* (illustrated by Barrie Mitchell), Puffin, 1981; *The Great Green Mouse Disaster* (picture book; illustrated by Philippe Dupasquier), Andersen, 1981; *Napper Strikes Again* (illustrated by B. Mitchell), Puffin, 1981; *Harriet and the Crocodiles* (illustrated by Mark Burgess), Abelard, 1982, Little, Brown, 1984; *The House under the Stairs*, Methuen, 1983; (editor) *A Tale to Tell*, Northern Ireland Arts Council, 1983; *Harriet and the Phantom School*, Abelard, 1984; *Napper's Golden Goals*, Puffin, 1984; *Going West* (illustrated by P. Dupasquier), Harper, 1984; *The Mystery Squad and the Whistling Teeth*, Blackie & Son, 1984; *The Mystery Squad and Mr.*

Midnight, Blackie & Son, 1984; *The Mystery Squad and the Artful Dodger*, Blackie & Son, 1984; *Big Bad Bertie* (illustrated by Glynis Ambrus), Methuen, 1984; *The Mystery Squad and the Creeping Castle*, Blackie & Son, 1985; *The Mystery Squad and the Gemini Job*, Blackie & Son, 1985; *The Budgie said GRRRR* (illustrated by G. Ambrus), Methuen, 1985; *Harriet and the Robot* (illustrated by M. Burgess), Abelard, 1985; *The School Reporter's Notebook*, Beaver, 1985; *Owl and Billy*, Methuen, 1986; *The Mystery Squad and Cannonball Kid*, Blackie & Son, 1986; *Our Wild Weekend*, Methuen, 1986; *The Mystery Squad and the Robot's Revenge*, Blackie & Son, 1986.

Under pseudonym Catherine Sefton; juvenile novels: *In a Blue Velvet Dress: Almost a Ghost Story* (illustrated by Gareth Floyd), Faber, 1972, published as *In a Blue Velvet Dress* (illustrated by Eros Keith), Harper, 1973, new edition, Hamish Hamilton, 1985; *The Sleepers on the Hill*, Faber, 1973; *The Back House Ghosts*, Faber, 1974, published as *The Haunting of Ellen: A Story of Suspense*, Harper, 1975; *The Ghost and Bertie Boggin* (illustrated by Jill Bennett), Faber, 1980; *Emer's Ghost*, Hamish Hamilton, 1981; *The Finn Gang* (illustrated by Sally Holmes), Hamish Hamilton, 1981; *The Emma Dilemma* (illustrated by J. Bennett), Faber, 1982; *A Puff of Smoke* (illustrated by Thelma Lambert), Hamish Hamilton, 1982; *Island of the Strangers*, Hamish Hamilton, 1983; *It's My Gang* (il-

MARTIN WADDELL

. . . That seemed to be all there was to the book, and Jane laid it down with a distinct feeling that she had been cheated. ■ (From *In a Blue Velvet Dress* by Catherine Sefton. Illustrated by Eros Keith.)

lustrated by Catherine Bradbury), Hamish Hamilton, 1984; *The Ghost Girl*, Hamish Hamilton, 1985; *The Blue Misty Monsters*, Faber, 1985.

Adult novels: *Otley*, Stein & Day, 1966; *Otley Pursued*, Stein & Day, 1967; *Otley Forever*, Stein & Day, 1968; *Otley Victorious*, Stein & Day, 1969; *Come Back When I'm Sober*, Hodder & Stoughton, 1969; *A Little Bit British: Being the Diary of an Ulsterman, August, 1969*, Tom Stacey, 1970.

ADAPTATIONS: "Otley" (motion picture), starring Romy Schneider and Tom Courtenay, Columbia, 1969; *In a Blue Velvet Dress* was adapted for "Jackanory" reading for BBC-TV, 1974; *The Sleepers on the Hill* was adapted as a television serial in 1976.

WORK IN PROGRESS: Little Dracula at the Seaside, Little Dracula's Christmas, Little Dracula Goes to School, Little Dracula's First Bite, Once There Were Giants, all for Walker Books; *The Day It Rained Elephants; Starry Night* (under Sefton pseudonym); "The Life of Bill" series of books.

SIDELIGHTS: "Writing has always been in my family, but I came to it on the rebound, having failed to become a professional football player. Much of my work derives from watching and listening to children. I have three boys of my own, and, as they have grown, so have the stories. In addition, I live in a sea-side resort, and a lot of my material is gained from simply walking around in summer. Several books have been written as a result of visiting schools, which I do a great deal of, courtesy of the Northern Ireland Arts Council.

"I have begun to move toward stories such as *Island of the Strangers*, which deal, between-the-lines, with the Northern Ireland situation, although I'm always primarily concerned with the emotional lives of the principal characters. I believe that part of my job as a writer is to depict things as they *are*, but also to suggest how they could be—to make sense from the chaos. Two 'Martin Waddell' titles verge on emotional territory, *Going West* and *Our Wild Weekend*, and could properly be Catherine Sefton titles! The tiny forthcoming picture book *Once There Were Giants* is another in this category, and probably one of the best books I have ever written.

"Most of my Martin Waddell titles are intended as pure fun although emotion does form the base of *The House under the Stairs* and *Owl and Billy*. The (hopefully) forthcoming *Starry Night* is a Catherine Sefton book for the fifteen- to sixteen-year-old age group. It deals with an illegitimate child's discovery of the fact of her illegitimacy, and is set in a house right on the border between Northern Ireland and the Republic. Hopefully her confusion with her own identity will also illuminate areas of confusion in the national identity. That being said, the aim is still 'A good story!'

"I am becoming more and more interested in the picture book, and what can be done with it, as in *The Great Green Mouse Disaster*—a wordless book, and *Going West* which deals with the death of a small child against an American Pioneer background.

"My books with Glynis Ambrus (*Big Bad Bertie, The Budgie Said GRRR*, and *The Day It Rained Elephants*) are totally daft. *Once There Were Giants* [in progress] is a tender emotional statement. The 'Little Dracula' series [in progress] is mad ghoulish humour. Waiting in the wings, if I can find someone to publish it, is a series of six to eight books entitled 'The Life of Bill,' intended to deal straightforwardly with life from the cradle to the grave, for four- to six-year-olds! 'Bill' requires

a publisher with nerve, because of the commitment involved and the nature of the subject matter. I know it *can* be done.

"My books for adults were written before I learned how to write, and suffer from padding to make the length. Only one, *A Little Bit British* deserves to stand. It was written in anger and shows it. I could do it better now!"

HOBBIES AND OTHER INTERESTS: Chess.

FOR MORE INFORMATION SEE: Times Literary Supplement, March 16, 1967, November 6, 1969, November 23, 1973, December 6, 1974, November 20, 1981; *New York Times Book Review*, May 21, 1967, July 28, 1968, February 1, 1970, May 4, 1975, March 25, 1984; *Saturday Review*, June 24, 1967.

WINN, Janet Bruce   1928-

PERSONAL: Born May 21, 1928, in Orange, N.J.; daughter of A. Bruce (an executive) and Katherine (Baldwin) Boehm; married O. Howard Winn (a poet and teacher), July 15, 1950; children: Martin, Bruce, Kate, Martha. *Education:* Vassar College, B.A., 1950; Stanford University, M.A., 1951; State University of New York at Albany, Ph.D., 1984. *Politics:* "Independent (left)." *Home address:* Sheldon Dr., Poughkeepsie, N.Y. 12603. *Agent:* Heinle & Heinle, 29 Lexington Rd., Concord, Mass. 01742. *Office:* Department of Philosophy, State University College at New Paltz, New Paltz, N.Y. 12561.

CAREER: Ulster County Community College, Stone Ridge, N.Y., part-time instructor in philosophy, 1969-79; Dutchess Community College, Poughkeepsie, N.Y., part-time instructor in sociology, 1973—. Visiting lecturer in philosophy at State University of New York at New Paltz. Member of board of directors and director of public relations of Hudson Valley Philharmonic Society, 1960-70. *Member:* Phi Beta Kappa.

WRITINGS: Home in Flames (young adult novel), Follett, 1972; (with Bruce Boehm) *Connecticut Low* (young adult novel), Houghton, 1980.

Work represented in anthologies, including *Best Short Stories of 1968*, Houghton, 1968. Contributor of stories to magazines,

Janet Winn with her father, Bruce Boehm.

including *Evidence, Husk, Prairie Schooner,* and *Cimmaron Review.*

WORK IN PROGRESS: Blue Hills (tentative title), a historical novel for young adults; research on the rationality of social science.

SIDELIGHTS: ''What seems to motivate my fiction, my teaching, and my research in sociology and philosophy is a sense that much is askew ethically with the world. Nothing works the way it did in the children's books of the past: through Alice's looking glass is an uglier sight than Carroll knew. So into what I write seep ethical and political concerns, fed long ago by socially-concerned parents, by some extraordinary teachers, by a number of thinking, ethically-aware friends. These social concerns seem to have rung bells at a distance: a story of mine (concerning race relations, in part) has been translated and published in a Hungarian anthology.''

WISEMAN, David   1916-

PERSONAL: Born January 13, 1916, in Manchester, England; son of Oscar (a salesman) and Margaret (Hussey) Wiseman; married Cicely Hilda Mary Richards, September 2, 1939; children: Michael, Sally Hilda Wiseman Smith, Patrick, Deborah Margaret Wiseman Lucas. *Education:* Victoria University of Manchester, B.A. (with honors), 1937. *Home:* 25 Ellers Lane, Auckley, Doncaster, Yorkshire, DN9 3HY, England. *Agent:* June Hall, 19 College Cross, London N1 1PT, England.

CAREER: British Institute of Adult Education, London, England, 1946-50; *Journal of Adult Education,* London, England, editor, 1948-51; high school teacher in Worcestershire, Yorkshire and Cornwall, England, 1952-59; high school principal in Doncaster, England, 1959-63, and Cornwall, England, 1963-75; Cornwall Education Board, Cornwall, England, coordinator, teacher, in-service training, 1975-77. Member of Cornwall Education Committee, 1970-75. *Military service:* British Army, 1940-46; became major. *Member:* Society of Authors. *Awards, honors:* Preis der Leseratten, 1982, for *Jeremy Visick,* from ZDF T-V, West Germany.

WRITINGS: Jeremy Visick (juvenile; *Horn Book* Honor List), Houghton, 1981 (published in England as *The Fate of Jeremy Visick,* Kestrel, 1982), *Thimbles* (juvenile novel; ALA Notable Book), Houghton, 1982; *Blodwen and the Guardians* (juvenile novel), Houghton, 1983; *Adam's Common,* Houghton, 1984; *Pudding and Pie* (juvenile novel), Kestrel, 1986.

WORK IN PROGRESS: An untitled adult historical novel, based partly in the United States and partly in Cornwall between the years 1880-1920; *Johnny Shall Have a New Master,* a novel about school life for adults; a juvenile novel, tentatively entitled *The Holloway Brooch,* about the suffragettes' campaign and its relevance to present day struggles for women's equality.

SIDELIGHTS: ''I was trained as a historian and so am tempted to write of characters from history. But to me, history is all about us, in how we think and act. We are linked to our forebears: through us, they live; through them, our lives have

(Jacket illustration by Abigail Rorer from *Jeremy Visick* by David Wiseman.)

DAVID WISEMAN

become fuller, richer. Perhaps this is why, in many of my children's stories, my present-day characters are caught up with children of the past, so that neither can shake off the other. Though children may see my stories as 'ghost stories,' this is not how I see them. For me, the 'ghosts' are real.

"One of the influences from my own past is that of my grandmother, who was imprisoned for her beliefs in women's rights, as a suffragette in England. She was a formidable woman and I remember her vividly. I also remember seeing, when she was in her nineties, my great-grandmother. She had come to England, from Ireland, in the mid-nineteenth century, to work in a Lancashire cotton mill. She had only one son (my grandfather), born the illegitimate child of a French apprentice at the mill (says family legend).

"I was brought up in a working class district of Manchester, England. At the end of the road was a public library, with a delightfully welcoming children's room. Here I spent hours. And in my home books were cherished. This love of books is still with me, so that I get almost as much pleasure from handling a book as I do from reading it. Among the books I read as a boy, Ernest Thompson Seton's *Two Little Savages* stayed with me longest, but I read and enjoyed everything from Dumas to Marryat, from Richmal Crompton to Edgar Wallace, from *Oblomov* to *The Dynasts*.

"I write now with the same enjoyment and commitment as I read then. Writing is both a joy and an obsession. I am unhappiest when circumstances prevent me from writing.

"I enjoy meeting others interested in writing, and I like talking about writing and its problems, especially with children.

"I like drawing and painting but, with my involvement with writing, now find it difficult to give time to them. I write regularly, from nine in the morning to one in the afternoon, a routine which my wife helps me to maintain.

"We both enjoy travelling, visiting a son and daughter in the United States and another son in Germany. I promise myself I will one day return to Paris (a city I love and which is the setting for a historical novel I am researching), Geneva (where I once studied), and Italy (where I can practise Italian, a language in which I was once fluent). But when I can fix all these visits between my writing I do not know. I need forty-eight hours in every day."

CUMULATIVE INDEX TO
ILLUSTRATIONS AND AUTHORS

Illustrations Index

(In the following index, the number of the volume in which an illustrator's work appears is given *before* the colon, and the page on which it appears is given *after* the colon. For example, a drawing by Adams, Adrienne appears in Volume 2 on page 6, another drawing by her appears in Volume 3 on page 80, another drawing in Volume 8 on page 1, and another drawing in Volume 15 on page 107.)

YABC

Index citations including this abbreviation refer to listings appearing in *Yesterday's Authors of Books for Children*, also published by the Gale Research Company, which covers authors who died prior to 1960.

Author Index

The following index gives the number of the volume in which an author's biographical sketch, Brief Entry, or Obituary appears.

This index includes references to all entries in the following series, which are also published by Gale Research Company.

YABC—*Yesterday's Authors of Books for Children: Facts and Pictures about Authors and Illustrators of Books for Young People from Early Times to 1960*, Volumes 1-2
CLR—*Children's Literature Review: Excerpts from Reviews, Criticism, and Commentary on Books for Children*, Volumes 1-9
SAAS—*Something about the Author Autobiography Series*, Volume 1

Author Index

D

K

N

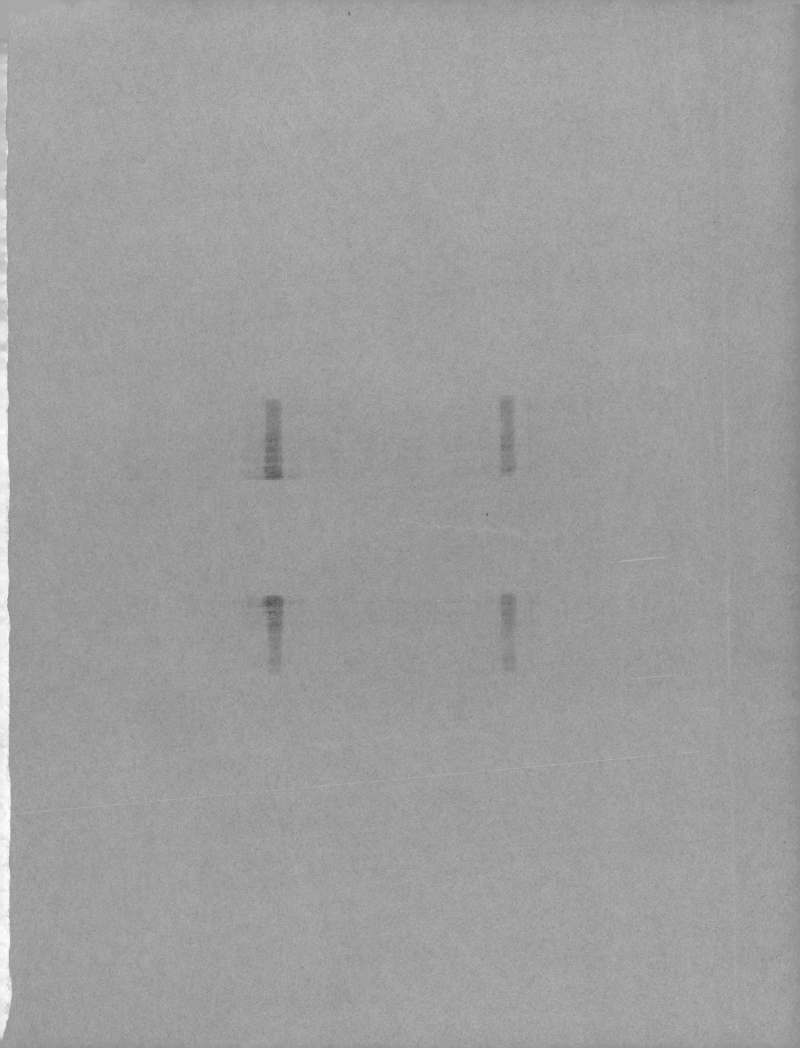